THE RATVOLUTION WILL NOT BE TELEVISED

Other *Pearls Before Swine* Books

This Little Piggy Stayed Home
BLTs Taste So Darn Good
Sgt. Piggy's Lonely Hearts Club Comic
Nighthogs

THE RATVOLUTION WILL NOT BE TELEVISED

A *Pearls Before Swine* Collection
by *Stephan Pastis*

Andrews McMeel
Publishing

Kansas City

Pearls Before Swine is distributed internationally by United Feature Syndicate, Inc.

06 07 08 09 10 BBG 10 9 8 7 6 5 4 3 2 1

ISBN-13: 978-0-7407-5674-0
ISBN-10: 0-7407-5674-5

Library of Congress Control Number: 2005933863

www.andrewsmcmeel.com

Pearls Before Swine can be viewed on the Internet at
www.comics.com/comics/pearls.

These strips appeared in newspapers from April 19, 2004 to January 23, 2005.

——— **ATTENTION: SCHOOLS AND BUSINESSES** ———

Andrews McMeel books are available at quantity discounts with bulk purchase for educational, business, or sales promotional use. For information, please write to: Special Sales Department, Andrews McMeel Publishing, LLC, 4520 Main Street, Kansas City, Missouri 64111

For my friend Emilio, a guy who lost almost his entire
baseball card collection playing pool against me
in the summer of 1979.

Those were the days.

Introduction

You never know when the good ideas will strike.

Sometimes it's in the car, sometimes it's in the bathroom, and sometimes it's when you're walking by your strange neighbor's house.

But if you're a cartoonist responsible for coming up with 365 new ideas a year, you write it down. Because if you don't, and you forget it, it's never coming back. It slips into the void. The Comic That Never Was.

What makes it especially painful is that you *are* able to remember how funny it was. You just can't recall the joke. And since I can't turn in blank panels with the note, "Man, did I have a great idea yesterday. You'll just have to believe me," it's not much help.

So you grab whatever you can and you write it down. On business cards, napkins, receipts, parking stubs, paper towels, brochures, the borders of newspapers, and when all else fails, the back of your hand. Sometimes, when I'm driving on the freeway and can't stop to write something down, I'll tell it to my son in the backseat, who will write it down with a crayon or pen in the white space of one of the books he is reading. (I should admit here that the book he is usually reading is *Garfield*, a sad irony given the amount of time I spend making fun of it in *Pearls*. I'd call him a traitor and kick him out of the house, but I'd feel bad. He's only seven.)

I also make sure to always keep notepads in key places, like in the drawer by the side of the bed. That notepad is key, because for some reason, ideas like to strike just as you're falling asleep. I think they do it to taunt you. They make you choose between sleep and a career. It's not kind. You begin to doze off, the idea hits, and you think, "Ahh, I'll remember it in the morning," but you won't. So you sit up, and you get out the notepad and you write it down the best you can. In the dark. Semiconscious.

Remarkably, this system usually works. In the morning, I see the note and it makes total sense to me. All I need is a few words of the joke and I'll remember the rest.

But then there was . . .

The Strip.

You see, one night, about two years ago, as I was fading into sleep, I stumbled upon a comic strip idea. And not just any idea. It was, if I may say, a *great* idea. So I got up, and there, in the dark, I wrote it down. And as I drifted off, I remember thinking, "*This* is the best *Pearls* strip I have ever written." Better than "Box O' Stupid People," better than anything. It was, truly . . . The Strip.

And so in the morning I awoke. And grabbed the piece of paper.
And this is what I saw:

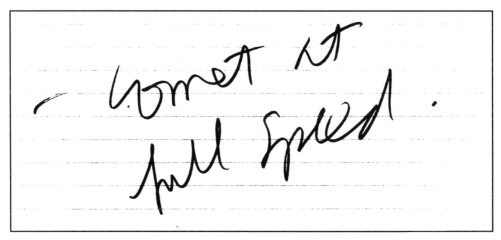

    That semilegible scrawl says, "Comet at full speed." And that's all it says. Just "Comet at full speed."
    I stared at it. Dumbfounded. "What the hell does this mean?" I thought.
    Hours went by. And still, nothing. I tried and tried. Nothing. "This can't be," I thought. "Think, Stephan, think." I agonized. Comets. At *full* speed. Why full speed? Why comets? Which comet? Halley's comet? The Hale-Bopp comet? Those guys who died in that big house with Nikes on waiting for a comet? Spaceships? Aliens? 'Comet' the bathroom disinfectant? Oh, Lord, please. No, no, no. Please. Come back. Please. Please. Please. And yet, nothing.
    I could not remember the joke.
    The greatest *Pearls* strip ever written had slipped into the Darkness. The Void. Never to be seen or heard from again. The Jimmy Hoffa of comic strips.
    Sometimes, pathetically, I will get out the note above and just stare at it. A shadow of a joke. A ghost of what might have been. A tragic keepsake. Forever haunted by a phrase.
    "Comet at full speed."
    In closing, I can only say that the joke hidden in the bowels of that phrase was, is, and always will be, my Funniest Joke Ever.
    Of this there can be no doubt.
    You'll just have to believe me.

—Stephan Pastis
March 2006

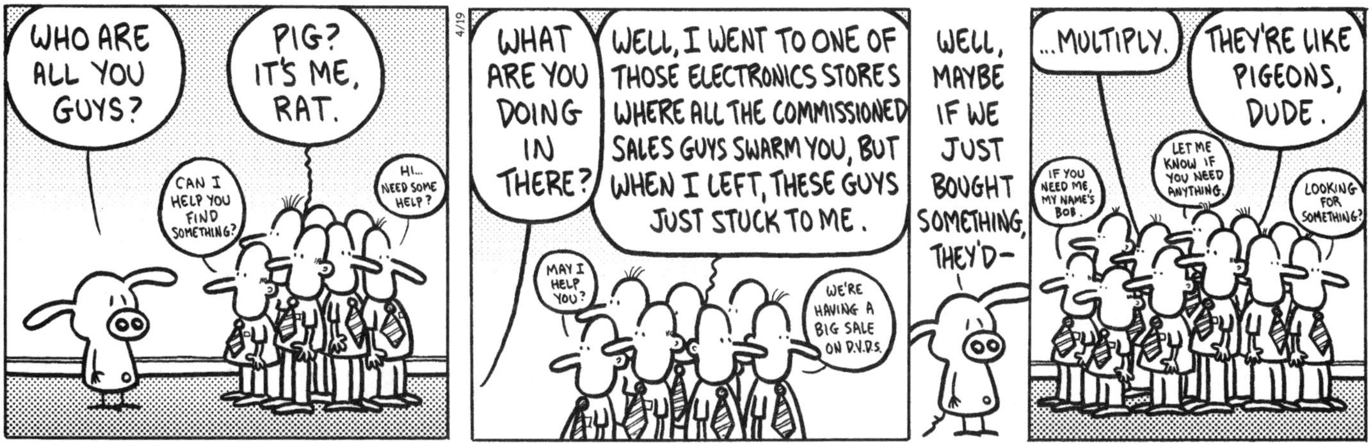
WHO ARE ALL YOU GUYS?
PIG? IT'S ME, RAT.
CAN I HELP YOU FIND SOMETHING?
HI... NEED SOME HELP?
4/19
WHAT ARE YOU DOING IN THERE?
WELL, I WENT TO ONE OF THOSE ELECTRONICS STORES WHERE ALL THE COMMISSIONED SALES GUYS SWARM YOU, BUT WHEN I LEFT, THESE GUYS JUST STUCK TO ME.
MAY I HELP YOU?
WE'RE HAVING A BIG SALE ON D.V.D.S.
WELL, MAYBE IF WE JUST BOUGHT SOMETHING, THEY'D–
...MULTIPLY.
THEY'RE LIKE PIGEONS, DUDE.
IF YOU NEED ME, MY NAME'S BOB.
LET ME KNOW IF YOU NEED ANYTHING.
LOOKING FOR SOMETHING?

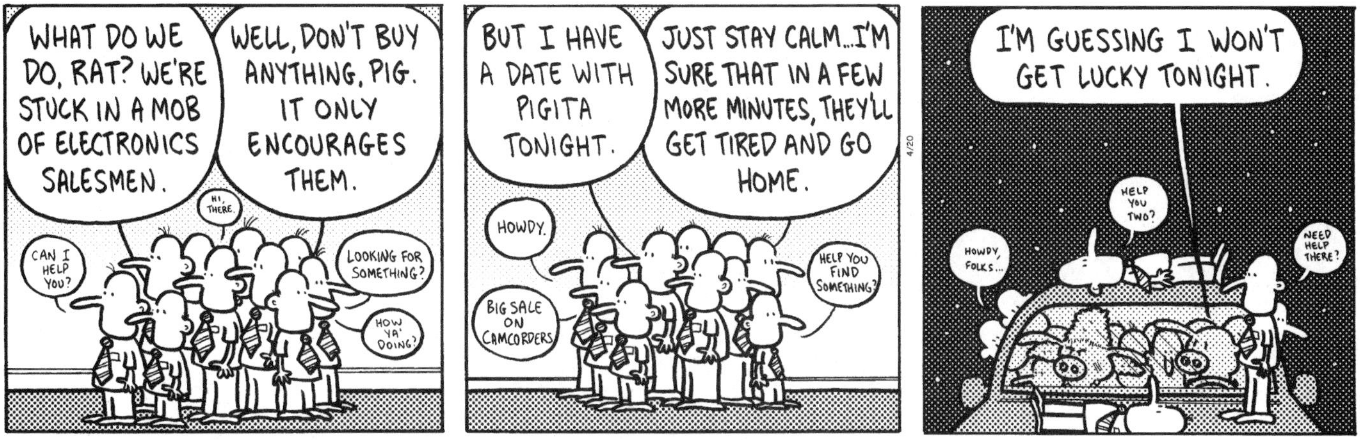
WHAT DO WE DO, RAT? WE'RE STUCK IN A MOB OF ELECTRONICS SALESMEN.
WELL, DON'T BUY ANYTHING, PIG. IT ONLY ENCOURAGES THEM.
CAN I HELP YOU?
HI, THERE.
LOOKING FOR SOMETHING?
HOW YA' DOING?
BUT I HAVE A DATE WITH PIGITA TONIGHT.
JUST STAY CALM...I'M SURE THAT IN A FEW MORE MINUTES, THEY'LL GET TIRED AND GO HOME.
HOWDY.
BIG SALE ON CAMCORDERS
HELP YOU FIND SOMETHING?
4/20
I'M GUESSING I WON'T GET LUCKY TONIGHT.
HOWDY, FOLKS...
HELP YOU TWO?
NEED HELP THERE?

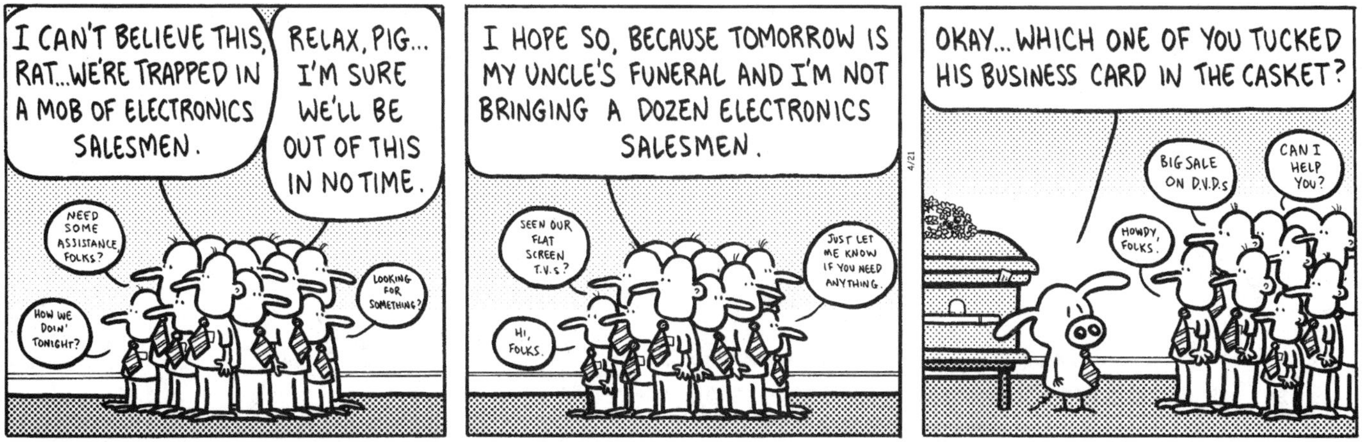
I CAN'T BELIEVE THIS, RAT...WE'RE TRAPPED IN A MOB OF ELECTRONICS SALESMEN.
RELAX, PIG... I'M SURE WE'LL BE OUT OF THIS IN NO TIME.
NEED SOME ASSISTANCE, FOLKS?
HOW WE DOIN' TONIGHT?
LOOKING FOR SOMETHING?
I HOPE SO, BECAUSE TOMORROW IS MY UNCLE'S FUNERAL AND I'M NOT BRINGING A DOZEN ELECTRONICS SALESMEN.
SEEN OUR FLAT SCREEN T.V.S?
JUST LET ME KNOW IF YOU NEED ANYTHING.
HI, FOLKS.
4/21
OKAY...WHICH ONE OF YOU TUCKED HIS BUSINESS CARD IN THE CASKET?
BIG SALE ON D.V.D.S
CAN I HELP YOU?
HOWDY, FOLKS.

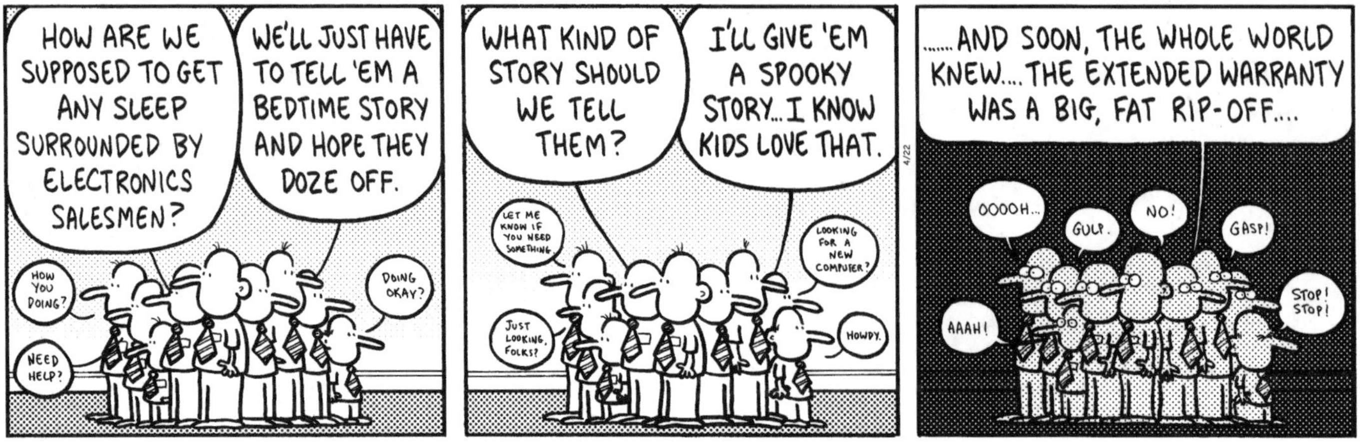
HOW ARE WE SUPPOSED TO GET ANY SLEEP SURROUNDED BY ELECTRONICS SALESMEN?
WE'LL JUST HAVE TO TELL 'EM A BEDTIME STORY AND HOPE THEY DOZE OFF.
HOW YOU DOING?
NEED HELP?
DOING OKAY?
WHAT KIND OF STORY SHOULD WE TELL THEM?
I'LL GIVE 'EM A SPOOKY STORY... I KNOW KIDS LOVE THAT.
LET ME KNOW IF YOU NEED SOMETHING.
JUST LOOKING, FOLKS?
LOOKING FOR A NEW COMPUTER?
HOWDY.
4/22
...... AND SOON, THE WHOLE WORLD KNEW.... THE EXTENDED WARRANTY WAS A BIG, FAT RIP-OFF....
OOOOH...
GULP.
NO!
GASP!
AAAH!
STOP! STOP!

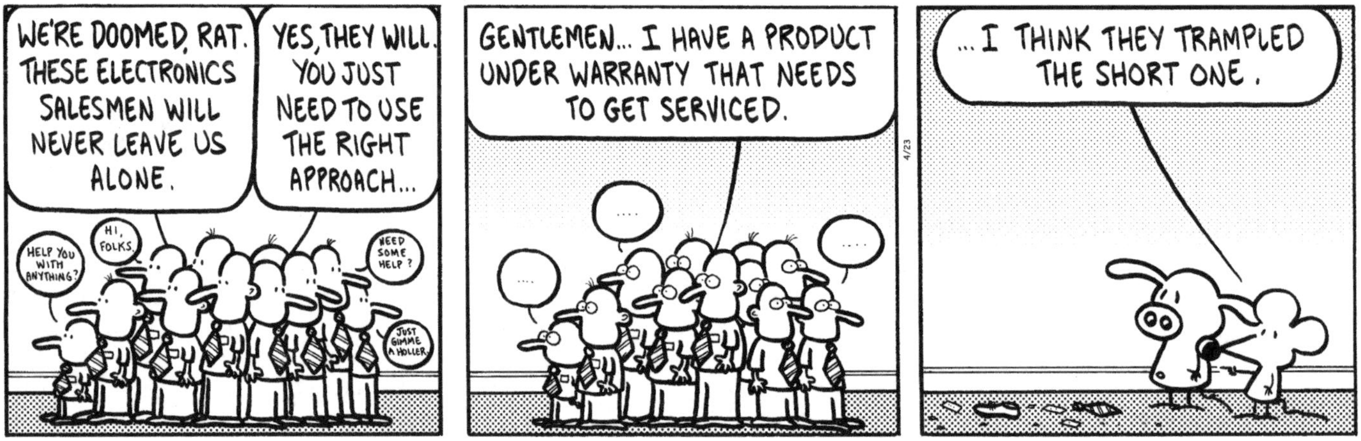
WE'RE DOOMED, RAT. THESE ELECTRONICS SALESMEN WILL NEVER LEAVE US ALONE.
YES, THEY WILL. YOU JUST NEED TO USE THE RIGHT APPROACH...
HELP YOU WITH ANYTHING?
HI, FOLKS.
NEED SOME HELP?
JUST GIMME A HOLLER.
GENTLEMEN... I HAVE A PRODUCT UNDER WARRANTY THAT NEEDS TO GET SERVICED.
....
....
....
4/23
... I THINK THEY TRAMPLED THE SHORT ONE.

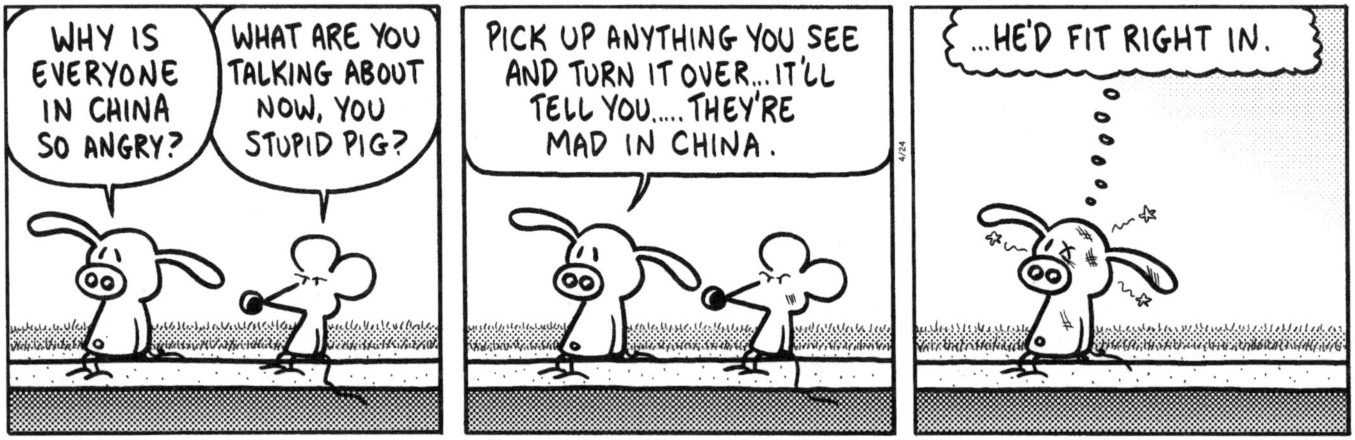
WHY IS EVERYONE IN CHINA SO ANGRY?
WHAT ARE YOU TALKING ABOUT NOW, YOU STUPID PIG?
PICK UP ANYTHING YOU SEE AND TURN IT OVER... IT'LL TELL YOU..... THEY'RE MAD IN CHINA.
4/24
...HE'D FIT RIGHT IN.

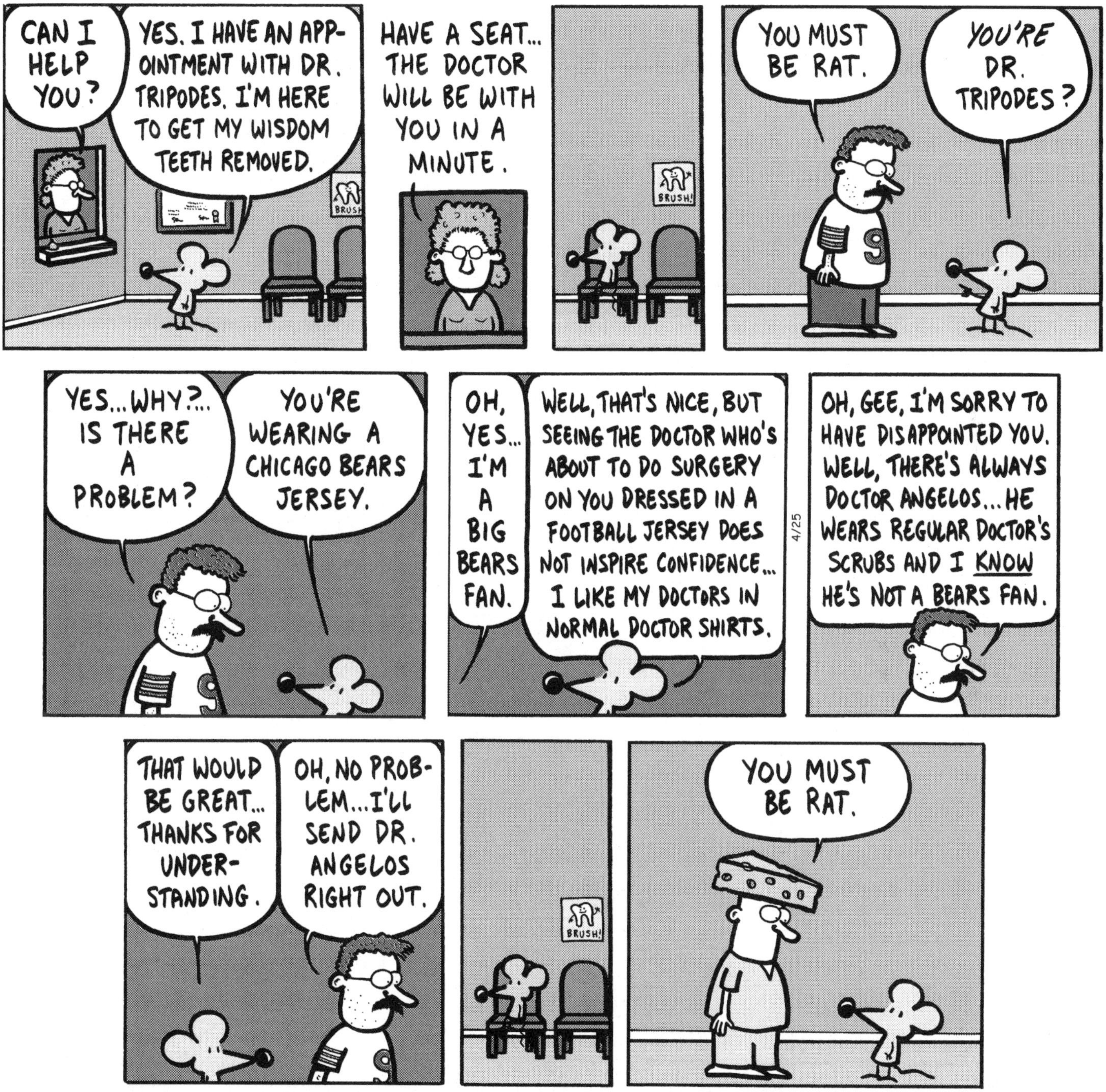
CAN I HELP YOU?
YES. I HAVE AN APPOINTMENT WITH DR. TRIPODES. I'M HERE TO GET MY WISDOM TEETH REMOVED.
BRUSH
HAVE A SEAT... THE DOCTOR WILL BE WITH YOU IN A MINUTE.
BRUSH!
YOU MUST BE RAT.
YOU'RE DR. TRIPODES?
YES...WHY?... IS THERE A PROBLEM?
YOU'RE WEARING A CHICAGO BEARS JERSEY.
OH, YES... I'M A BIG BEARS FAN.
WELL, THAT'S NICE, BUT SEEING THE DOCTOR WHO'S ABOUT TO DO SURGERY ON YOU DRESSED IN A FOOTBALL JERSEY DOES NOT INSPIRE CONFIDENCE... I LIKE MY DOCTORS IN NORMAL DOCTOR SHIRTS.
4/25
OH, GEE, I'M SORRY TO HAVE DISAPPOINTED YOU. WELL, THERE'S ALWAYS DOCTOR ANGELOS... HE WEARS REGULAR DOCTOR'S SCRUBS AND I KNOW HE'S NOT A BEARS FAN.
THAT WOULD BE GREAT... THANKS FOR UNDERSTANDING.
OH, NO PROBLEM... I'LL SEND DR. ANGELOS RIGHT OUT.
BRUSH!
YOU MUST BE RAT.

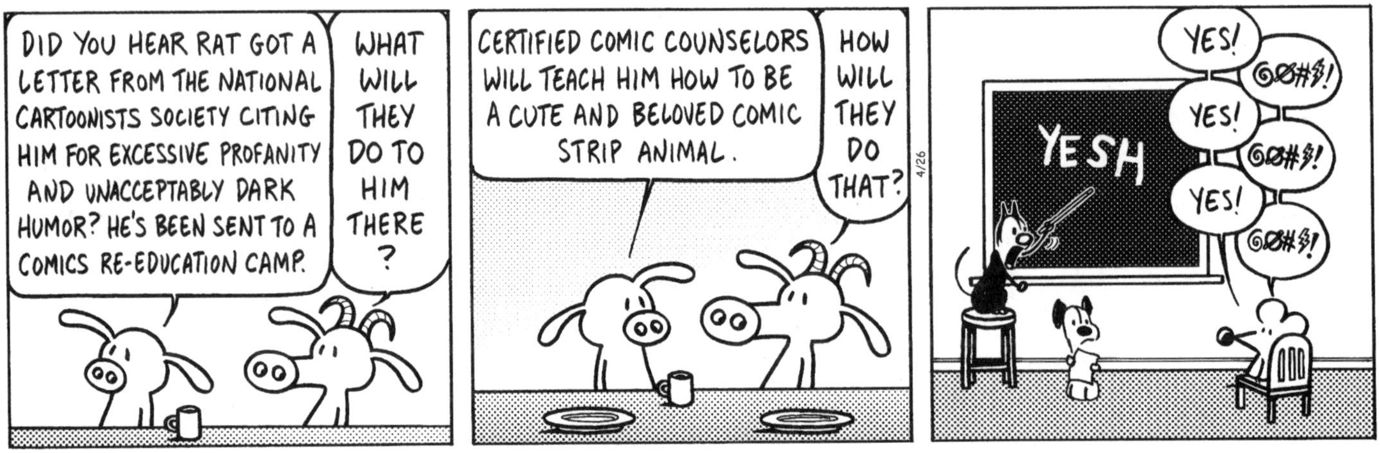
DID YOU HEAR RAT GOT A LETTER FROM THE NATIONAL CARTOONISTS SOCIETY CITING HIM FOR EXCESSIVE PROFANITY AND UNACCEPTABLY DARK HUMOR? HE'S BEEN SENT TO A COMICS RE-EDUCATION CAMP.
WHAT WILL THEY DO TO HIM THERE?
CERTIFIED COMIC COUNSELORS WILL TEACH HIM HOW TO BE A CUTE AND BELOVED COMIC STRIP ANIMAL.
HOW WILL THEY DO THAT?
4/26
YESH
YES!
YES!
YES!

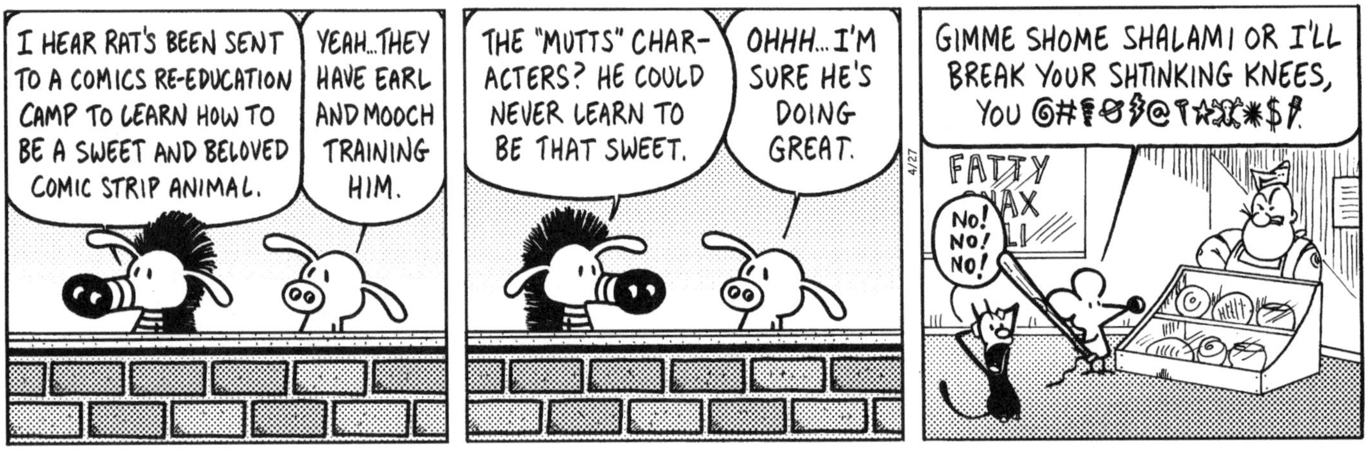
I HEAR RAT'S BEEN SENT TO A COMICS RE-EDUCATION CAMP TO LEARN HOW TO BE A SWEET AND BELOVED COMIC STRIP ANIMAL.
YEAH...THEY HAVE EARL AND MOOCH TRAINING HIM.
THE "MUTTS" CHARACTERS? HE COULD NEVER LEARN TO BE THAT SWEET.
OHHH...I'M SURE HE'S DOING GREAT.
4/27
GIMME SHOME SHALAMI OR I'LL BREAK YOUR SHTINKING KNEES, YOU
NO! NO! NO!

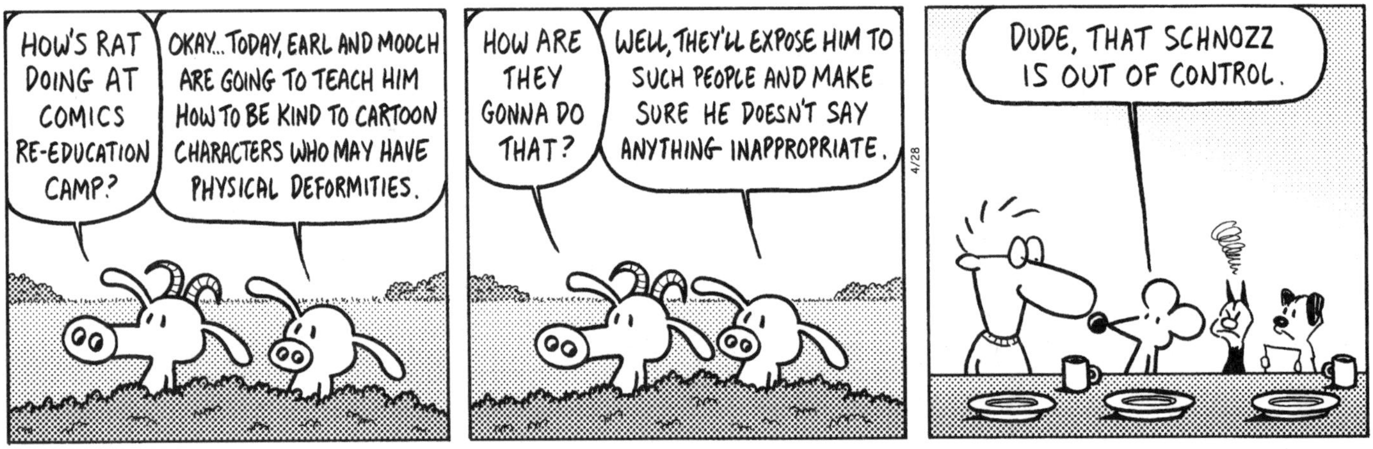
HOW'S RAT DOING AT COMICS RE-EDUCATION CAMP?
OKAY...TODAY, EARL AND MOOCH ARE GOING TO TEACH HIM HOW TO BE KIND TO CARTOON CHARACTERS WHO MAY HAVE PHYSICAL DEFORMITIES.
HOW ARE THEY GONNA DO THAT?
WELL, THEY'LL EXPOSE HIM TO SUCH PEOPLE AND MAKE SURE HE DOESN'T SAY ANYTHING INAPPROPRIATE.
4/28
DUDE, THAT SCHNOZZ IS OUT OF CONTROL.

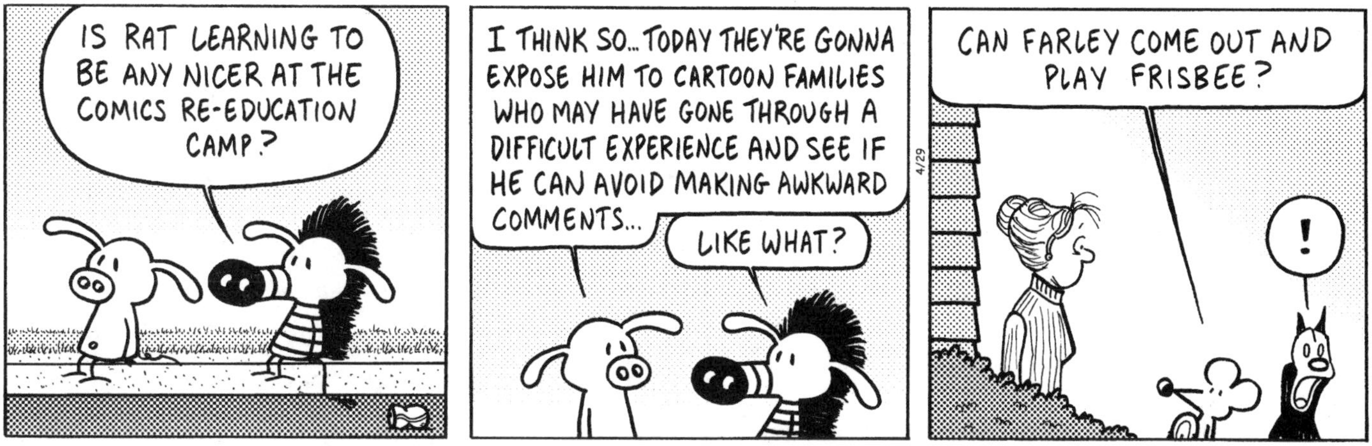
IS RAT LEARNING TO BE ANY NICER AT THE COMICS RE-EDUCATION CAMP?
I THINK SO... TODAY THEY'RE GONNA EXPOSE HIM TO CARTOON FAMILIES WHO MAY HAVE GONE THROUGH A DIFFICULT EXPERIENCE AND SEE IF HE CAN AVOID MAKING AWKWARD COMMENTS...
LIKE WHAT?
4/29
CAN FARLEY COME OUT AND PLAY FRISBEE?
!

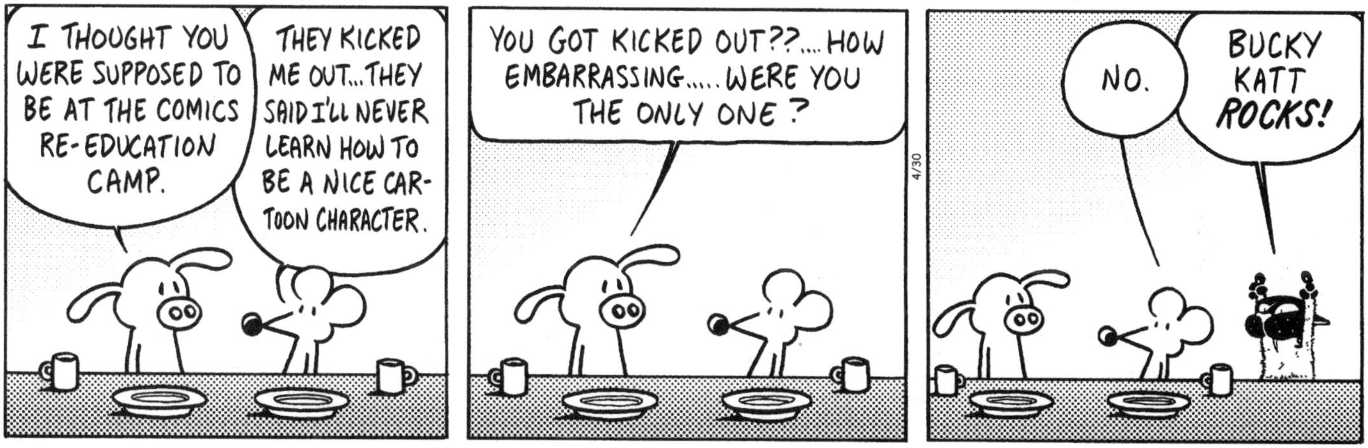
I THOUGHT YOU WERE SUPPOSED TO BE AT THE COMICS RE-EDUCATION CAMP.
THEY KICKED ME OUT... THEY SAID I'LL NEVER LEARN HOW TO BE A NICE CARTOON CHARACTER.
YOU GOT KICKED OUT??.... HOW EMBARRASSING..... WERE YOU THE ONLY ONE?
4/30
NO.
BUCKY KATT ROCKS!

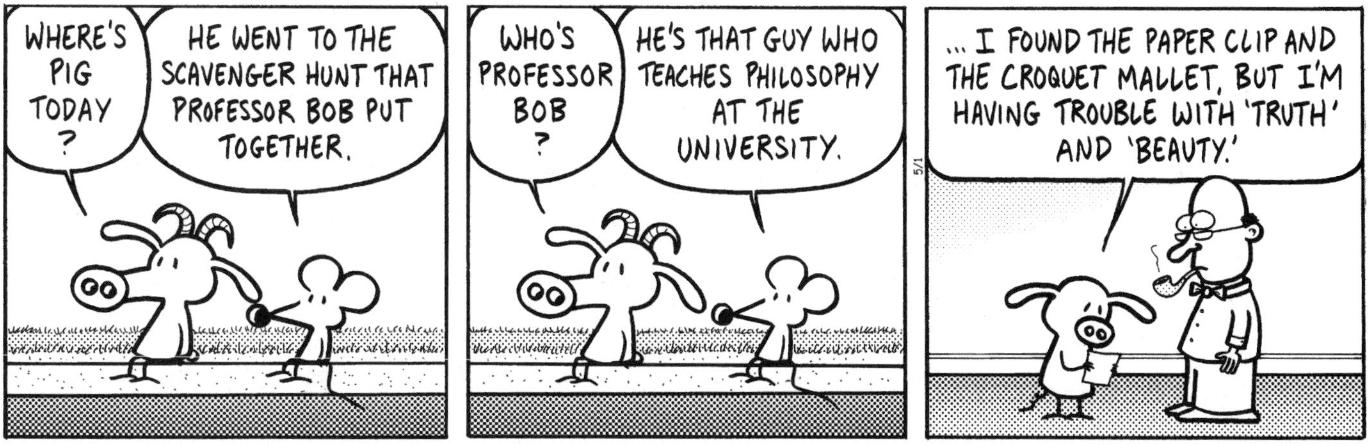
WHERE'S PIG TODAY?
HE WENT TO THE SCAVENGER HUNT THAT PROFESSOR BOB PUT TOGETHER.
WHO'S PROFESSOR BOB?
HE'S THAT GUY WHO TEACHES PHILOSOPHY AT THE UNIVERSITY.
5/1
... I FOUND THE PAPER CLIP AND THE CROQUET MALLET, BUT I'M HAVING TROUBLE WITH 'TRUTH' AND 'BEAUTY.'

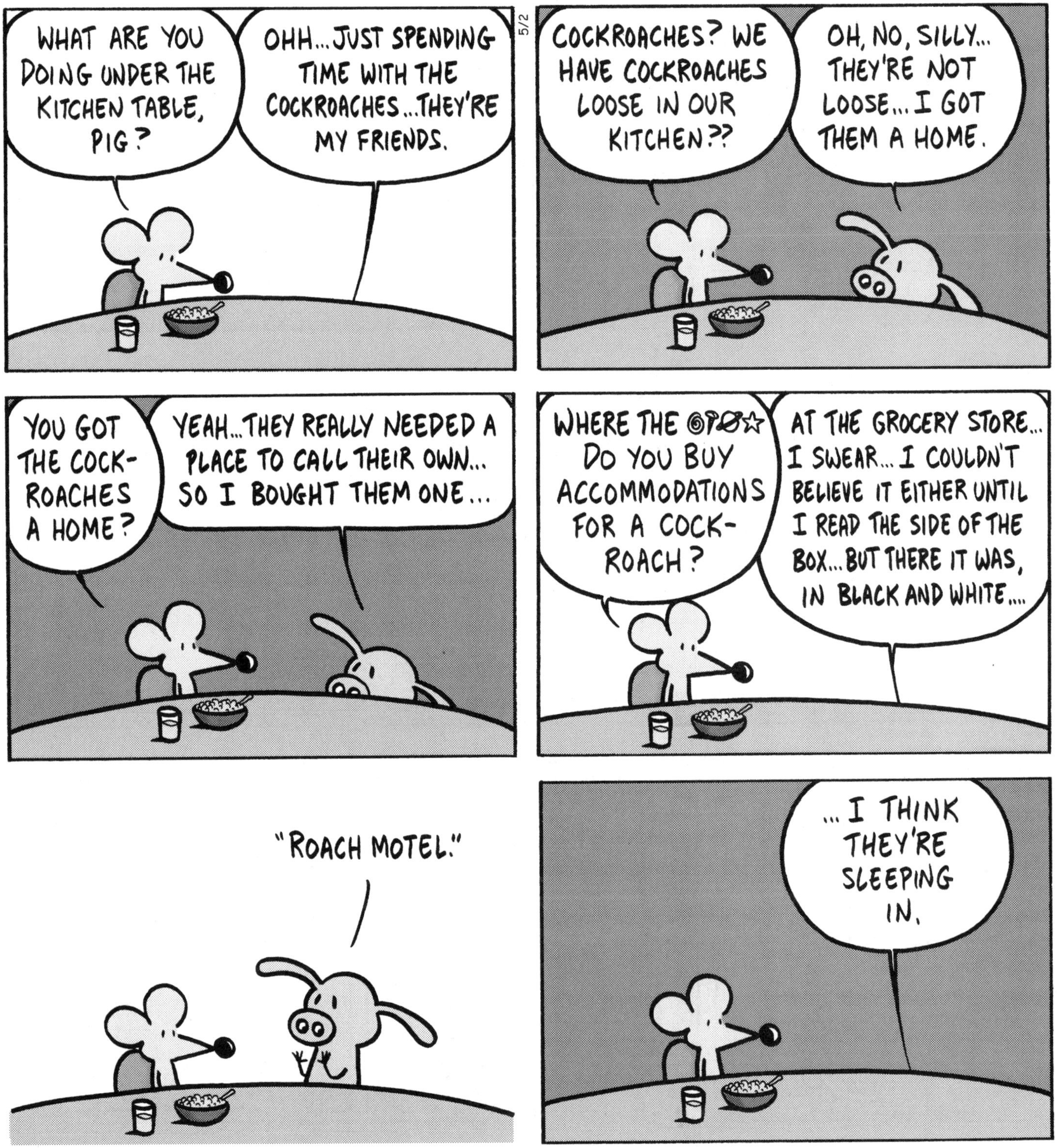
5/2
WHAT ARE YOU DOING UNDER THE KITCHEN TABLE, PIG?
OHH...JUST SPENDING TIME WITH THE COCKROACHES...THEY'RE MY FRIENDS.
COCKROACHES? WE HAVE COCKROACHES LOOSE IN OUR KITCHEN??
OH, NO, SILLY... THEY'RE NOT LOOSE...I GOT THEM A HOME.
YOU GOT THE COCK-ROACHES A HOME?
YEAH...THEY REALLY NEEDED A PLACE TO CALL THEIR OWN... SO I BOUGHT THEM ONE...
WHERE THE @?Ø☆ DO YOU BUY ACCOMMODATIONS FOR A COCK-ROACH?
AT THE GROCERY STORE... I SWEAR... I COULDN'T BELIEVE IT EITHER UNTIL I READ THE SIDE OF THE BOX...BUT THERE IT WAS, IN BLACK AND WHITE....
"ROACH MOTEL."
...I THINK THEY'RE SLEEPING IN.

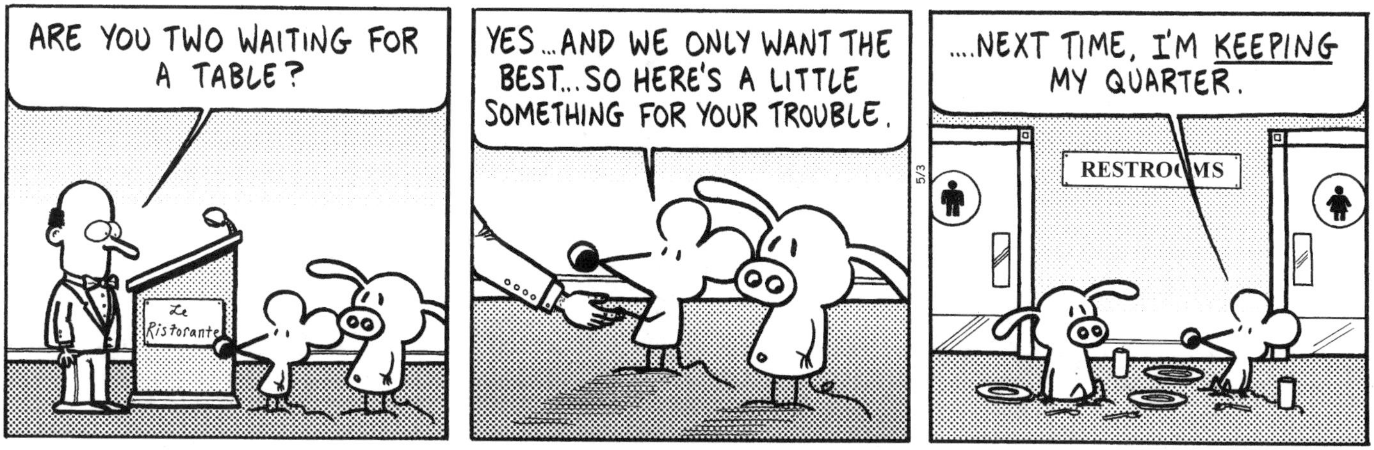
ARE YOU TWO WAITING FOR A TABLE?
Le Ristorante
YES...AND WE ONLY WANT THE BEST...SO HERE'S A LITTLE SOMETHING FOR YOUR TROUBLE.
5/3
....NEXT TIME, I'M KEEPING MY QUARTER.

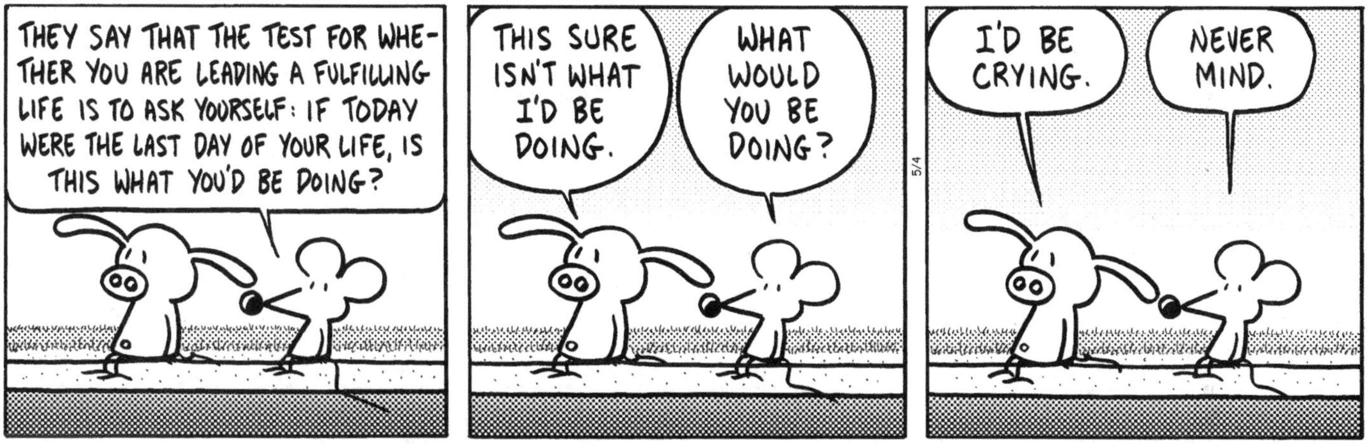
THEY SAY THAT THE TEST FOR WHETHER YOU ARE LEADING A FULFILLING LIFE IS TO ASK YOURSELF: IF TODAY WERE THE LAST DAY OF YOUR LIFE, IS THIS WHAT YOU'D BE DOING?
THIS SURE ISN'T WHAT I'D BE DOING.
WHAT WOULD YOU BE DOING?
5/4
I'D BE CRYING.
NEVER MIND.

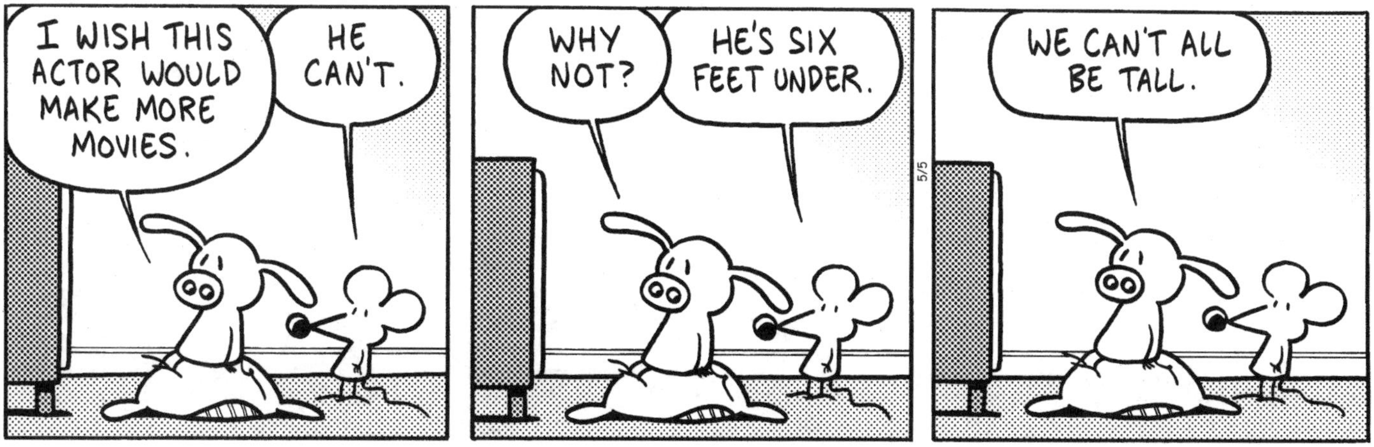
I WISH THIS ACTOR WOULD MAKE MORE MOVIES.
HE CAN'T.
WHY NOT?
HE'S SIX FEET UNDER.
5/5
WE CAN'T ALL BE TALL.

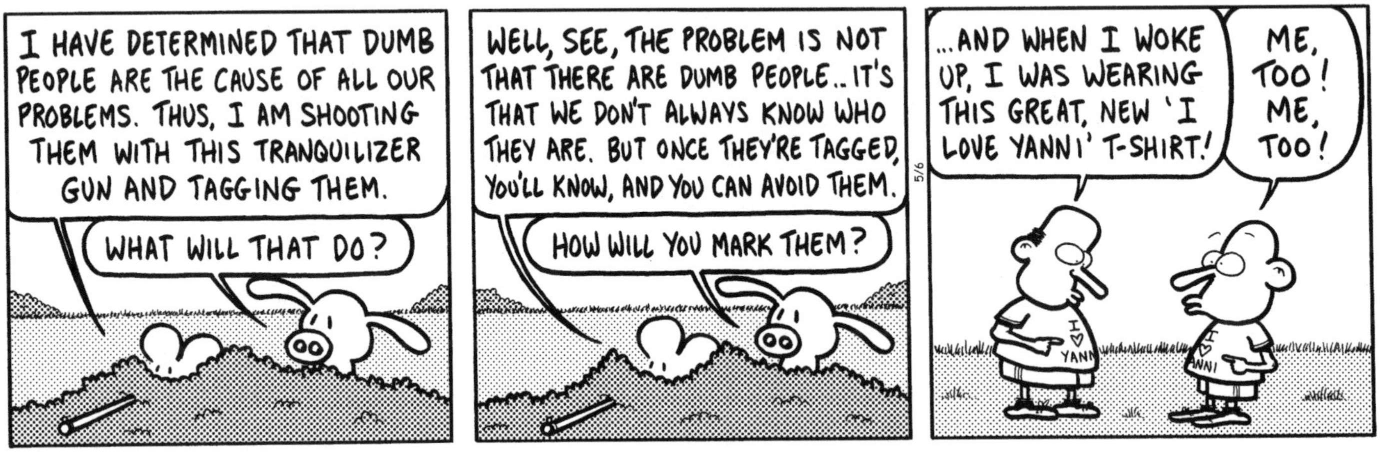
I HAVE DETERMINED THAT DUMB PEOPLE ARE THE CAUSE OF ALL OUR PROBLEMS. THUS, I AM SHOOTING THEM WITH THIS TRANQUILIZER GUN AND TAGGING THEM.
WHAT WILL THAT DO?
WELL, SEE, THE PROBLEM IS NOT THAT THERE ARE DUMB PEOPLE.. IT'S THAT WE DON'T ALWAYS KNOW WHO THEY ARE. BUT ONCE THEY'RE TAGGED, YOU'LL KNOW, AND YOU CAN AVOID THEM.
HOW WILL YOU MARK THEM?
...AND WHEN I WOKE UP, I WAS WEARING THIS GREAT, NEW 'I LOVE YANNI' T-SHIRT!
ME, TOO! ME, TOO!
5/6

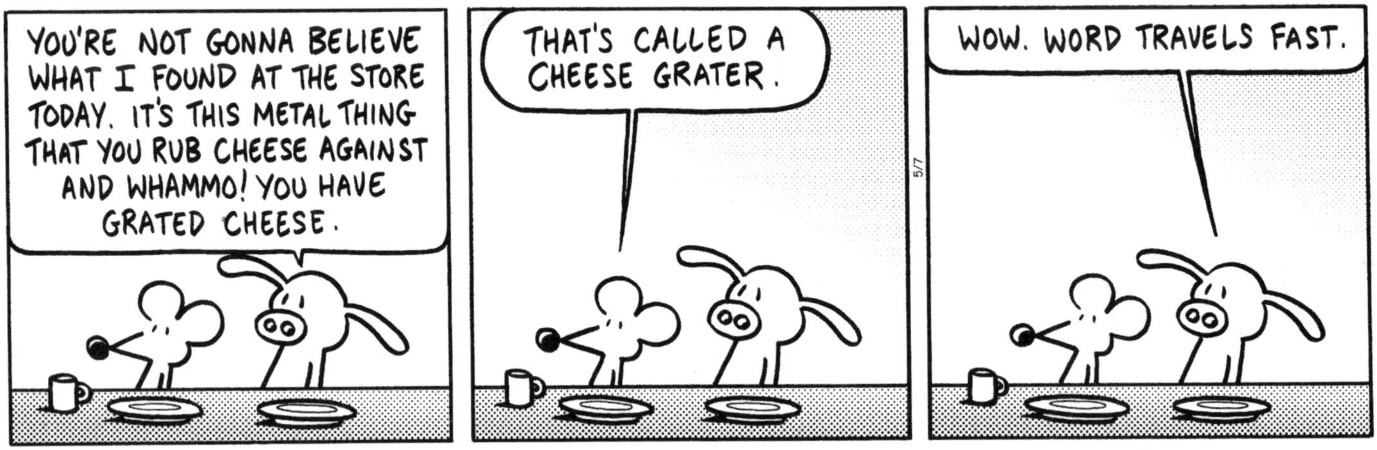
YOU'RE NOT GONNA BELIEVE WHAT I FOUND AT THE STORE TODAY. IT'S THIS METAL THING THAT YOU RUB CHEESE AGAINST AND WHAMMO! YOU HAVE GRATED CHEESE.
THAT'S CALLED A CHEESE GRATER.
WOW. WORD TRAVELS FAST.
5/7

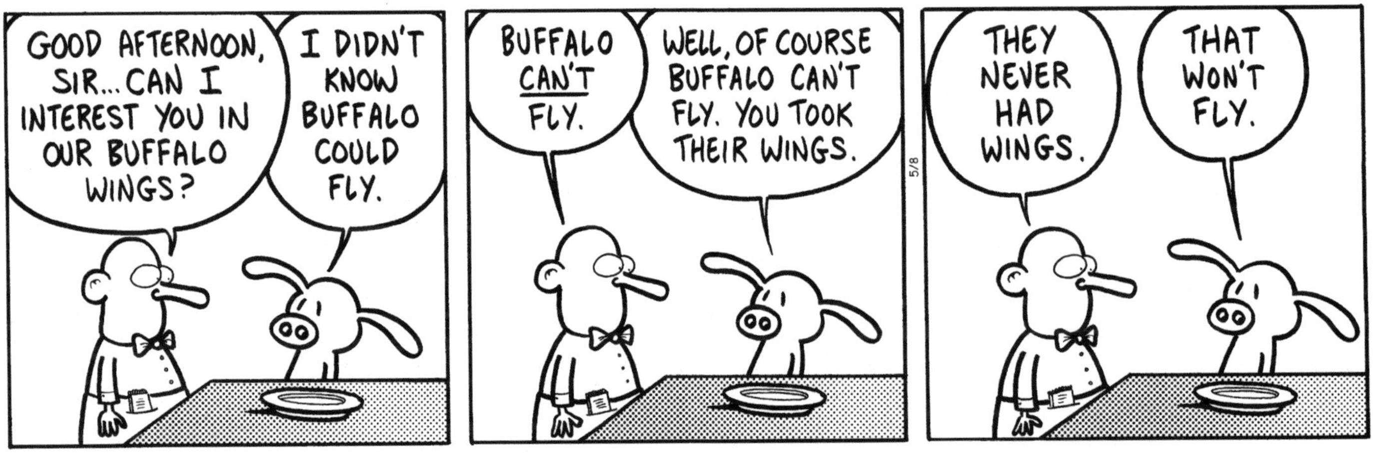
GOOD AFTERNOON, SIR... CAN I INTEREST YOU IN OUR BUFFALO WINGS?
I DIDN'T KNOW BUFFALO COULD FLY.
BUFFALO CAN'T FLY.
WELL, OF COURSE BUFFALO CAN'T FLY. YOU TOOK THEIR WINGS.
THEY NEVER HAD WINGS.
THAT WON'T FLY.
5/8

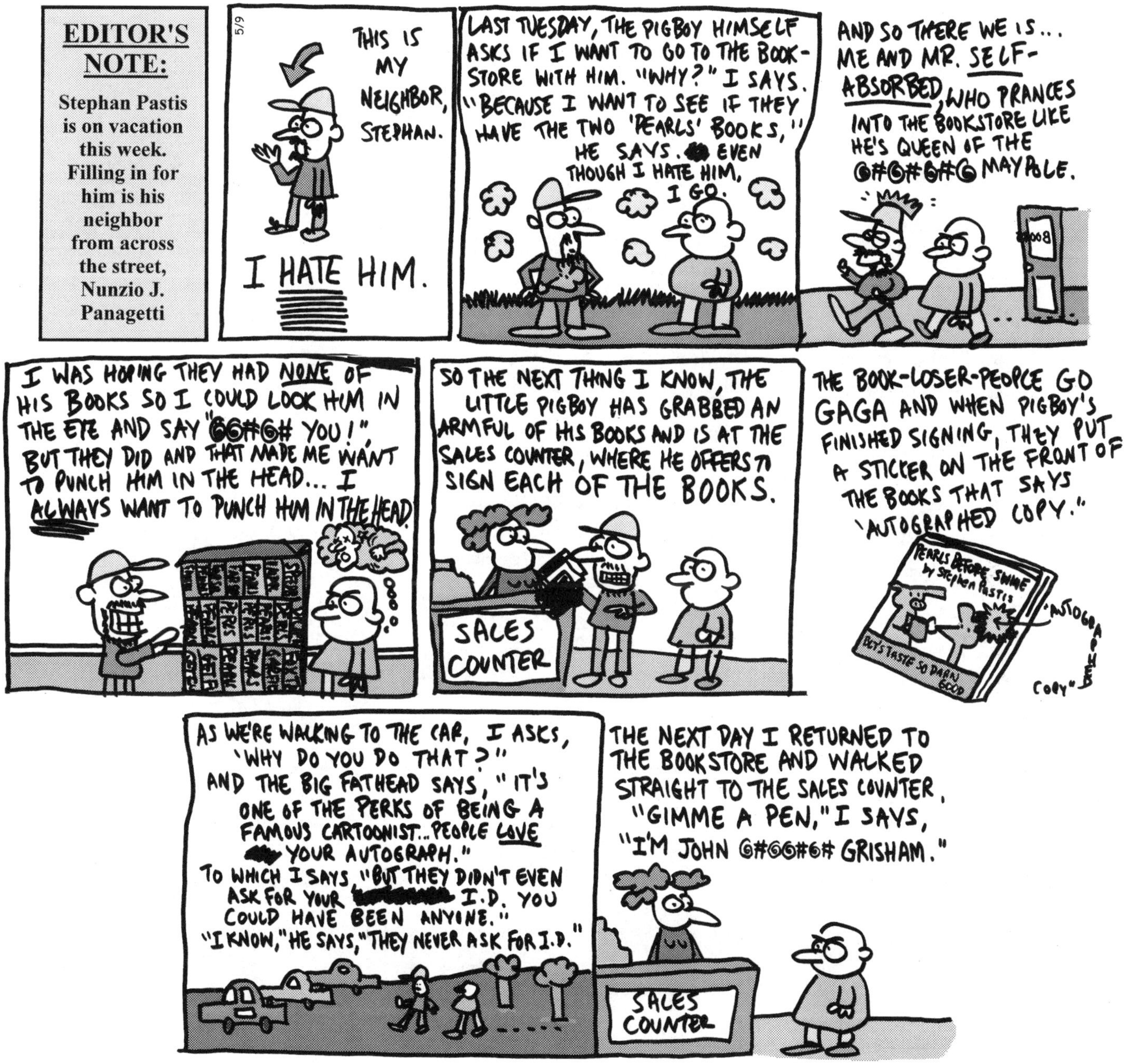
EDITOR'S NOTE:
Stephan Pastis is on vacation this week. Filling in for him is his neighbor from across the street, Nunzio J. Panagetti
5/9
THIS IS MY NEIGHBOR, STEPHAN.
I HATE HIM.
LAST TUESDAY, THE PIGBOY HIMSELF ASKS IF I WANT TO GO TO THE BOOKSTORE WITH HIM. "WHY?" I SAYS. "BECAUSE I WANT TO SEE IF THEY HAVE THE TWO 'PEARLS' BOOKS," HE SAYS. [redacted] EVEN THOUGH I HATE HIM, I GO.
AND SO THERE WE IS... ME AND MR. SELF-ABSORBED, WHO PRANCES INTO THE BOOKSTORE LIKE HE'S QUEEN OF THE @#@#@#@ MAYPOLE.
I WAS HOPING THEY HAD NONE OF HIS BOOKS SO I COULD LOOK HIM IN THE EYE AND SAY "@@#@# YOU!", BUT THEY DID AND THAT MADE ME WANT TO PUNCH HIM IN THE HEAD... I ALWAYS WANT TO PUNCH HIM IN THE HEAD.
SO THE NEXT THING I KNOW, THE LITTLE PIGBOY HAS GRABBED AN ARMFUL OF HIS BOOKS AND IS AT THE SALES COUNTER, WHERE HE OFFERS TO SIGN EACH OF THE BOOKS.
SALES COUNTER
THE BOOK-LOSER-PEOPLE GO GAGA AND WHEN PIGBOY'S FINISHED SIGNING, THEY PUT A STICKER ON THE FRONT OF THE BOOKS THAT SAYS "AUTOGRAPHED COPY."
PEARLS BEFORE SWINE by Stephan Pastis
BLT'S TASTE SO DARN GOOD
"AUTOGRAPHED COPY"
AS WE'RE WALKING TO THE CAR, I ASKS, "WHY DO YOU DO THAT?" AND THE BIG FATHEAD SAYS, "IT'S ONE OF THE PERKS OF BEING A FAMOUS CARTOONIST... PEOPLE LOVE [redacted] YOUR AUTOGRAPH." TO WHICH I SAYS, "BUT THEY DIDN'T EVEN ASK FOR YOUR [redacted] I.D. YOU COULD HAVE BEEN ANYONE." "I KNOW," HE SAYS, "THEY NEVER ASK FOR I.D."
THE NEXT DAY I RETURNED TO THE BOOKSTORE AND WALKED STRAIGHT TO THE SALES COUNTER. "GIMME A PEN," I SAYS, "I'M JOHN @#@@#@# GRISHAM."
SALES COUNTER

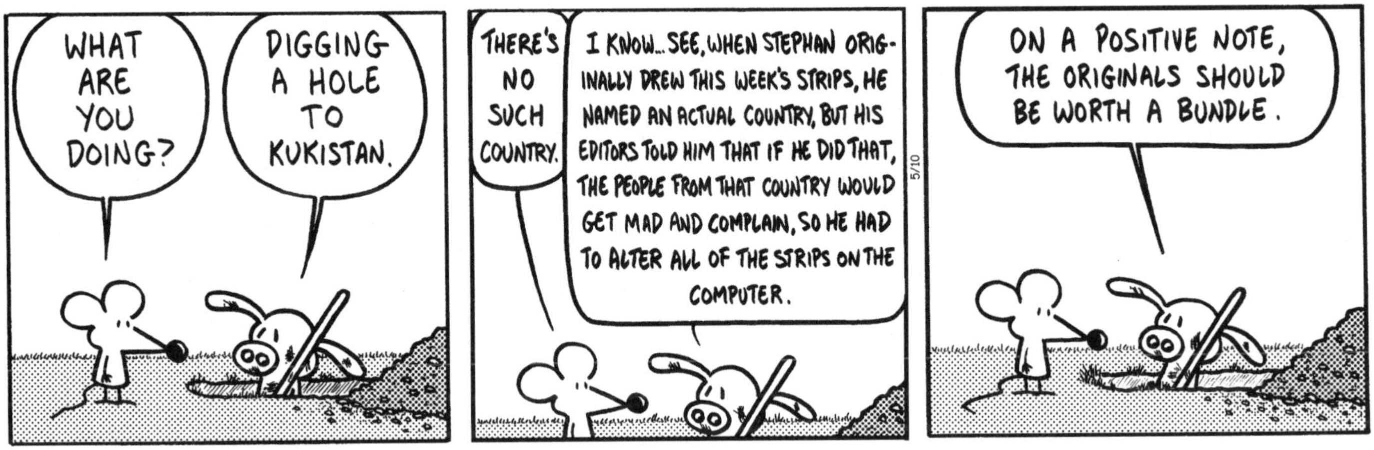
WHAT ARE YOU DOING?
DIGGING A HOLE TO KUKISTAN.
THERE'S NO SUCH COUNTRY.
I KNOW... SEE, WHEN STEPHAN ORIGINALLY DREW THIS WEEK'S STRIPS, HE NAMED AN ACTUAL COUNTRY, BUT HIS EDITORS TOLD HIM THAT IF HE DID THAT, THE PEOPLE FROM THAT COUNTRY WOULD GET MAD AND COMPLAIN, SO HE HAD TO ALTER ALL OF THE STRIPS ON THE COMPUTER.
5/10
ON A POSITIVE NOTE, THE ORIGINALS SHOULD BE WORTH A BUNDLE.

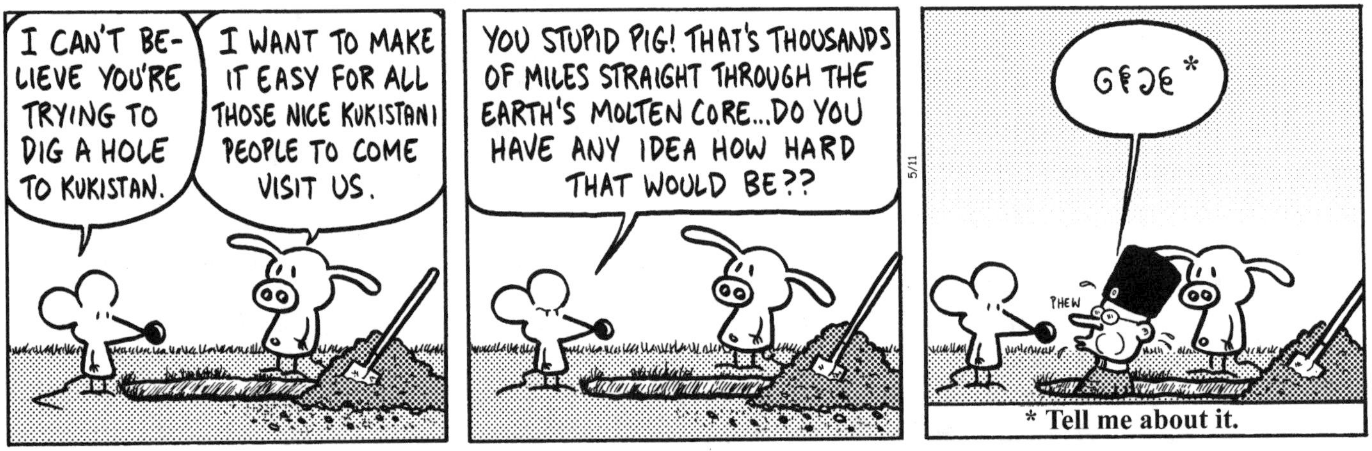
I CAN'T BELIEVE YOU'RE TRYING TO DIG A HOLE TO KUKISTAN.
I WANT TO MAKE IT EASY FOR ALL THOSE NICE KUKISTANI PEOPLE TO COME VISIT US.
YOU STUPID PIG! THAT'S THOUSANDS OF MILES STRAIGHT THROUGH THE EARTH'S MOLTEN CORE...DO YOU HAVE ANY IDEA HOW HARD THAT WOULD BE??
5/11
PHEW
* Tell me about it.

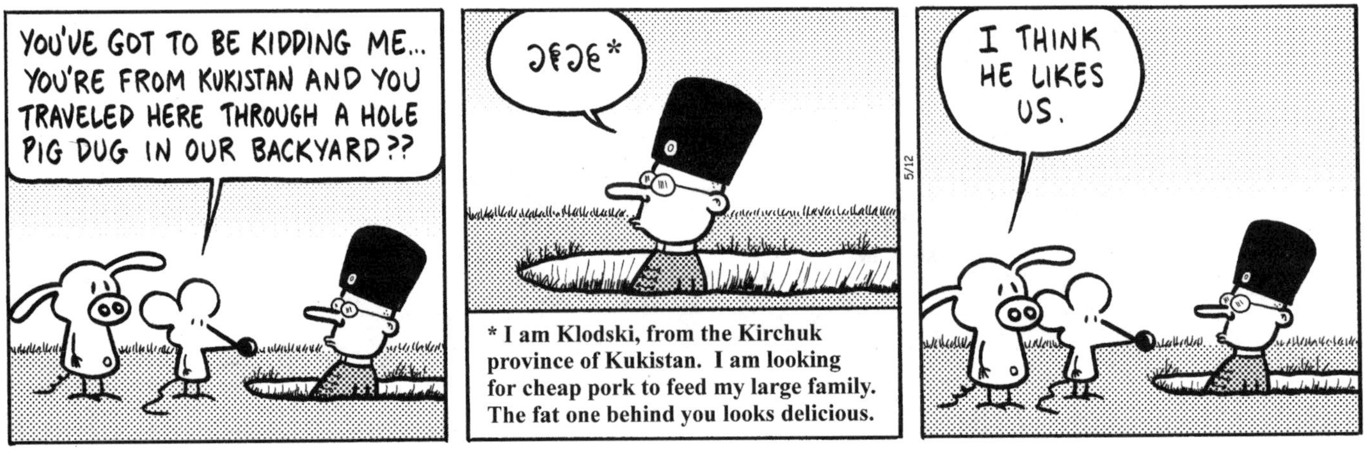
YOU'VE GOT TO BE KIDDING ME... YOU'RE FROM KUKISTAN AND YOU TRAVELED HERE THROUGH A HOLE PIG DUG IN OUR BACKYARD??
* I am Klodski, from the Kirchuk province of Kukistan. I am looking for cheap pork to feed my large family. The fat one behind you looks delicious.
5/12
I THINK HE LIKES US.

WHERE ARE YOU GOING, PIG?

I'M GOING BACK TO KUKISTAN WITH MY NEW KUKISTANI FRIEND... I CAN'T WAIT TO SEE KUKISTANI CULTURE UP CLOSE.

ϵϝϽϵ*

*The only thing you will see up close is the inside of a frying pan, you big, fat succulent pig.

...I HOPE THE LANGUAGE ISN'T A PROBLEM.

IN THE KIRCHUK PROVINCE OF KUKISTAN

ϝϽϵ*

ϝ**

* Klodski, you are back...Did you find good, cheap pork?

** Yes, I -- Holy Trotsky!...I lost him!

Ͻ*

ϝ**

*Lost him? Didn't you explain to him when he jumped into the hole that he needed to slow down as soon as he saw daylight, or else he would risk blowing right through the other side of the earth?

** Please, woman...Even a stupid pig would know that.

NUTS.

WE GOT A PROBLEM, GOAT... PASTIS LAUNCHED PIG INTO ORBIT IN THE LAST STRIP, AND HE CAN'T THINK OF A CLEVER, LOGICAL WAY TO GET HIM BACK.

DON'T WORRY, RAT...PASTIS IS A SMART GUY... I'M SURE HE'LL FIGURE OUT SOMETHING CREATIVE INVOLVING SPACE TRAVEL OR ALIEN LIFE WHERE PIG GETS RETURNED TO EARTH IN SOME ELABORATE, INSIGHTFUL WAY.

AAAAAAAAAHHHHH

THUD!!

DID YOU HEAR SOMETHING?

THIS IS MY NEW FRIEND, FROLO, THE COMEBACK CLOWN.

FROLO REBOUNDS FROM EVERYTHING.

PUSH

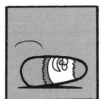

SPROING!

BAD TIMES. SETBACKS. DISAPPOINTMENTS. FROLO ALWAYS POPS BACK UP.

PUSH

SPROING!

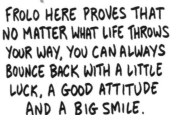

FROLO HERE PROVES THAT NO MATTER WHAT LIFE THROWS YOUR WAY, YOU CAN ALWAYS BOUNCE BACK WITH A LITTLE LUCK, A GOOD ATTITUDE AND A BIG SMILE.

POP! POP!

5/16

Foooooosshhhh

YOUR THEORY HAS HOLES.

Panel 1: BEHOLD...I HAVE INVENTED SOMETHING WHICH WILL HELP ME TO RESOLVE DISPUTES WITH DUMB PEOPLE. I CALL IT THE "MALLET O' UNDERSTANDING."

HOW DOES IT WORK?

Panel 2: WHEN PEOPLE ACT DUMB, I SMASH THEM OVER THE HEAD.

HOW DOES THAT PROMOTE UNDERSTANDING?

5/17

Panel 3: FRANKLY, I HAVEN'T THOUGHT THAT FAR AHEAD.

Panel 4: 5/18

BEHOLD...THE "MALLET O' UNDERSTANDING"...DESIGNED TO HELP ME AMICABLY RESOLVE DISPUTES WITH THOSE WHO DISAGREE WITH ME.

HOW'S IT WORK?

Panel 5: IF YOU DISAGREE WITH ME, I SMASH YOU OVER THE HEAD.

THAT'S HARDLY AMICABLE.

Panel 6: SMASH

Panel 7: SADLY, YOU WERE UNCLEAR ON THE CONCEPT.

Panel 8: BEHOLD...THE "MALLET O' UNDERSTANDING"...DESIGNED TO HELP ME AMICABLY RESOLVE DISPUTES WITH DUMB PEOPLE.

HOW DOES IT WORK?

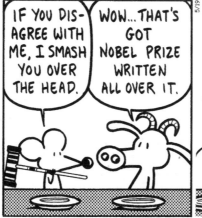

Panel 9: 5/19

IF YOU DISAGREE WITH ME, I SMASH YOU OVER THE HEAD.

WOW...THAT'S GOT NOBEL PRIZE WRITTEN ALL OVER IT.

Panel 10: SMASH

Panel 11: SNOOTY SARCASM IS NOT PRUDENT.

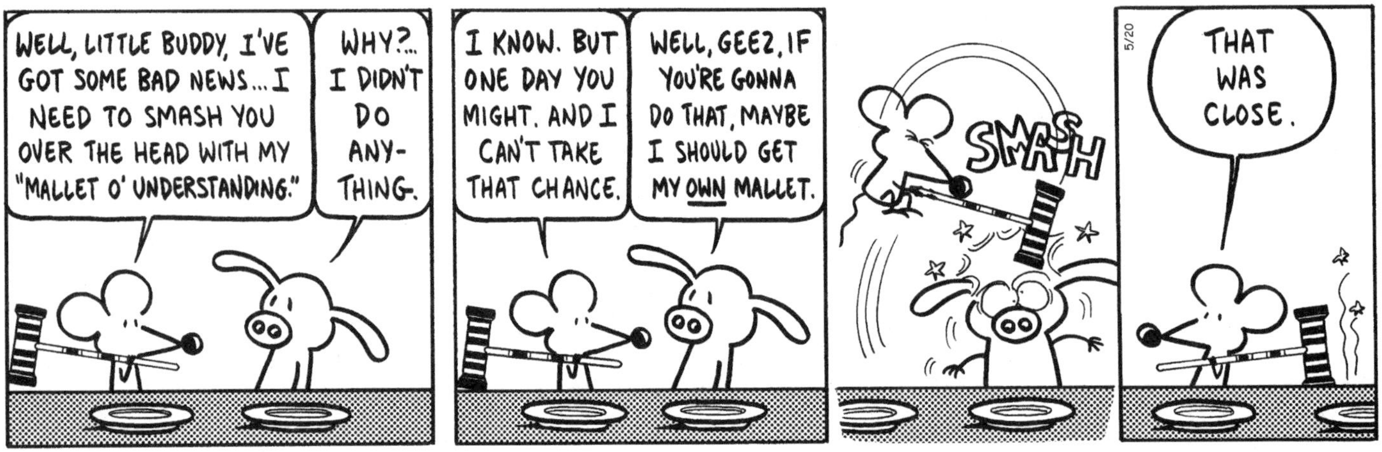
WELL, LITTLE BUDDY, I'VE GOT SOME BAD NEWS... I NEED TO SMASH YOU OVER THE HEAD WITH MY "MALLET O' UNDERSTANDING."
WHY?... I DIDN'T DO ANYTHING.
I KNOW. BUT ONE DAY YOU MIGHT. AND I CAN'T TAKE THAT CHANCE.
WELL, GEEZ, IF YOU'RE GONNA DO THAT, MAYBE I SHOULD GET MY OWN MALLET.
SMASH
5/20
THAT WAS CLOSE.

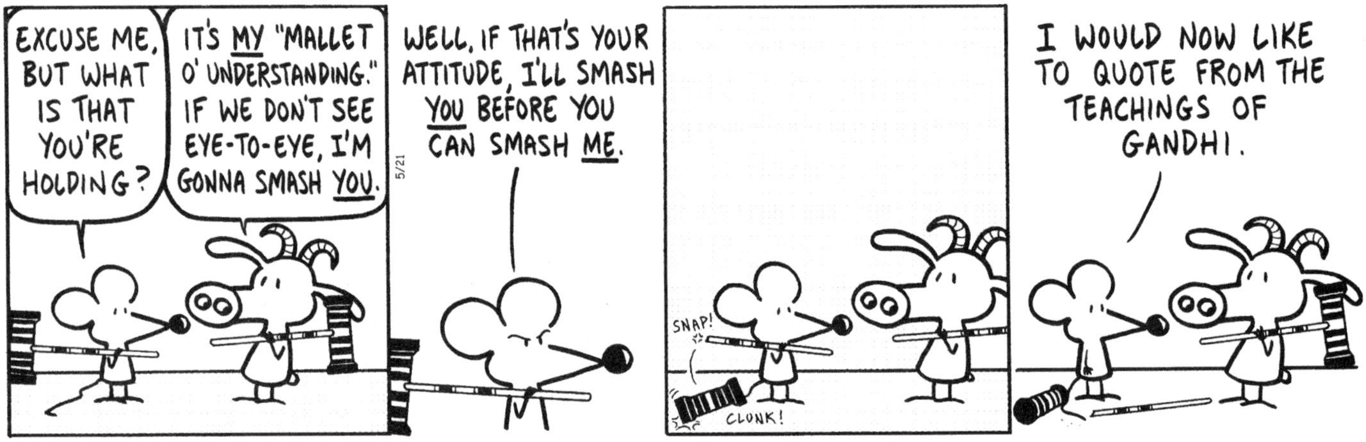
EXCUSE ME, BUT WHAT IS THAT YOU'RE HOLDING?
IT'S MY "MALLET O' UNDERSTANDING." IF WE DON'T SEE EYE-TO-EYE, I'M GONNA SMASH YOU.
5/21
WELL, IF THAT'S YOUR ATTITUDE, I'LL SMASH YOU BEFORE YOU CAN SMASH ME.
SNAP!
CLUNK!
I WOULD NOW LIKE TO QUOTE FROM THE TEACHINGS OF GANDHI.

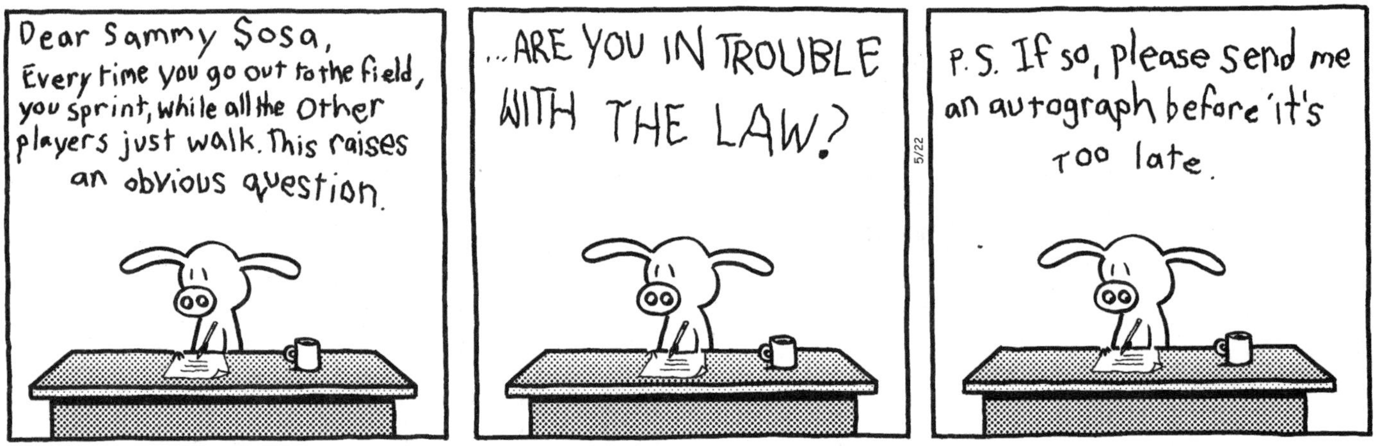
Dear Sammy Sosa,
Every time you go out to the field, you sprint, while all the other players just walk. This raises an obvious question.
...ARE YOU IN TROUBLE WITH THE LAW?
5/22
P.S. If so, please send me an autograph before it's too late.

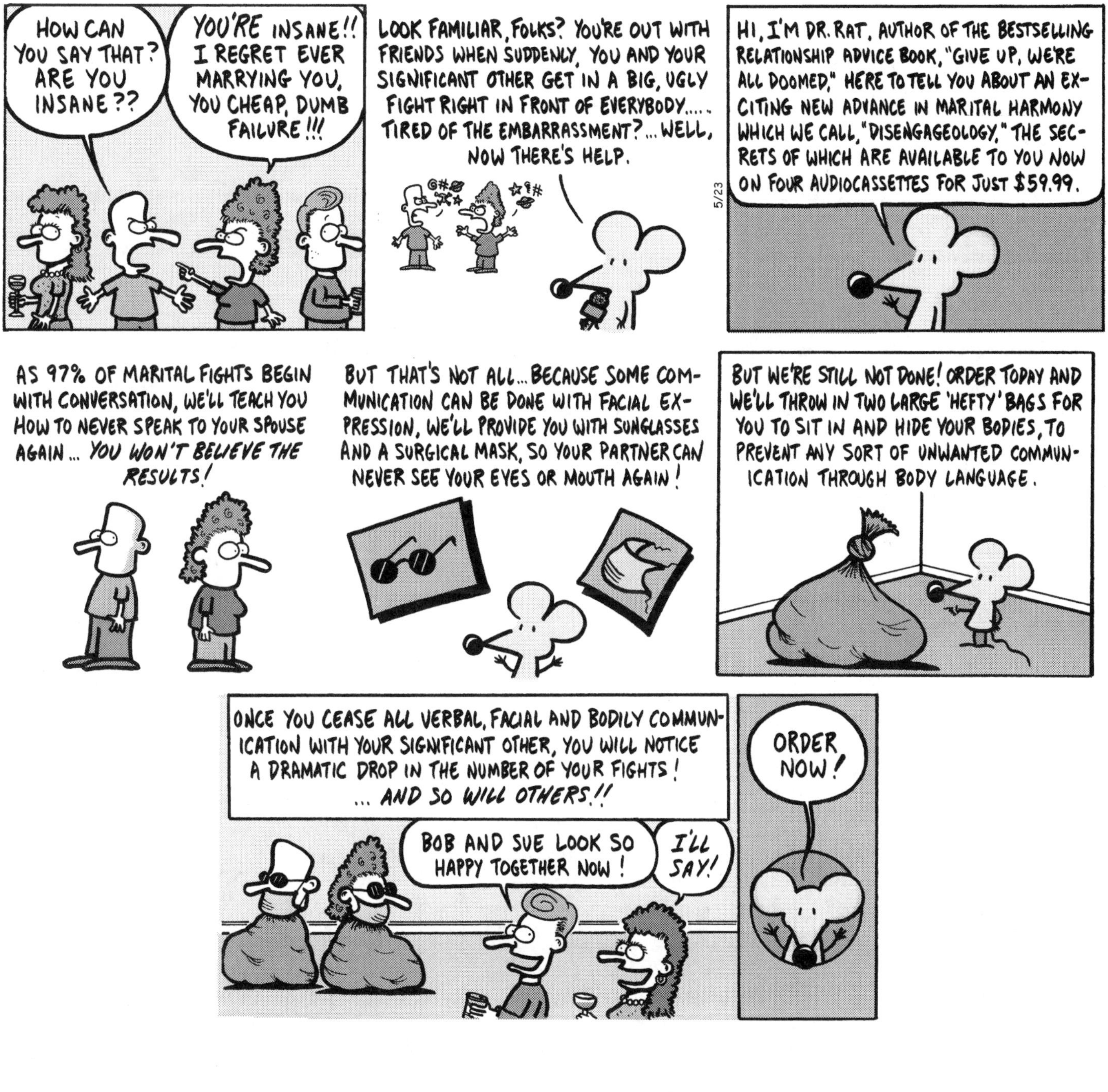
HOW CAN YOU SAY THAT? ARE YOU INSANE??
YOU'RE INSANE!! I REGRET EVER MARRYING YOU, YOU CHEAP, DUMB FAILURE!!!
LOOK FAMILIAR, FOLKS? YOU'RE OUT WITH FRIENDS WHEN SUDDENLY, YOU AND YOUR SIGNIFICANT OTHER GET IN A BIG, UGLY FIGHT RIGHT IN FRONT OF EVERYBODY..... TIRED OF THE EMBARRASSMENT?... WELL, NOW THERE'S HELP.
5/23
HI, I'M DR. RAT, AUTHOR OF THE BESTSELLING RELATIONSHIP ADVICE BOOK, "GIVE UP, WE'RE ALL DOOMED," HERE TO TELL YOU ABOUT AN EXCITING NEW ADVANCE IN MARITAL HARMONY WHICH WE CALL, "DISENGAGEOLOGY," THE SECRETS OF WHICH ARE AVAILABLE TO YOU NOW ON FOUR AUDIOCASSETTES FOR JUST $59.99.
AS 97% OF MARITAL FIGHTS BEGIN WITH CONVERSATION, WE'LL TEACH YOU HOW TO NEVER SPEAK TO YOUR SPOUSE AGAIN... YOU WON'T BELIEVE THE RESULTS!
BUT THAT'S NOT ALL... BECAUSE SOME COMMUNICATION CAN BE DONE WITH FACIAL EXPRESSION, WE'LL PROVIDE YOU WITH SUNGLASSES AND A SURGICAL MASK, SO YOUR PARTNER CAN NEVER SEE YOUR EYES OR MOUTH AGAIN!
BUT WE'RE STILL NOT DONE! ORDER TODAY AND WE'LL THROW IN TWO LARGE 'HEFTY' BAGS FOR YOU TO SIT IN AND HIDE YOUR BODIES, TO PREVENT ANY SORT OF UNWANTED COMMUNICATION THROUGH BODY LANGUAGE.
ONCE YOU CEASE ALL VERBAL, FACIAL AND BODILY COMMUNICATION WITH YOUR SIGNIFICANT OTHER, YOU WILL NOTICE A DRAMATIC DROP IN THE NUMBER OF YOUR FIGHTS! ... AND SO WILL OTHERS!!
BOB AND SUE LOOK SO HAPPY TOGETHER NOW!
I'LL SAY!
ORDER NOW!

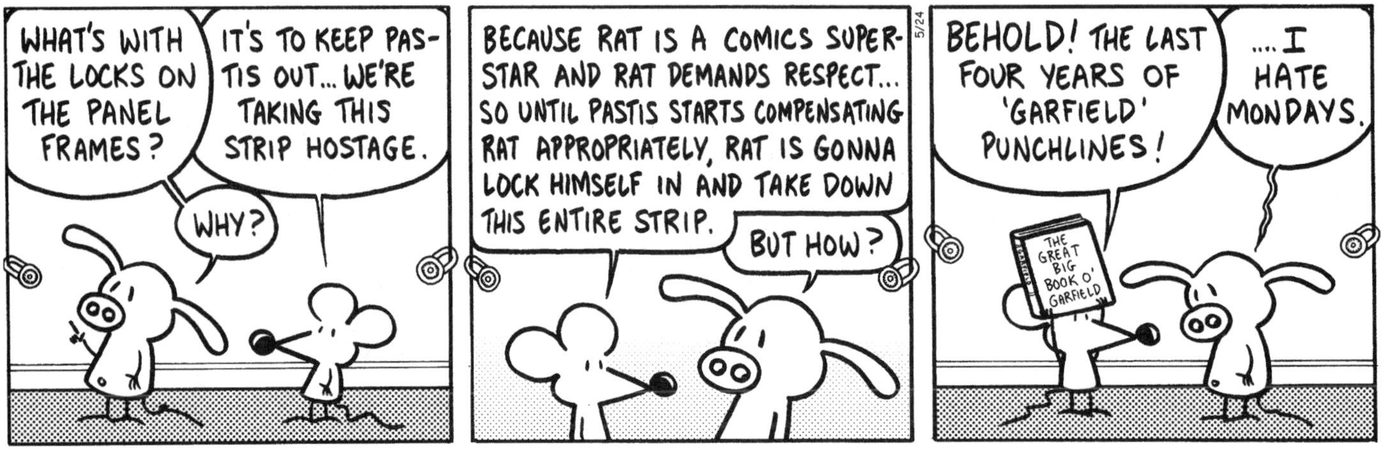
WHAT'S WITH THE LOCKS ON THE PANEL FRAMES?
IT'S TO KEEP PASTIS OUT... WE'RE TAKING THIS STRIP HOSTAGE.
WHY?
BECAUSE RAT IS A COMICS SUPERSTAR AND RAT DEMANDS RESPECT... SO UNTIL PASTIS STARTS COMPENSATING RAT APPROPRIATELY, RAT IS GONNA LOCK HIMSELF IN AND TAKE DOWN THIS ENTIRE STRIP.
BUT HOW?
5/24
BEHOLD! THE LAST FOUR YEARS OF 'GARFIELD' PUNCHLINES!
THE GREAT BIG BOOK O' GARFIELD
....I HATE MONDAYS.

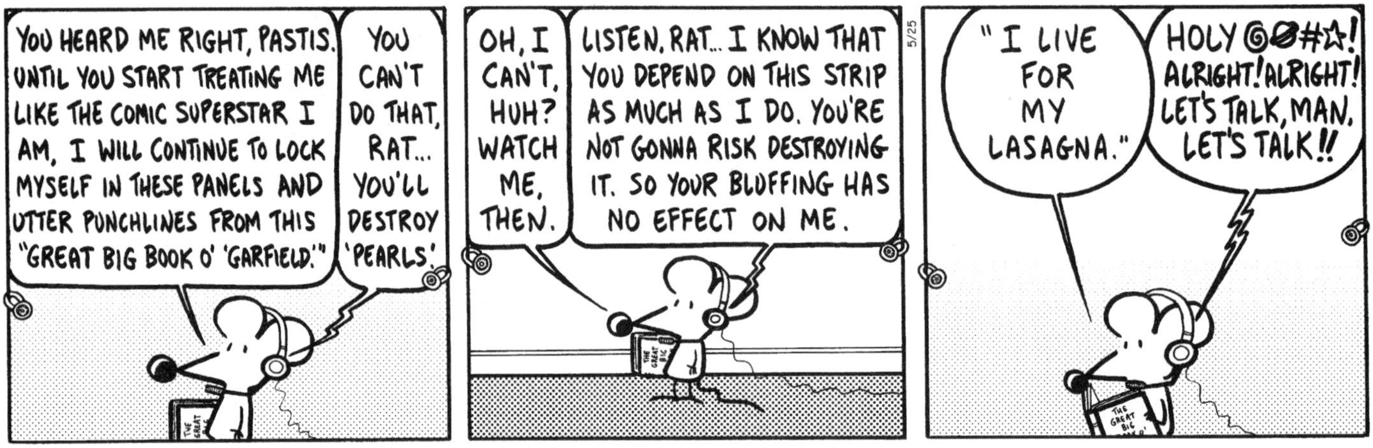
YOU HEARD ME RIGHT, PASTIS. UNTIL YOU START TREATING ME LIKE THE COMIC SUPERSTAR I AM, I WILL CONTINUE TO LOCK MYSELF IN THESE PANELS AND UTTER PUNCHLINES FROM THIS "GREAT BIG BOOK O' 'GARFIELD.'"
YOU CAN'T DO THAT, RAT... YOU'LL DESTROY 'PEARLS.'
OH, I CAN'T, HUH? WATCH ME, THEN.
LISTEN, RAT... I KNOW THAT YOU DEPEND ON THIS STRIP AS MUCH AS I DO. YOU'RE NOT GONNA RISK DESTROYING IT. SO YOUR BLUFFING HAS NO EFFECT ON ME.
5/25
"I LIVE FOR MY LASAGNA."
HOLY @@#☆! ALRIGHT! ALRIGHT! LET'S TALK, MAN. LET'S TALK!!

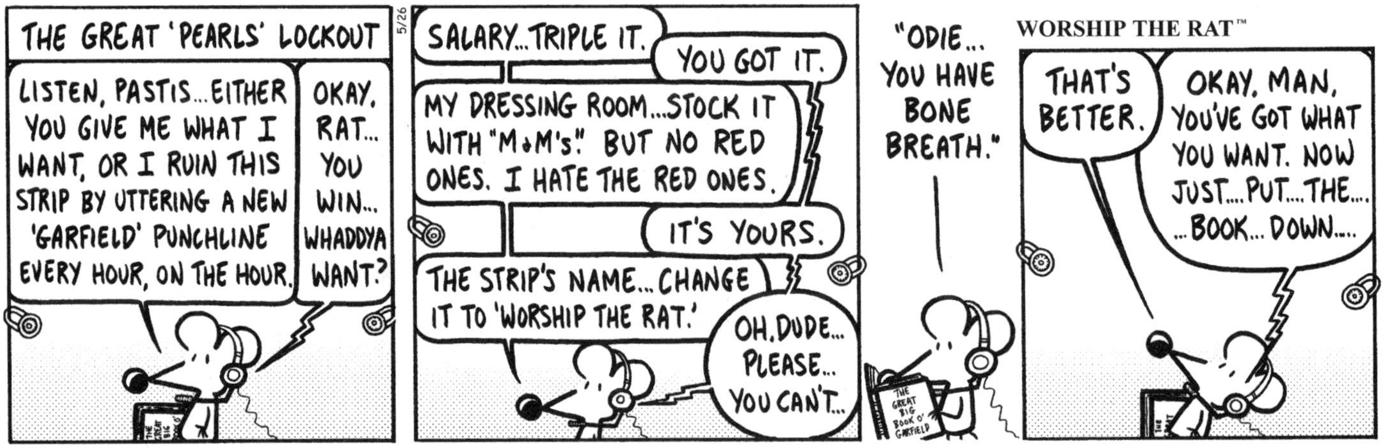
THE GREAT 'PEARLS' LOCKOUT
LISTEN, PASTIS... EITHER YOU GIVE ME WHAT I WANT, OR I RUIN THIS STRIP BY UTTERING A NEW 'GARFIELD' PUNCHLINE EVERY HOUR, ON THE HOUR.
OKAY, RAT... YOU WIN... WHADDYA WANT?
5/26
SALARY... TRIPLE IT.
YOU GOT IT.
MY DRESSING ROOM... STOCK IT WITH "M&M's." BUT NO RED ONES. I HATE THE RED ONES.
IT'S YOURS.
THE STRIP'S NAME... CHANGE IT TO 'WORSHIP THE RAT.'
OH, DUDE... PLEASE... YOU CAN'T...
"ODIE... YOU HAVE BONE BREATH."
THE GREAT BIG BOOK O' GARFIELD
WORSHIP THE RAT™
THAT'S BETTER.
OKAY, MAN, YOU'VE GOT WHAT YOU WANT. NOW JUST.... PUT.... THE.... ...BOOK... DOWN....

WORSHIP THE RAT™

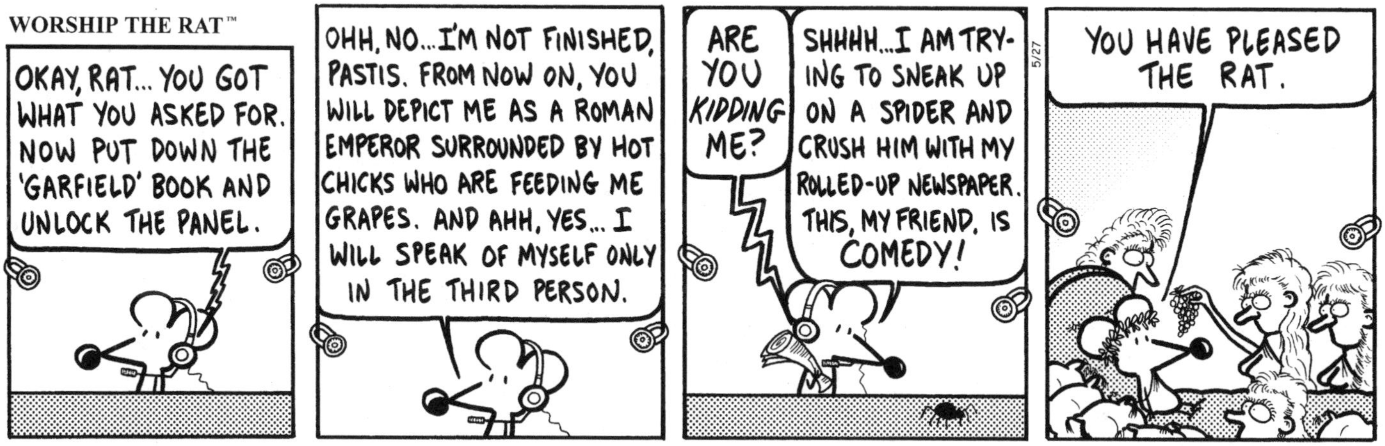
OKAY, RAT... YOU GOT WHAT YOU ASKED FOR. NOW PUT DOWN THE 'GARFIELD' BOOK AND UNLOCK THE PANEL.
OHH, NO... I'M NOT FINISHED, PASTIS. FROM NOW ON, YOU WILL DEPICT ME AS A ROMAN EMPEROR SURROUNDED BY HOT CHICKS WHO ARE FEEDING ME GRAPES. AND AHH, YES... I WILL SPEAK OF MYSELF ONLY IN THE THIRD PERSON.
ARE YOU KIDDING ME?
SHHHH... I AM TRYING TO SNEAK UP ON A SPIDER AND CRUSH HIM WITH MY ROLLED-UP NEWSPAPER. THIS, MY FRIEND, IS COMEDY!
5/27
YOU HAVE PLEASED THE RAT.

WORSHIP THE RAT™

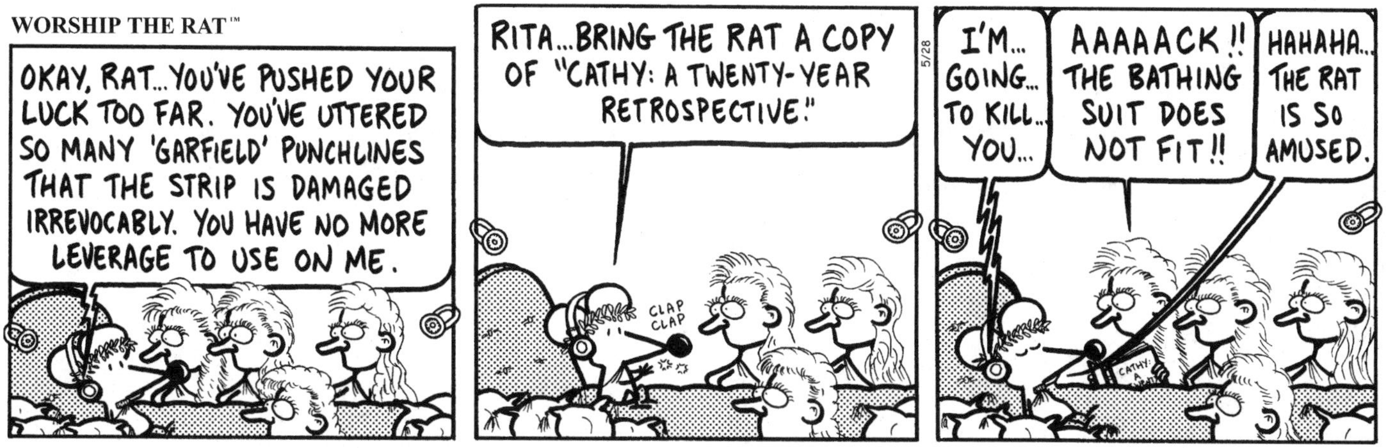
OKAY, RAT... YOU'VE PUSHED YOUR LUCK TOO FAR. YOU'VE UTTERED SO MANY 'GARFIELD' PUNCHLINES THAT THE STRIP IS DAMAGED IRREVOCABLY. YOU HAVE NO MORE LEVERAGE TO USE ON ME.
RITA... BRING THE RAT A COPY OF "CATHY: A TWENTY-YEAR RETROSPECTIVE."
CLAP CLAP
5/28
I'M... GOING... TO KILL... YOU...
AAAAACK!! THE BATHING SUIT DOES NOT FIT!!
HAHAHA... THE RAT IS SO AMUSED.

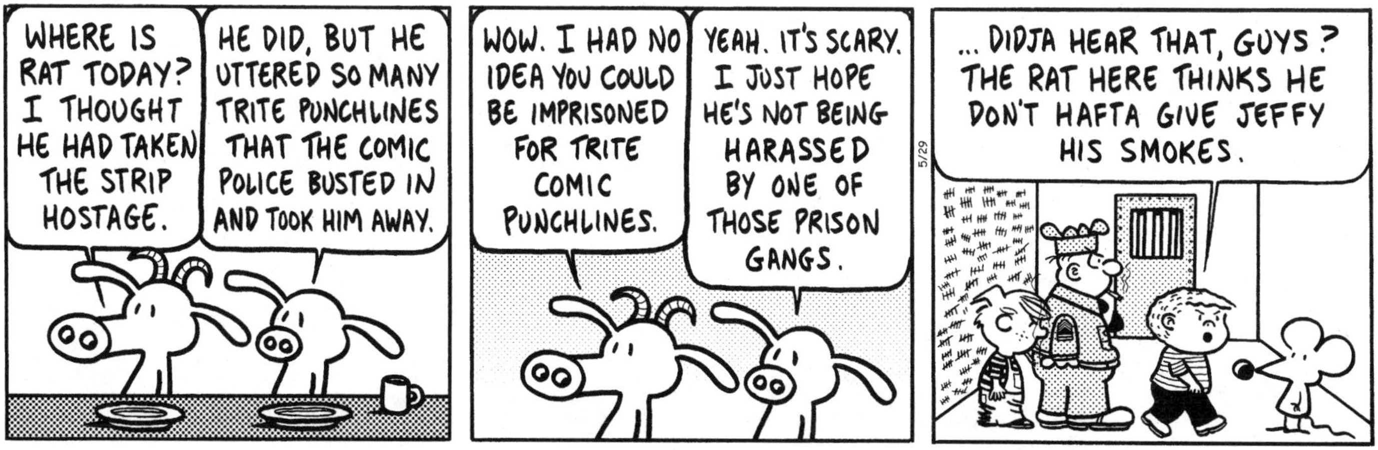
WHERE IS RAT TODAY? I THOUGHT HE HAD TAKEN THE STRIP HOSTAGE.
HE DID, BUT HE UTTERED SO MANY TRITE PUNCHLINES THAT THE COMIC POLICE BUSTED IN AND TOOK HIM AWAY.
WOW. I HAD NO IDEA YOU COULD BE IMPRISONED FOR TRITE COMIC PUNCHLINES.
YEAH. IT'S SCARY. I JUST HOPE HE'S NOT BEING HARASSED BY ONE OF THOSE PRISON GANGS.
5/29
... DIDJA HEAR THAT, GUYS? THE RAT HERE THINKS HE DON'T HAFTA GIVE JEFFY HIS SMOKES.

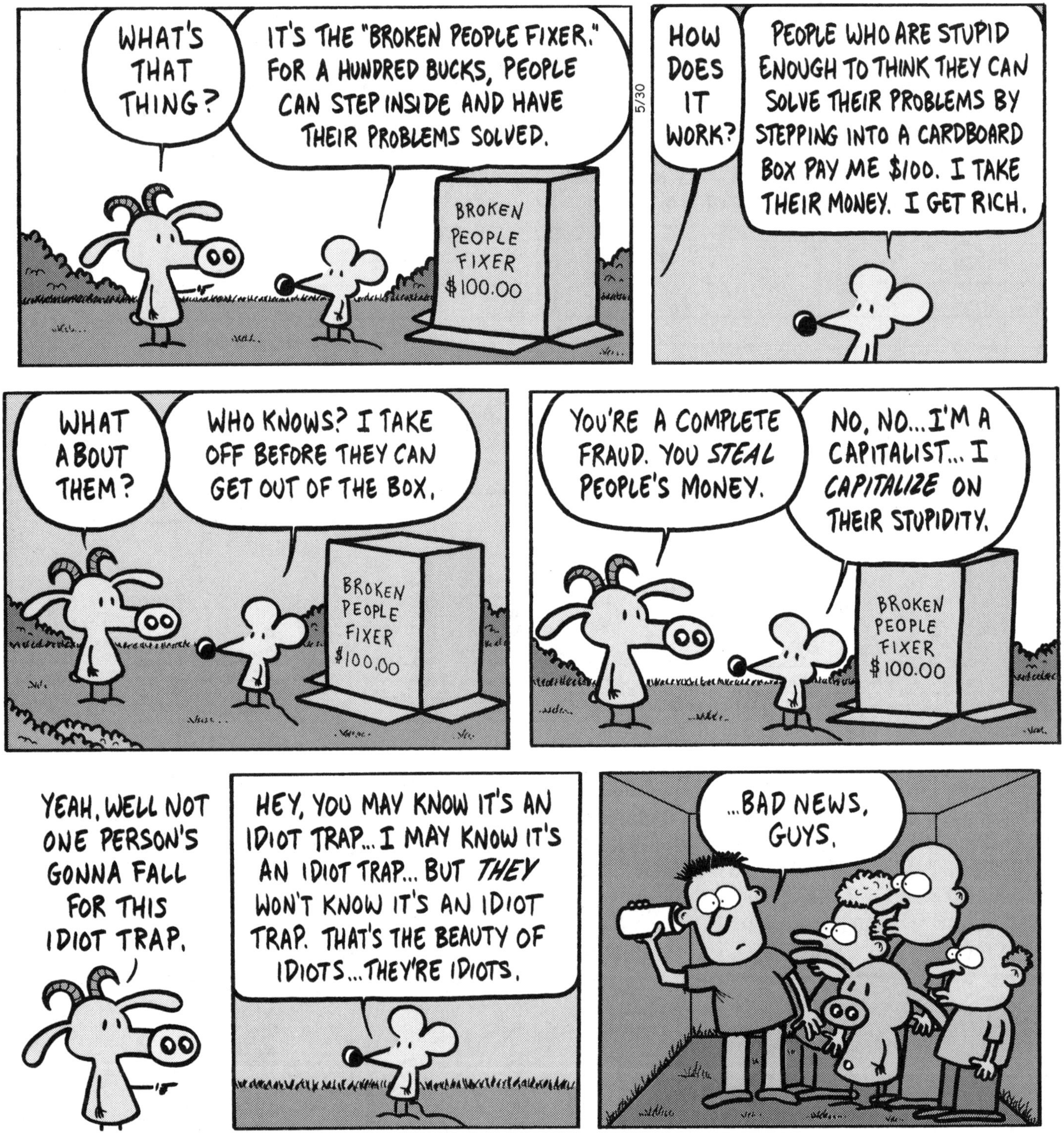
WHAT'S THAT THING?
IT'S THE "BROKEN PEOPLE FIXER." FOR A HUNDRED BUCKS, PEOPLE CAN STEP INSIDE AND HAVE THEIR PROBLEMS SOLVED.
BROKEN PEOPLE FIXER $100.00
5/30
HOW DOES IT WORK?
PEOPLE WHO ARE STUPID ENOUGH TO THINK THEY CAN SOLVE THEIR PROBLEMS BY STEPPING INTO A CARDBOARD BOX PAY ME $100. I TAKE THEIR MONEY. I GET RICH.
WHAT ABOUT THEM?
WHO KNOWS? I TAKE OFF BEFORE THEY CAN GET OUT OF THE BOX.
BROKEN PEOPLE FIXER $100.00
YOU'RE A COMPLETE FRAUD. YOU *STEAL* PEOPLE'S MONEY.
NO, NO...I'M A CAPITALIST... I *CAPITALIZE* ON THEIR STUPIDITY.
BROKEN PEOPLE FIXER $100.00
YEAH, WELL NOT ONE PERSON'S GONNA FALL FOR THIS IDIOT TRAP.
HEY, YOU MAY KNOW IT'S AN IDIOT TRAP...I MAY KNOW IT'S AN IDIOT TRAP... BUT *THEY* WON'T KNOW IT'S AN IDIOT TRAP. THAT'S THE BEAUTY OF IDIOTS...THEY'RE IDIOTS.
...BAD NEWS, GUYS.

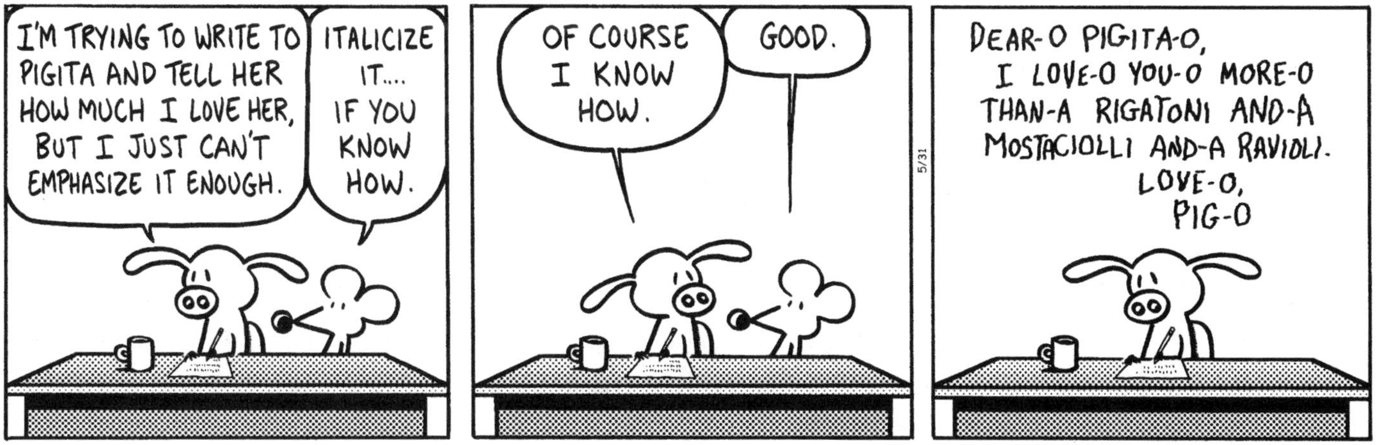
I'M TRYING TO WRITE TO PIGITA AND TELL HER HOW MUCH I LOVE HER, BUT I JUST CAN'T EMPHASIZE IT ENOUGH.
ITALICIZE IT.... IF YOU KNOW HOW.
OF COURSE I KNOW HOW.
GOOD.
5/31
DEAR-O PIGITA-O,
I LOVE-O YOU-O MORE-O THAN-A RIGATONI AND-A MOSTACIOLLI AND-A RAVIOLI.
LOVE-O,
PIG-O

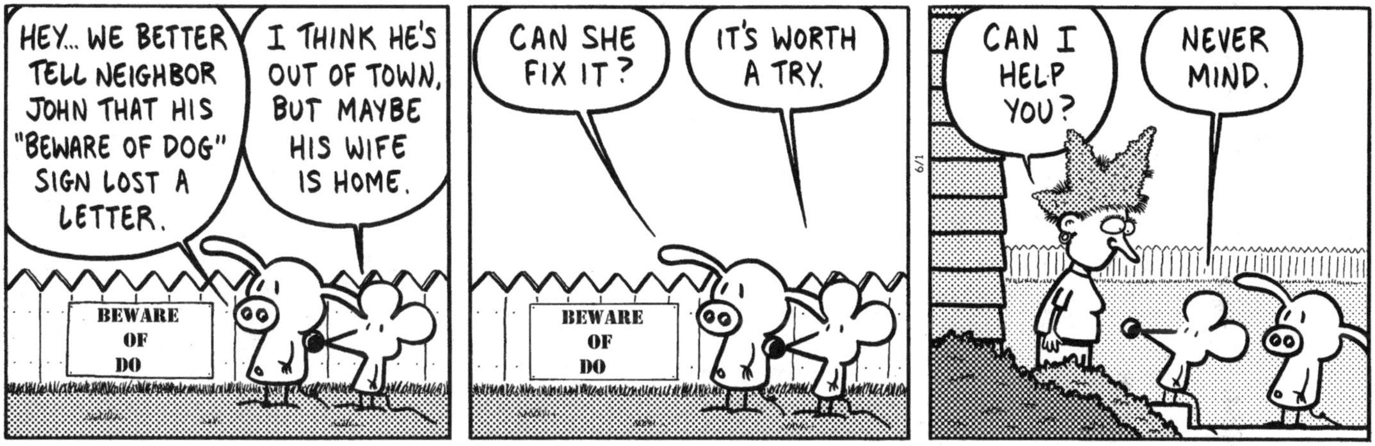
HEY... WE BETTER TELL NEIGHBOR JOHN THAT HIS "BEWARE OF DOG" SIGN LOST A LETTER.
I THINK HE'S OUT OF TOWN, BUT MAYBE HIS WIFE IS HOME.
BEWARE OF DO
CAN SHE FIX IT?
IT'S WORTH A TRY.
BEWARE OF DO
6/1
CAN I HELP YOU?
NEVER MIND.

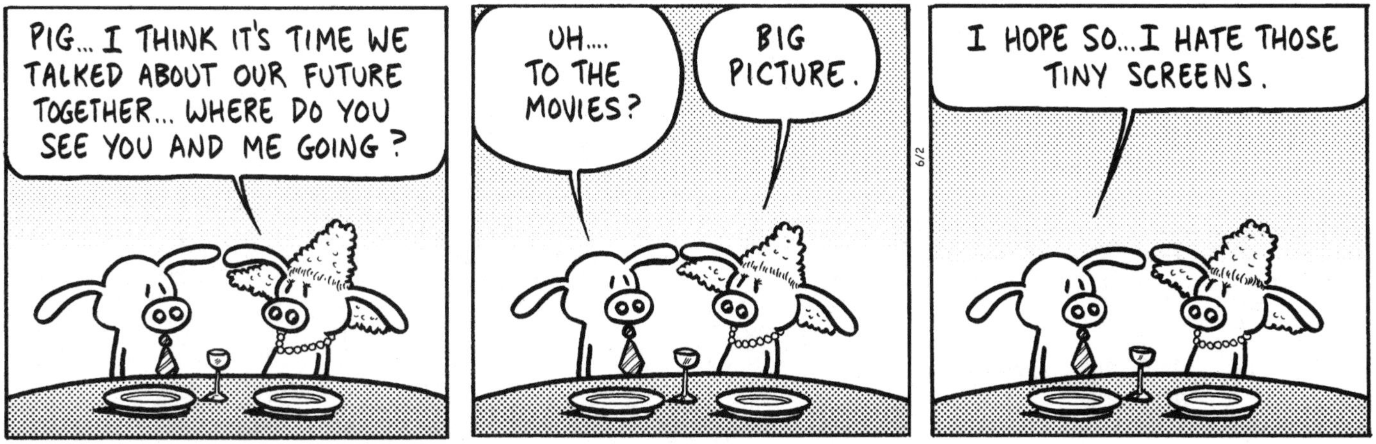
PIG... I THINK IT'S TIME WE TALKED ABOUT OUR FUTURE TOGETHER... WHERE DO YOU SEE YOU AND ME GOING?
UH.... TO THE MOVIES?
BIG PICTURE.
6/2
I HOPE SO... I HATE THOSE TINY SCREENS.

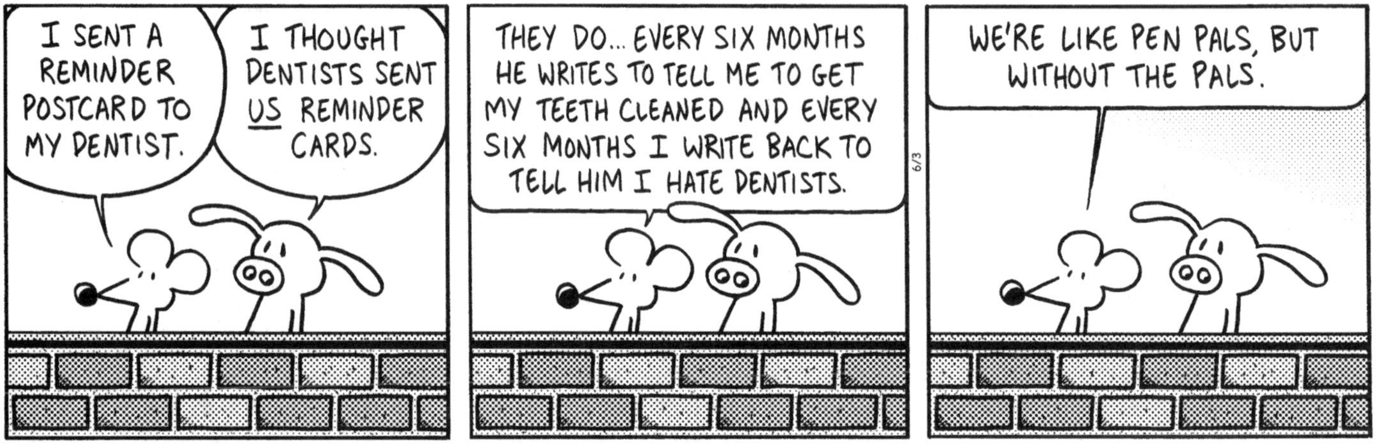
I SENT A REMINDER POSTCARD TO MY DENTIST.
I THOUGHT DENTISTS SENT US REMINDER CARDS.
THEY DO... EVERY SIX MONTHS HE WRITES TO TELL ME TO GET MY TEETH CLEANED AND EVERY SIX MONTHS I WRITE BACK TO TELL HIM I HATE DENTISTS.
6/3
WE'RE LIKE PEN PALS, BUT WITHOUT THE PALS.

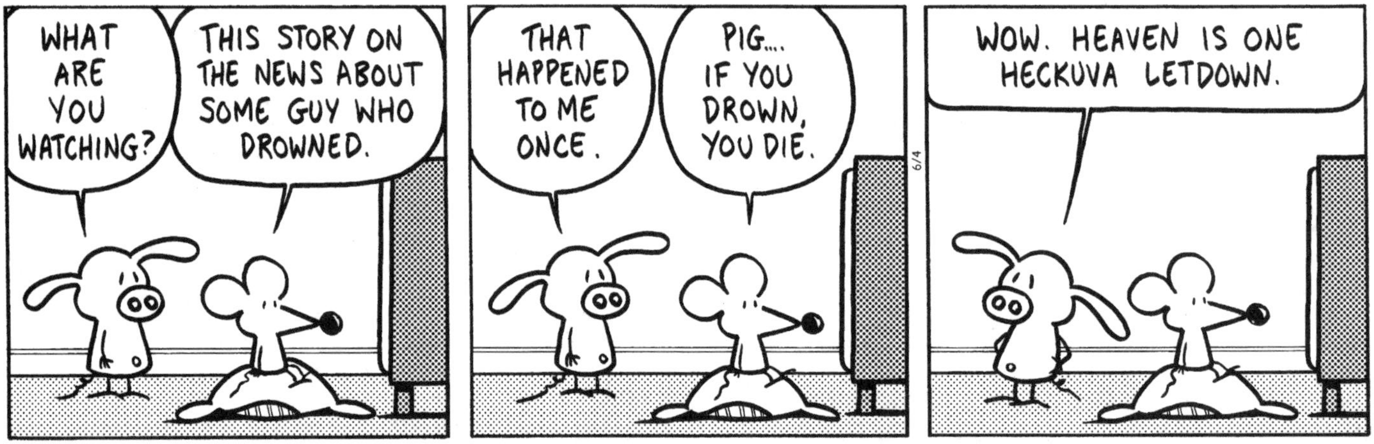
WHAT ARE YOU WATCHING?
THIS STORY ON THE NEWS ABOUT SOME GUY WHO DROWNED.
THAT HAPPENED TO ME ONCE.
PIG.... IF YOU DROWN, YOU DIE.
6/4
WOW. HEAVEN IS ONE HECKUVA LETDOWN.

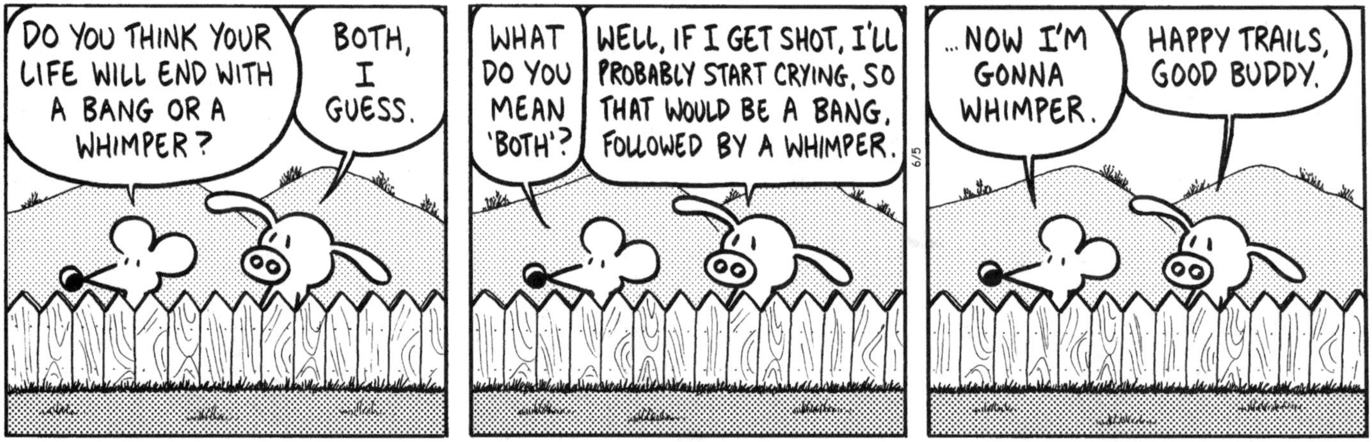
DO YOU THINK YOUR LIFE WILL END WITH A BANG OR A WHIMPER?
BOTH, I GUESS.
WHAT DO YOU MEAN 'BOTH'?
WELL, IF I GET SHOT, I'LL PROBABLY START CRYING, SO THAT WOULD BE A BANG, FOLLOWED BY A WHIMPER.
6/5
...NOW I'M GONNA WHIMPER.
HAPPY TRAILS, GOOD BUDDY.

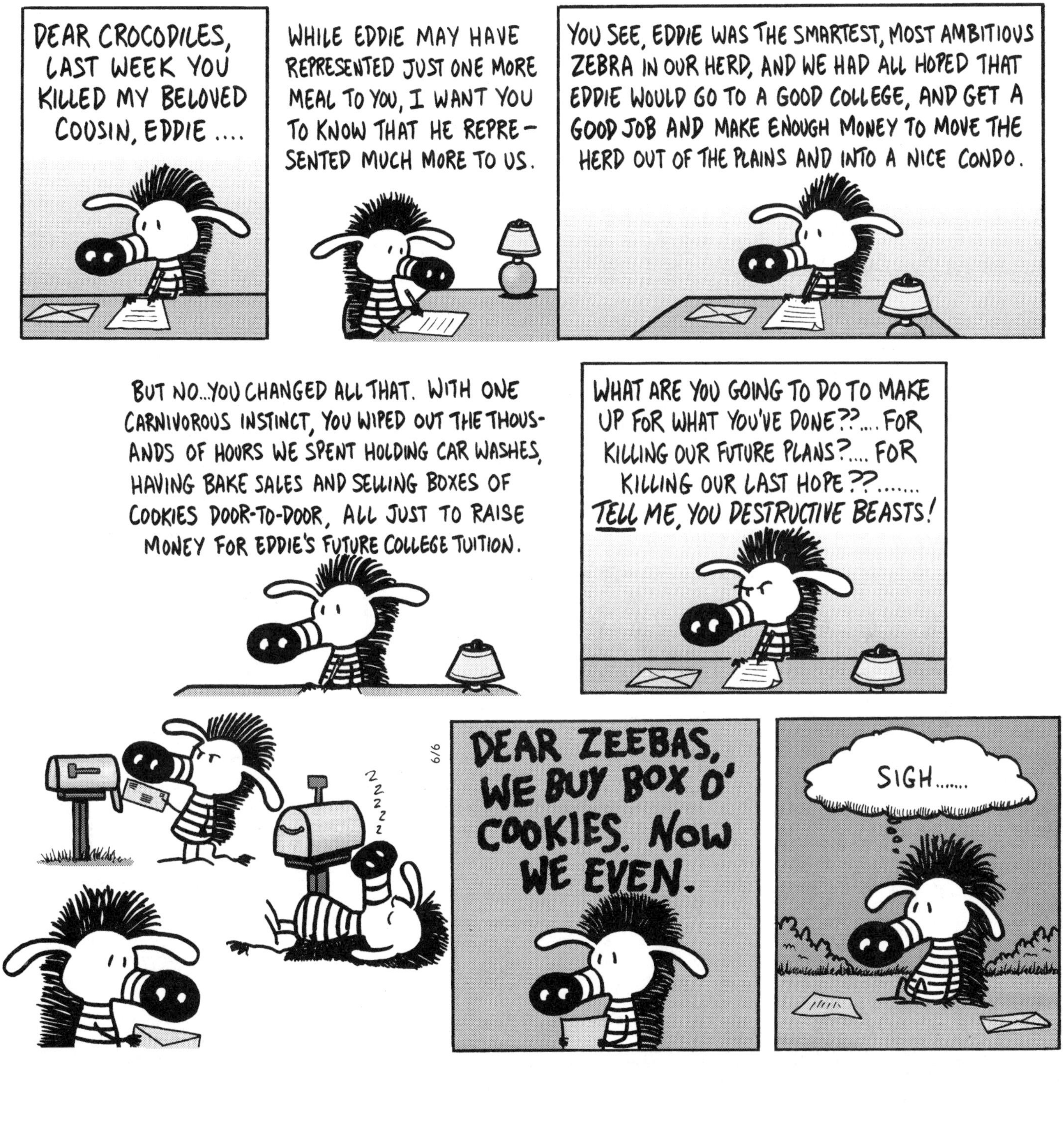
DEAR CROCODILES, LAST WEEK YOU KILLED MY BELOVED COUSIN, EDDIE....
WHILE EDDIE MAY HAVE REPRESENTED JUST ONE MORE MEAL TO YOU, I WANT YOU TO KNOW THAT HE REPRE-SENTED MUCH MORE TO US.
YOU SEE, EDDIE WAS THE SMARTEST, MOST AMBITIOUS ZEBRA IN OUR HERD, AND WE HAD ALL HOPED THAT EDDIE WOULD GO TO A GOOD COLLEGE, AND GET A GOOD JOB AND MAKE ENOUGH MONEY TO MOVE THE HERD OUT OF THE PLAINS AND INTO A NICE CONDO.
BUT NO...YOU CHANGED ALL THAT. WITH ONE CARNIVOROUS INSTINCT, YOU WIPED OUT THE THOUS-ANDS OF HOURS WE SPENT HOLDING CAR WASHES, HAVING BAKE SALES AND SELLING BOXES OF COOKIES DOOR-TO-DOOR, ALL JUST TO RAISE MONEY FOR EDDIE'S FUTURE COLLEGE TUITION.
WHAT ARE YOU GOING TO DO TO MAKE UP FOR WHAT YOU'VE DONE??.... FOR KILLING OUR FUTURE PLANS?.... FOR KILLING OUR LAST HOPE??....... TELL ME, YOU DESTRUCTIVE BEASTS!
Z Z Z Z Z
6/6
DEAR ZEEBAS, WE BUY BOX O' COOKIES. NOW WE EVEN.
SIGH.......

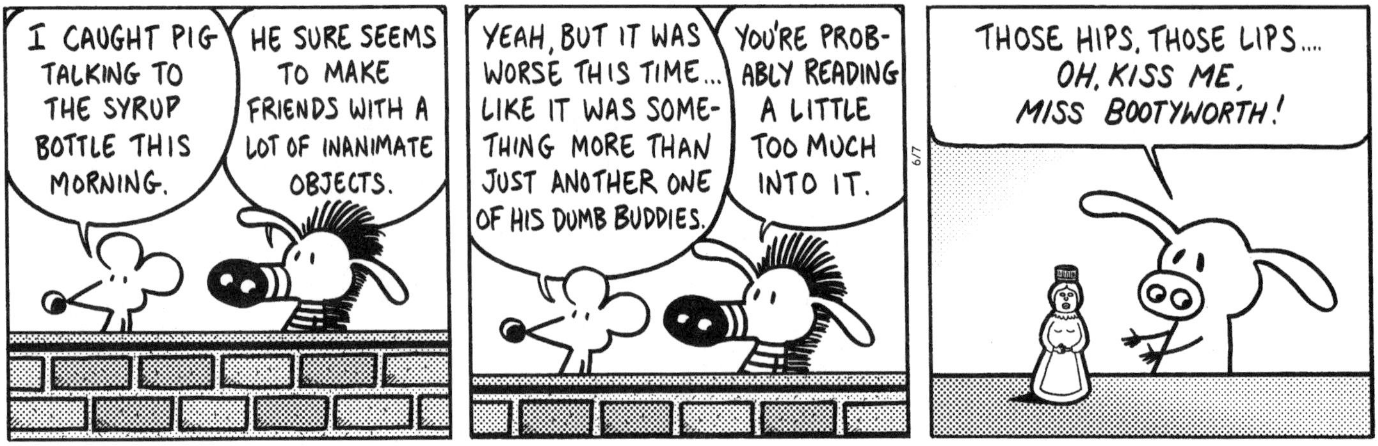
I CAUGHT PIG TALKING TO THE SYRUP BOTTLE THIS MORNING.
HE SURE SEEMS TO MAKE FRIENDS WITH A LOT OF INANIMATE OBJECTS.
YEAH, BUT IT WAS WORSE THIS TIME... LIKE IT WAS SOMETHING MORE THAN JUST ANOTHER ONE OF HIS DUMB BUDDIES.
YOU'RE PROBABLY READING A LITTLE TOO MUCH INTO IT.
6/7
THOSE HIPS, THOSE LIPS.... *OH, KISS ME, MISS BOOTYWORTH!*

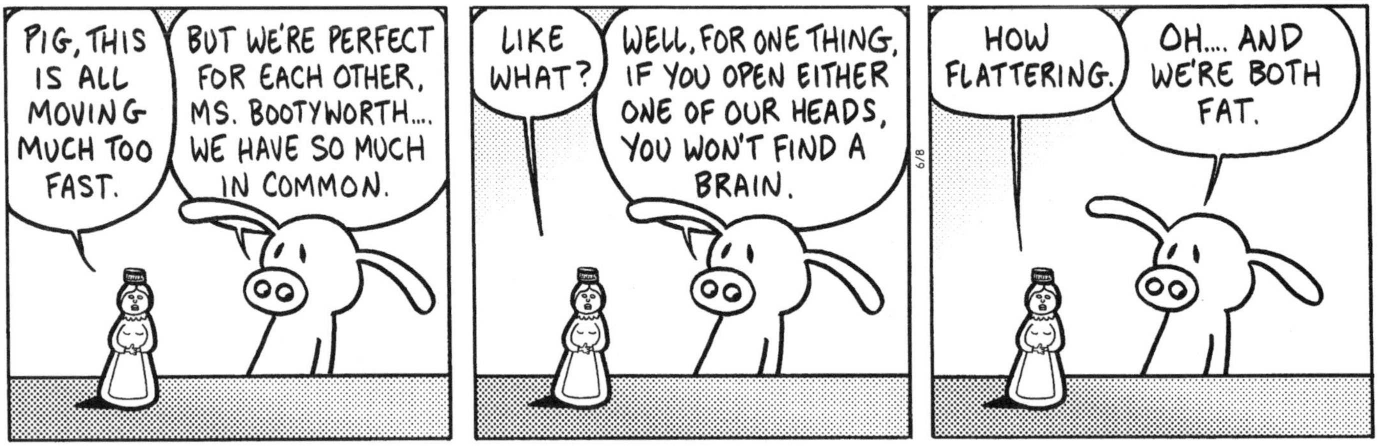
PIG, THIS IS ALL MOVING MUCH TOO FAST.
BUT WE'RE PERFECT FOR EACH OTHER, MS. BOOTYWORTH.... WE HAVE SO MUCH IN COMMON.
LIKE WHAT?
WELL, FOR ONE THING, IF YOU OPEN EITHER ONE OF OUR HEADS, YOU WON'T FIND A BRAIN.
6/8
HOW FLATTERING.
OH.... AND WE'RE BOTH FAT.

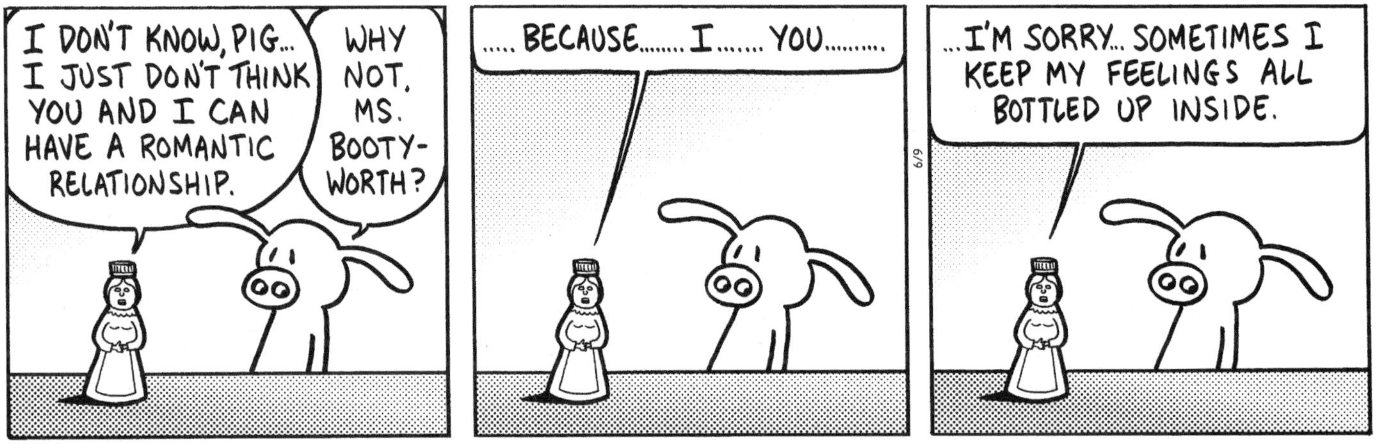
I DON'T KNOW, PIG... I JUST DON'T THINK YOU AND I CAN HAVE A ROMANTIC RELATIONSHIP.
WHY NOT, MS. BOOTYWORTH?
..... BECAUSE........ I....... YOU..........
6/9
...I'M SORRY... SOMETIMES I KEEP MY FEELINGS ALL BOTTLED UP INSIDE.

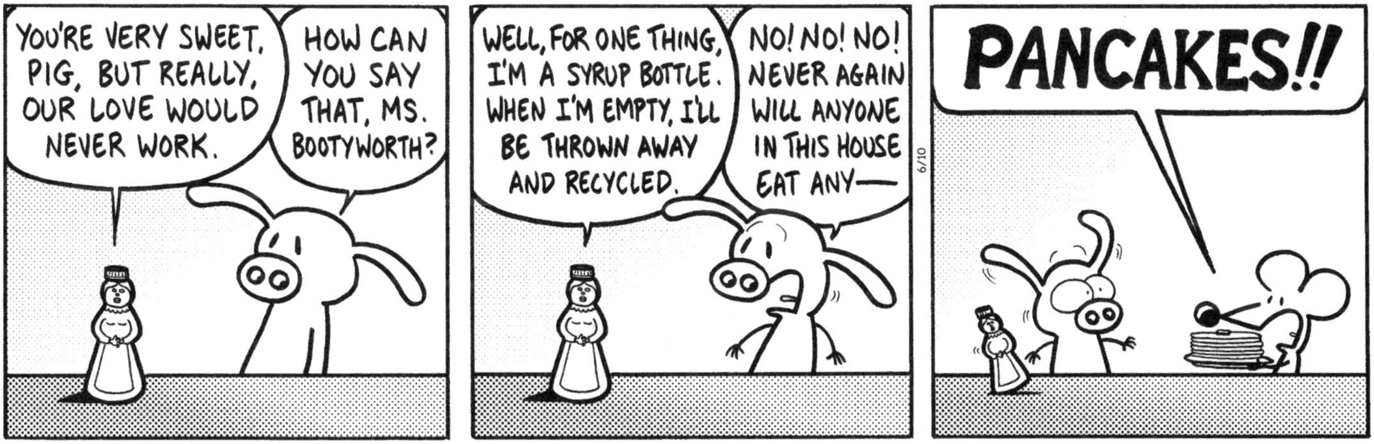
YOU'RE VERY SWEET, PIG, BUT REALLY, OUR LOVE WOULD NEVER WORK.
HOW CAN YOU SAY THAT, MS. BOOTYWORTH?
WELL, FOR ONE THING, I'M A SYRUP BOTTLE. WHEN I'M EMPTY, I'LL BE THROWN AWAY AND RECYCLED.
NO! NO! NO! NEVER AGAIN WILL ANYONE IN THIS HOUSE EAT ANY—
6/10
PANCAKES!!

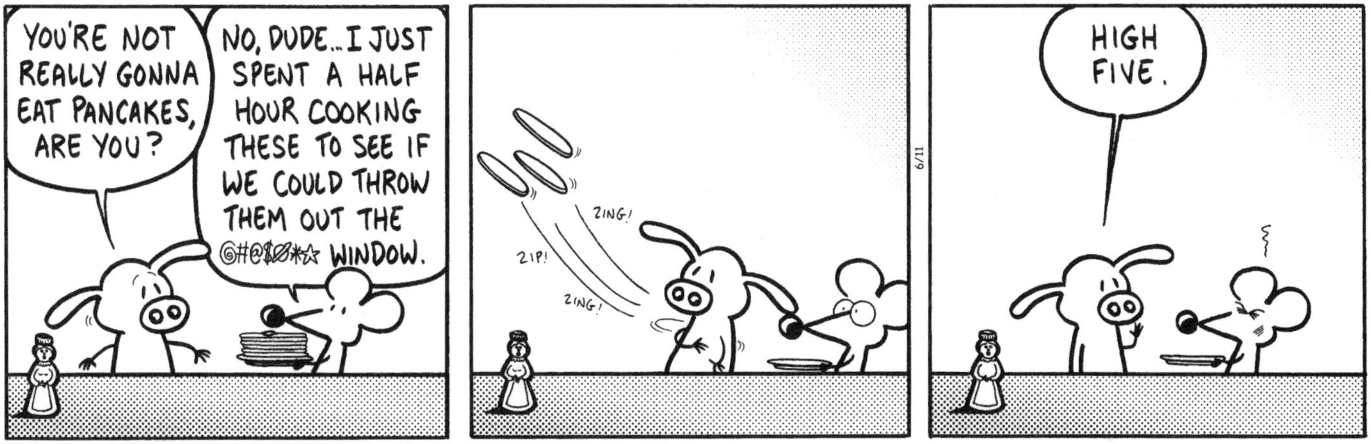
YOU'RE NOT REALLY GONNA EAT PANCAKES, ARE YOU?
NO, DUDE... I JUST SPENT A HALF HOUR COOKING THESE TO SEE IF WE COULD THROW THEM OUT THE @#@$Ø*✩ WINDOW.
ZING!
ZIP!
ZING!
6/11
HIGH FIVE.

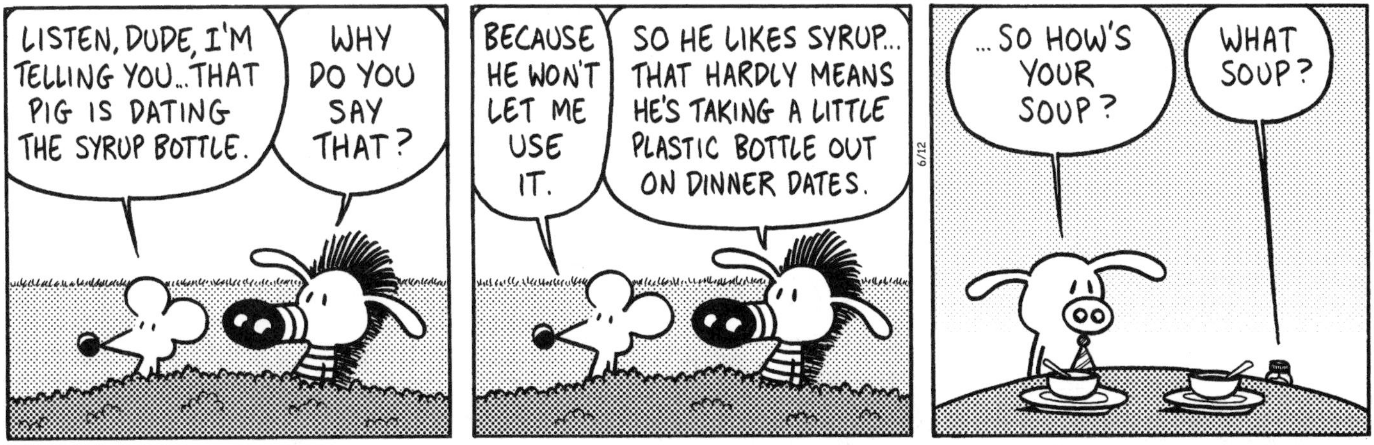
LISTEN, DUDE, I'M TELLING YOU... THAT PIG IS DATING THE SYRUP BOTTLE.
WHY DO YOU SAY THAT?
BECAUSE HE WON'T LET ME USE IT.
SO HE LIKES SYRUP... THAT HARDLY MEANS HE'S TAKING A LITTLE PLASTIC BOTTLE OUT ON DINNER DATES.
6/12
...SO HOW'S YOUR SOUP?
WHAT SOUP?

 DEAR CROCODILES, RECENTLY, I TOLD YOU ABOUT MY COUSIN EDDIE, WHO YOU KILLED.

 I TOLD YOU HOW WE HAD SPENT THOU-SANDS OF HOURS SELLING COOKIES DOOR-TO-DOOR TO RAISE MONEY FOR EDDIE'S FUTURE COLLEGE TUITION, SO THAT EDDIE COULD ONE DAY GET A GOOD JOB AND RESCUE OUR HERD FROM THE PLAINS.

 EVEN THOUGH EDDIE IS NOW DEAD, AND THERE IS NO MORE NEED TO RAISE MONEY, YOU OFFERED TO BUY ONE BOX OF COOKIES. WHILE WE SHOULD HAVE REJECTED YOUR USELESS GESTURE, WE ACTED IN GOOD FAITH BY SHIPPING YOU A BOX OF THIN MINT COOKIES AND BILLING YOU $2.76.

6/13

 TO DATE, YOU HAVE NOT PAID US A DIME.

 CAN YOU PLEASE TELL US WHY YOU WISH TO LOP THIS PETTY, AGGRAVATING HUMILIATION ATOP YOUR SIN OF MURDERING MY COUSIN?

 U.S. MAIL

DEER ZEEBAS. BEEG CASH FRO PROBBEMS. PEESE BEE PAYSHUNT.

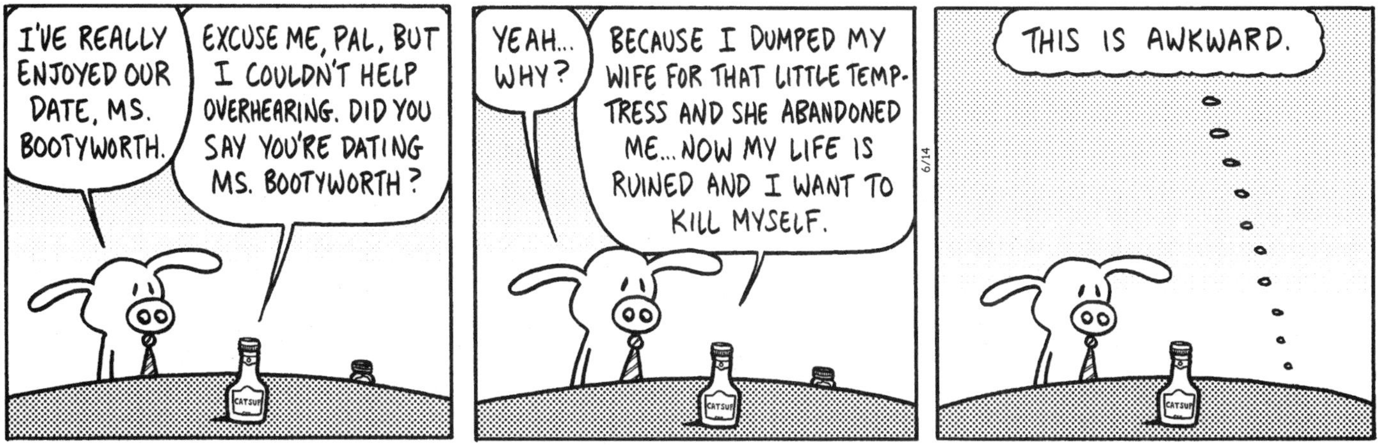
I'VE REALLY ENJOYED OUR DATE, MS. BOOTYWORTH.
EXCUSE ME, PAL, BUT I COULDN'T HELP OVERHEARING. DID YOU SAY YOU'RE DATING MS. BOOTYWORTH?
CATSUP
YEAH... WHY?
BECAUSE I DUMPED MY WIFE FOR THAT LITTLE TEMPTRESS AND SHE ABANDONED ME... NOW MY LIFE IS RUINED AND I WANT TO KILL MYSELF.
6/14
THIS IS AWKWARD.

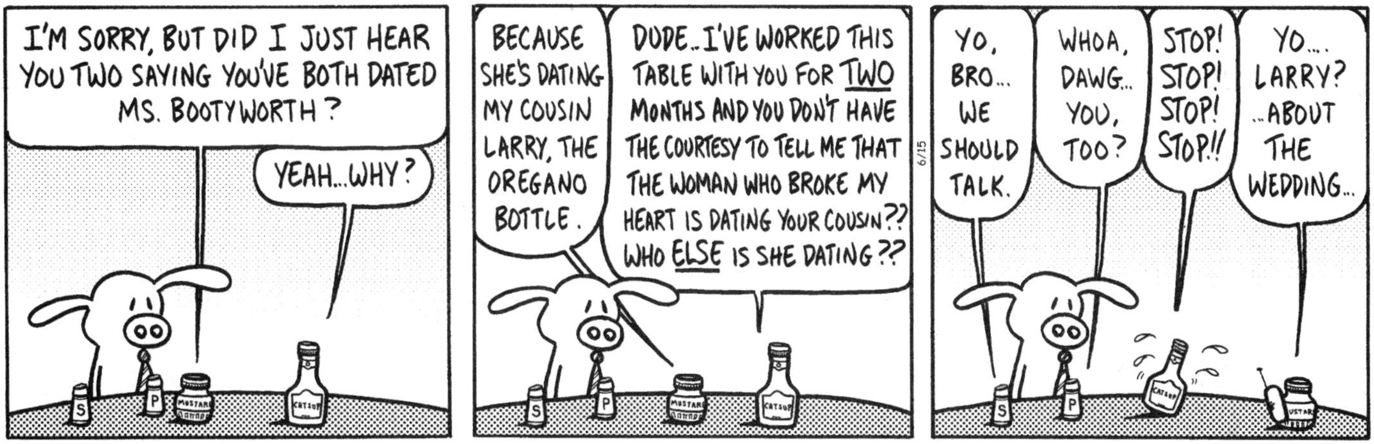
I'M SORRY, BUT DID I JUST HEAR YOU TWO SAYING YOU'VE BOTH DATED MS. BOOTYWORTH?
YEAH...WHY?
BECAUSE SHE'S DATING MY COUSIN LARRY, THE OREGANO BOTTLE.
DUDE..I'VE WORKED THIS TABLE WITH YOU FOR TWO MONTHS AND YOU DON'T HAVE THE COURTESY TO TELL ME THAT THE WOMAN WHO BROKE MY HEART IS DATING YOUR COUSIN?? WHO ELSE IS SHE DATING??
6/15
YO, BRO... WE SHOULD TALK.
WHOA, DAWG... YOU, TOO?
STOP! STOP! STOP! STOP!!
YO.... LARRY? ...ABOUT THE WEDDING...

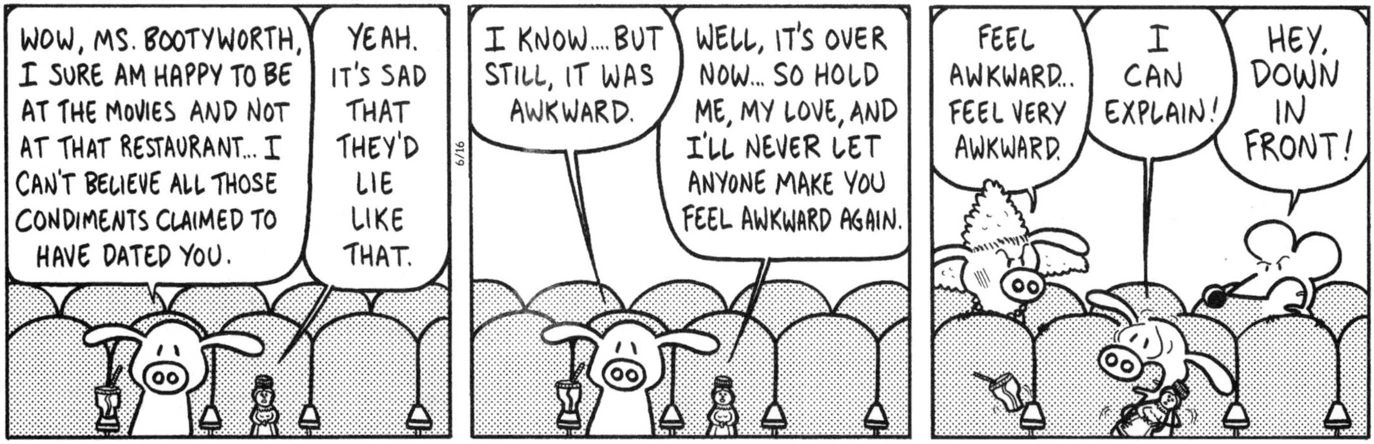
WOW, MS. BOOTYWORTH, I SURE AM HAPPY TO BE AT THE MOVIES AND NOT AT THAT RESTAURANT... I CAN'T BELIEVE ALL THOSE CONDIMENTS CLAIMED TO HAVE DATED YOU.
YEAH. IT'S SAD THAT THEY'D LIE LIKE THAT.
6/16
I KNOW.... BUT STILL, IT WAS AWKWARD.
WELL, IT'S OVER NOW... SO HOLD ME, MY LOVE, AND I'LL NEVER LET ANYONE MAKE YOU FEEL AWKWARD AGAIN.
FEEL AWKWARD.. FEEL VERY AWKWARD.
I CAN EXPLAIN!
HEY, DOWN IN FRONT!

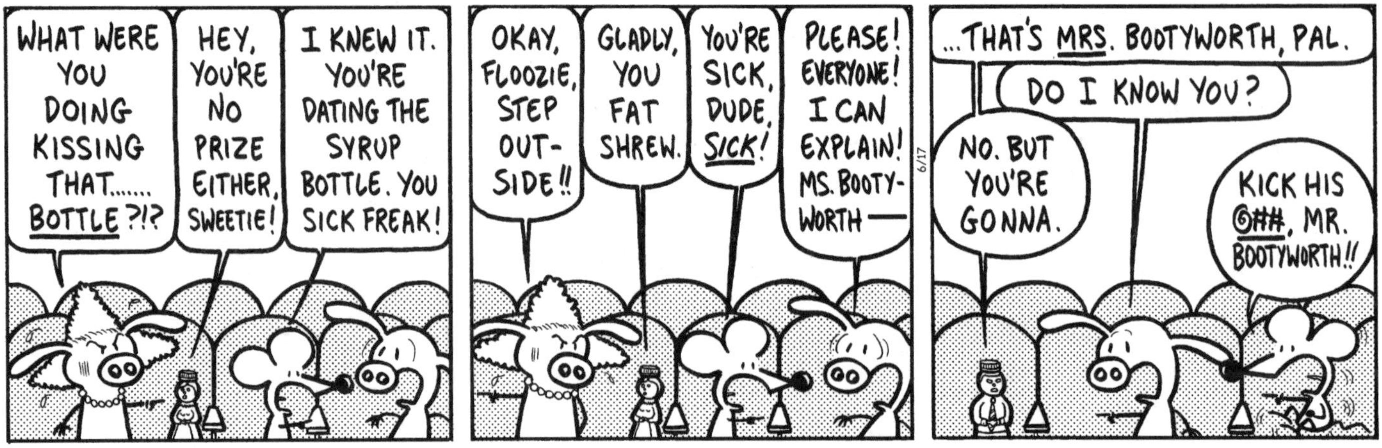
WHAT WERE YOU DOING KISSING THAT....... BOTTLE?!?
HEY, YOU'RE NO PRIZE EITHER, SWEETIE!
I KNEW IT. YOU'RE DATING THE SYRUP BOTTLE. YOU SICK FREAK!
OKAY, FLOOZIE, STEP OUT-SIDE!!
GLADLY, YOU FAT SHREW.
YOU'RE SICK, DUDE, SICK!
PLEASE! EVERYONE! I CAN EXPLAIN! MS. BOOTY-WORTH —
6/17
...THAT'S MRS. BOOTYWORTH, PAL.
DO I KNOW YOU?
NO. BUT YOU'RE GONNA.
KICK HIS @##, MR. BOOTYWORTH!!

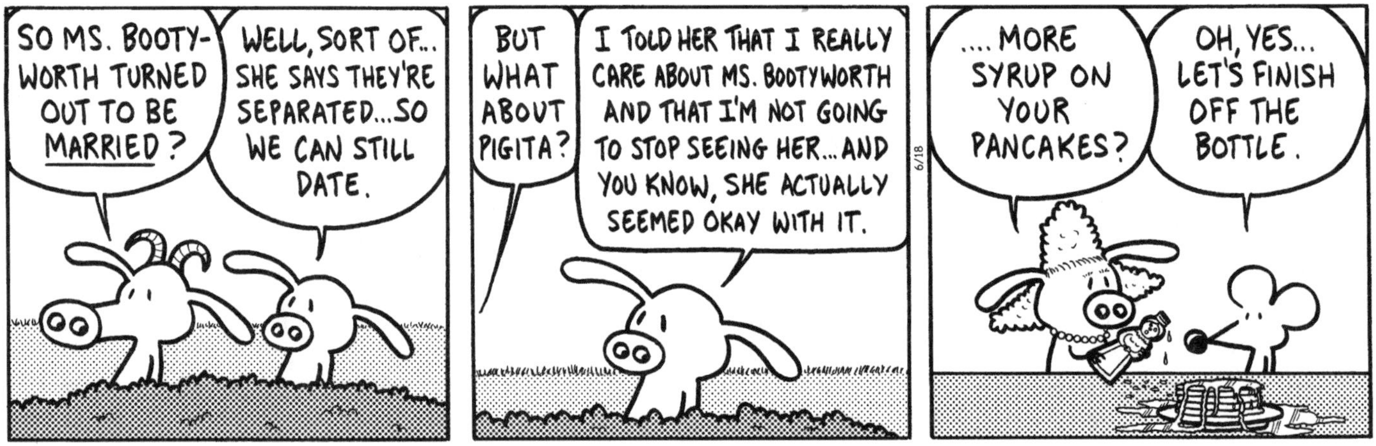
SO MS. BOOTY-WORTH TURNED OUT TO BE MARRIED?
WELL, SORT OF... SHE SAYS THEY'RE SEPARATED...SO WE CAN STILL DATE.
BUT WHAT ABOUT PIGITA?
I TOLD HER THAT I REALLY CARE ABOUT MS. BOOTYWORTH AND THAT I'M NOT GOING TO STOP SEEING HER...AND YOU KNOW, SHE ACTUALLY SEEMED OKAY WITH IT.
6/18
....MORE SYRUP ON YOUR PANCAKES?
OH, YES... LET'S FINISH OFF THE BOTTLE.

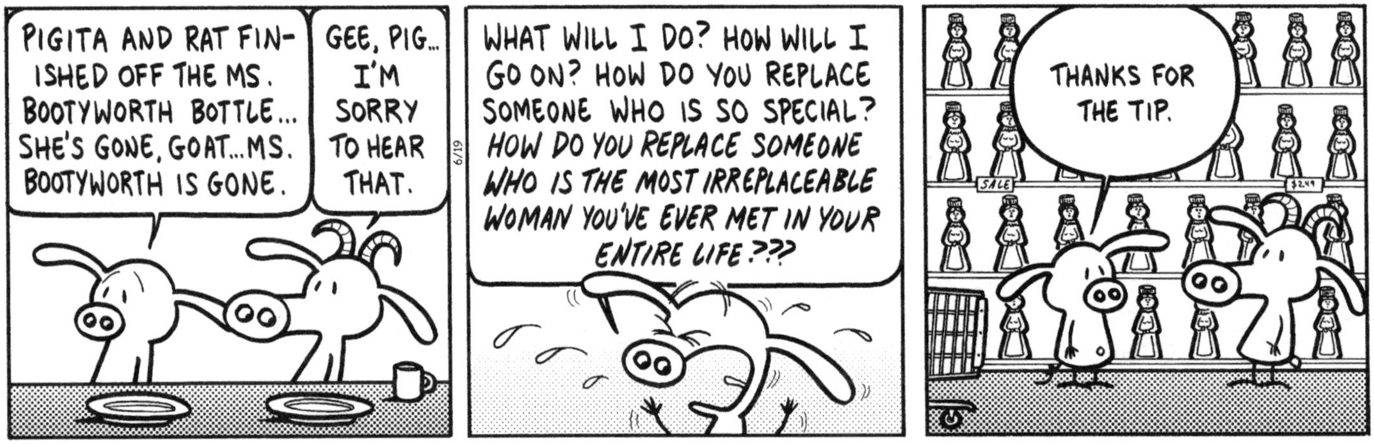
PIGITA AND RAT FIN-ISHED OFF THE MS. BOOTYWORTH BOTTLE... SHE'S GONE, GOAT...MS. BOOTYWORTH IS GONE.
GEE, PIG... I'M SORRY TO HEAR THAT.
6/19
WHAT WILL I DO? HOW WILL I GO ON? HOW DO YOU REPLACE SOMEONE WHO IS SO SPECIAL? HOW DO YOU REPLACE SOMEONE WHO IS THE MOST IRREPLACEABLE WOMAN YOU'VE EVER MET IN YOUR ENTIRE LIFE???
SALE
THANKS FOR THE TIP.

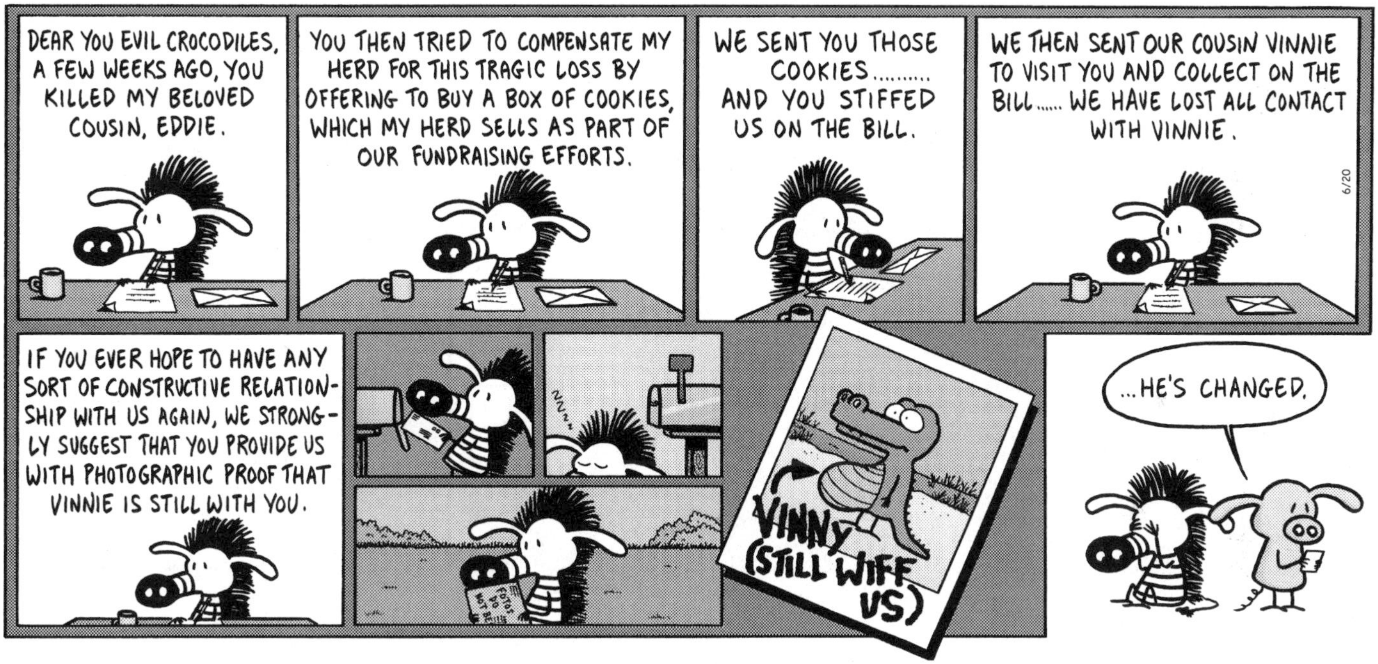
DEAR YOU EVIL CROCODILES, A FEW WEEKS AGO, YOU KILLED MY BELOVED COUSIN, EDDIE.
YOU THEN TRIED TO COMPENSATE MY HERD FOR THIS TRAGIC LOSS BY OFFERING TO BUY A BOX OF COOKIES, WHICH MY HERD SELLS AS PART OF OUR FUNDRAISING EFFORTS.
WE SENT YOU THOSE COOKIES.......... AND YOU STIFFED US ON THE BILL.
WE THEN SENT OUR COUSIN VINNIE TO VISIT YOU AND COLLECT ON THE BILL...... WE HAVE LOST ALL CONTACT WITH VINNIE.
6/20
IF YOU EVER HOPE TO HAVE ANY SORT OF CONSTRUCTIVE RELATIONSHIP WITH US AGAIN, WE STRONGLY SUGGEST THAT YOU PROVIDE US WITH PHOTOGRAPHIC PROOF THAT VINNIE IS STILL WITH YOU.
VINNY (STILL WIFF US)
...HE'S CHANGED.

WELL, FOLKS, IT'S TIME ONCE AGAIN FOR THE 'PEARLS' MAILBAG, WHERE WE ANSWER SOME OF THE MANY E-MAILS THAT POUR IN EVERY WEEK HERE AT 'PEARLS, INC.'

OUR FIRST E-MAIL IS FROM CELIA L., OF SAN FRANCISCO, CA, WHO WRITES, "PIG IS SO CUTE AND KIND AND HUMBLE. HAS HIS SUDDEN POPULARITY CHANGED HIM AT ALL?"... WELL, CELIA, LET'S ASK PIG.

YO, GIRL, P. DIDDY PIGGY DON'T WANT NO PLAYAH HATAHS.

THE 'PEARLS' MAILBAG

THIS 'PEARLS' READER WRITES, "IF I GAVE YOU $500, WOULD YOU NAME A CHARACTER IN THE STRIP AFTER ME?"

PLEASE, PEOPLE... AS MUCH AS WE'D LIKE TO ACCOMMODATE ALL FAN REQUESTS, WE ARE SIMPLY NOT GOING TO SACRIFICE THE INTEGRITY OF THE STRIP TO TURN A QUICK PROFIT.

ISN'T THAT RIGHT, THEODORE JAMES HAWKINS?

CALL ME TEDDY.

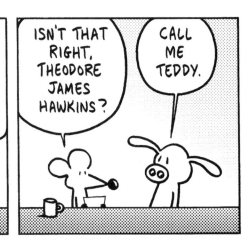

THE 'PEARLS' MAILBAG

OUR NEXT E-MAIL IS FROM STEPHEN H., OF BERKELEY, CA, WHO ASKS, "IS RAT AS RUDE IN REAL LIFE AS HE APPEARS TO BE IN THE COMIC STRIP?"

WELL, STEVE, PERHAPS YOU DON'T UNDERSTAND THAT I'M ONLY A DRAWING. WITH JUST A COUPLE SWIPES OF THE ERASER, I CEASE TO EXIST.

THIS CHANGES EVERYTHING....

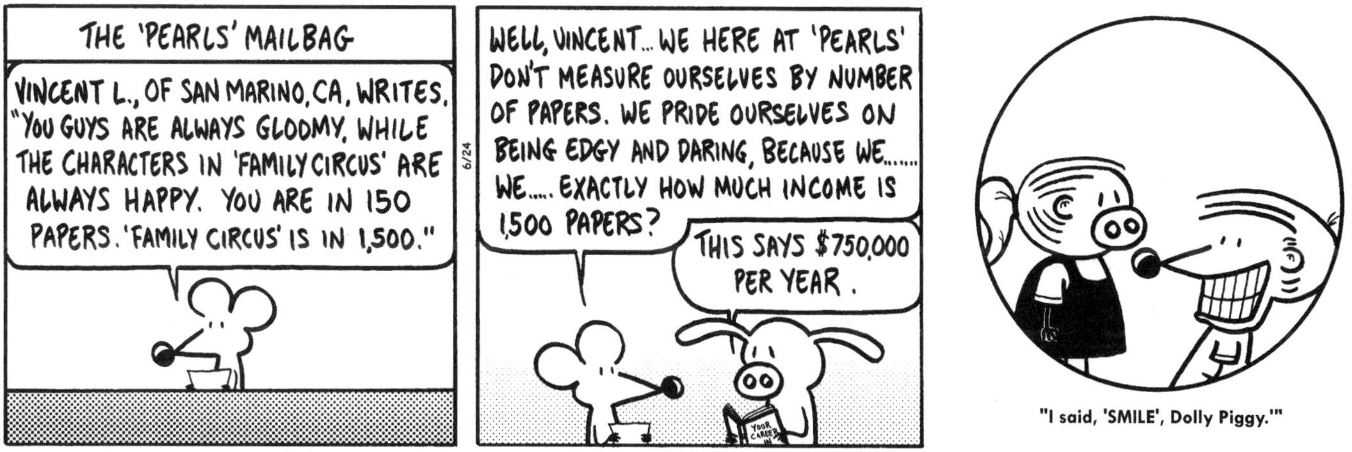
THE 'PEARLS' MAILBAG
VINCENT L., OF SAN MARINO, CA, WRITES, "YOU GUYS ARE ALWAYS GLOOMY, WHILE THE CHARACTERS IN 'FAMILY CIRCUS' ARE ALWAYS HAPPY. YOU ARE IN 150 PAPERS. 'FAMILY CIRCUS' IS IN 1,500."
6/24
WELL, VINCENT... WE HERE AT 'PEARLS' DON'T MEASURE OURSELVES BY NUMBER OF PAPERS. WE PRIDE OURSELVES ON BEING EDGY AND DARING, BECAUSE WE...... WE..... EXACTLY HOW MUCH INCOME IS 1,500 PAPERS?
THIS SAYS $750,000 PER YEAR.
YOUR CAREER
"I said, 'SMILE', Dolly Piggy.'"

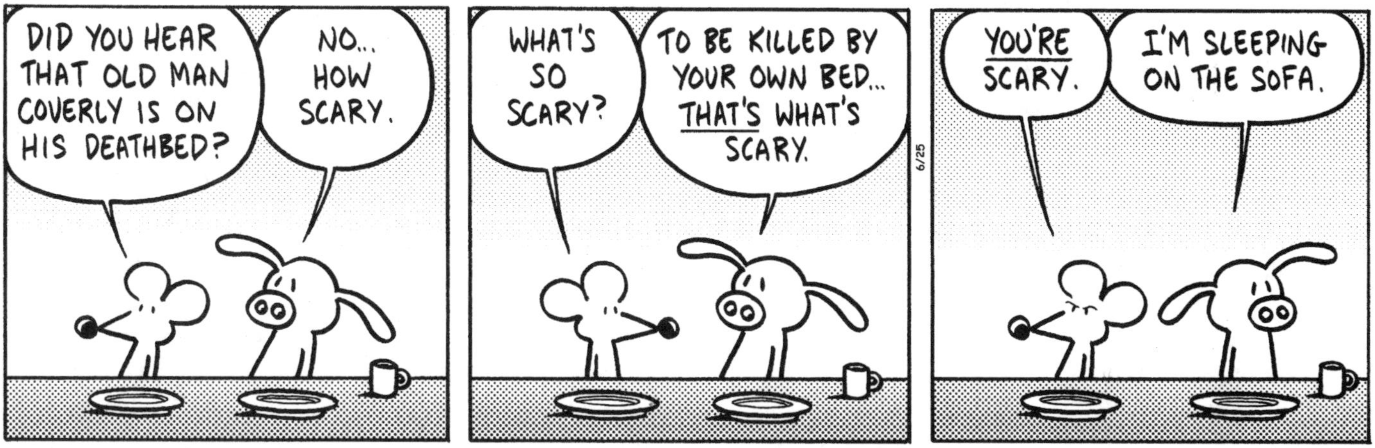
DID YOU HEAR THAT OLD MAN COVERLY IS ON HIS DEATHBED?
NO... HOW SCARY.
WHAT'S SO SCARY?
TO BE KILLED BY YOUR OWN BED... THAT'S WHAT'S SCARY.
6/25
YOU'RE SCARY.
I'M SLEEPING ON THE SOFA.

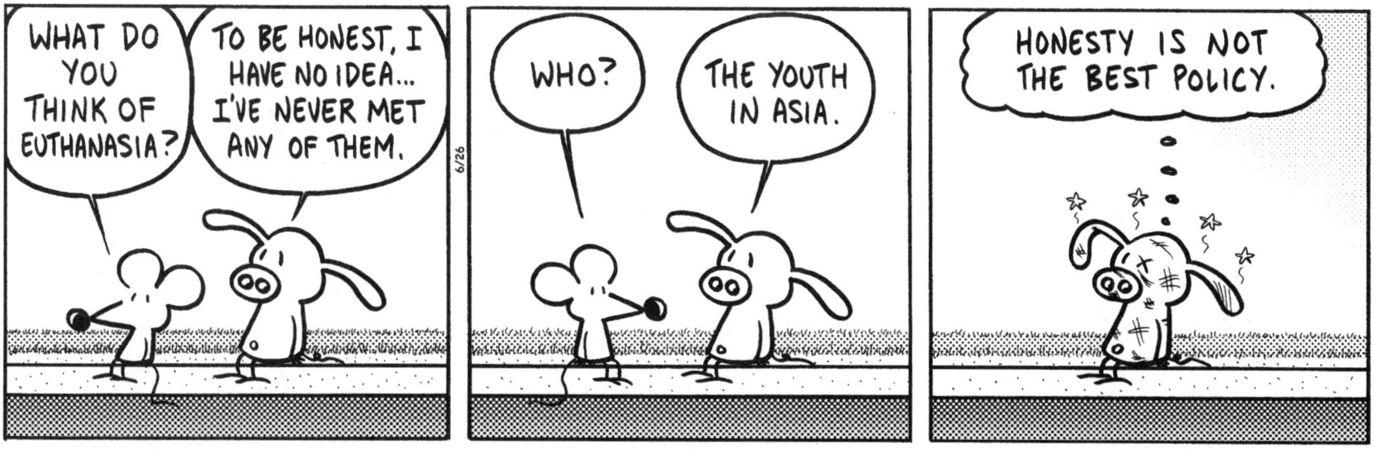
WHAT DO YOU THINK OF EUTHANASIA?
TO BE HONEST, I HAVE NO IDEA... I'VE NEVER MET ANY OF THEM.
6/26
WHO?
THE YOUTH IN ASIA.
HONESTY IS NOT THE BEST POLICY.

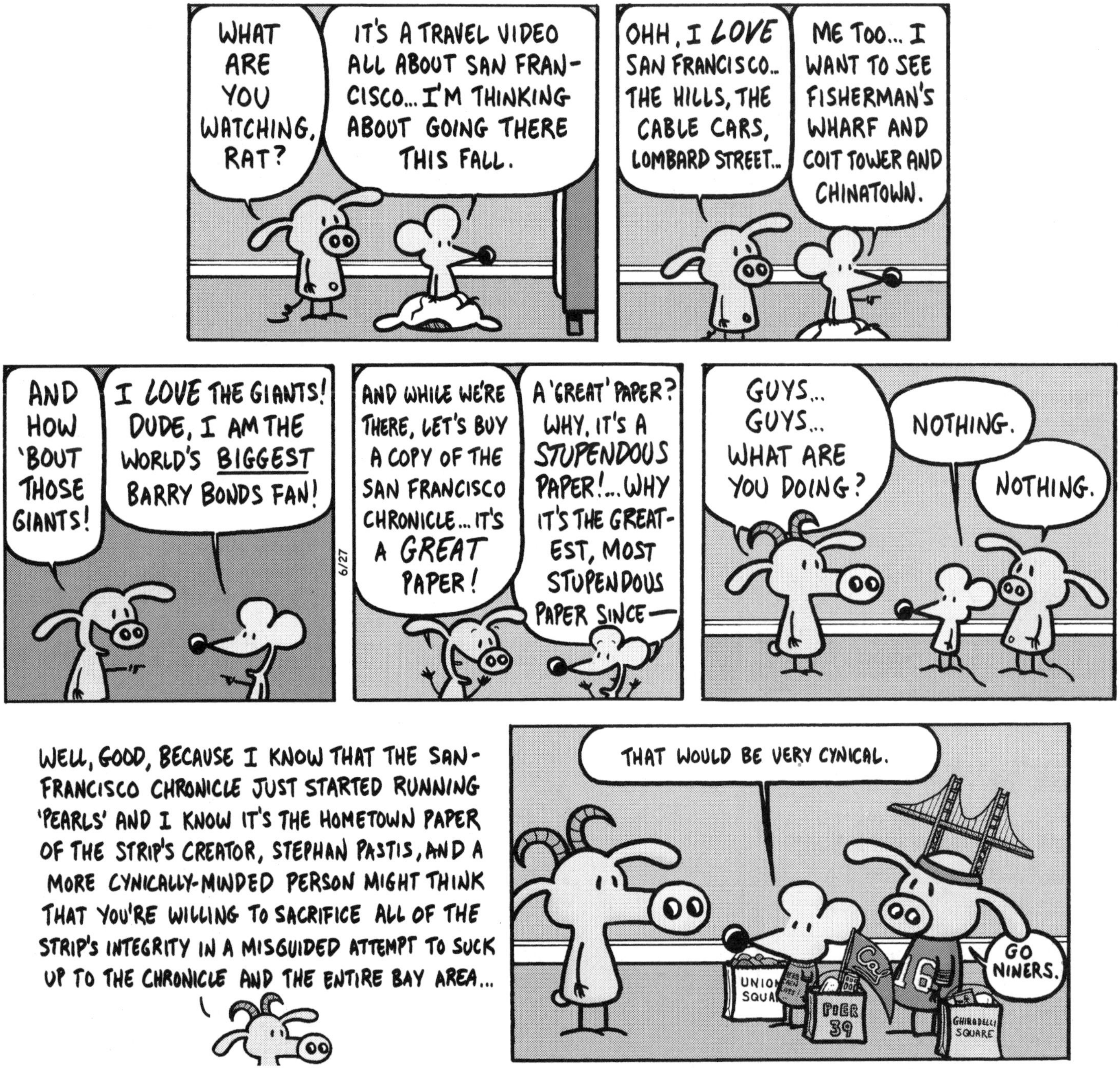
WHAT ARE YOU WATCHING, RAT?
IT'S A TRAVEL VIDEO ALL ABOUT SAN FRANCISCO... I'M THINKING ABOUT GOING THERE THIS FALL.
OHH, I LOVE SAN FRANCISCO.. THE HILLS, THE CABLE CARS, LOMBARD STREET..
ME TOO... I WANT TO SEE FISHERMAN'S WHARF AND COIT TOWER AND CHINATOWN.
AND HOW 'BOUT THOSE GIANTS!
I LOVE THE GIANTS! DUDE, I AM THE WORLD'S BIGGEST BARRY BONDS FAN!
6/27
AND WHILE WE'RE THERE, LET'S BUY A COPY OF THE SAN FRANCISCO CHRONICLE... IT'S A GREAT PAPER!
A 'GREAT' PAPER? WHY, IT'S A STUPENDOUS PAPER!... WHY IT'S THE GREATEST, MOST STUPENDOUS PAPER SINCE—
GUYS... GUYS... WHAT ARE YOU DOING?
NOTHING.
NOTHING.
WELL, GOOD, BECAUSE I KNOW THAT THE SAN-FRANCISCO CHRONICLE JUST STARTED RUNNING 'PEARLS' AND I KNOW IT'S THE HOMETOWN PAPER OF THE STRIP'S CREATOR, STEPHAN PASTIS, AND A MORE CYNICALLY-MINDED PERSON MIGHT THINK THAT YOU'RE WILLING TO SACRIFICE ALL OF THE STRIP'S INTEGRITY IN A MISGUIDED ATTEMPT TO SUCK UP TO THE CHRONICLE AND THE ENTIRE BAY AREA...
THAT WOULD BE VERY CYNICAL.
GO NINERS.
Cal
16
PIER 39
GHIRADELLI SQUARE

Panel 1: I JUST BOUGHT THIS MODEL OF THE SOLAR SYSTEM, BUT IT'S MISSING SATURN.

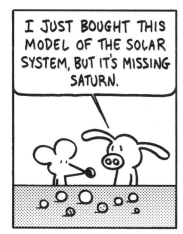

Panel 2: GEEZ... WHAT A ◎#❋⌀⚆☆ RIP-OFF.

Panel 3: GEEZ... WHAT A ◎#❋⌀⚆☆ RIP-OFF.

Panel 4: THERE ARE ADVANTAGES TO HAVING A FOUL MOUTH IN THE FUNNY PAGES.

Panel 5: HEY, BUDDY, I'LL DRAW YOUR PORTRAIT FOR TEN BUCKS. / ARE YOU ANY GOOD AT REALLY CAPTURING SOMEONE'S LIKENESS?

PORTRAITS TEN BUCKS

Panel 6: NO.

PORTRAITS TEN BUCKS

Panel 7: JUMP FOR JOY, YOU HOMELY CRETIN.

PORTRAITS TEN BUCKS

Panel 8: HEY, PAL, DO A PORTRAIT OF MY WIFE.

PORTRAITS TEN BUCKS

Panel 9: SCRIBBLE SCRIBBLE SCRIBBLE

Panel 10: WHAT THE?? WHY'D YOU DRAW THAT COW IN THE BACKGROUND? / THAT'S THE FOREGROUND.

PORTRAITS TEN BUCKS

Panel 11: SURE... BLAME THE MESSENGER.

PORTRAITS TEN BUCKS

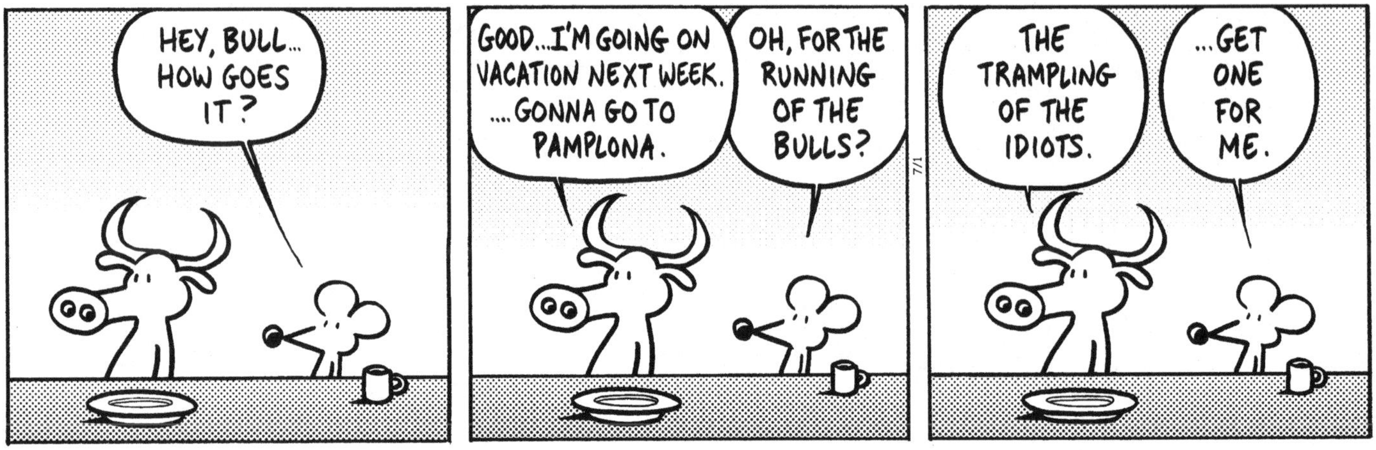
HEY, BULL... HOW GOES IT?
GOOD...I'M GOING ON VACATION NEXT WEEK. ....GONNA GO TO PAMPLONA.
OH, FOR THE RUNNING OF THE BULLS?
7/1
THE TRAMPLING OF THE IDIOTS.
...GET ONE FOR ME.

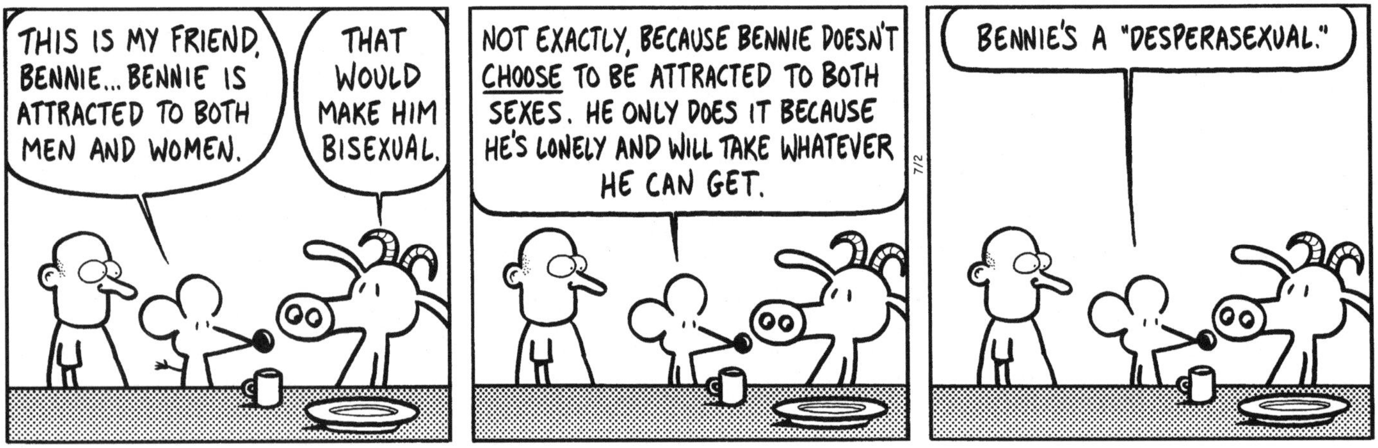
THIS IS MY FRIEND, BENNIE... BENNIE IS ATTRACTED TO BOTH MEN AND WOMEN.
THAT WOULD MAKE HIM BISEXUAL.
NOT EXACTLY, BECAUSE BENNIE DOESN'T CHOOSE TO BE ATTRACTED TO BOTH SEXES. HE ONLY DOES IT BECAUSE HE'S LONELY AND WILL TAKE WHATEVER HE CAN GET.
7/2
BENNIE'S A "DESPERASEXUAL."

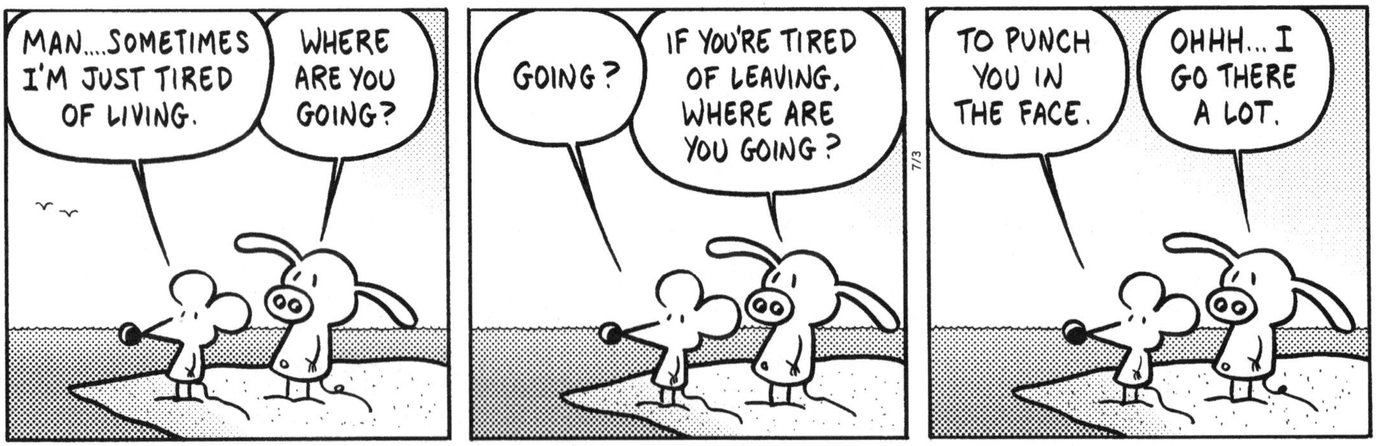
MAN....SOMETIMES I'M JUST TIRED OF LIVING.
WHERE ARE YOU GOING?
GOING?
IF YOU'RE TIRED OF LEAVING, WHERE ARE YOU GOING?
7/3
TO PUNCH YOU IN THE FACE.
OHHH... I GO THERE A LOT.

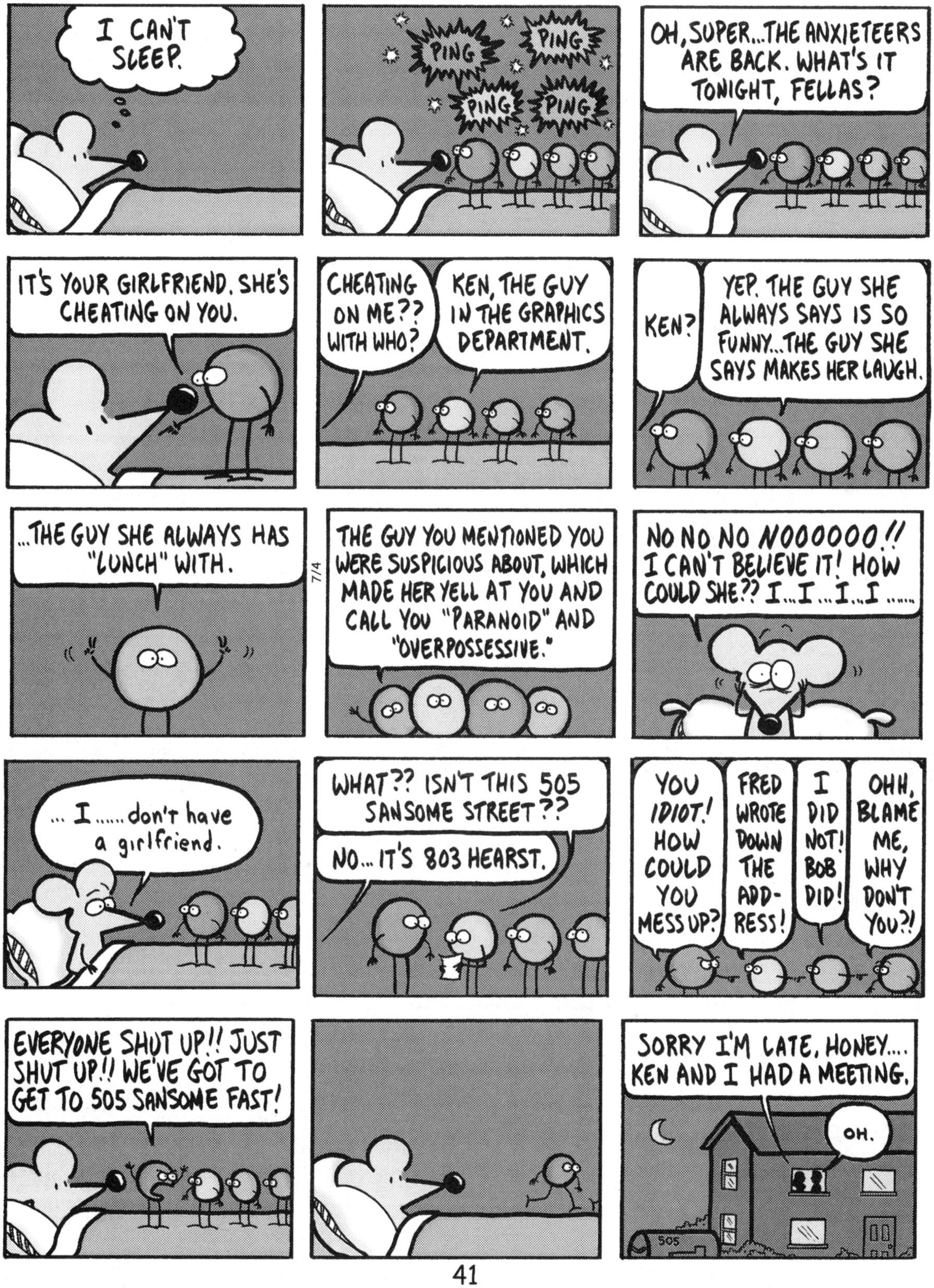
I CAN'T SLEEP.
PING
PING
PING
PING
OH, SUPER...THE ANXIETEERS ARE BACK. WHAT'S IT TONIGHT, FELLAS?
IT'S YOUR GIRLFRIEND. SHE'S CHEATING ON YOU.
CHEATING ON ME?? WITH WHO?
KEN, THE GUY IN THE GRAPHICS DEPARTMENT.
KEN?
YEP. THE GUY SHE ALWAYS SAYS IS SO FUNNY...THE GUY SHE SAYS MAKES HER LAUGH,
...THE GUY SHE ALWAYS HAS "LUNCH" WITH.
THE GUY YOU MENTIONED YOU WERE SUSPICIOUS ABOUT, WHICH MADE HER YELL AT YOU AND CALL YOU "PARANOID" AND "OVERPOSSESSIVE."
NO NO NO NOOOOOO!! I CAN'T BELIEVE IT! HOW COULD SHE?? I...I...I...I......
... I...... don't have a girlfriend.
WHAT?? ISN'T THIS 505 SANSOME STREET??
NO... IT'S 803 HEARST.
YOU IDIOT! HOW COULD YOU MESS UP?
FRED WROTE DOWN THE ADD-RESS!
I DID NOT! BOB DID!
OHH, BLAME ME, WHY DON'T YOU?!
EVERYONE SHUT UP!! JUST SHUT UP!! WE'VE GOT TO GET TO 505 SANSOME FAST!
SORRY I'M LATE, HONEY.... KEN AND I HAD A MEETING.
OH.
505

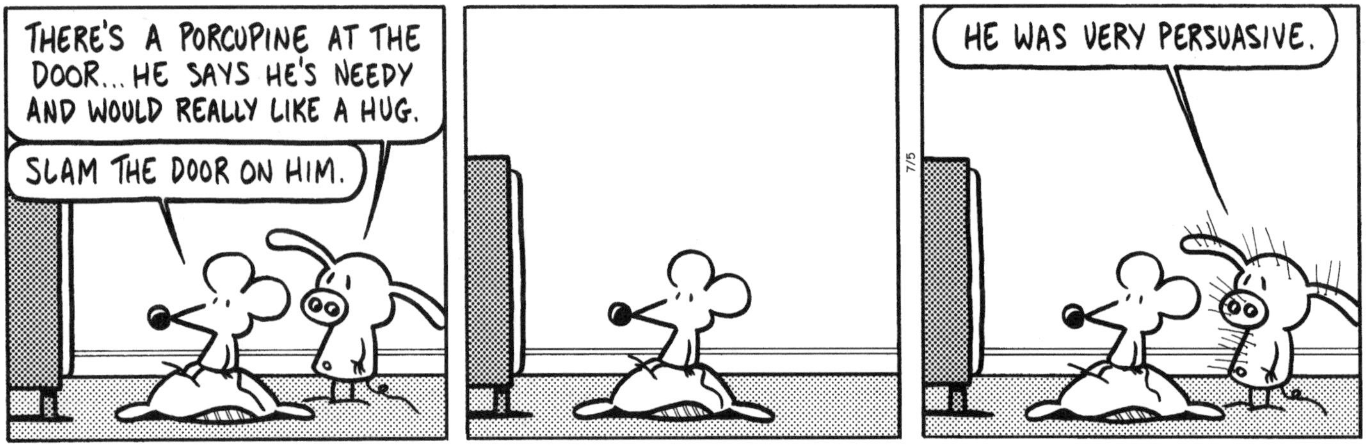
THERE'S A PORCUPINE AT THE DOOR... HE SAYS HE'S NEEDY AND WOULD REALLY LIKE A HUG.
SLAM THE DOOR ON HIM.
7/5
HE WAS VERY PERSUASIVE.

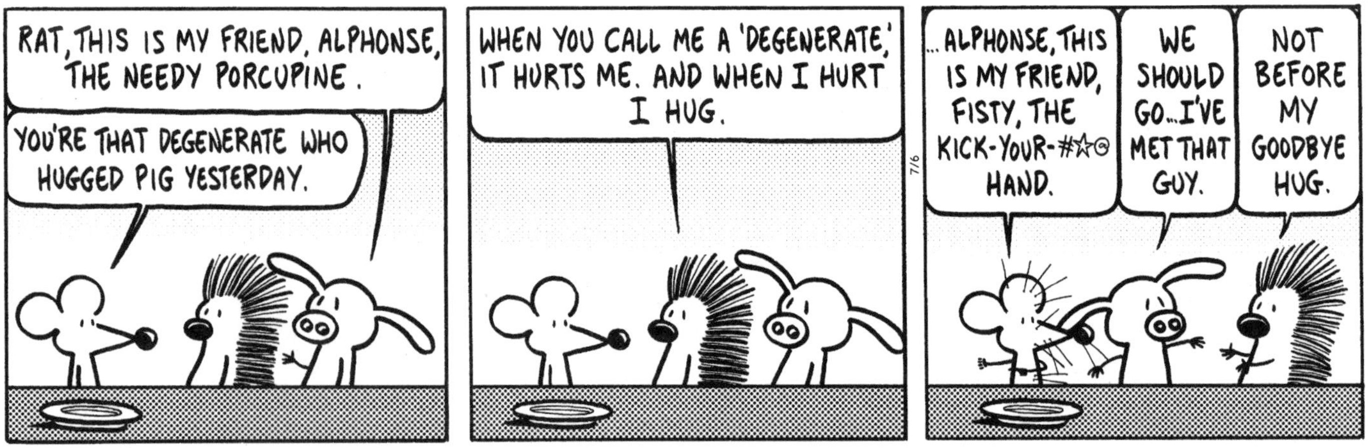
RAT, THIS IS MY FRIEND, ALPHONSE, THE NEEDY PORCUPINE.
YOU'RE THAT DEGENERATE WHO HUGGED PIG YESTERDAY.
WHEN YOU CALL ME A 'DEGENERATE,' IT HURTS ME. AND WHEN I HURT I HUG.
7/6
...ALPHONSE, THIS IS MY FRIEND, FISTY, THE KICK-YOUR-#☆@ HAND.
WE SHOULD GO...I'VE MET THAT GUY.
NOT BEFORE MY GOODBYE HUG.

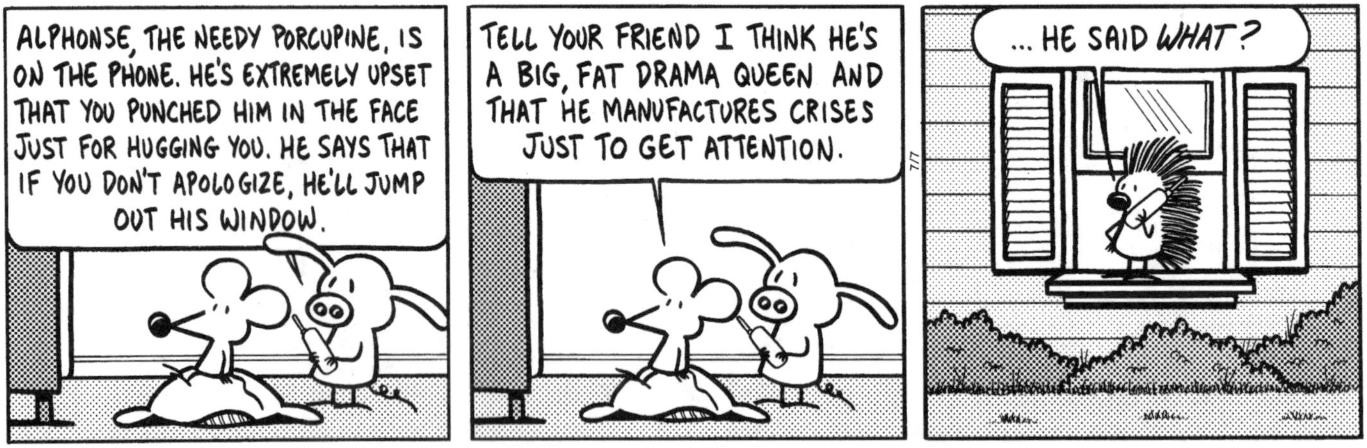
ALPHONSE, THE NEEDY PORCUPINE, IS ON THE PHONE. HE'S EXTREMELY UPSET THAT YOU PUNCHED HIM IN THE FACE JUST FOR HUGGING YOU. HE SAYS THAT IF YOU DON'T APOLOGIZE, HE'LL JUMP OUT HIS WINDOW.
TELL YOUR FRIEND I THINK HE'S A BIG, FAT DRAMA QUEEN AND THAT HE MANUFACTURES CRISES JUST TO GET ATTENTION.
7/7
... HE SAID *WHAT?*

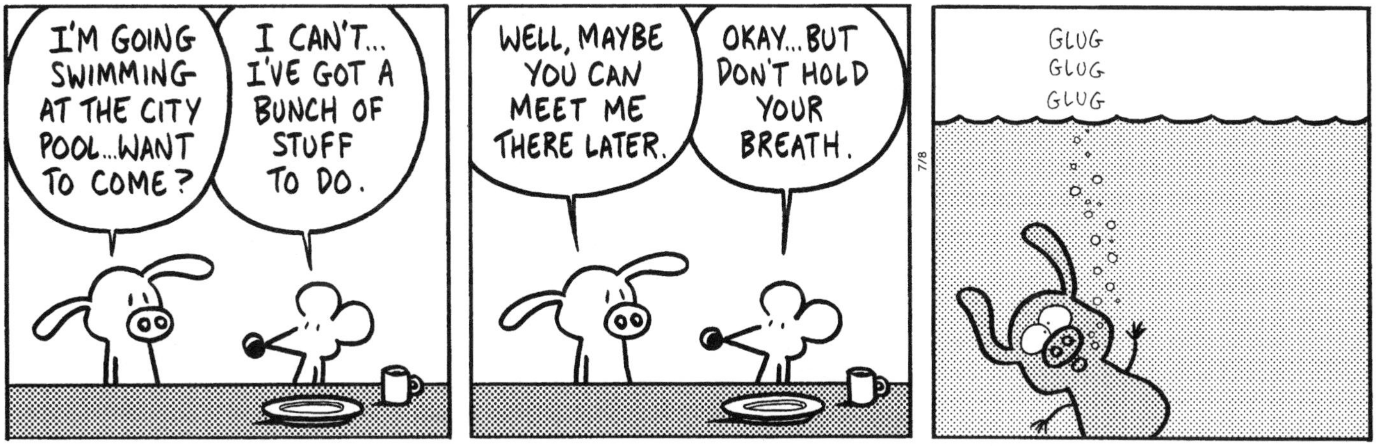
I'M GOING SWIMMING AT THE CITY POOL...WANT TO COME?
I CAN'T... I'VE GOT A BUNCH OF STUFF TO DO.
WELL, MAYBE YOU CAN MEET ME THERE LATER.
OKAY...BUT DON'T HOLD YOUR BREATH.
7/8
GLUG
GLUG
GLUG

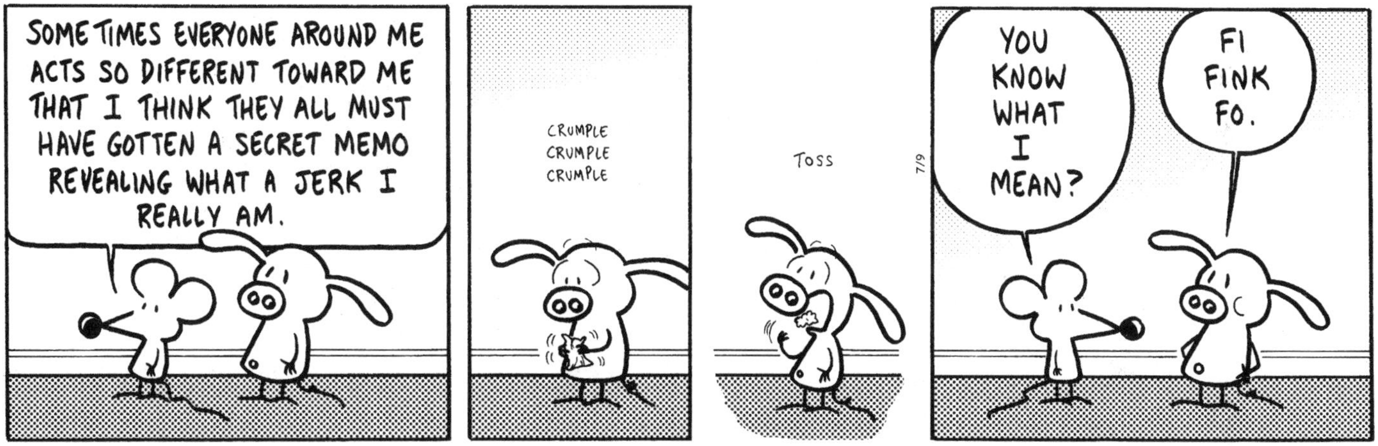
SOMETIMES EVERYONE AROUND ME ACTS SO DIFFERENT TOWARD ME THAT I THINK THEY ALL MUST HAVE GOTTEN A SECRET MEMO REVEALING WHAT A JERK I REALLY AM.
CRUMPLE
CRUMPLE
CRUMPLE
TOSS
7/9
YOU KNOW WHAT I MEAN?
FI FINK FO.

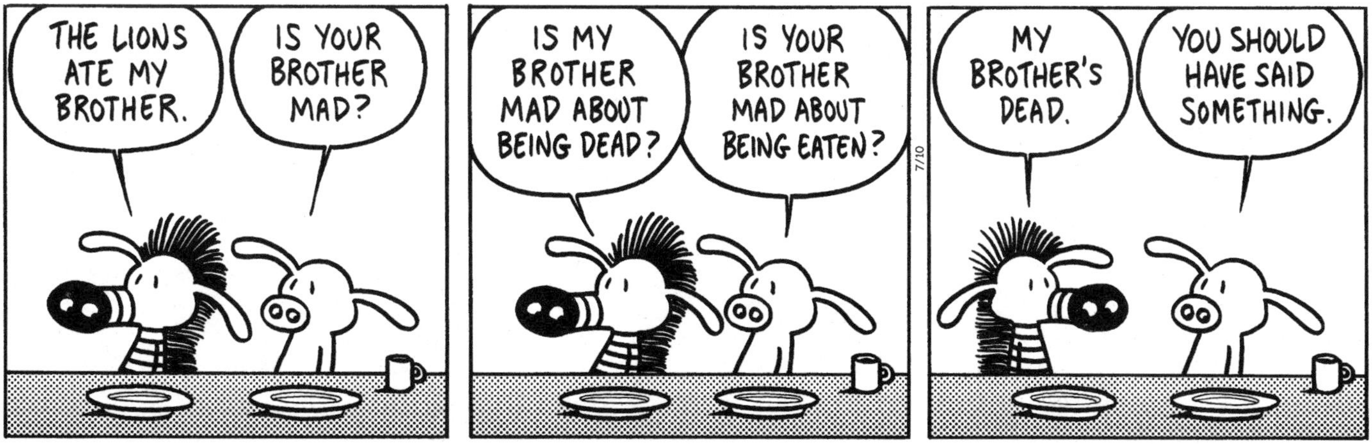
THE LIONS ATE MY BROTHER.
IS YOUR BROTHER MAD?
IS MY BROTHER MAD ABOUT BEING DEAD?
IS YOUR BROTHER MAD ABOUT BEING EATEN?
7/10
MY BROTHER'S DEAD.
YOU SHOULD HAVE SAID SOMETHING.

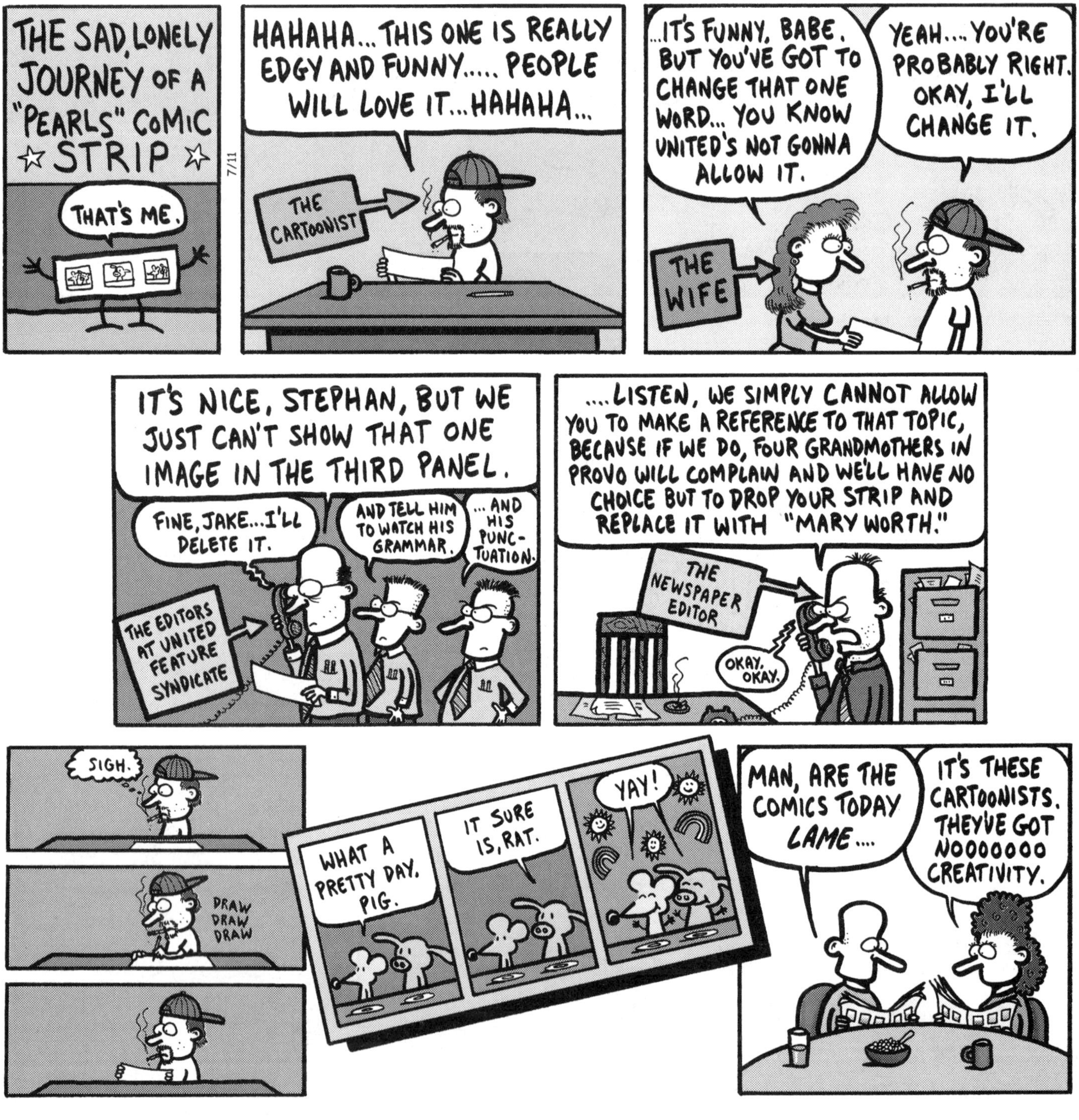
THE SAD, LONELY JOURNEY OF A "PEARLS" COMIC STRIP
THAT'S ME.
7/11
HAHAHA... THIS ONE IS REALLY EDGY AND FUNNY..... PEOPLE WILL LOVE IT... HAHAHA...
THE CARTOONIST
...IT'S FUNNY, BABE. BUT YOU'VE GOT TO CHANGE THAT ONE WORD... YOU KNOW UNITED'S NOT GONNA ALLOW IT.
YEAH.... YOU'RE PROBABLY RIGHT. OKAY, I'LL CHANGE IT.
THE WIFE
IT'S NICE, STEPHAN, BUT WE JUST CAN'T SHOW THAT ONE IMAGE IN THE THIRD PANEL.
FINE, JAKE... I'LL DELETE IT.
AND TELL HIM TO WATCH HIS GRAMMAR.
... AND HIS PUNC-TUATION.
THE EDITORS AT UNITED FEATURE SYNDICATE
....LISTEN, WE SIMPLY CANNOT ALLOW YOU TO MAKE A REFERENCE TO THAT TOPIC, BECAUSE IF WE DO, FOUR GRANDMOTHERS IN PROVO WILL COMPLAIN AND WE'LL HAVE NO CHOICE BUT TO DROP YOUR STRIP AND REPLACE IT WITH "MARY WORTH."
THE NEWSPAPER EDITOR
OKAY. OKAY.
SIGH.
DRAW DRAW DRAW
WHAT A PRETTY DAY, PIG.
IT SURE IS, RAT.
YAY!
MAN, ARE THE COMICS TODAY LAME....
IT'S THESE CARTOONISTS. THEY'VE GOT NOOOOOOO CREATIVITY.

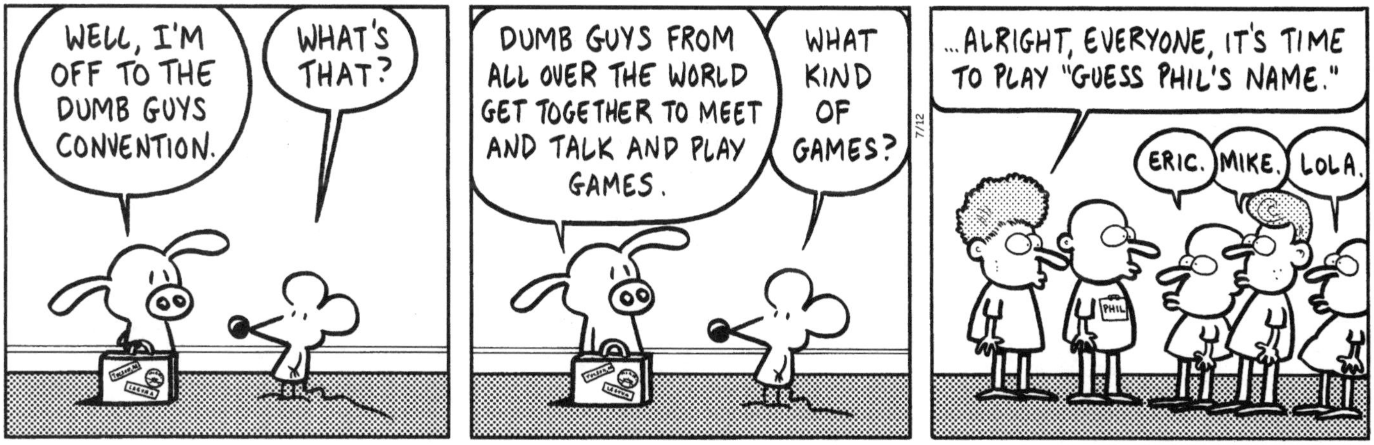
WELL, I'M OFF TO THE DUMB GUYS CONVENTION.
WHAT'S THAT?
DUMB GUYS FROM ALL OVER THE WORLD GET TOGETHER TO MEET AND TALK AND PLAY GAMES.
WHAT KIND OF GAMES?
7/12
...ALRIGHT, EVERYONE, IT'S TIME TO PLAY "GUESS PHIL'S NAME."
PHIL
ERIC.
MIKE.
LOLA.

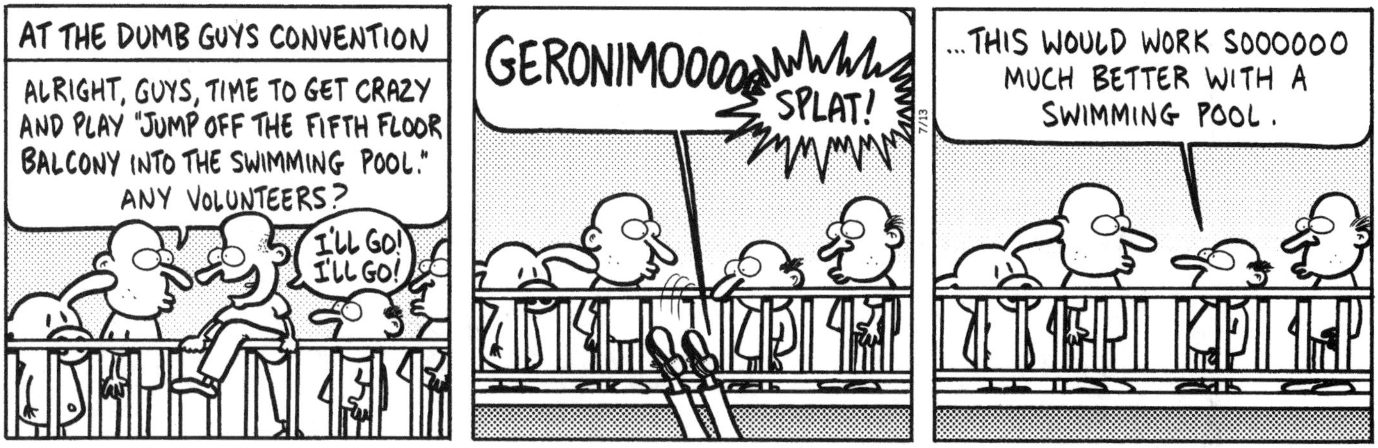
AT THE DUMB GUYS CONVENTION
ALRIGHT, GUYS, TIME TO GET CRAZY AND PLAY "JUMP OFF THE FIFTH FLOOR BALCONY INTO THE SWIMMING POOL." ANY VOLUNTEERS?
I'LL GO! I'LL GO!
GERONIMOOOOO
SPLAT!
7/13
...THIS WOULD WORK SOOOOOO MUCH BETTER WITH A SWIMMING POOL.

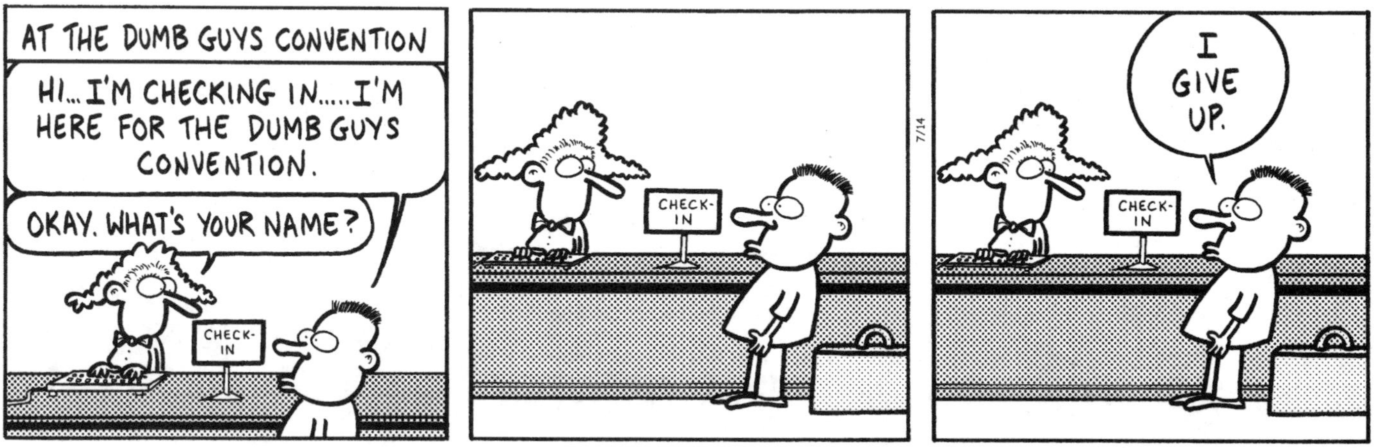
AT THE DUMB GUYS CONVENTION
HI... I'M CHECKING IN..... I'M HERE FOR THE DUMB GUYS CONVENTION.
OKAY. WHAT'S YOUR NAME?
CHECK-IN
CHECK-IN
7/14
I GIVE UP.
CHECK-IN

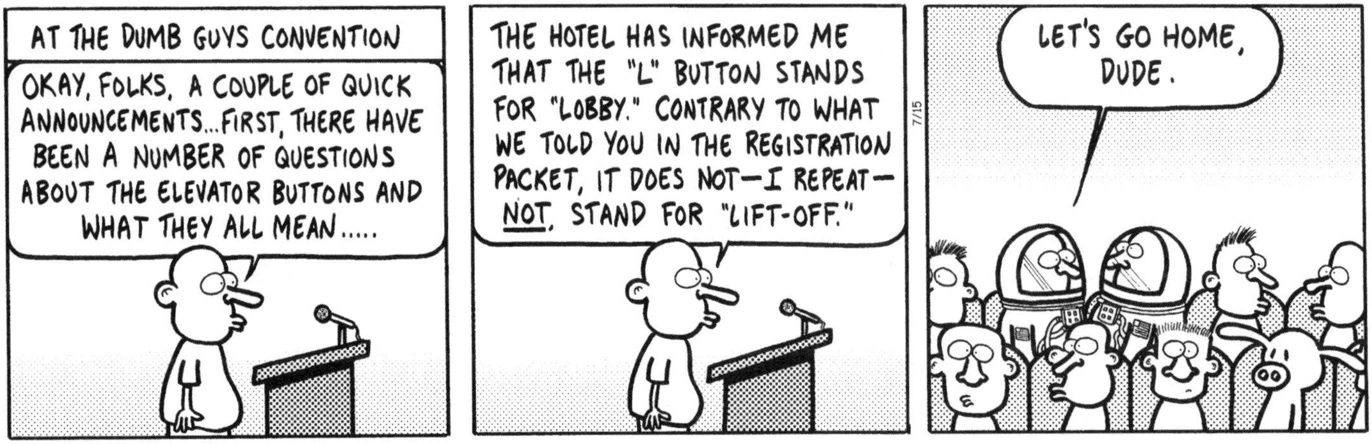
AT THE DUMB GUYS CONVENTION
OKAY, FOLKS, A COUPLE OF QUICK ANNOUNCEMENTS...FIRST, THERE HAVE BEEN A NUMBER OF QUESTIONS ABOUT THE ELEVATOR BUTTONS AND WHAT THEY ALL MEAN.....
THE HOTEL HAS INFORMED ME THAT THE "L" BUTTON STANDS FOR "LOBBY." CONTRARY TO WHAT WE TOLD YOU IN THE REGISTRATION PACKET, IT DOES NOT—I REPEAT—NOT, STAND FOR "LIFT-OFF."
7/15
LET'S GO HOME, DUDE.

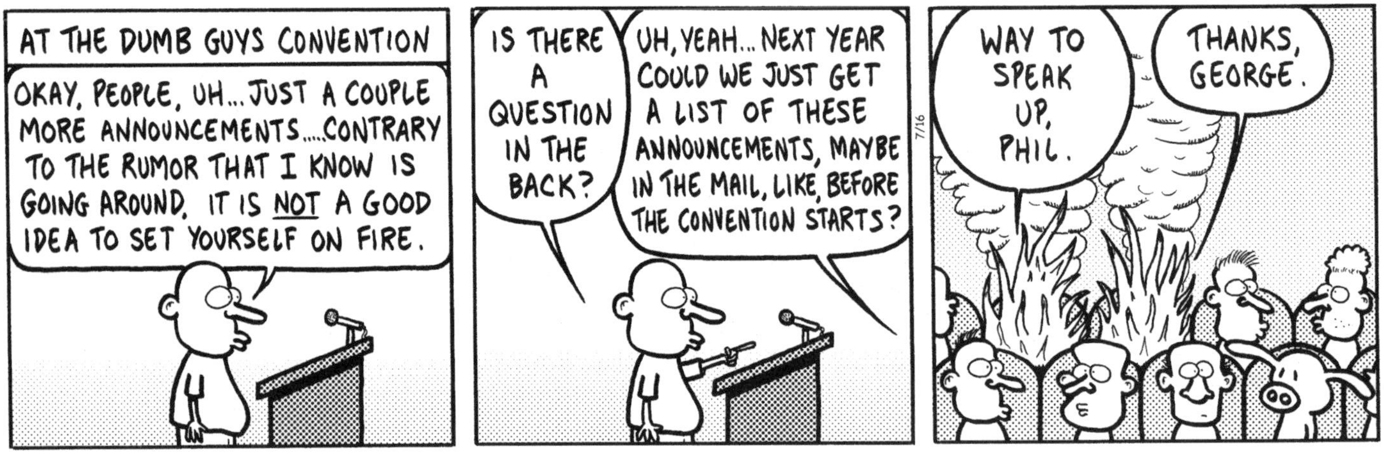
AT THE DUMB GUYS CONVENTION
OKAY, PEOPLE, UH...JUST A COUPLE MORE ANNOUNCEMENTS.....CONTRARY TO THE RUMOR THAT I KNOW IS GOING AROUND, IT IS NOT A GOOD IDEA TO SET YOURSELF ON FIRE.
IS THERE A QUESTION IN THE BACK?
UH, YEAH... NEXT YEAR COULD WE JUST GET A LIST OF THESE ANNOUNCEMENTS, MAYBE IN THE MAIL, LIKE, BEFORE THE CONVENTION STARTS?
7/16
WAY TO SPEAK UP, PHIL.
THANKS, GEORGE.

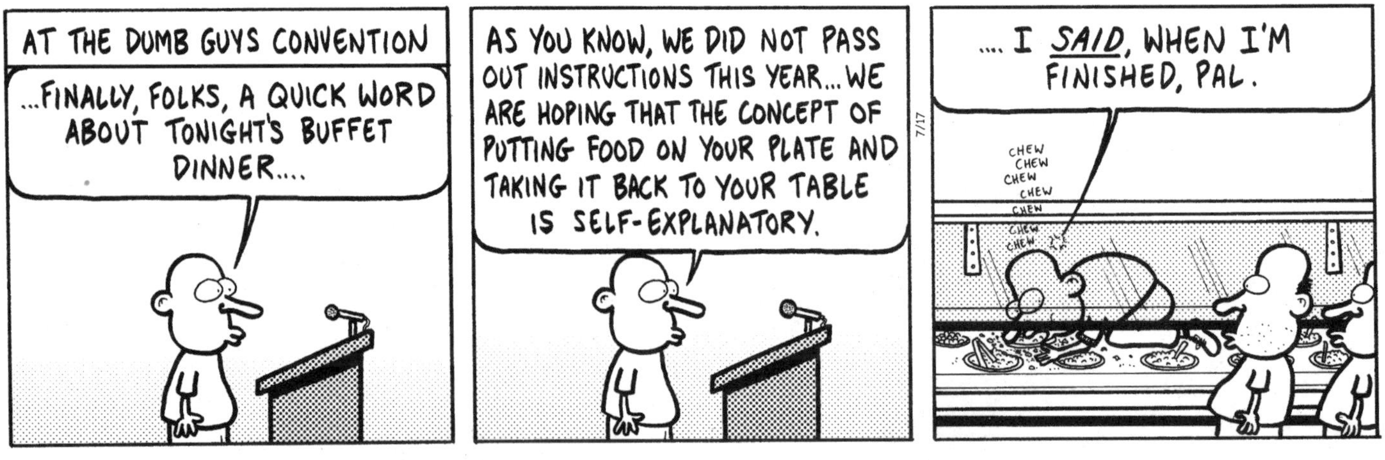
AT THE DUMB GUYS CONVENTION
...FINALLY, FOLKS, A QUICK WORD ABOUT TONIGHT'S BUFFET DINNER....
AS YOU KNOW, WE DID NOT PASS OUT INSTRUCTIONS THIS YEAR...WE ARE HOPING THAT THE CONCEPT OF PUTTING FOOD ON YOUR PLATE AND TAKING IT BACK TO YOUR TABLE IS SELF-EXPLANATORY.
7/17
.... I SAID, WHEN I'M FINISHED, PAL.
CHEW CHEW CHEW CHEW CHEW CHEW CHEW

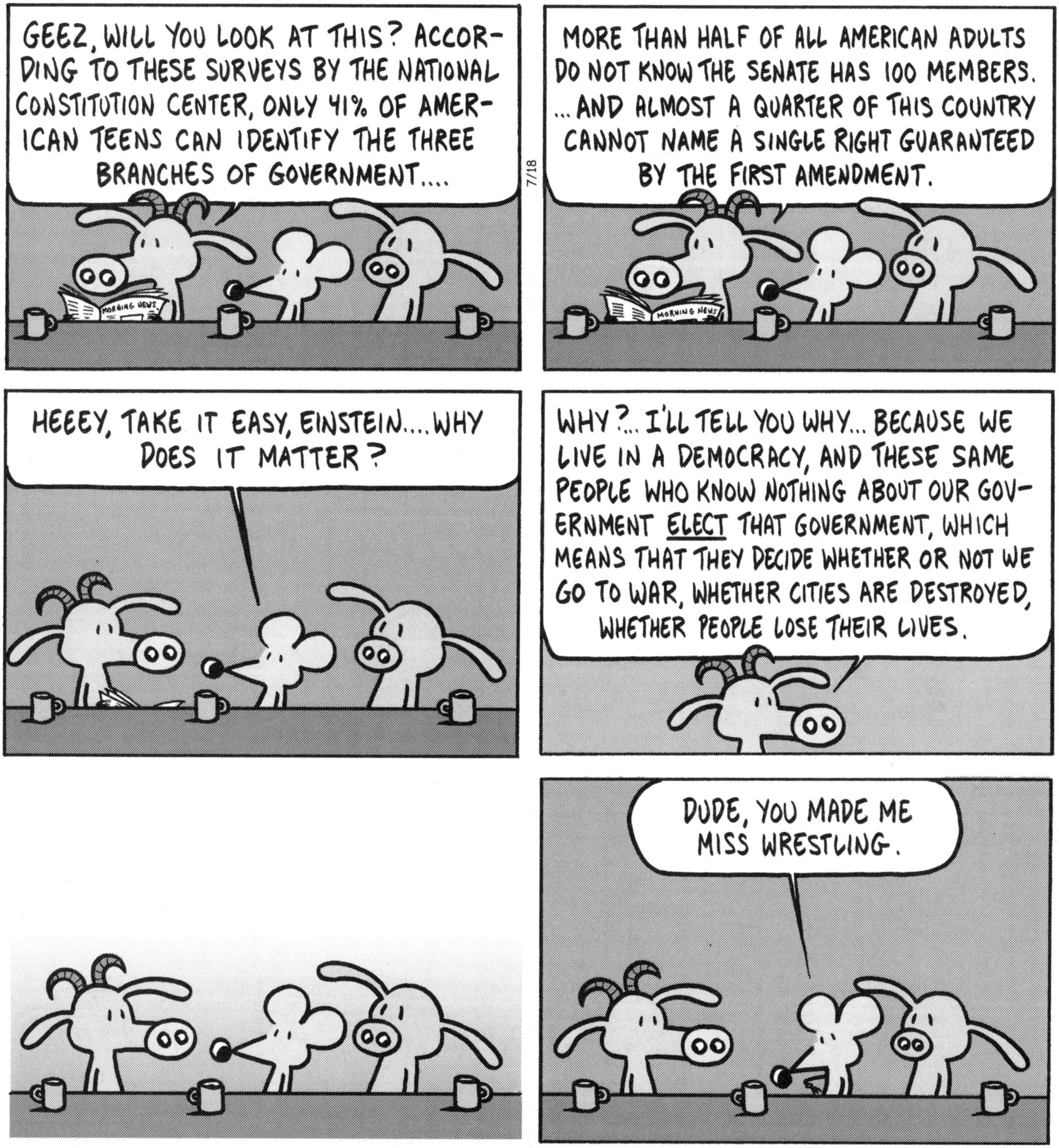
GEEZ, WILL YOU LOOK AT THIS? ACCORDING TO THESE SURVEYS BY THE NATIONAL CONSTITUTION CENTER, ONLY 41% OF AMERICAN TEENS CAN IDENTIFY THE THREE BRANCHES OF GOVERNMENT....
MORNING NEWS
7/18
MORE THAN HALF OF ALL AMERICAN ADULTS DO NOT KNOW THE SENATE HAS 100 MEMBERS. ...AND ALMOST A QUARTER OF THIS COUNTRY CANNOT NAME A SINGLE RIGHT GUARANTEED BY THE FIRST AMENDMENT.
MORNING NEWS
HEEEY, TAKE IT EASY, EINSTEIN....WHY DOES IT MATTER?
WHY?... I'LL TELL YOU WHY... BECAUSE WE LIVE IN A DEMOCRACY, AND THESE SAME PEOPLE WHO KNOW NOTHING ABOUT OUR GOVERNMENT ELECT THAT GOVERNMENT, WHICH MEANS THAT THEY DECIDE WHETHER OR NOT WE GO TO WAR, WHETHER CITIES ARE DESTROYED, WHETHER PEOPLE LOSE THEIR LIVES.
DUDE, YOU MADE ME MISS WRESTLING.

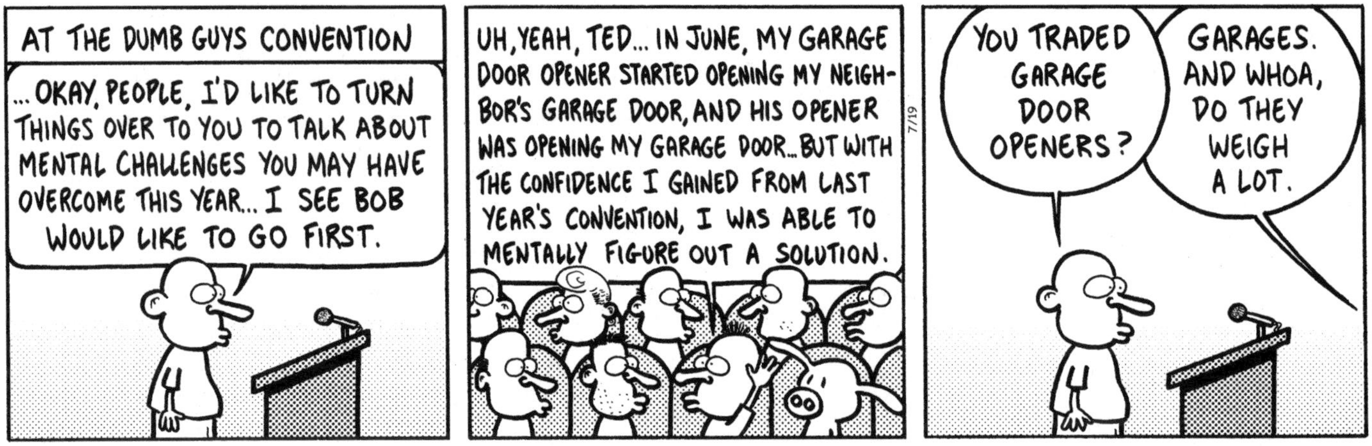
AT THE DUMB GUYS CONVENTION
...OKAY, PEOPLE, I'D LIKE TO TURN THINGS OVER TO YOU TO TALK ABOUT MENTAL CHALLENGES YOU MAY HAVE OVERCOME THIS YEAR... I SEE BOB WOULD LIKE TO GO FIRST.
UH, YEAH, TED... IN JUNE, MY GARAGE DOOR OPENER STARTED OPENING MY NEIGHBOR'S GARAGE DOOR, AND HIS OPENER WAS OPENING MY GARAGE DOOR... BUT WITH THE CONFIDENCE I GAINED FROM LAST YEAR'S CONVENTION, I WAS ABLE TO MENTALLY FIGURE OUT A SOLUTION.
7/19
YOU TRADED GARAGE DOOR OPENERS?
GARAGES. AND WHOA, DO THEY WEIGH A LOT.

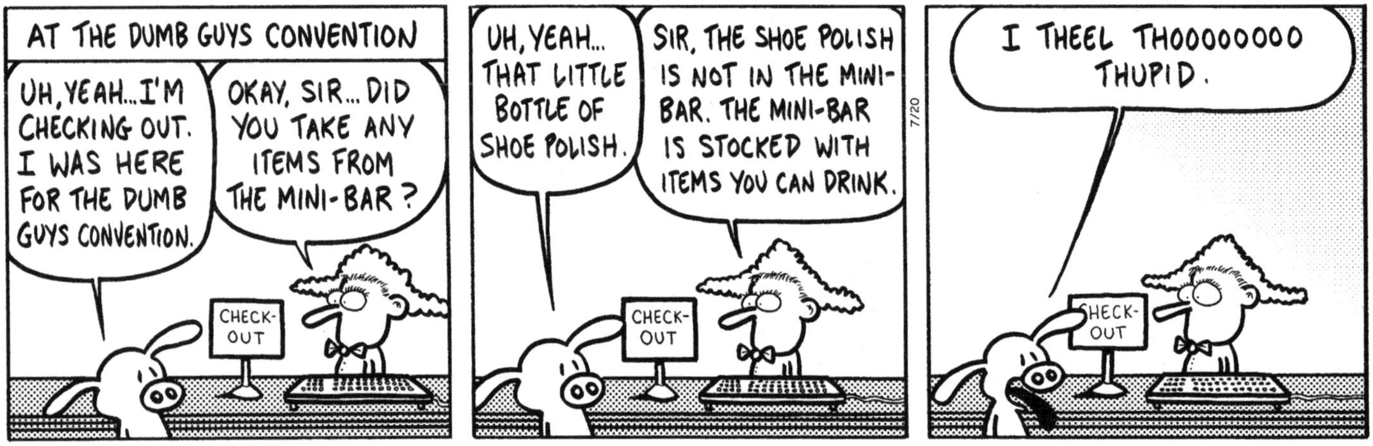
AT THE DUMB GUYS CONVENTION
UH, YEAH... I'M CHECKING OUT. I WAS HERE FOR THE DUMB GUYS CONVENTION.
OKAY, SIR... DID YOU TAKE ANY ITEMS FROM THE MINI-BAR?
CHECK-OUT
UH, YEAH... THAT LITTLE BOTTLE OF SHOE POLISH.
SIR, THE SHOE POLISH IS NOT IN THE MINI-BAR. THE MINI-BAR IS STOCKED WITH ITEMS YOU CAN DRINK.
7/20
I THEEL THOOOOOOOO THUPID.

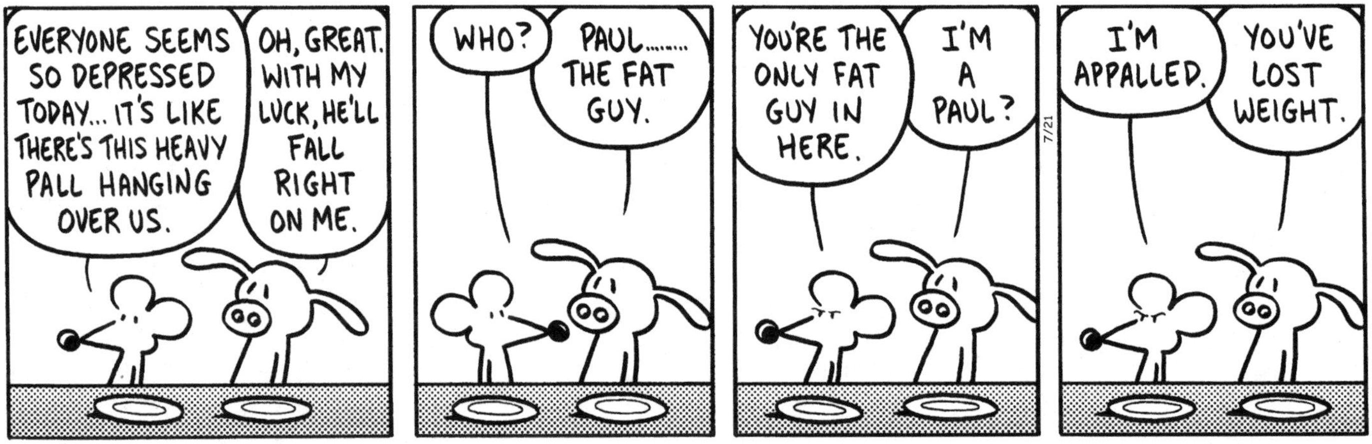
EVERYONE SEEMS SO DEPRESSED TODAY... IT'S LIKE THERE'S THIS HEAVY PALL HANGING OVER US.
OH, GREAT. WITH MY LUCK, HE'LL FALL RIGHT ON ME.
WHO?
PAUL........ THE FAT GUY.
YOU'RE THE ONLY FAT GUY IN HERE.
I'M A PAUL?
7/21
I'M APPALLED.
YOU'VE LOST WEIGHT.

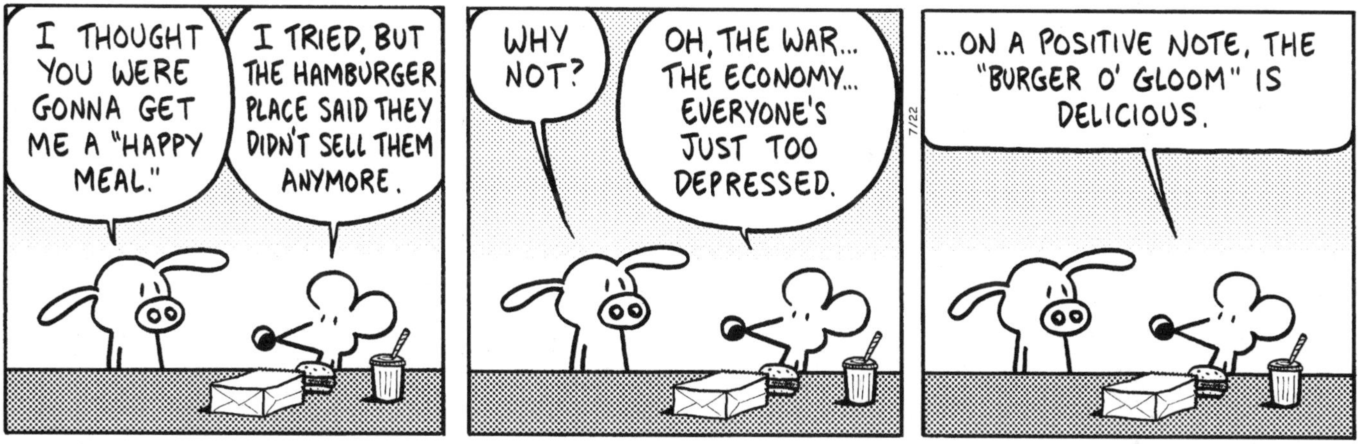
I THOUGHT YOU WERE GONNA GET ME A "HAPPY MEAL."
I TRIED, BUT THE HAMBURGER PLACE SAID THEY DIDN'T SELL THEM ANYMORE.
WHY NOT?
OH, THE WAR... THE ECONOMY... EVERYONE'S JUST TOO DEPRESSED.
7/22
...ON A POSITIVE NOTE, THE "BURGER O' GLOOM" IS DELICIOUS.

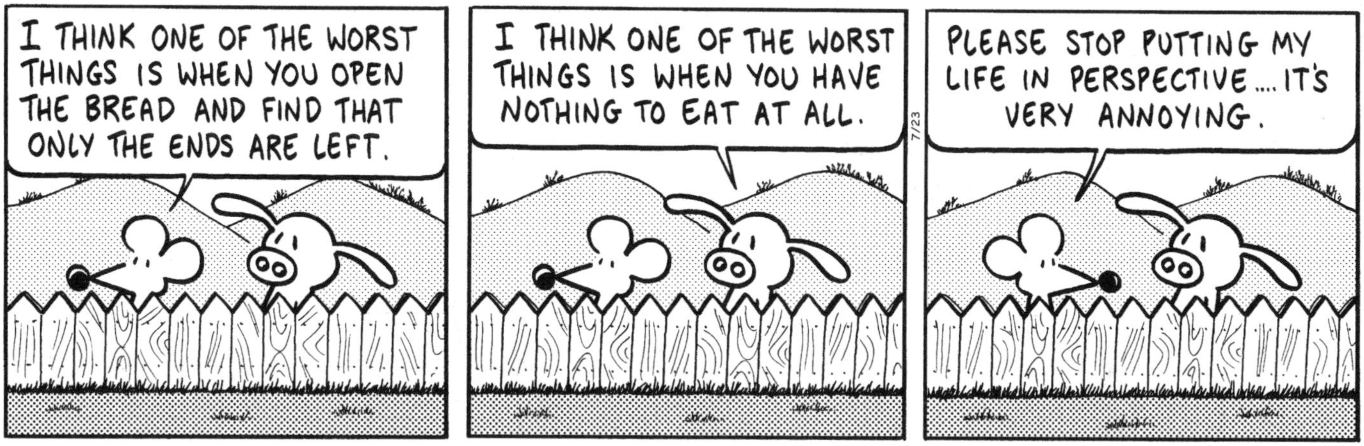
I THINK ONE OF THE WORST THINGS IS WHEN YOU OPEN THE BREAD AND FIND THAT ONLY THE ENDS ARE LEFT.
I THINK ONE OF THE WORST THINGS IS WHEN YOU HAVE NOTHING TO EAT AT ALL.
7/23
PLEASE STOP PUTTING MY LIFE IN PERSPECTIVE.... IT'S VERY ANNOYING.

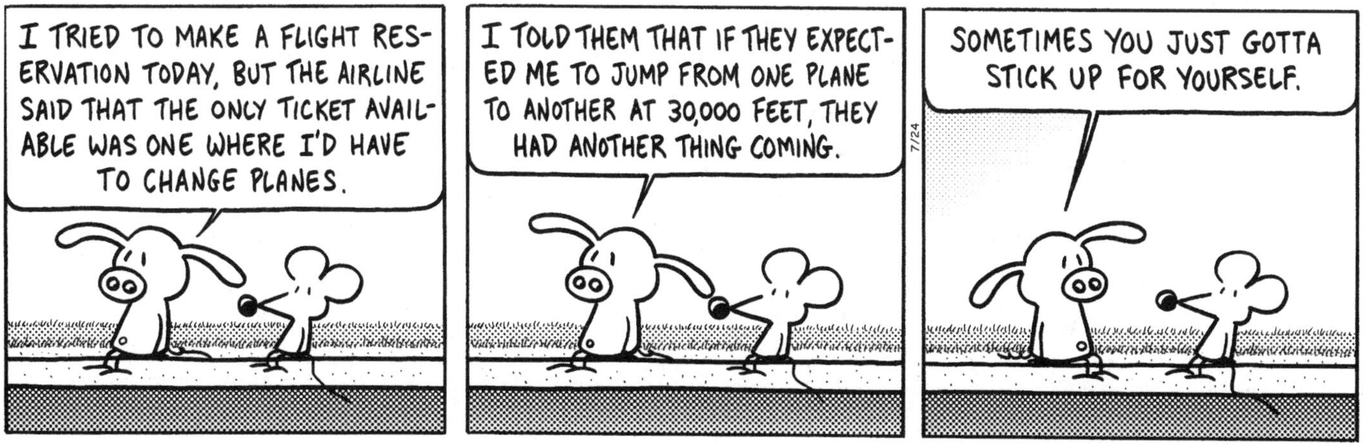
I TRIED TO MAKE A FLIGHT RESERVATION TODAY, BUT THE AIRLINE SAID THAT THE ONLY TICKET AVAILABLE WAS ONE WHERE I'D HAVE TO CHANGE PLANES.
I TOLD THEM THAT IF THEY EXPECTED ME TO JUMP FROM ONE PLANE TO ANOTHER AT 30,000 FEET, THEY HAD ANOTHER THING COMING.
7/24
SOMETIMES YOU JUST GOTTA STICK UP FOR YOURSELF.

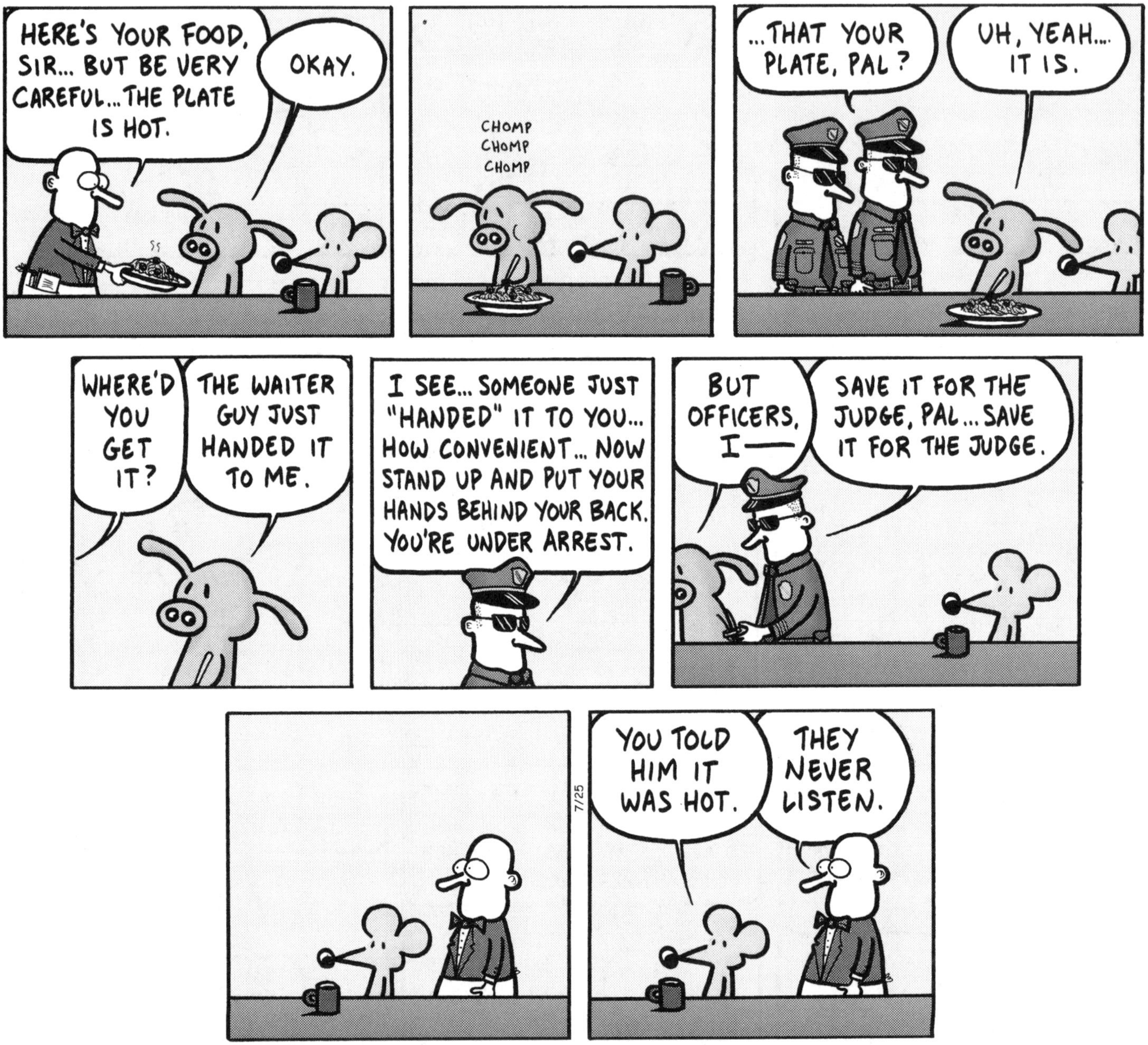
HERE'S YOUR FOOD, SIR... BUT BE VERY CAREFUL... THE PLATE IS HOT.
OKAY.
CHOMP CHOMP CHOMP
...THAT YOUR PLATE, PAL?
UH, YEAH.... IT IS.
WHERE'D YOU GET IT?
THE WAITER GUY JUST HANDED IT TO ME.
I SEE... SOMEONE JUST "HANDED" IT TO YOU... HOW CONVENIENT... NOW STAND UP AND PUT YOUR HANDS BEHIND YOUR BACK. YOU'RE UNDER ARREST.
BUT OFFICERS, I—
SAVE IT FOR THE JUDGE, PAL... SAVE IT FOR THE JUDGE.
7/25
YOU TOLD HIM IT WAS HOT.
THEY NEVER LISTEN.

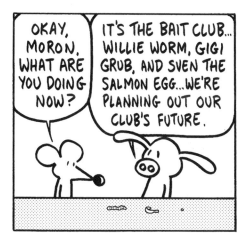

Panel 1: OKAY, MORON, WHAT ARE YOU DOING NOW?

IT'S THE BAIT CLUB... WILLIE WORM, GIGI GRUB, AND SVEN THE SALMON EGG...WE'RE PLANNING OUT OUR CLUB'S FUTURE.

Panel 2: WELL, DON'T PLAN TOO MUCH, BECAUSE I'M GOING TROUT FISHING TOMORROW AND YOU'RE ALL GONNA DIE.

7/26

Panel 3: SUDDENLY, THE ISSUE OF WHERE TO BUILD OUR RETIREMENT HOME DOES NOT LOOK SO PRESSING.

Panel 4: THE MEETING OF THE BAIT CLUB

YOU KNOW, I THINK WE REALLY NEED TO BE FOCUSING ON NEXT SUNDAY'S PANCAKE BREAKFAST FUNDRAISER. WE HAVEN'T RENTED THE TABLES. WE HAVEN'T PUT UP THE FLYERS. WE STILL NEED THE COFFEE.

Panel 5: GIGI...THE RAT JUST TOLD US THAT HE'S GOING FISHING TOMORROW AND THAT WE ARE ALL GOING TO DIE.

7/27

Panel 6: HEY... I DIDN'T INTERRUPT **YOU**.

Panel 7: YOU KNOW, THE WORST PART ABOUT BEING BAIT IS THAT WE'RE JUST AN AFTERTHOUGHT. EVERY TREE HUGGER IN THE WORLD COMPLAINS IF YOU USE THE WRONG TYPE OF HOOK ON THE POOR FISH, BUT NO ONE CARES ABOUT WILLIE WORM.

Panel 8: HEY...MAYBE WE SHOULD ORGANIZE OUR OWN PROTEST...WILLIE HERE CAN CLIMB TO THE TOP OF A REDWOOD AND JUST SIT THERE FOR WEEKS... IT'LL BE A BIG MEDIA EVENT.

7/28

Panel 9: SVEN..... A BIRD WILL EAT ME.

HEY, TAKE ONE FOR THE TEAM, DUDE.

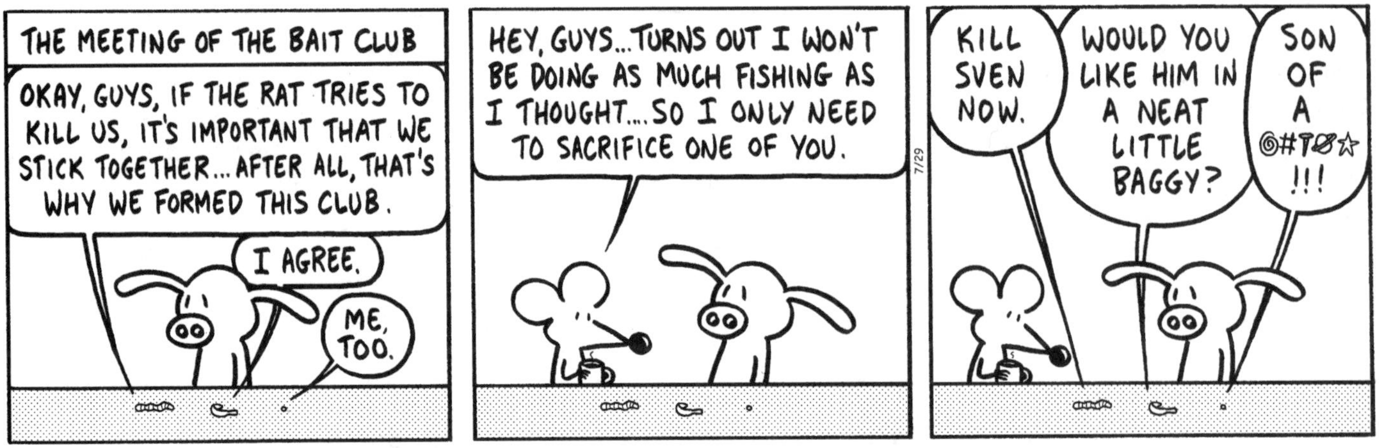
THE MEETING OF THE BAIT CLUB
OKAY, GUYS, IF THE RAT TRIES TO KILL US, IT'S IMPORTANT THAT WE STICK TOGETHER... AFTER ALL, THAT'S WHY WE FORMED THIS CLUB.
I AGREE.
ME, TOO.
HEY, GUYS... TURNS OUT I WON'T BE DOING AS MUCH FISHING AS I THOUGHT.... SO I ONLY NEED TO SACRIFICE ONE OF YOU.
7/29
KILL SVEN NOW.
WOULD YOU LIKE HIM IN A NEAT LITTLE BAGGY?
SON OF A
!!!

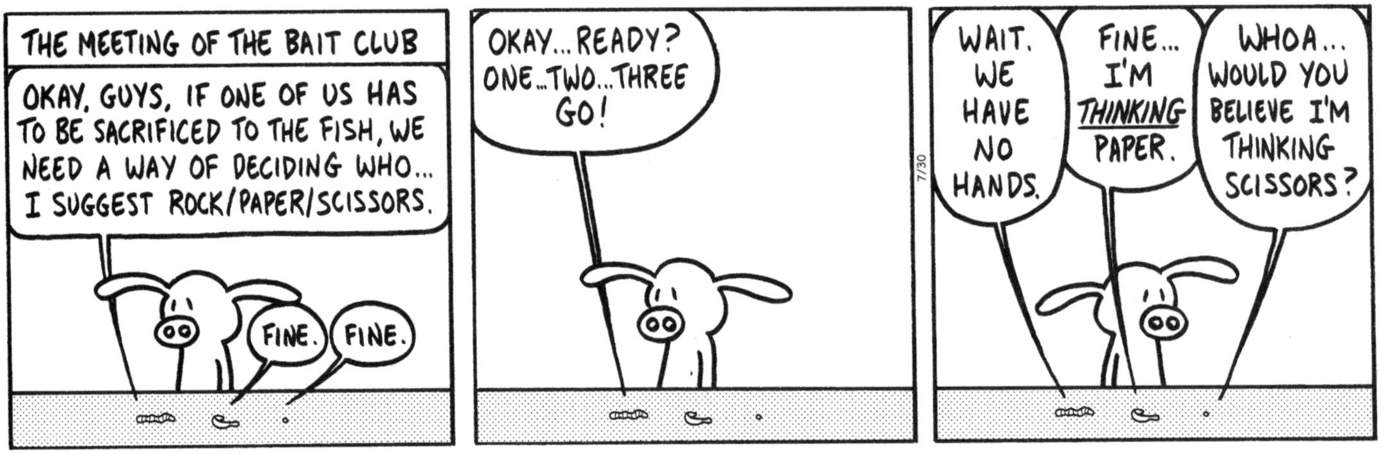
THE MEETING OF THE BAIT CLUB
OKAY, GUYS, IF ONE OF US HAS TO BE SACRIFICED TO THE FISH, WE NEED A WAY OF DECIDING WHO... I SUGGEST ROCK/PAPER/SCISSORS.
FINE.
FINE.
OKAY... READY? ONE... TWO... THREE GO!
7/30
WAIT. WE HAVE NO HANDS.
FINE... I'M THINKING PAPER.
WHOA... WOULD YOU BELIEVE I'M THINKING SCISSORS?

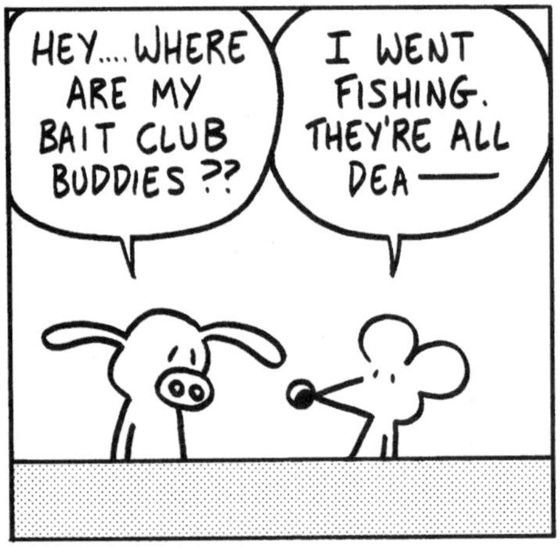
HEY.... WHERE ARE MY BAIT CLUB BUDDIES??
I WENT FISHING. THEY'RE ALL DEA——

AUTHOR'S NOTE: It has come to my attention that virtually all "Pearls" series that are centered upon new, peripheral characters end in death. Whether it be the Fruit Buddies, Angry Bob or Tooty the Gingerbread Man, the newbies always die. As comedy is founded upon the unexpected, and death in these panels is all too expected, we now introduce a totally unexplored concept in "Pearls"... the happy, sappy ending. True "Pearls" diehards may wish to look away.

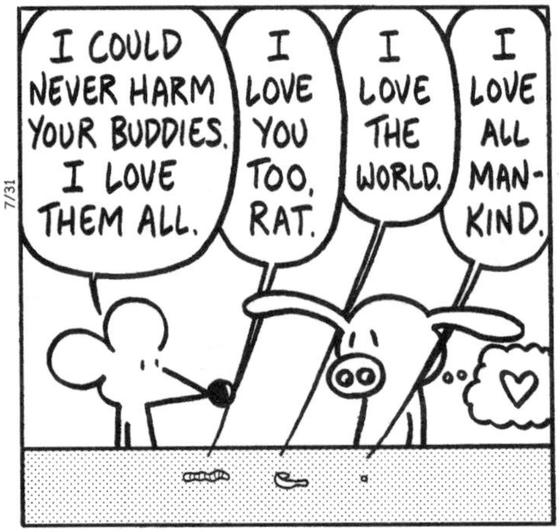
7/31
I COULD NEVER HARM YOUR BUDDIES. I LOVE THEM ALL.
I LOVE YOU TOO, RAT.
I LOVE THE WORLD.
I LOVE ALL MAN-KIND.

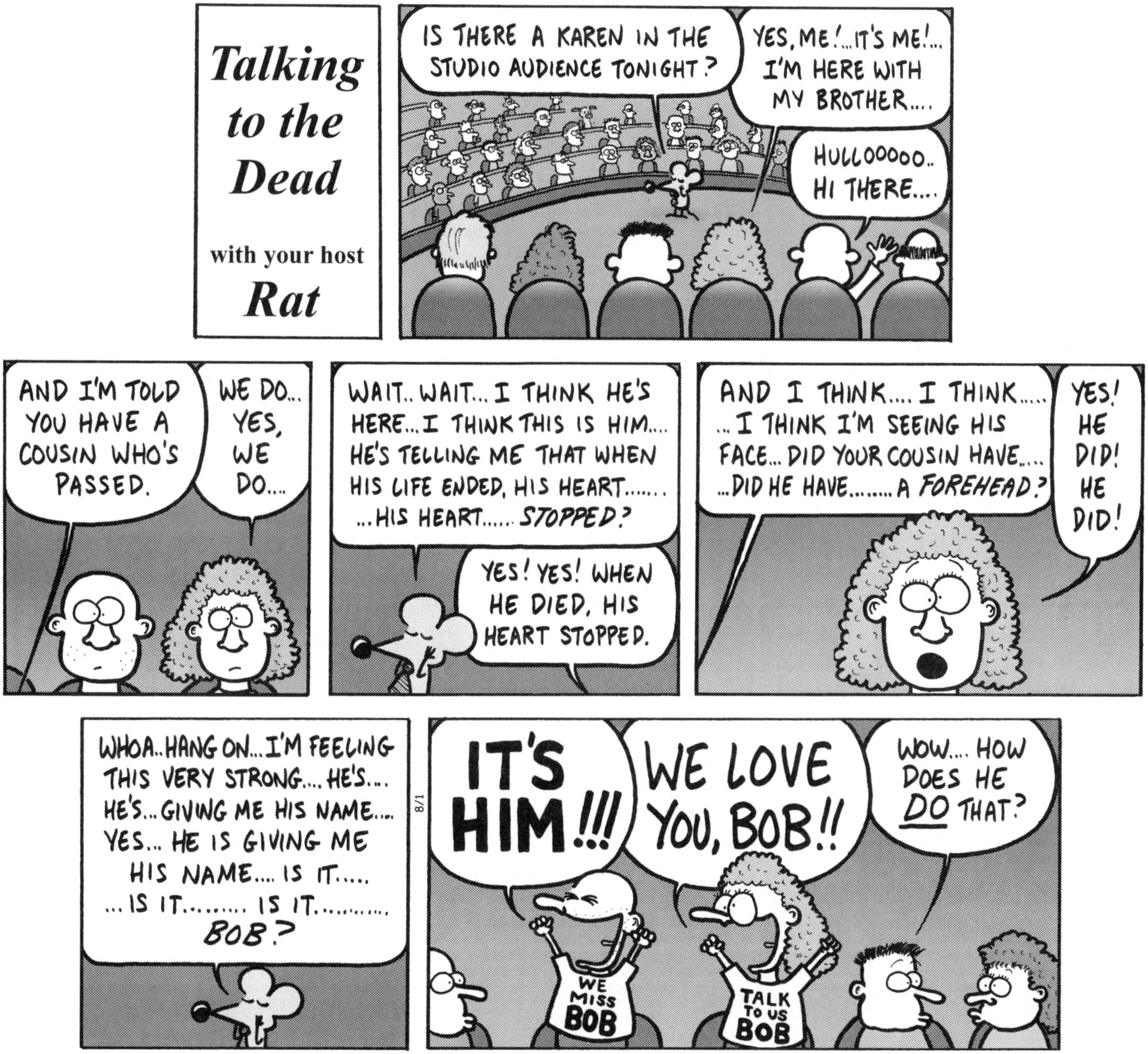
Talking to the Dead
with your host
Rat
IS THERE A KAREN IN THE STUDIO AUDIENCE TONIGHT?
YES, ME!...IT'S ME!... I'M HERE WITH MY BROTHER....
HULLOOOOO.. HI THERE....
AND I'M TOLD YOU HAVE A COUSIN WHO'S PASSED.
WE DO... YES, WE DO....
WAIT.. WAIT... I THINK HE'S HERE... I THINK THIS IS HIM.... HE'S TELLING ME THAT WHEN HIS LIFE ENDED, HIS HEART....... ...HIS HEART...... STOPPED?
YES! YES! WHEN HE DIED, HIS HEART STOPPED.
AND I THINK.... I THINK..... ...I THINK I'M SEEING HIS FACE... DID YOUR COUSIN HAVE..... ...DID HE HAVE........ A FOREHEAD?
YES! HE DID! HE DID!
WHOA.. HANG ON... I'M FEELING THIS VERY STRONG.... HE'S.... HE'S... GIVING ME HIS NAME.... YES... HE IS GIVING ME HIS NAME.... IS IT..... ...IS IT......... IS IT........... BOB?
8/1
IT'S HIM!!!
WE LOVE YOU, BOB!!
WOW.... HOW DOES HE DO THAT?
WE MISS BOB
TALK TO US BOB

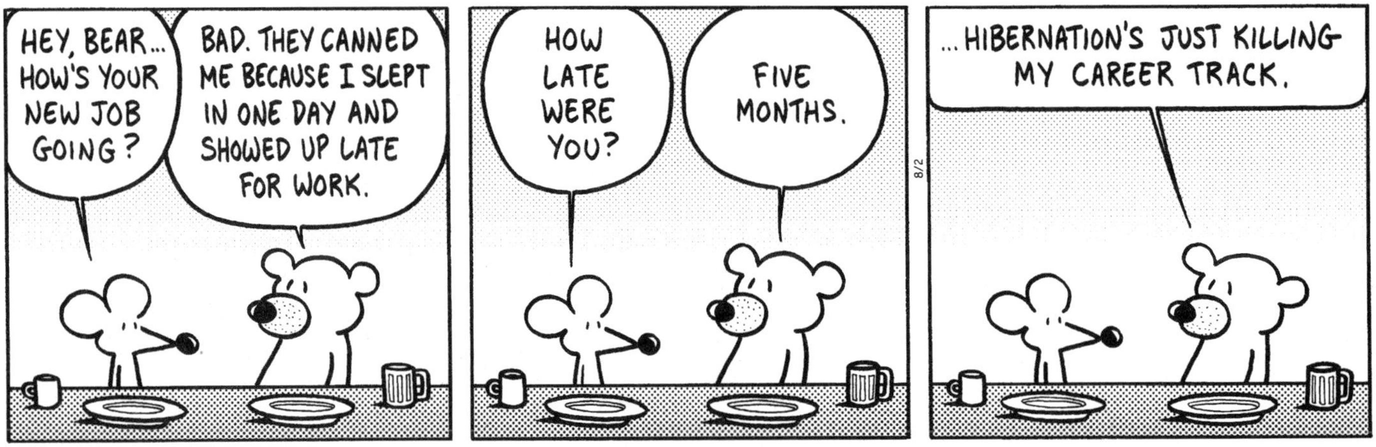
HEY, BEAR... HOW'S YOUR NEW JOB GOING?
BAD. THEY CANNED ME BECAUSE I SLEPT IN ONE DAY AND SHOWED UP LATE FOR WORK.
HOW LATE WERE YOU?
FIVE MONTHS.
8/2
...HIBERNATION'S JUST KILLING MY CAREER TRACK.

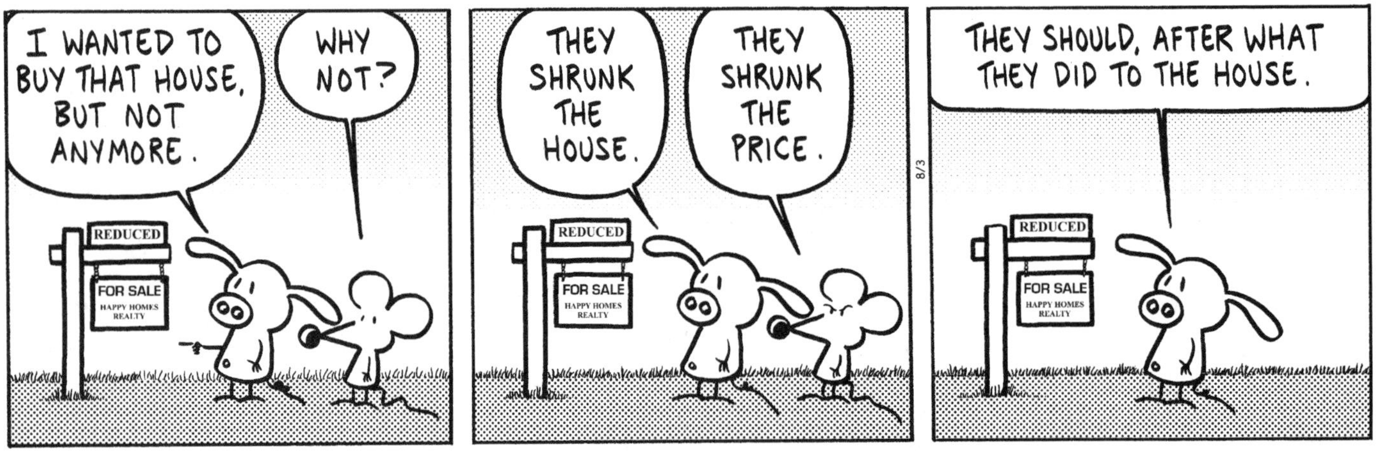
I WANTED TO BUY THAT HOUSE, BUT NOT ANYMORE.
WHY NOT?
REDUCED
FOR SALE
HAPPY HOMES REALTY
THEY SHRUNK THE HOUSE.
THEY SHRUNK THE PRICE.
8/3
THEY SHOULD, AFTER WHAT THEY DID TO THE HOUSE.

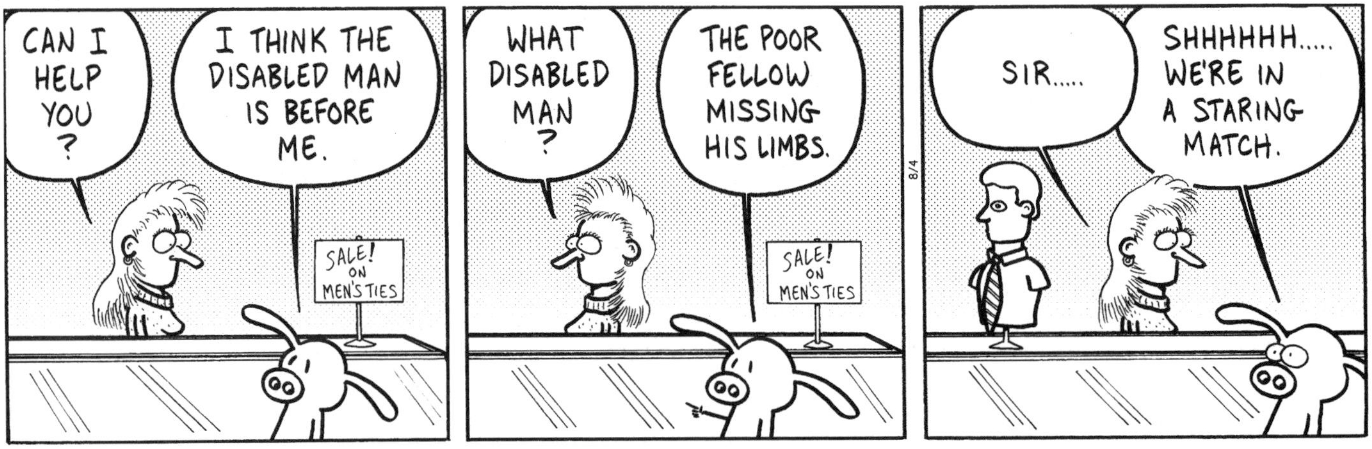
CAN I HELP YOU?
I THINK THE DISABLED MAN IS BEFORE ME.
SALE! ON MEN'S TIES
WHAT DISABLED MAN?
THE POOR FELLOW MISSING HIS LIMBS.
8/4
SIR.....
SHHHHHH..... WE'RE IN A STARING MATCH.

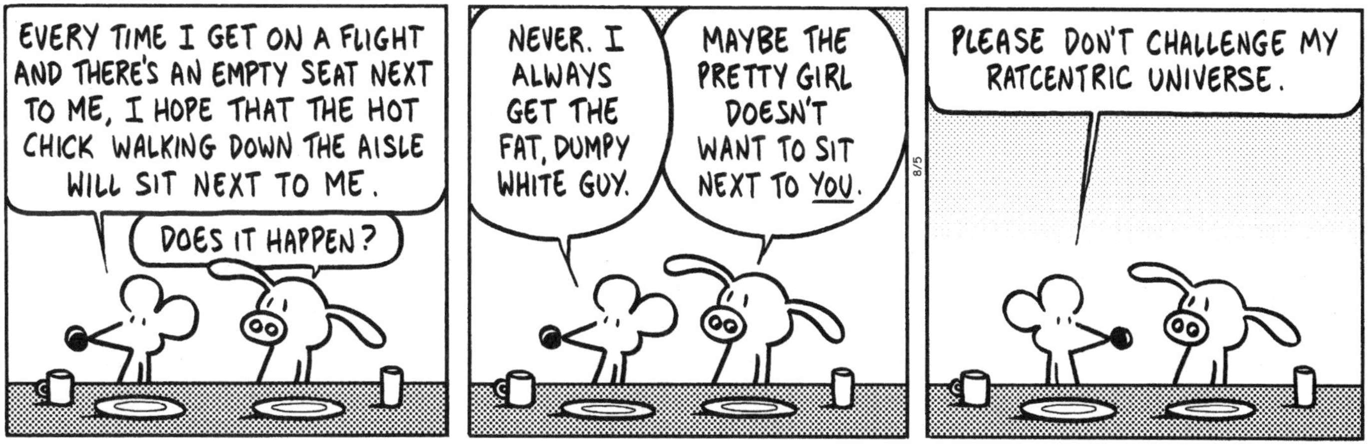
EVERY TIME I GET ON A FLIGHT AND THERE'S AN EMPTY SEAT NEXT TO ME, I HOPE THAT THE HOT CHICK WALKING DOWN THE AISLE WILL SIT NEXT TO ME.
DOES IT HAPPEN?
NEVER. I ALWAYS GET THE FAT, DUMPY WHITE GUY.
MAYBE THE PRETTY GIRL DOESN'T WANT TO SIT NEXT TO YOU.
8/5
PLEASE DON'T CHALLENGE MY RATCENTRIC UNIVERSE.

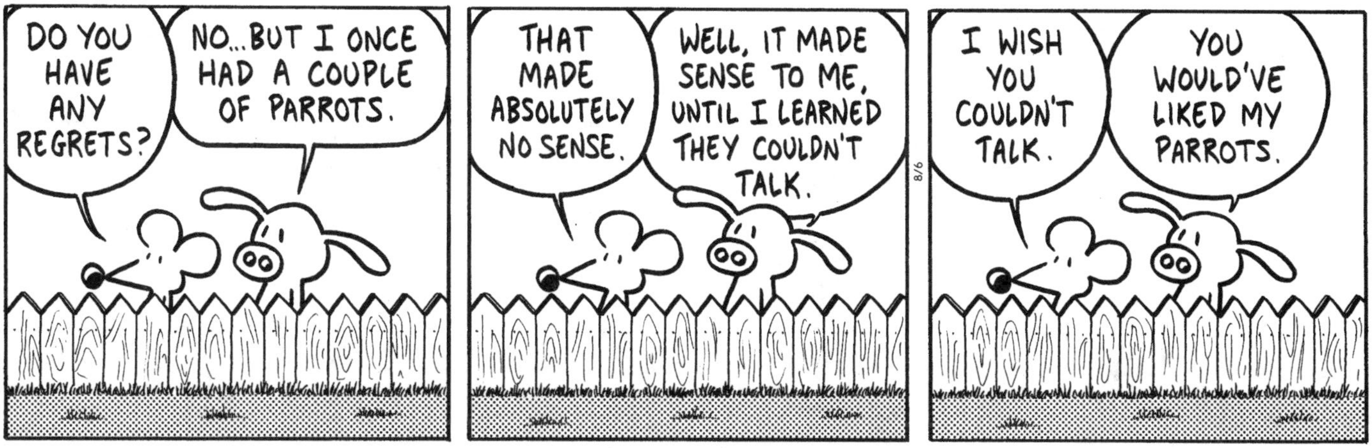
DO YOU HAVE ANY REGRETS?
NO...BUT I ONCE HAD A COUPLE OF PARROTS.
THAT MADE ABSOLUTELY NO SENSE.
WELL, IT MADE SENSE TO ME, UNTIL I LEARNED THEY COULDN'T TALK.
8/6
I WISH YOU COULDN'T TALK.
YOU WOULD'VE LIKED MY PARROTS.

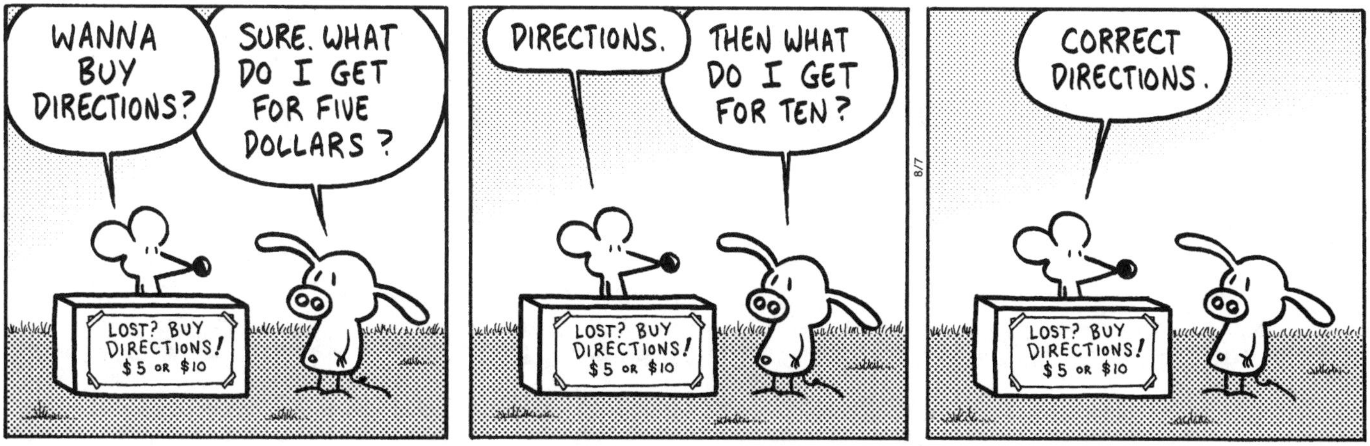
WANNA BUY DIRECTIONS?
SURE. WHAT DO I GET FOR FIVE DOLLARS?
LOST? BUY DIRECTIONS! $5 OR $10
DIRECTIONS.
THEN WHAT DO I GET FOR TEN?
8/7
CORRECT DIRECTIONS.

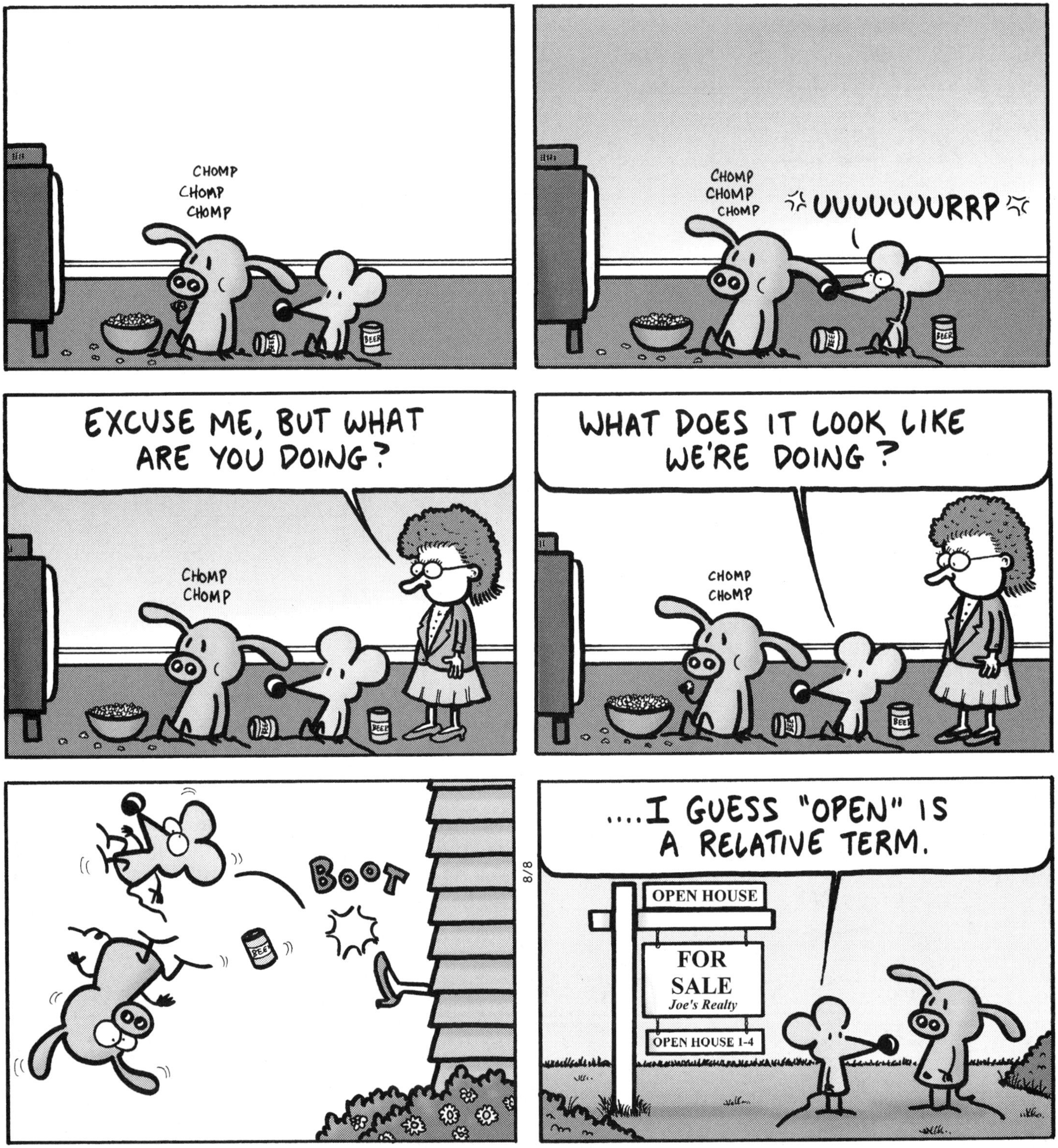
CHOMP
CHOMP
CHOMP
CHOMP
CHOMP
CHOMP
UUUUUUURRP
EXCUSE ME, BUT WHAT ARE YOU DOING?
CHOMP
CHOMP
WHAT DOES IT LOOK LIKE WE'RE DOING?
CHOMP
CHOMP
BOOT
8/8
....I GUESS "OPEN" IS A RELATIVE TERM.
OPEN HOUSE
FOR SALE
Joe's Realty
OPEN HOUSE 1-4

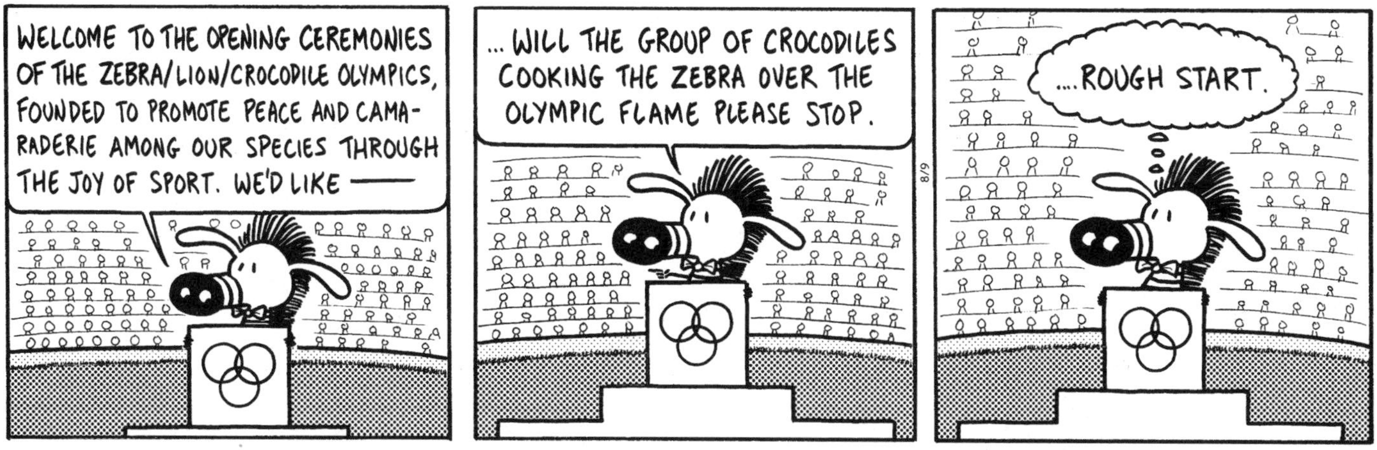
WELCOME TO THE OPENING CEREMONIES OF THE ZEBRA/LION/CROCODILE OLYMPICS, FOUNDED TO PROMOTE PEACE AND CAMARADERIE AMONG OUR SPECIES THROUGH THE JOY OF SPORT. WE'D LIKE ——
... WILL THE GROUP OF CROCODILES COOKING THE ZEBRA OVER THE OLYMPIC FLAME PLEASE STOP.
8/9
.... ROUGH START.

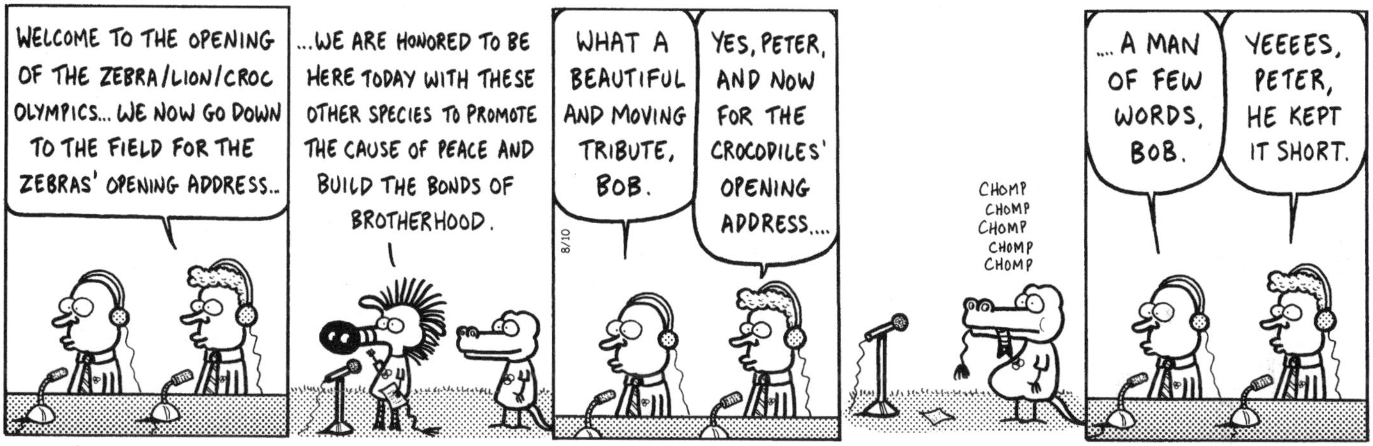
WELCOME TO THE OPENING OF THE ZEBRA/LION/CROC OLYMPICS... WE NOW GO DOWN TO THE FIELD FOR THE ZEBRAS' OPENING ADDRESS...
... WE ARE HONORED TO BE HERE TODAY WITH THESE OTHER SPECIES TO PROMOTE THE CAUSE OF PEACE AND BUILD THE BONDS OF BROTHERHOOD.
8/10
WHAT A BEAUTIFUL AND MOVING TRIBUTE, BOB.
YES, PETER, AND NOW FOR THE CROCODILES' OPENING ADDRESS....
CHOMP CHOMP CHOMP CHOMP CHOMP
.... A MAN OF FEW WORDS, BOB.
YEEEES, PETER, HE KEPT IT SHORT.

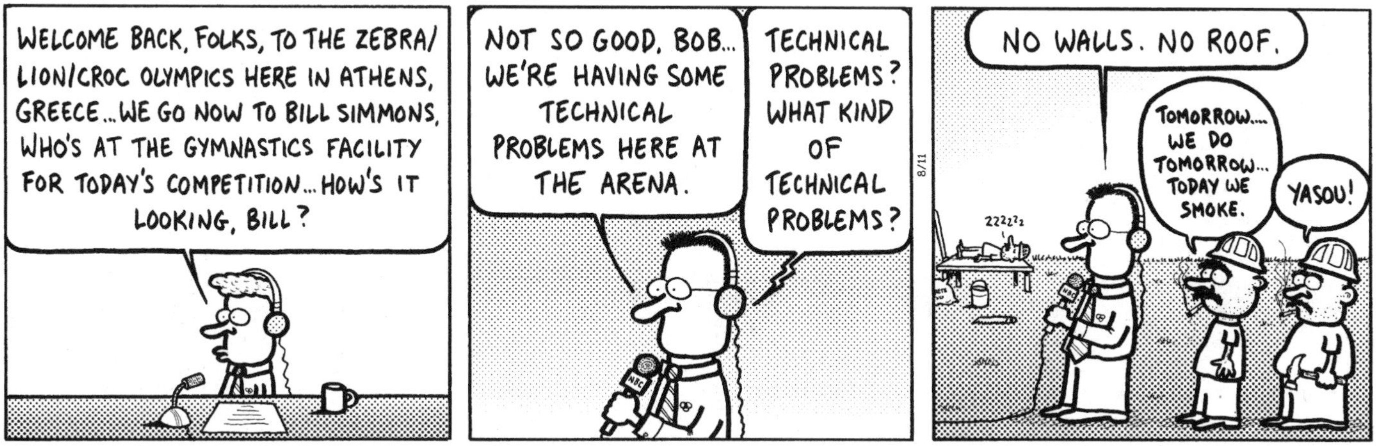
WELCOME BACK, FOLKS, TO THE ZEBRA/LION/CROC OLYMPICS HERE IN ATHENS, GREECE... WE GO NOW TO BILL SIMMONS, WHO'S AT THE GYMNASTICS FACILITY FOR TODAY'S COMPETITION... HOW'S IT LOOKING, BILL?
NOT SO GOOD, BOB... WE'RE HAVING SOME TECHNICAL PROBLEMS HERE AT THE ARENA.
TECHNICAL PROBLEMS? WHAT KIND OF TECHNICAL PROBLEMS?
8/11
NO WALLS. NO ROOF.
TOMORROW.... WE DO TOMORROW... TODAY WE SMOKE.
YASOU!
ZZZZZZ

Panel 1: WELCOME BACK, FOLKS, TO THE ZEBRA/LION/CROC OLYMPICS... TODAY'S EVENT IS SYNCHRONIZED SWIMMING, AND IT LOOKS LIKE OUR FIRST ZEBRA/CROC DUO ARE ALREADY IN THE POOL... HOW'S IT LOOKING, BOB?

Panel 2: YEEEES, PETER... THE PAIRING OF THESE TWO UNLIKELY SPECIES IS UNPRECEDENTED, AND REEEALLY SHOWS THE ENERGY AND SPIRIT THAT IS THE HALLMARK OF.........

Panel 3: AAAAAAAAAHH! CHOMP CHOMP CHOMP CHOMP CHOMP CHOMP CHOMP CHOMP

Panel 4: ......A HUNGRY CROCODILE?

THAT'S GONNA BE A BIIIIIG POINT DEDUCTION, PETER....

Panel 5: FOLKS, THIS JUST IN.... THE REMAINDER OF THE ZEBRA/LION/CROC OLYMPICS HAVE BEEN CANCELLED... THE OLYMPIC COMMITTEE CITED THE GREEKS' FAILURE TO PROTECT THE ZEBRAS AND THEIR FAILURE TO COMPLETE CONSTRUCTION OF THE FACILITIES.

Panel 6: THE GREEKS, FOR THEIR PART, HAVE DENIED THE ACCUSATIONS... WE GO NOW TO BILL SIMMONS, WHO'S AT THE TRACK AND FIELD FACILITIES WITH SOME OF THE ZEBRAS... UH.... WELL, HE'S *SUPPOSED TO* BE WITH THE ZEBRAS... G#§# IT, BILL, WHERE ARE THE G#§#*G# ZEBRAS??

Panel 7: CRUSHED BY A BACKHOE, BOB.

WHERE HE COME FROM?

WHO CARE? TIME FOR COKE BREAK.

PEPSI! NO COKE!

Panel 8: WE HAD TO CANCEL THE ZEBRA/LION/CROC OLYMPICS... THE GREEKS WEREN'T READY AND THE CROCS KEPT KILLING US.

THAT'S THE WAY IT GOES, DUDE.

Panel 9: YEAH, BUT WHAT A WASTE... WE BOUGHT ALL THOSE MEDALS FOR NOTHING.

GIVE 'EM TO SOME LOSER WHO'LL APPRECIATE 'EM 'CAUSE HE'S TOO LAME TO WIN AWARDS ON HIS OWN.

Panel 10: NOT SO LOUD.

WHAT ARE YOU DOING, PIG?
I'M THE GRAND PEA, AND I'M COMBATING VEGETABLEISM.
8/15
YOU'RE COMBATING *WHAT?*
VEGETABLEISM.... THE DISCRIMINATORY TREATMENT OF CERTAIN VEGETABLES BASED SOLELY UPON THE TYPE OF VEGETABLE THEY ARE.
ARE YOU G#&$G#@ KIDDING ME?? HAVE YOU LOST YER G#@☆#&@ MIND??
HARDLY. LOOK BEHIND YOU.
RESTRICTED BEACH AREA P EAS KEEP OUT

YOU IDIOT! THAT SIGN JUST LOST A COUPLE OF LETTERS... IT'S SUPPOSED TO SAY "*PLEASE*," NOT "*PEAS*."
PLEASE TELL ME YOU KNEW THAT.
I DID.
...AND THAT YOU'RE NOT THAT STUPID.
I'M NOT.
...AND THAT YOU WOULDN'T ORGANIZE A PROTEST OVER A MISREADING OF A SIGN.
I WOULDN'T.
GOOD.
GOOD.
SEE YA.
BYE.

FIRST, THE GOOD NEWS....
WE'RE HERE! WE'RE GREEN! GET USED TO IT!
NO PEAS! NO JUSTICE!
WHAT'S SO FUNNY ABOUT PEAS, LOVE AND UNDERSTANDING?

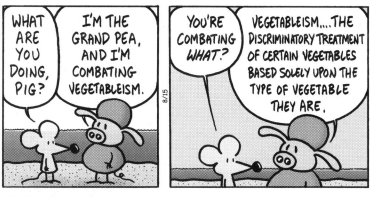

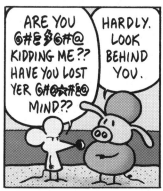

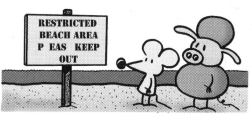

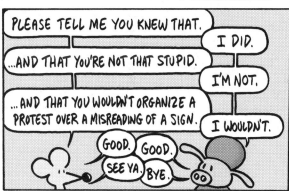

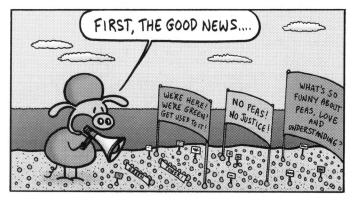

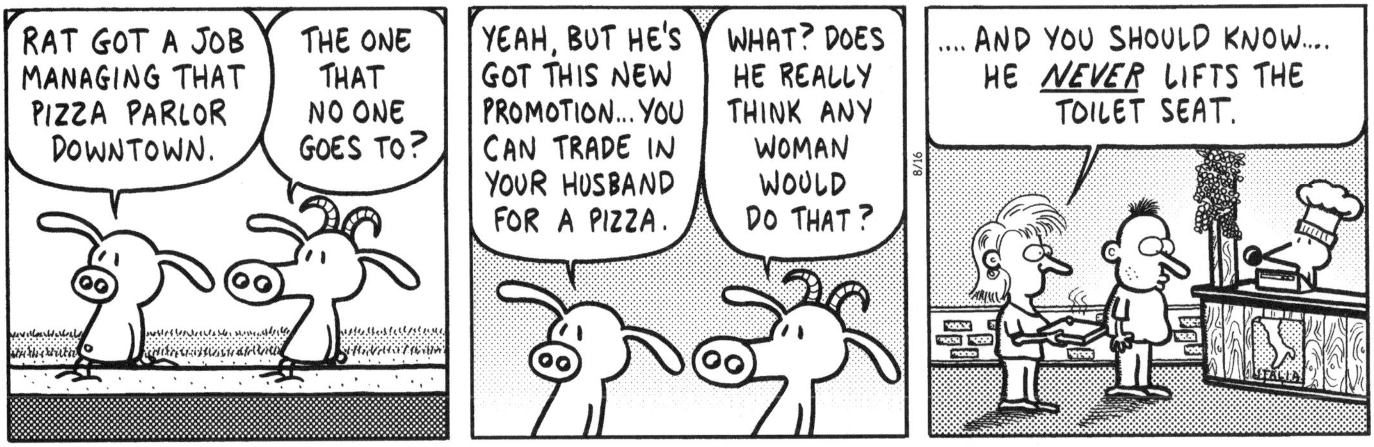
RAT GOT A JOB MANAGING THAT PIZZA PARLOR DOWNTOWN.
THE ONE THAT NO ONE GOES TO?
YEAH, BUT HE'S GOT THIS NEW PROMOTION... YOU CAN TRADE IN YOUR HUSBAND FOR A PIZZA.
WHAT? DOES HE REALLY THINK ANY WOMAN WOULD DO THAT?
8/16
.... AND YOU SHOULD KNOW.... HE NEVER LIFTS THE TOILET SEAT.
ITALIA

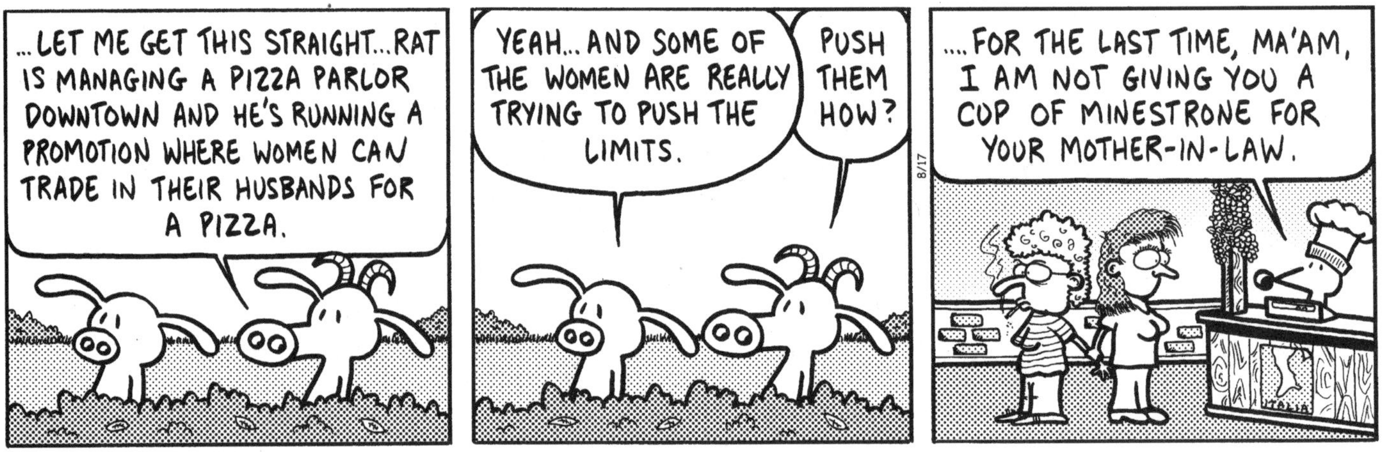
...LET ME GET THIS STRAIGHT...RAT IS MANAGING A PIZZA PARLOR DOWNTOWN AND HE'S RUNNING A PROMOTION WHERE WOMEN CAN TRADE IN THEIR HUSBANDS FOR A PIZZA.
YEAH... AND SOME OF THE WOMEN ARE REALLY TRYING TO PUSH THE LIMITS.
PUSH THEM HOW?
8/17
....FOR THE LAST TIME, MA'AM, I AM NOT GIVING YOU A CUP OF MINESTRONE FOR YOUR MOTHER-IN-LAW.
ITALIA

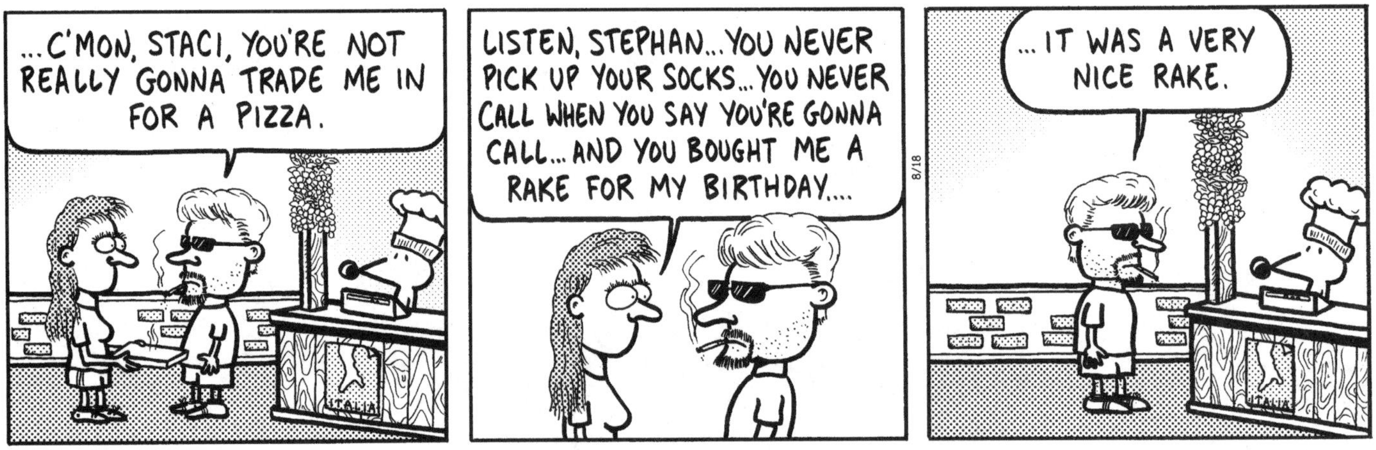
...C'MON, STACI, YOU'RE NOT REALLY GONNA TRADE ME IN FOR A PIZZA.
ITALIA
LISTEN, STEPHAN... YOU NEVER PICK UP YOUR SOCKS... YOU NEVER CALL WHEN YOU SAY YOU'RE GONNA CALL... AND YOU BOUGHT ME A RAKE FOR MY BIRTHDAY....
8/18
... IT WAS A VERY NICE RAKE.
ITALIA

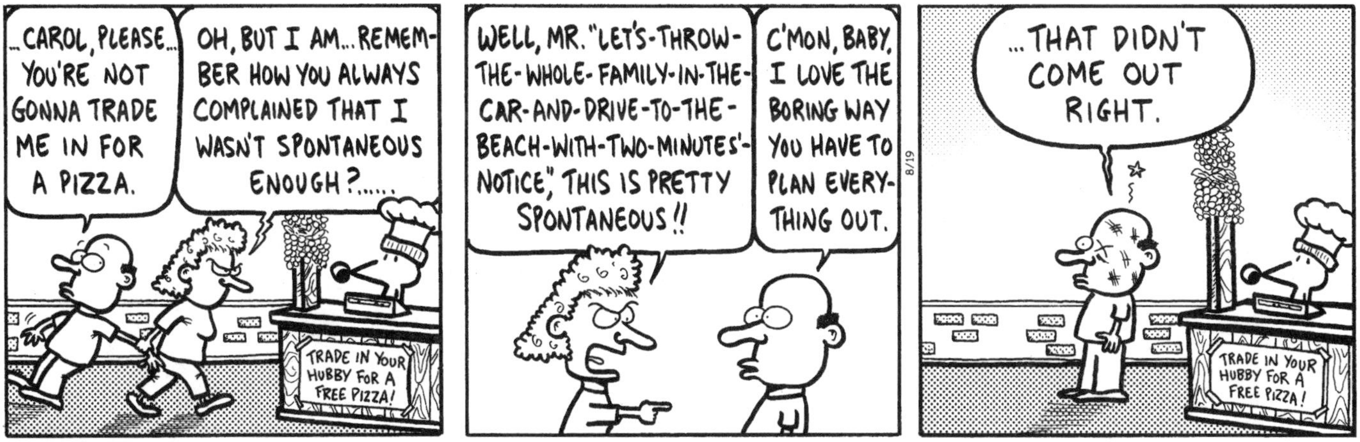
...CAROL, PLEASE... YOU'RE NOT GONNA TRADE ME IN FOR A PIZZA.
OH, BUT I AM... REMEMBER HOW YOU ALWAYS COMPLAINED THAT I WASN'T SPONTANEOUS ENOUGH?......
TRADE IN YOUR HUBBY FOR A FREE PIZZA!
WELL, MR. "LET'S-THROW-THE-WHOLE-FAMILY-IN-THE-CAR-AND-DRIVE-TO-THE-BEACH-WITH-TWO-MINUTES'-NOTICE," THIS IS PRETTY SPONTANEOUS!!
C'MON, BABY, I LOVE THE BORING WAY YOU HAVE TO PLAN EVERYTHING OUT.
8/19
...THAT DIDN'T COME OUT RIGHT.
TRADE IN YOUR HUBBY FOR A FREE PIZZA!

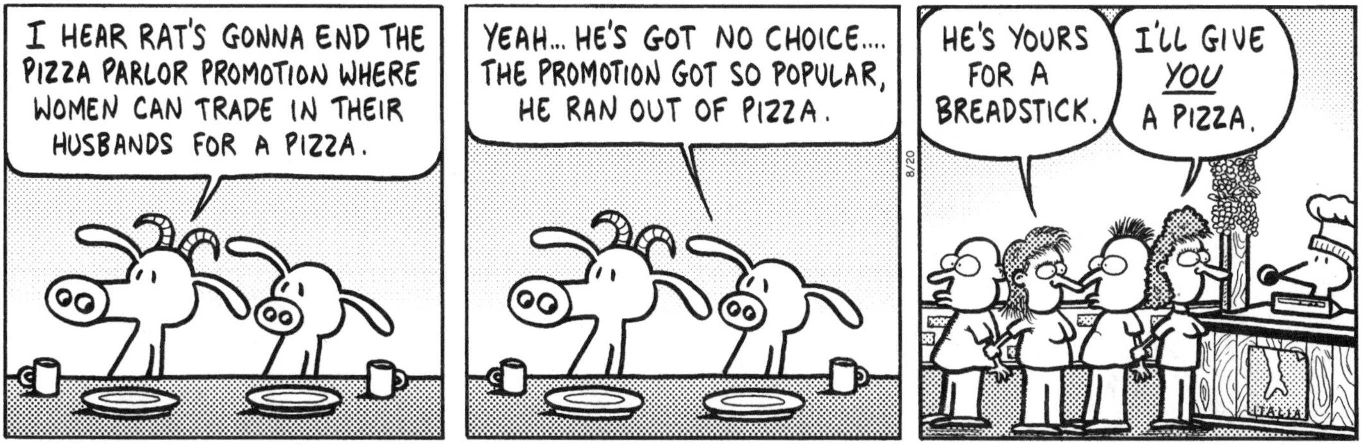
I HEAR RAT'S GONNA END THE PIZZA PARLOR PROMOTION WHERE WOMEN CAN TRADE IN THEIR HUSBANDS FOR A PIZZA.
YEAH... HE'S GOT NO CHOICE.... THE PROMOTION GOT SO POPULAR, HE RAN OUT OF PIZZA.
8/20
HE'S YOURS FOR A BREADSTICK.
I'LL GIVE YOU A PIZZA.

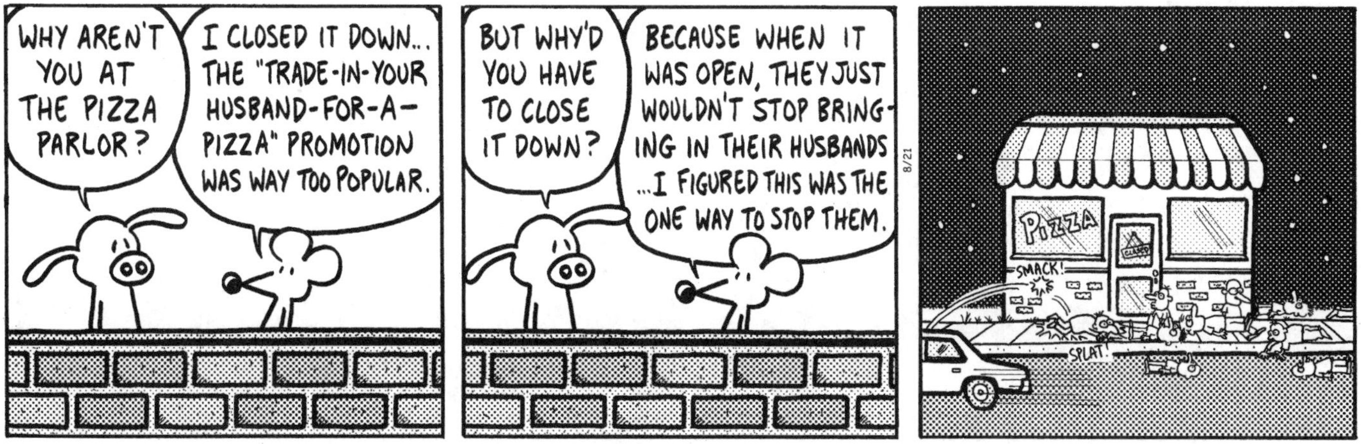
WHY AREN'T YOU AT THE PIZZA PARLOR?
I CLOSED IT DOWN... THE "TRADE-IN-YOUR-HUSBAND-FOR-A-PIZZA" PROMOTION WAS WAY TOO POPULAR.
BUT WHY'D YOU HAVE TO CLOSE IT DOWN?
BECAUSE WHEN IT WAS OPEN, THEY JUST WOULDN'T STOP BRINGING IN THEIR HUSBANDS ...I FIGURED THIS WAS THE ONE WAY TO STOP THEM.
8/21
PIZZA
SMACK!
SPLAT!

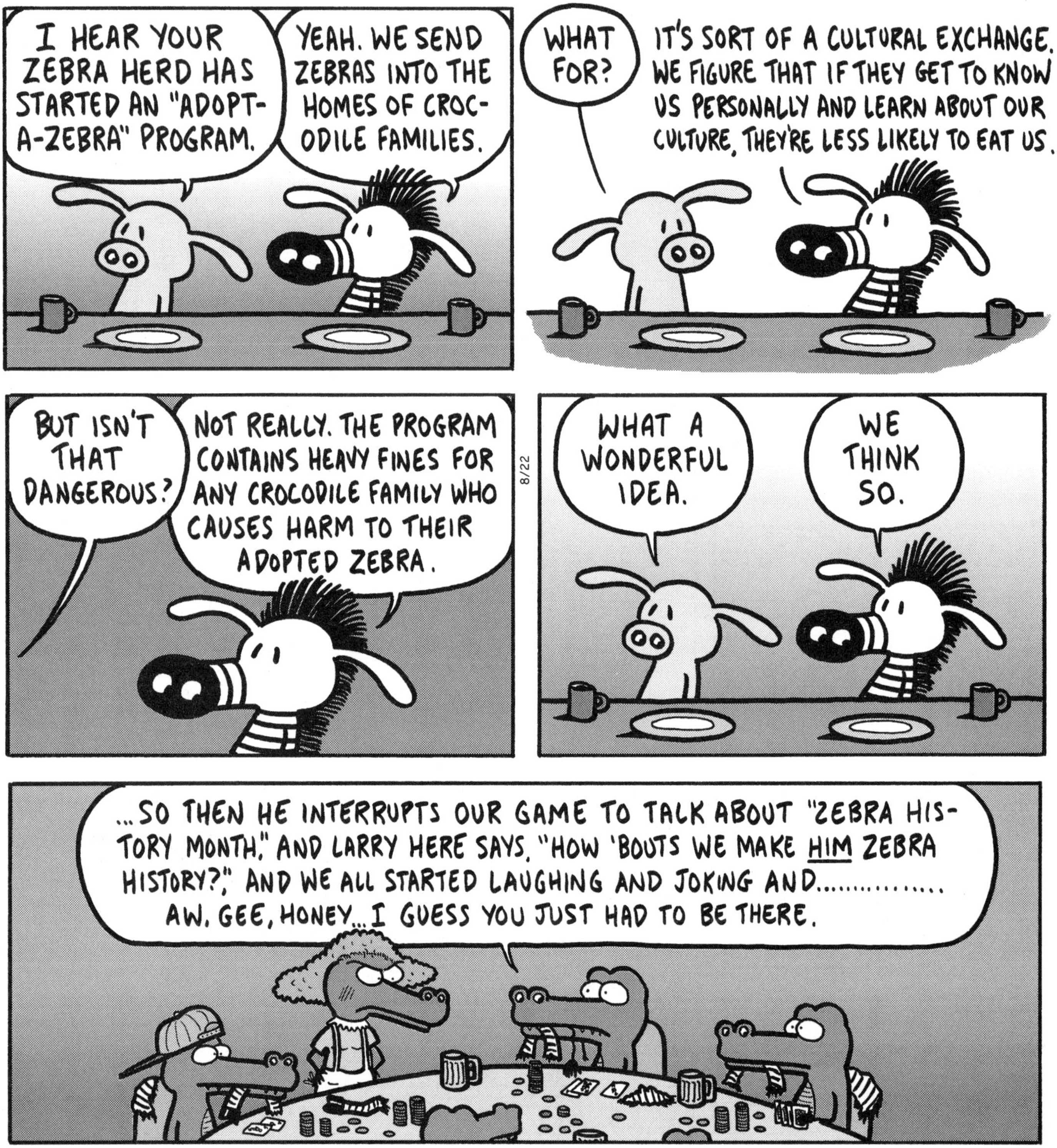
I HEAR YOUR ZEBRA HERD HAS STARTED AN "ADOPT-A-ZEBRA" PROGRAM.
YEAH. WE SEND ZEBRAS INTO THE HOMES OF CROC-ODILE FAMILIES.
WHAT FOR?
IT'S SORT OF A CULTURAL EXCHANGE. WE FIGURE THAT IF THEY GET TO KNOW US PERSONALLY AND LEARN ABOUT OUR CULTURE, THEY'RE LESS LIKELY TO EAT US.
BUT ISN'T THAT DANGEROUS?
NOT REALLY. THE PROGRAM CONTAINS HEAVY FINES FOR ANY CROCODILE FAMILY WHO CAUSES HARM TO THEIR ADOPTED ZEBRA.
8/22
WHAT A WONDERFUL IDEA.
WE THINK SO.
...SO THEN HE INTERRUPTS OUR GAME TO TALK ABOUT "ZEBRA HIS-TORY MONTH," AND LARRY HERE SAYS, "HOW 'BOUTS WE MAKE HIM ZEBRA HISTORY?," AND WE ALL STARTED LAUGHING AND JOKING AND............... AW, GEE, HONEY... I GUESS YOU JUST HAD TO BE THERE.

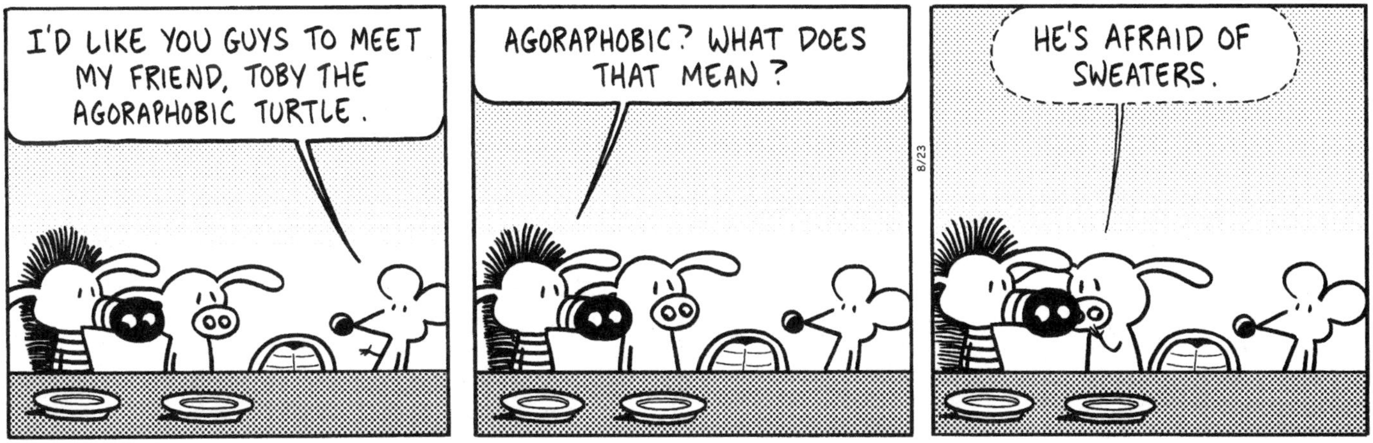
I'D LIKE YOU GUYS TO MEET MY FRIEND, TOBY THE AGORAPHOBIC TURTLE.
AGORAPHOBIC? WHAT DOES THAT MEAN?
8/23
HE'S AFRAID OF SWEATERS.

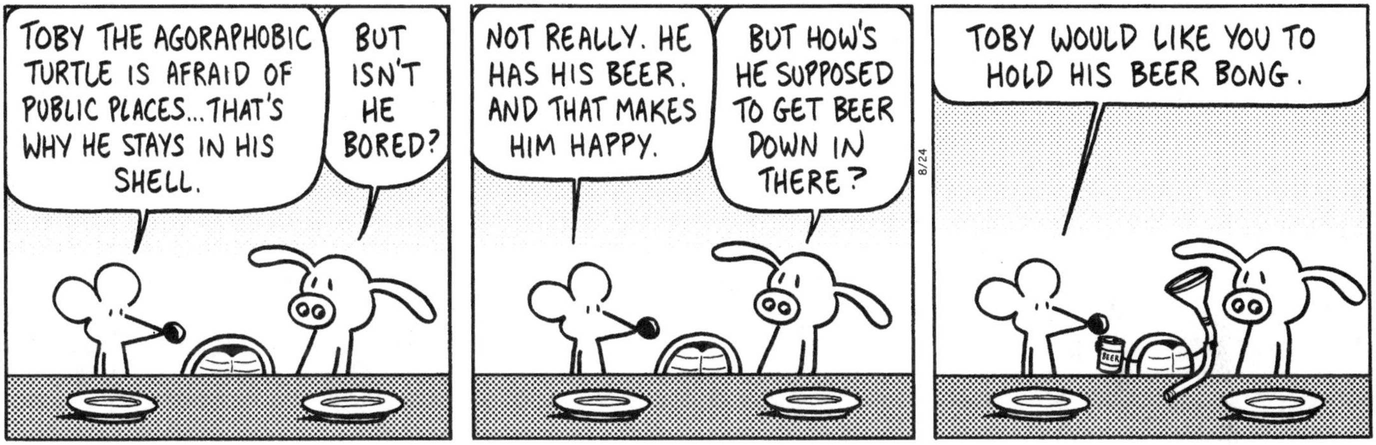
TOBY THE AGORAPHOBIC TURTLE IS AFRAID OF PUBLIC PLACES...THAT'S WHY HE STAYS IN HIS SHELL.
BUT ISN'T HE BORED?
NOT REALLY. HE HAS HIS BEER. AND THAT MAKES HIM HAPPY.
BUT HOW'S HE SUPPOSED TO GET BEER DOWN IN THERE?
8/24
TOBY WOULD LIKE YOU TO HOLD HIS BEER BONG.
BEER

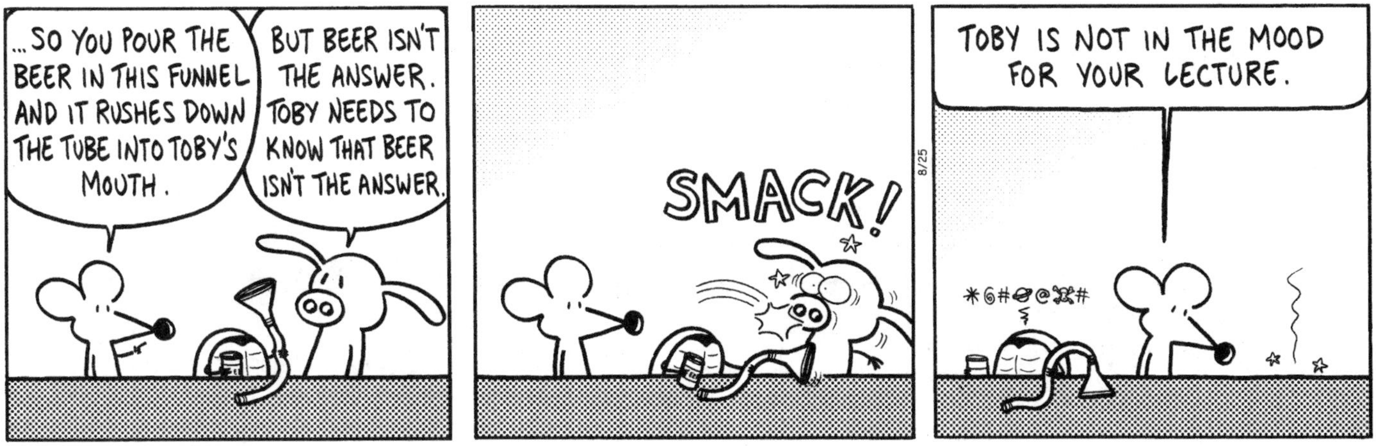
...SO YOU POUR THE BEER IN THIS FUNNEL AND IT RUSHES DOWN THE TUBE INTO TOBY'S MOUTH.
BUT BEER ISN'T THE ANSWER. TOBY NEEDS TO KNOW THAT BEER ISN'T THE ANSWER.
8/25
SMACK!
TOBY IS NOT IN THE MOOD FOR YOUR LECTURE.

Panel 1: JUST BECAUSE TOBY THE AGORAPHOBIC TURTLE IS AFRAID OF PUBLIC PLACES IS NO REASON FOR HIM TO LIVE IN HIS SHELL AND GUZZLE FROM A BEER BONG.

Panel 2: ...I THINK THAT LIFE IS BEAUTIFUL AND WONDERFUL ...AND MAYBE WITH HELP, TOBY CAN REALIZE THAT, TOO.

Panel 3: HIIYAA!!

POW!

8/26

Panel 4: TOBY REJECTS YOUR THEORY.

@#Ø*$%

Panel 5: GOAT, THIS IS MY FRIEND, TOBY THE AGORAPHOBIC TURTLE... HE FEARS PUBLIC PLACES, SO HE STAYS IN HIS SHELL AND DRINKS FROM A BEER BONG.

Panel 6: IT'S... NICE... TO.... MEET...

POUR POUR POUR POUR
FOOOOOOOOSSHHH
GLUG GLUG GLUG GLUG
UUUUUUUUURP

8/27

Panel 7: YOU.

NUTS. PASSED OUT AGAIN.

Panel 8: ...HI, MR. PASTIS... PIG SAYS YOU CALLED.

YEAH... LISTEN, RAT...I FIRED YOUR PAL, TOBY, TODAY.....THERE'S JUST NO LICENSING POTENTIAL FOR AN AGORAPHOBIC TURTLE.

Panel 9: NO LICENSING POTENTIAL? HA! I KNEW YOU WERE A SELL-OUT, PASTIS! SO MUCH FOR YOUR BIG-TALKING "I'LL BE JUST LIKE BILL WATTERSON AND NEVER MASS-MARKET MY CHARACTERS" ACT! YOU HYPOCRITICAL WEASEL!

8/28

Panel 10: YOU'RE REALLY JUMPING TO CONCLUSIONS.

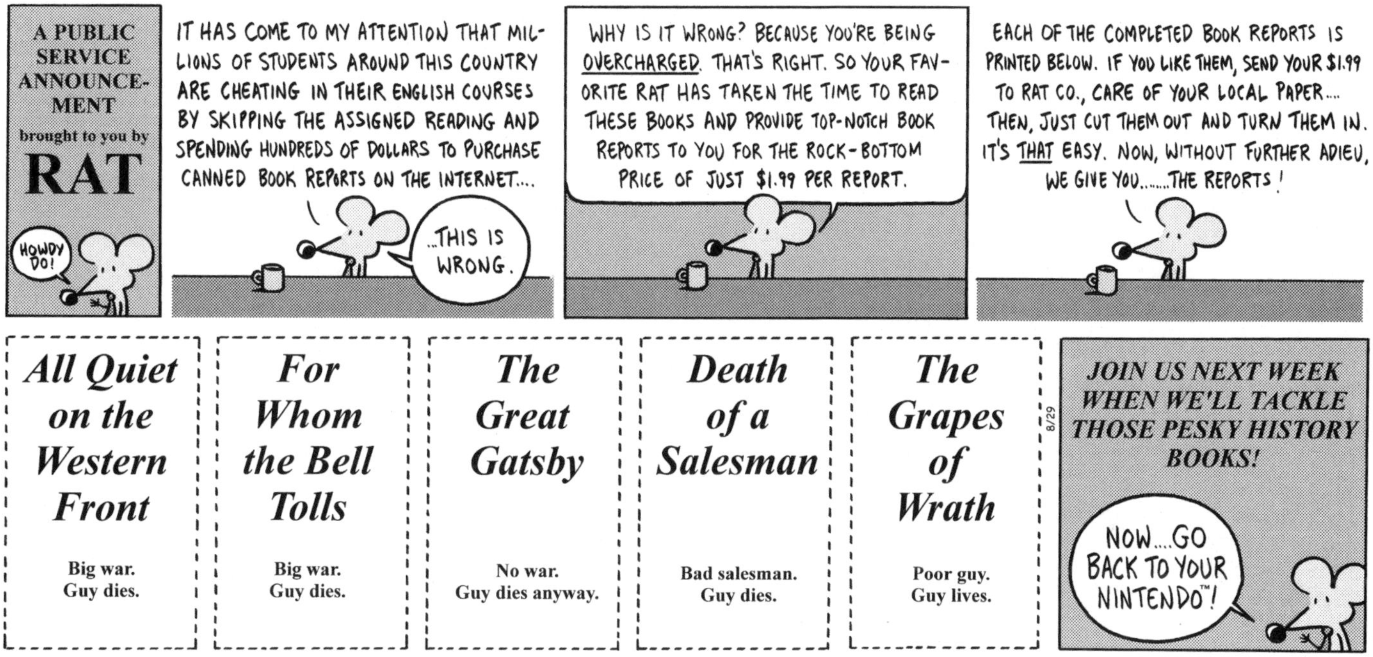
A PUBLIC SERVICE ANNOUNCEMENT brought to you by RAT
HOWDY DO!
IT HAS COME TO MY ATTENTION THAT MILLIONS OF STUDENTS AROUND THIS COUNTRY ARE CHEATING IN THEIR ENGLISH COURSES BY SKIPPING THE ASSIGNED READING AND SPENDING HUNDREDS OF DOLLARS TO PURCHASE CANNED BOOK REPORTS ON THE INTERNET....
...THIS IS WRONG.
WHY IS IT WRONG? BECAUSE YOU'RE BEING OVERCHARGED. THAT'S RIGHT. SO YOUR FAVORITE RAT HAS TAKEN THE TIME TO READ THESE BOOKS AND PROVIDE TOP-NOTCH BOOK REPORTS TO YOU FOR THE ROCK-BOTTOM PRICE OF JUST $1.99 PER REPORT.
EACH OF THE COMPLETED BOOK REPORTS IS PRINTED BELOW. IF YOU LIKE THEM, SEND YOUR $1.99 TO RAT CO., CARE OF YOUR LOCAL PAPER.... THEN, JUST CUT THEM OUT AND TURN THEM IN. IT'S THAT EASY. NOW, WITHOUT FURTHER ADIEU, WE GIVE YOU.......THE REPORTS!
All Quiet on the Western Front
Big war. Guy dies.
For Whom the Bell Tolls
Big war. Guy dies.
The Great Gatsby
No war. Guy dies anyway.
Death of a Salesman
Bad salesman. Guy dies.
The Grapes of Wrath
Poor guy. Guy lives.
8/29
JOIN US NEXT WEEK WHEN WE'LL TACKLE THOSE PESKY HISTORY BOOKS!
NOW....GO BACK TO YOUR NINTENDO™!

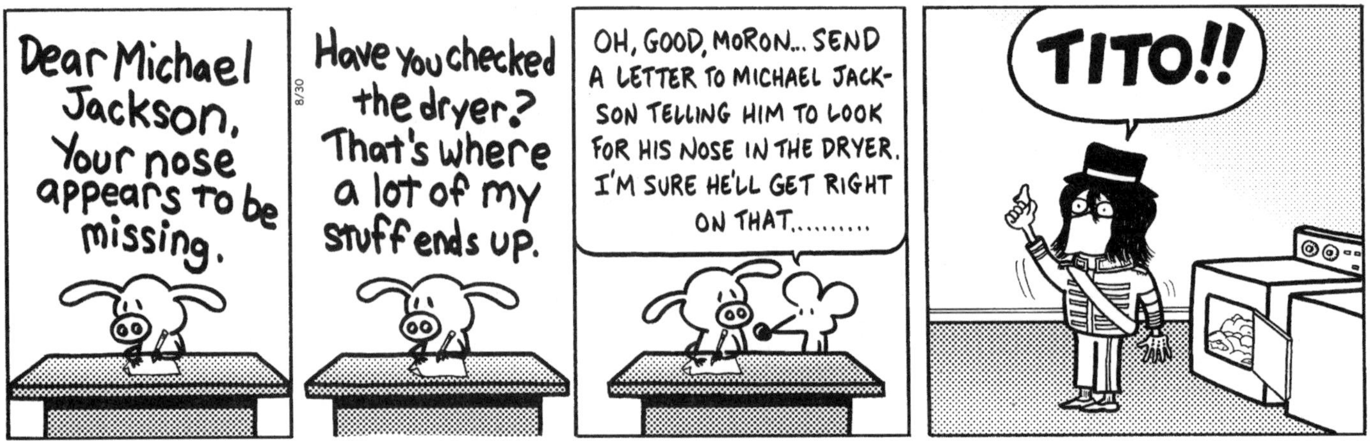
Dear Michael Jackson, Your nose appears to be missing.
8/30
Have you checked the dryer? That's where a lot of my stuff ends up.
OH, GOOD, MORON... SEND A LETTER TO MICHAEL JACKSON TELLING HIM TO LOOK FOR HIS NOSE IN THE DRYER. I'M SURE HE'LL GET RIGHT ON THAT.........
TITO!!

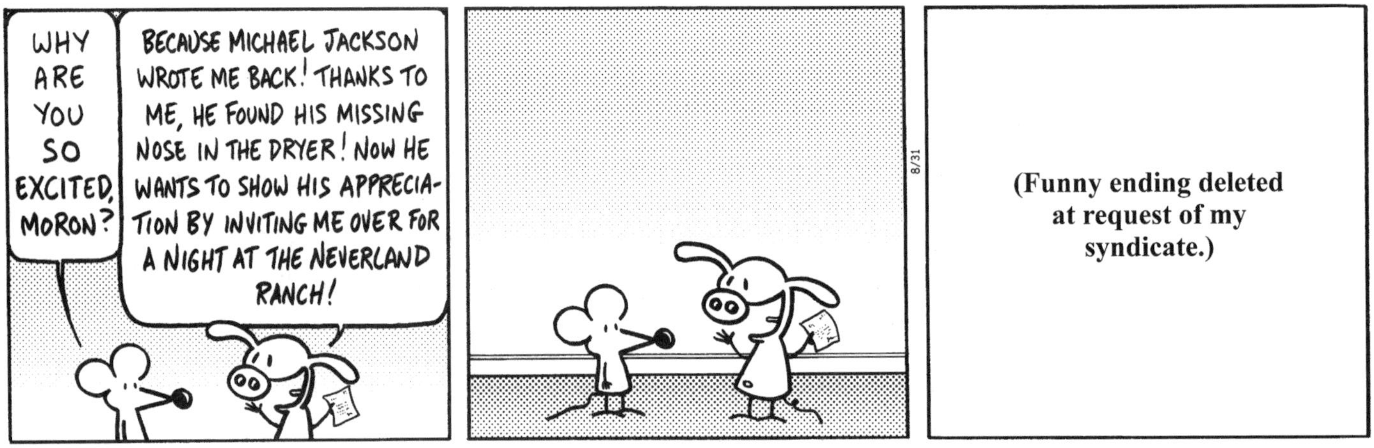
WHY ARE YOU SO EXCITED, MORON?
BECAUSE MICHAEL JACKSON WROTE ME BACK! THANKS TO ME, HE FOUND HIS MISSING NOSE IN THE DRYER! NOW HE WANTS TO SHOW HIS APPRECIATION BY INVITING ME OVER FOR A NIGHT AT THE NEVERLAND RANCH!
8/31
(Funny ending deleted at request of my syndicate.)

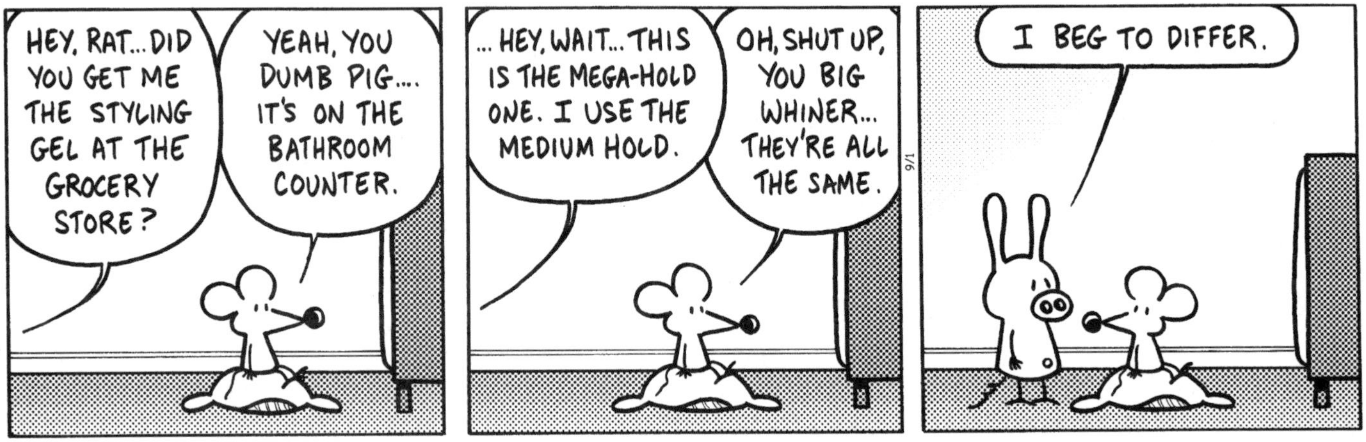
HEY, RAT...DID YOU GET ME THE STYLING GEL AT THE GROCERY STORE?
YEAH, YOU DUMB PIG.... IT'S ON THE BATHROOM COUNTER.
...HEY, WAIT...THIS IS THE MEGA-HOLD ONE. I USE THE MEDIUM HOLD.
OH, SHUT UP, YOU BIG WHINER... THEY'RE ALL THE SAME.
9/1
I BEG TO DIFFER.

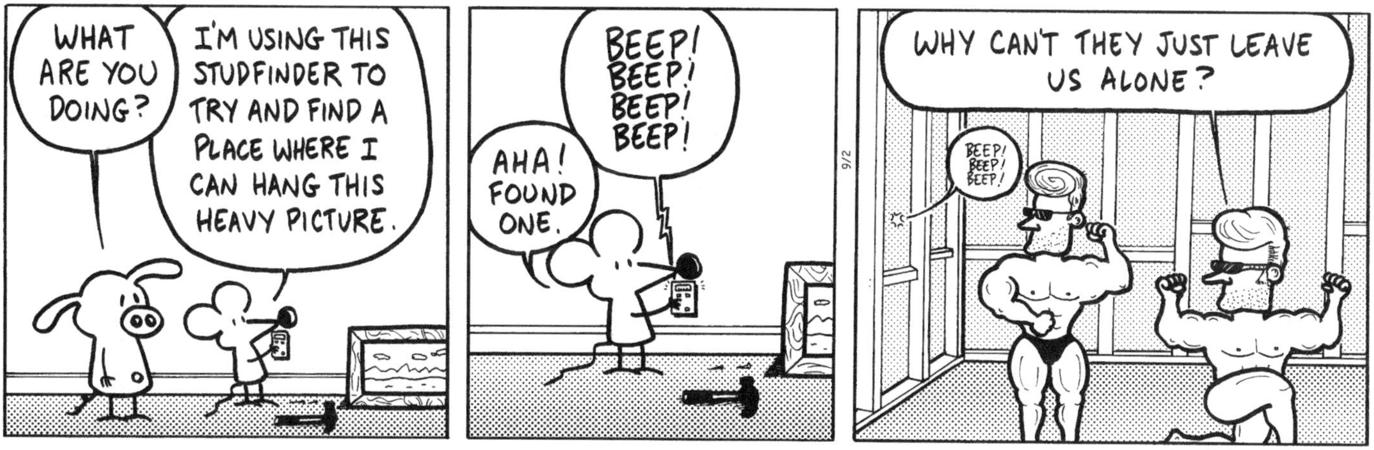
WHAT ARE YOU DOING?
I'M USING THIS STUDFINDER TO TRY AND FIND A PLACE WHERE I CAN HANG THIS HEAVY PICTURE.
BEEP! BEEP! BEEP! BEEP!
AHA! FOUND ONE.
9/2
BEEP! BEEP! BEEP!
WHY CAN'T THEY JUST LEAVE US ALONE?

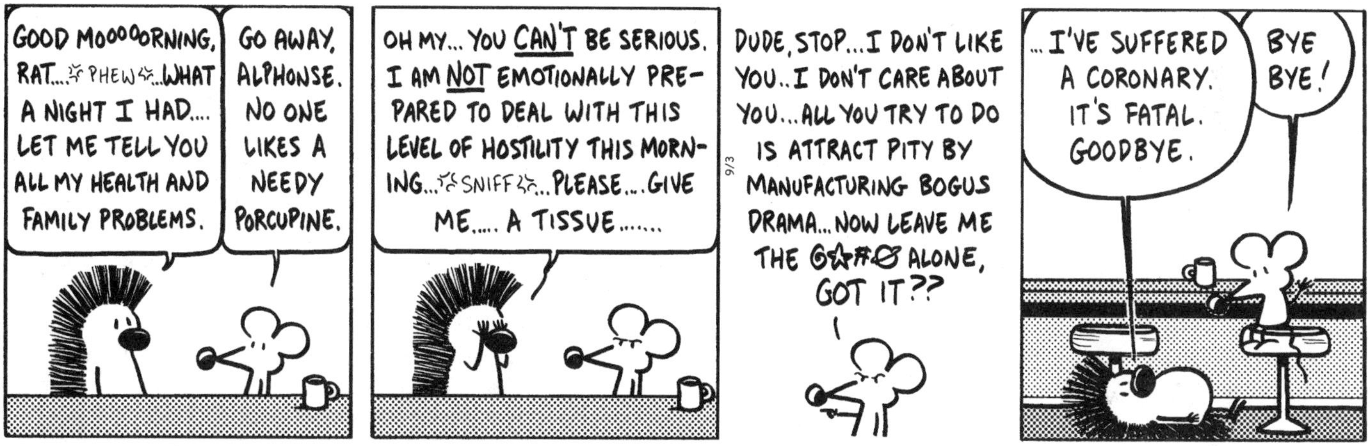
GOOD MOOOOORNING, RAT... PHEW... WHAT A NIGHT I HAD... LET ME TELL YOU ALL MY HEALTH AND FAMILY PROBLEMS.
GO AWAY, ALPHONSE. NO ONE LIKES A NEEDY PORCUPINE.
OH MY... YOU CAN'T BE SERIOUS. I AM NOT EMOTIONALLY PREPARED TO DEAL WITH THIS LEVEL OF HOSTILITY THIS MORNING... SNIFF... PLEASE.... GIVE ME..... A TISSUE.......
9/3
DUDE, STOP... I DON'T LIKE YOU.. I DON'T CARE ABOUT YOU... ALL YOU TRY TO DO IS ATTRACT PITY BY MANUFACTURING BOGUS DRAMA... NOW LEAVE ME THE @☆#@ ALONE, GOT IT??
... I'VE SUFFERED A CORONARY. IT'S FATAL. GOODBYE.
BYE BYE!

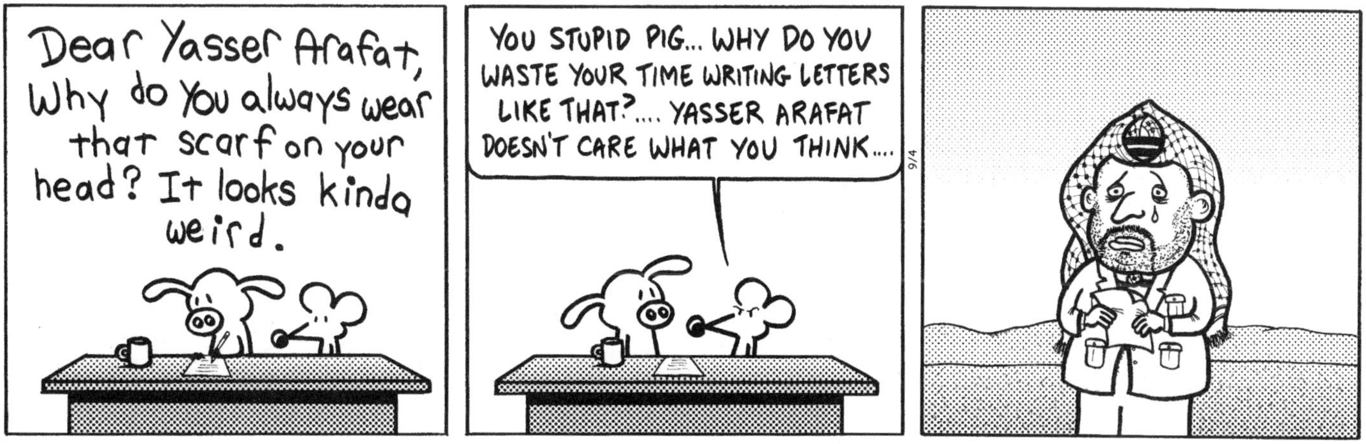
Dear Yasser Arafat, Why do you always wear that scarf on your head? It looks kinda weird.
YOU STUPID PIG... WHY DO YOU WASTE YOUR TIME WRITING LETTERS LIKE THAT?.... YASSER ARAFAT DOESN'T CARE WHAT YOU THINK....
9/4

AND NOW, A PUBLIC SERVICE ANNOUNCEMENT FROM YOUR FAVORITE RAT

HIYA.

KIDS, I DON'T KNOW ABOUT YOU, BUT FOR ME, THERE'S NOTHING WORSE THAN A TEACHER WHO MAKES YOU SLOG THROUGH BIG, FAT BOOKS ON AMERICAN HISTORY AND THEN FORCES YOU TO WRITE LAME REPORTS ABOUT EVENTS THAT HAVE NO RELEVANCE TO YOUR MTV UNIVERSE.

BUT NOW, THERE'S HOPE. YOUR FAVORITE RAT HAS READ THESE BOOKS AND DRAFTED INSIGHTFUL, CONCISE REPORTS ON EACH OF THE KEY EVENTS IN AMERICAN HISTORY. THESE REPORTS, WHICH ARE PRINTED IN FULL BELOW, ARE BEING OFFERED TO YOU FOR THE LOW, LOW PRICE OF $1.99 EACH.

SO, IF YOU LIKE THEM, SEND YOUR $1.99 TO RAT CO., C/O YOUR LOCAL PAPER. THEN, JUST CUT THEM OUT, TURN THEM IN, AND ENJOY ALL THE FREE TIME YOU'LL SAVE! SO, WITHOUT FURTHER DELAY, WE GIVE YOU RAT CO.'S TOP-NOTCH REPORTS.......

THE AMERICAN REVOLUTION

We don't like tea that comes from British people. So we kill them. Years later, we make up.

THE CIVIL WAR

Guys with beards take their states and go home. We shoot them. Years later, they star in "Dukes of Hazzard."

THE GREAT DEPRESSION

Poor people from Oklahoma go to California to pick grapes. Those who stay in Oklahoma are immortalized in the Merle Haggard song, "Okies from Muskogee."

WORLD WAR TWO

We save the French. They thank us by sitting in their cafes and smoking cigarettes.

And now back to *Total Request Live.*

I WANT MY MTV!!

68

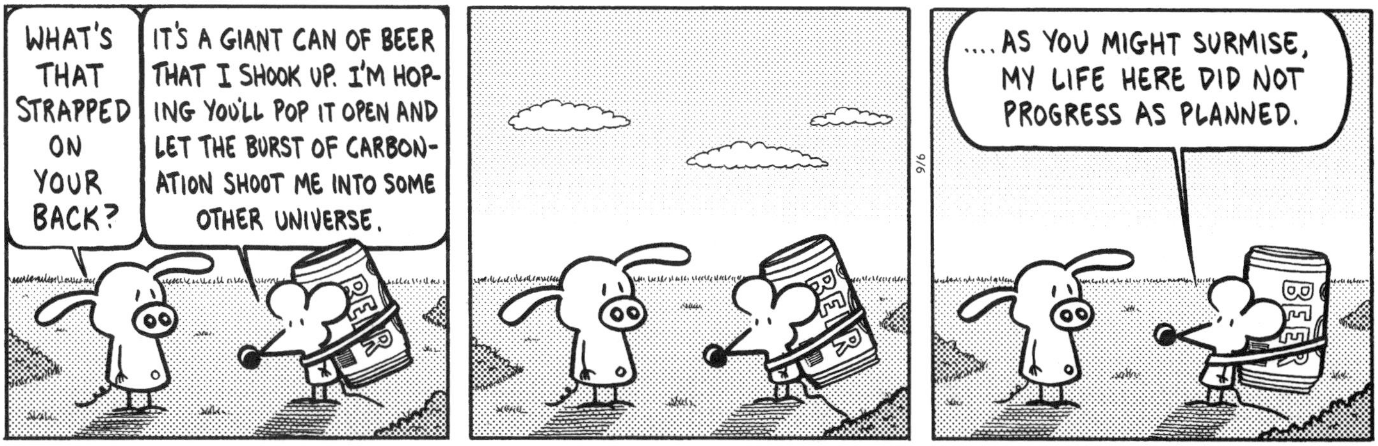
WHAT'S THAT STRAPPED ON YOUR BACK?
IT'S A GIANT CAN OF BEER THAT I SHOOK UP. I'M HOPING YOU'LL POP IT OPEN AND LET THE BURST OF CARBONATION SHOOT ME INTO SOME OTHER UNIVERSE.
BEER
9/6
....AS YOU MIGHT SURMISE, MY LIFE HERE DID NOT PROGRESS AS PLANNED.

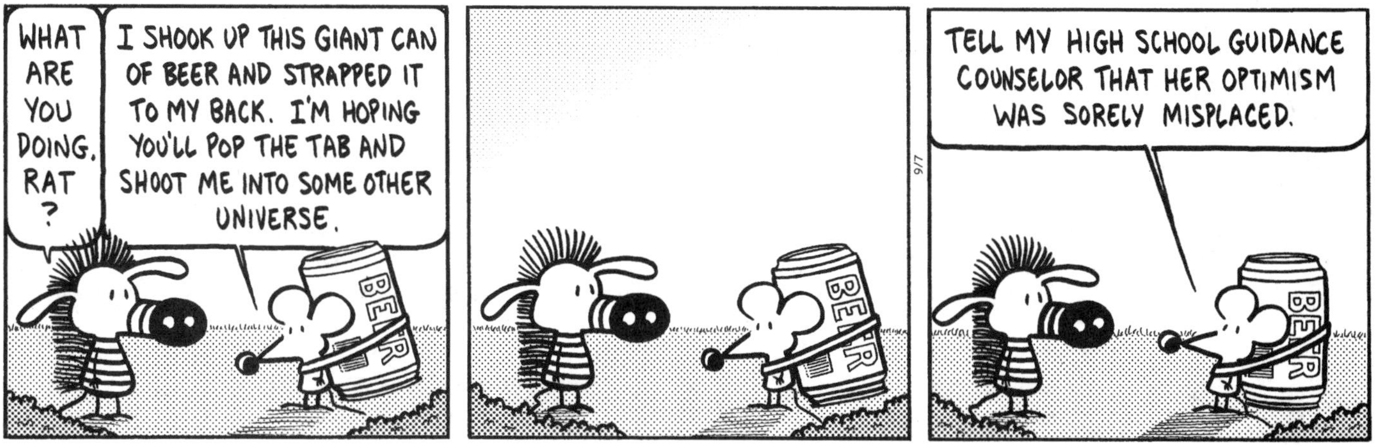
WHAT ARE YOU DOING, RAT?
I SHOOK UP THIS GIANT CAN OF BEER AND STRAPPED IT TO MY BACK. I'M HOPING YOU'LL POP THE TAB AND SHOOT ME INTO SOME OTHER UNIVERSE.
BEER
9/7
TELL MY HIGH SCHOOL GUIDANCE COUNSELOR THAT HER OPTIMISM WAS SORELY MISPLACED.

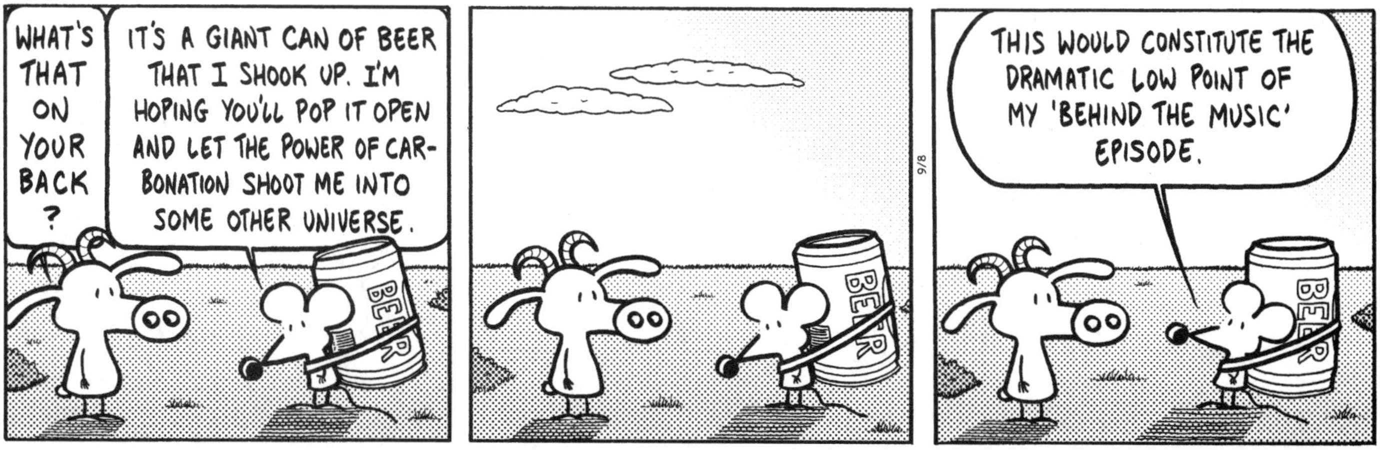
WHAT'S THAT ON YOUR BACK?
IT'S A GIANT CAN OF BEER THAT I SHOOK UP. I'M HOPING YOU'LL POP IT OPEN AND LET THE POWER OF CARBONATION SHOOT ME INTO SOME OTHER UNIVERSE.
BEER
9/8
THIS WOULD CONSTITUTE THE DRAMATIC LOW POINT OF MY 'BEHIND THE MUSIC' EPISODE.

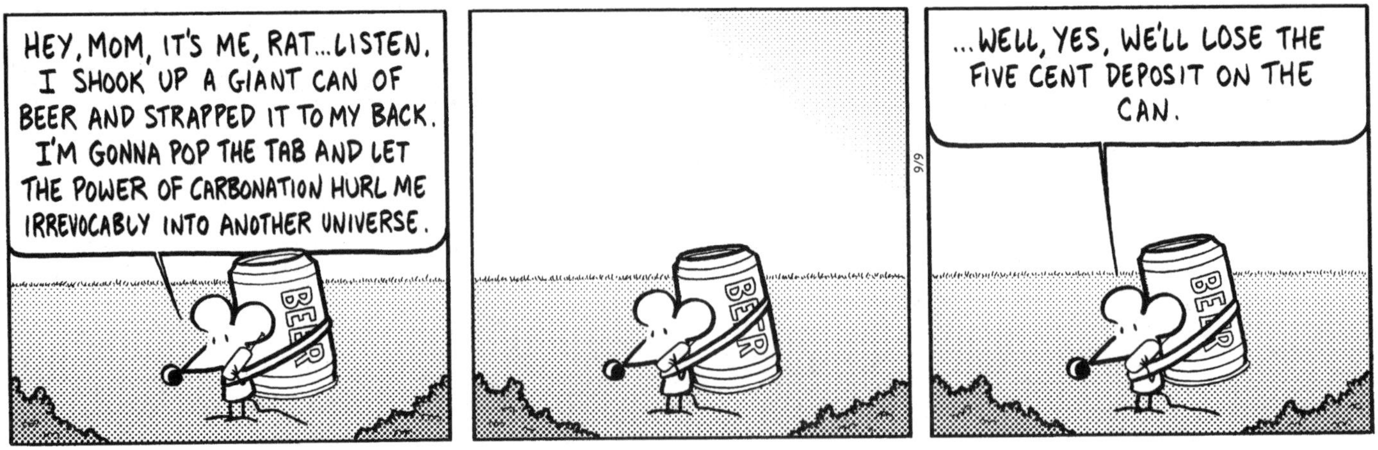
HEY, MOM, IT'S ME, RAT...LISTEN. I SHOOK UP A GIANT CAN OF BEER AND STRAPPED IT TO MY BACK. I'M GONNA POP THE TAB AND LET THE POWER OF CARBONATION HURL ME IRREVOCABLY INTO ANOTHER UNIVERSE.
BEER
9/9
...WELL, YES, WE'LL LOSE THE FIVE CENT DEPOSIT ON THE CAN.

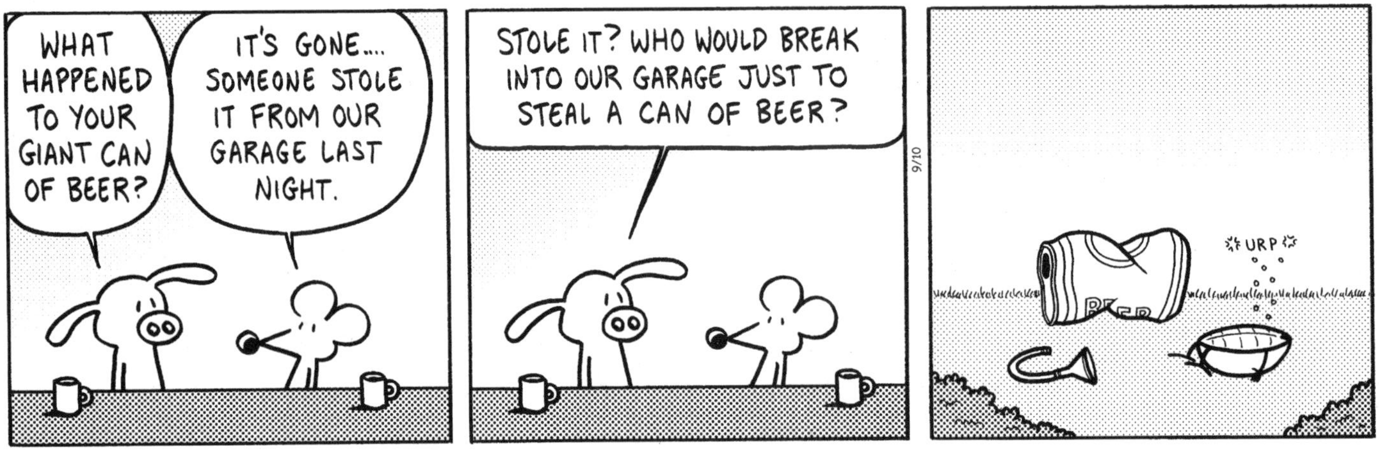
WHAT HAPPENED TO YOUR GIANT CAN OF BEER?
IT'S GONE.... SOMEONE STOLE IT FROM OUR GARAGE LAST NIGHT.
STOLE IT? WHO WOULD BREAK INTO OUR GARAGE JUST TO STEAL A CAN OF BEER?
9/10
URP

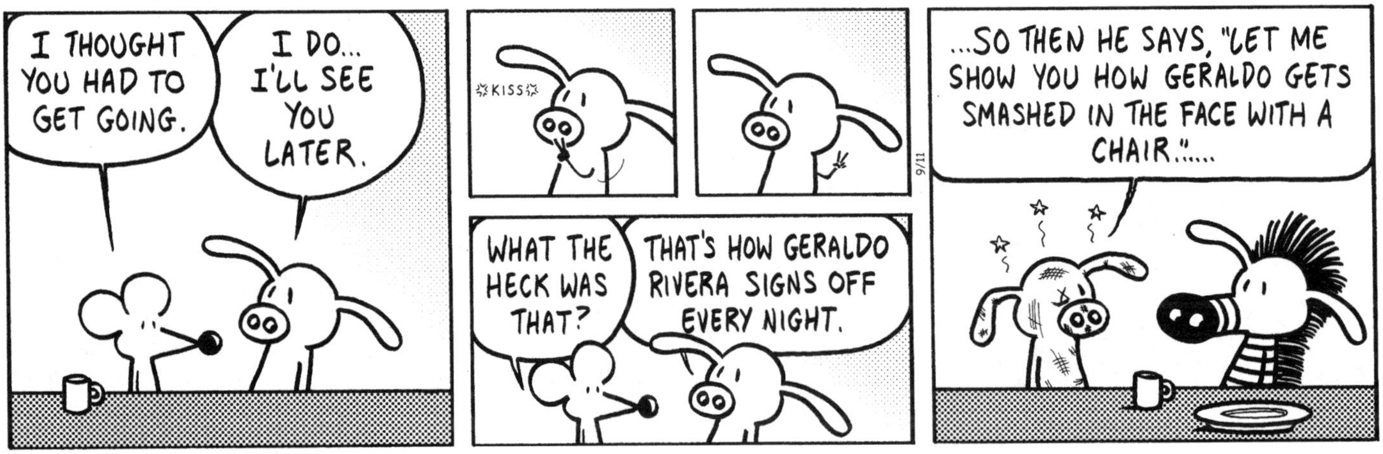
I THOUGHT YOU HAD TO GET GOING.
I DO... I'LL SEE YOU LATER.
KISS
9/11
WHAT THE HECK WAS THAT?
THAT'S HOW GERALDO RIVERA SIGNS OFF EVERY NIGHT.
...SO THEN HE SAYS, "LET ME SHOW YOU HOW GERALDO GETS SMASHED IN THE FACE WITH A CHAIR."....

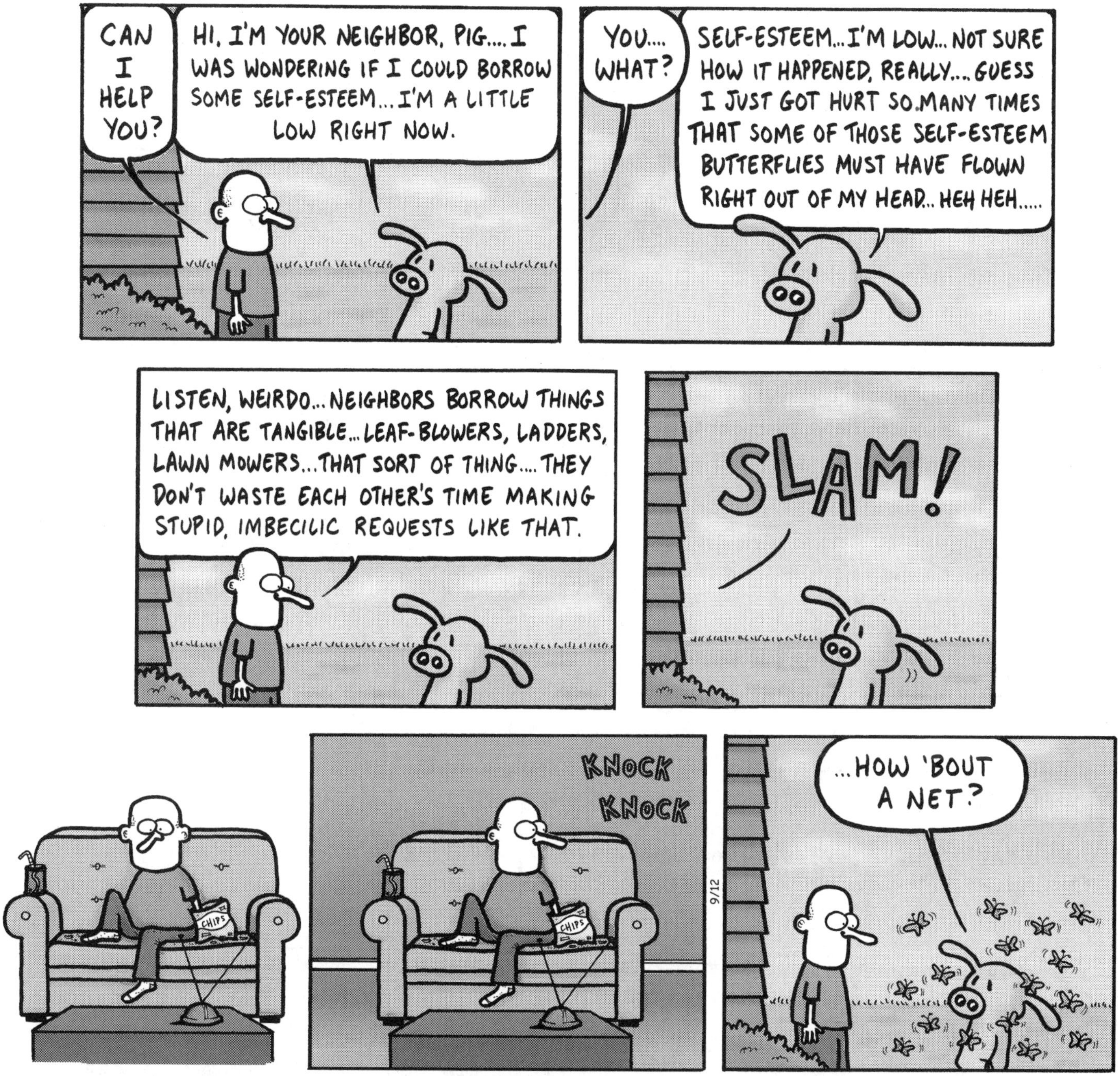
CAN I HELP YOU?
HI, I'M YOUR NEIGHBOR, PIG.... I WAS WONDERING IF I COULD BORROW SOME SELF-ESTEEM... I'M A LITTLE LOW RIGHT NOW.
YOU.... WHAT?
SELF-ESTEEM... I'M LOW... NOT SURE HOW IT HAPPENED, REALLY.... GUESS I JUST GOT HURT SO MANY TIMES THAT SOME OF THOSE SELF-ESTEEM BUTTERFLIES MUST HAVE FLOWN RIGHT OUT OF MY HEAD... HEH HEH.....
LISTEN, WEIRDO... NEIGHBORS BORROW THINGS THAT ARE TANGIBLE... LEAF-BLOWERS, LADDERS, LAWN MOWERS... THAT SORT OF THING.... THEY DON'T WASTE EACH OTHER'S TIME MAKING STUPID, IMBECILIC REQUESTS LIKE THAT.
SLAM!
CHIPS
KNOCK
KNOCK
CHIPS
9/12
...HOW 'BOUT A NET?

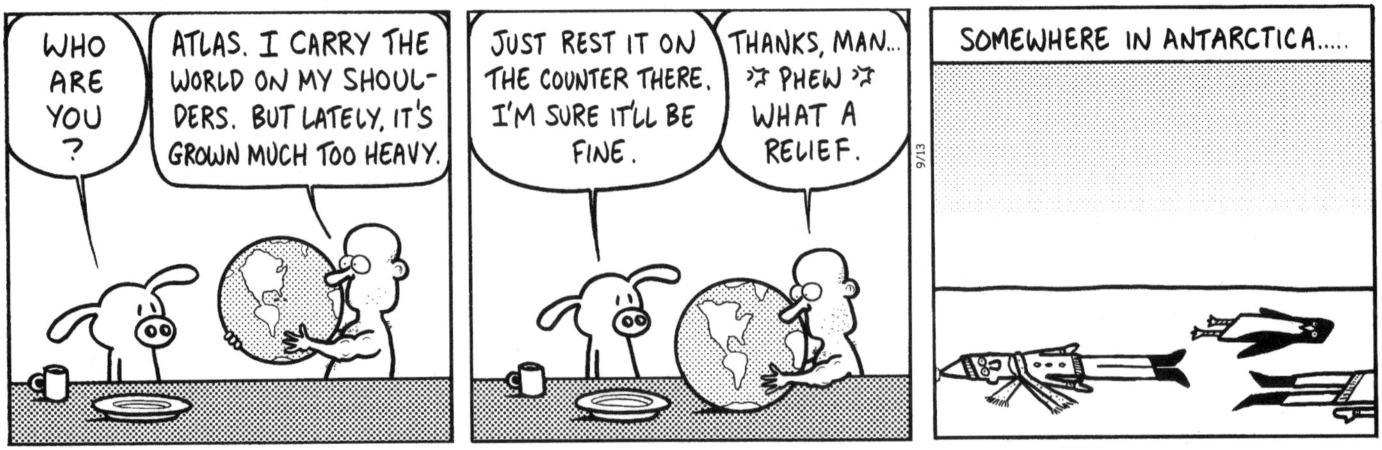
WHO ARE YOU ?
ATLAS. I CARRY THE WORLD ON MY SHOULDERS. BUT LATELY, IT'S GROWN MUCH TOO HEAVY.
JUST REST IT ON THE COUNTER THERE. I'M SURE IT'LL BE FINE.
THANKS, MAN... PHEW WHAT A RELIEF.
9/13
SOMEWHERE IN ANTARCTICA.....

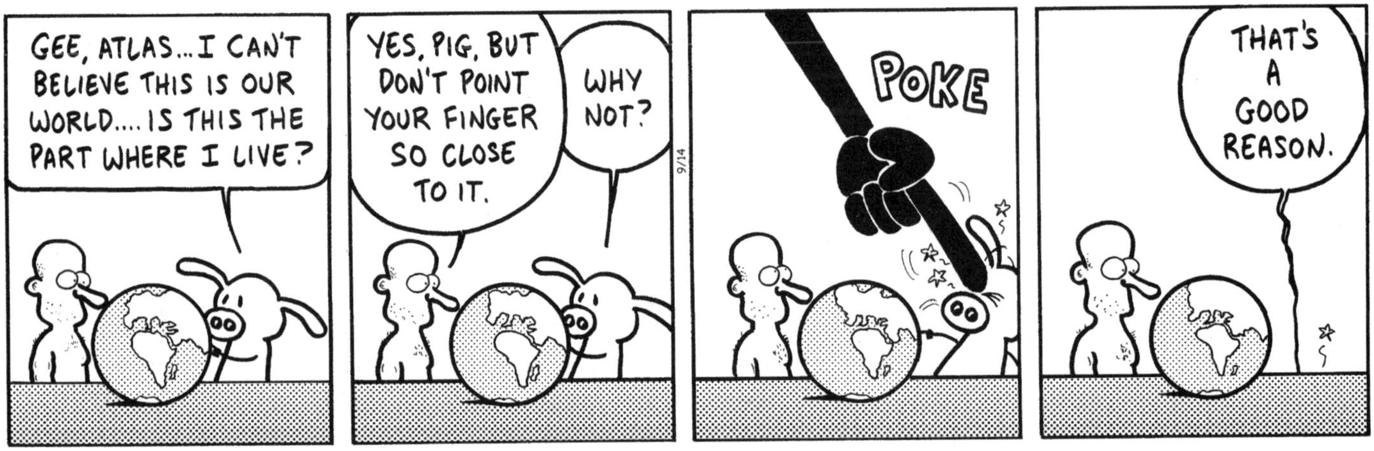
GEE, ATLAS...I CAN'T BELIEVE THIS IS OUR WORLD....IS THIS THE PART WHERE I LIVE?
YES, PIG, BUT DON'T POINT YOUR FINGER SO CLOSE TO IT.
WHY NOT?
9/14
POKE
THAT'S A GOOD REASON.

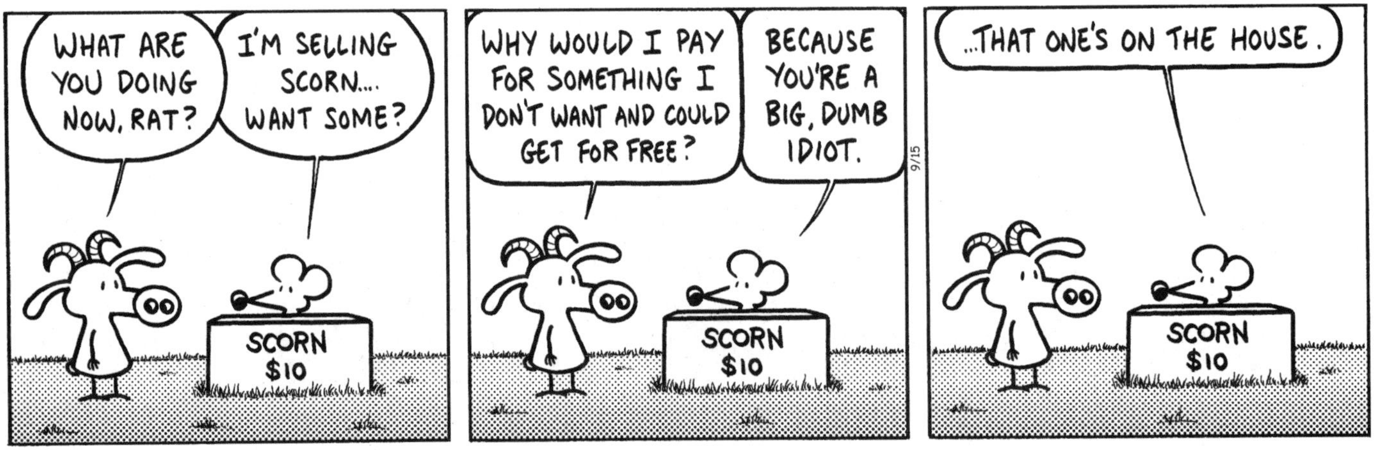
WHAT ARE YOU DOING NOW, RAT?
I'M SELLING SCORN... WANT SOME?
SCORN $10
WHY WOULD I PAY FOR SOMETHING I DON'T WANT AND COULD GET FOR FREE?
BECAUSE YOU'RE A BIG, DUMB IDIOT.
SCORN $10
9/15
...THAT ONE'S ON THE HOUSE.
SCORN $10

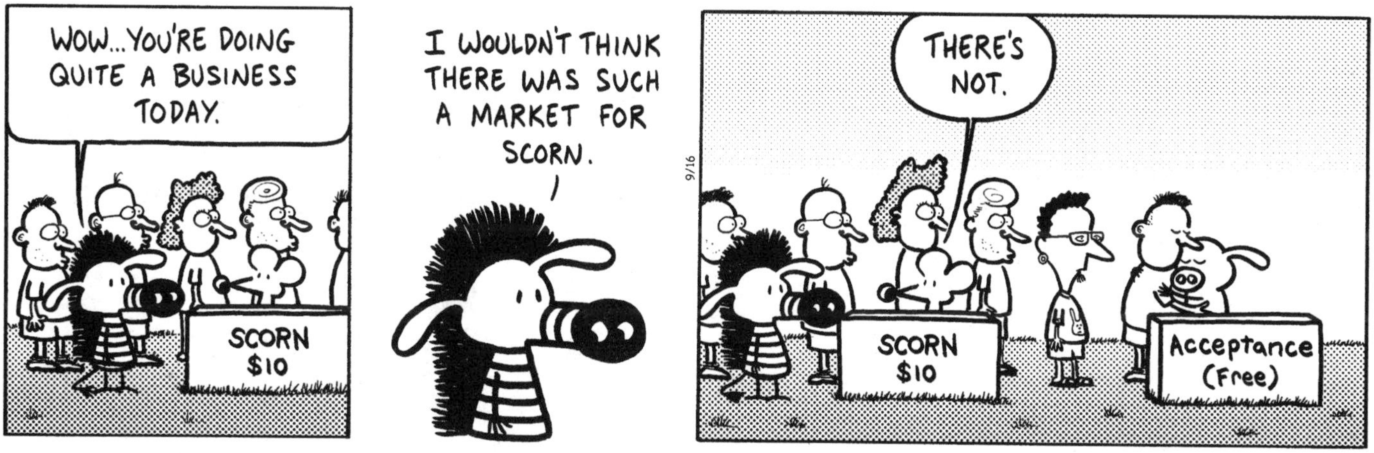
WOW...YOU'RE DOING QUITE A BUSINESS TODAY.
SCORN $10
I WOULDN'T THINK THERE WAS SUCH A MARKET FOR SCORN.
9/16
THERE'S NOT.
SCORN $10
Acceptance (Free)

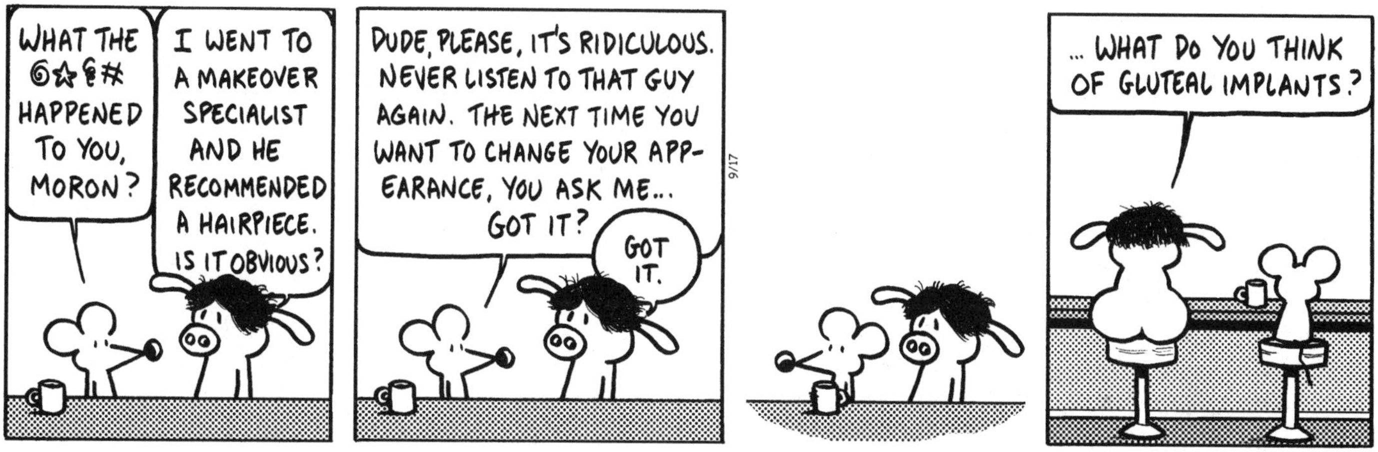
WHAT THE @☆$# HAPPENED TO YOU, MORON?
I WENT TO A MAKEOVER SPECIALIST AND HE RECOMMENDED A HAIRPIECE. IS IT OBVIOUS?
DUDE, PLEASE, IT'S RIDICULOUS. NEVER LISTEN TO THAT GUY AGAIN. THE NEXT TIME YOU WANT TO CHANGE YOUR APP-EARANCE, YOU ASK ME... GOT IT?
GOT IT.
9/17
...WHAT DO YOU THINK OF GLUTEAL IMPLANTS?

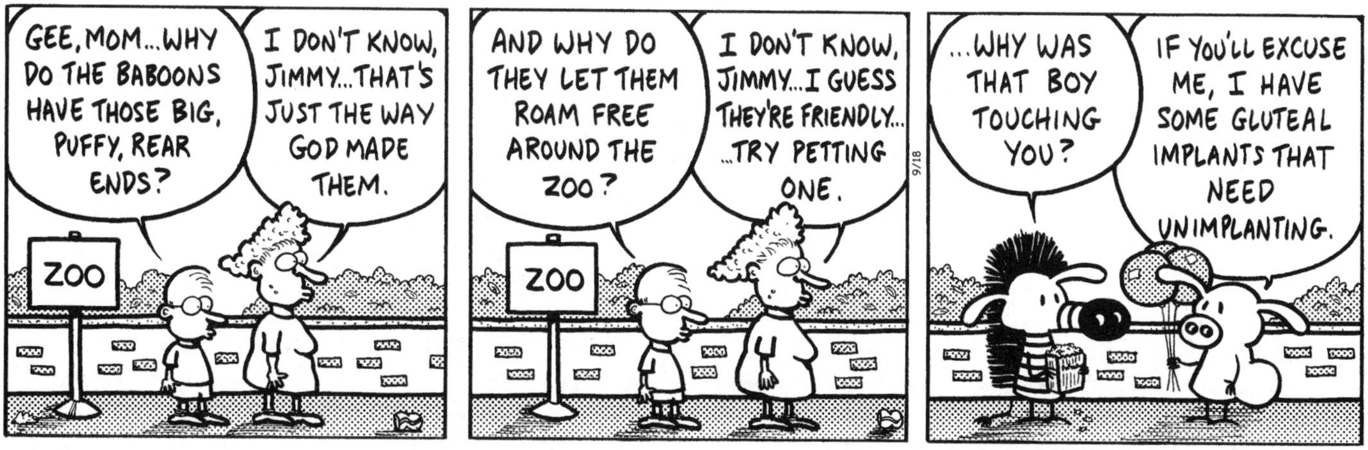
GEE, MOM...WHY DO THE BABOONS HAVE THOSE BIG, PUFFY, REAR ENDS?
I DON'T KNOW, JIMMY...THAT'S JUST THE WAY GOD MADE THEM.
ZOO
AND WHY DO THEY LET THEM ROAM FREE AROUND THE ZOO?
I DON'T KNOW, JIMMY...I GUESS THEY'RE FRIENDLY... ...TRY PETTING ONE.
ZOO
9/18
...WHY WAS THAT BOY TOUCHING YOU?
IF YOU'LL EXCUSE ME, I HAVE SOME GLUTEAL IMPLANTS THAT NEED UNIMPLANTING.

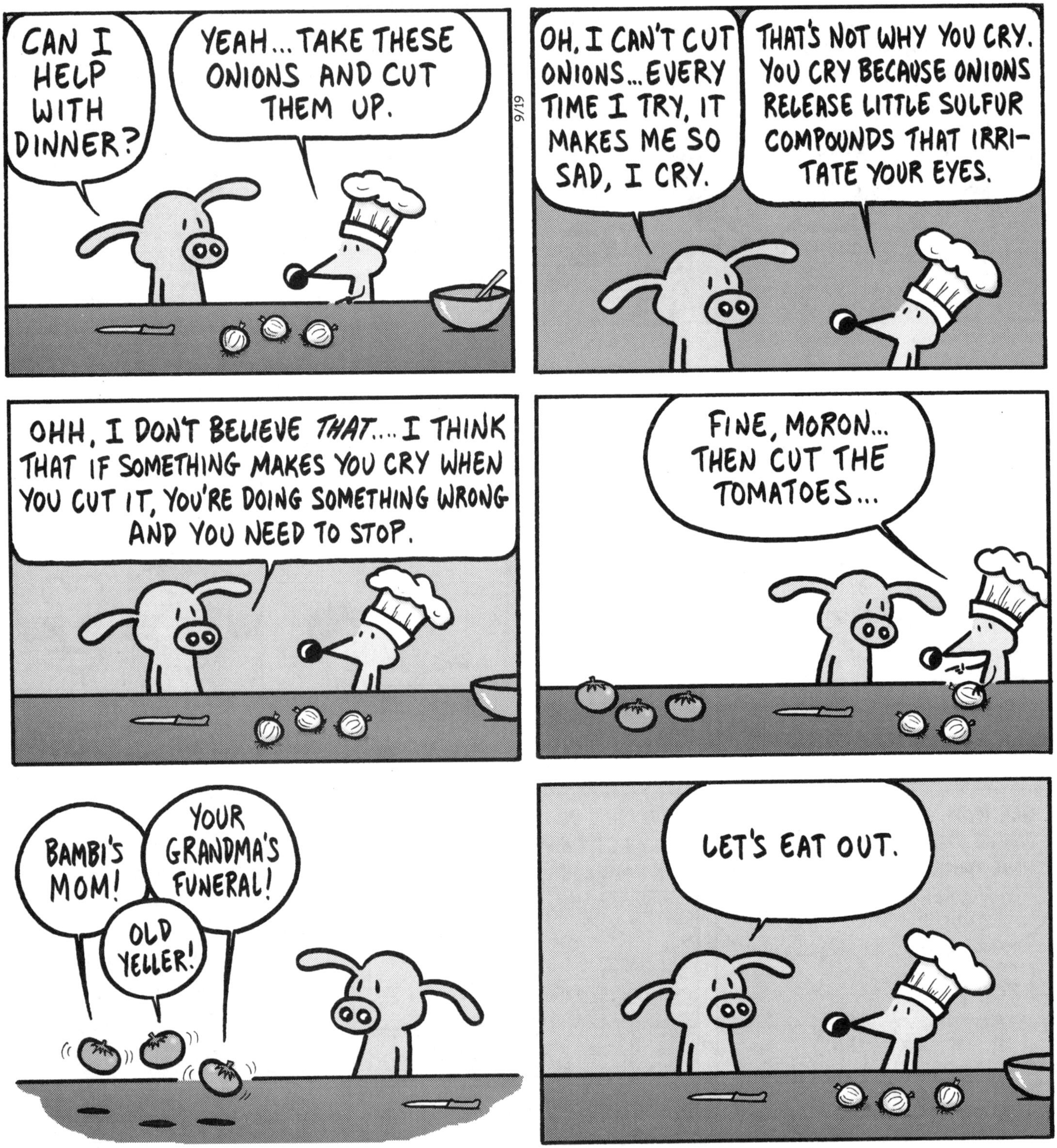
CAN I HELP WITH DINNER?
YEAH... TAKE THESE ONIONS AND CUT THEM UP.
9/19
OH, I CAN'T CUT ONIONS... EVERY TIME I TRY, IT MAKES ME SO SAD, I CRY.
THAT'S NOT WHY YOU CRY. YOU CRY BECAUSE ONIONS RELEASE LITTLE SULFUR COMPOUNDS THAT IRRITATE YOUR EYES.
OHH, I DON'T BELIEVE *THAT*.... I THINK THAT IF SOMETHING MAKES YOU CRY WHEN YOU CUT IT, YOU'RE DOING SOMETHING WRONG AND YOU NEED TO STOP.
FINE, MORON... THEN CUT THE TOMATOES...
BAMBI'S MOM!
YOUR GRANDMA'S FUNERAL!
OLD YELLER!
LET'S EAT OUT.

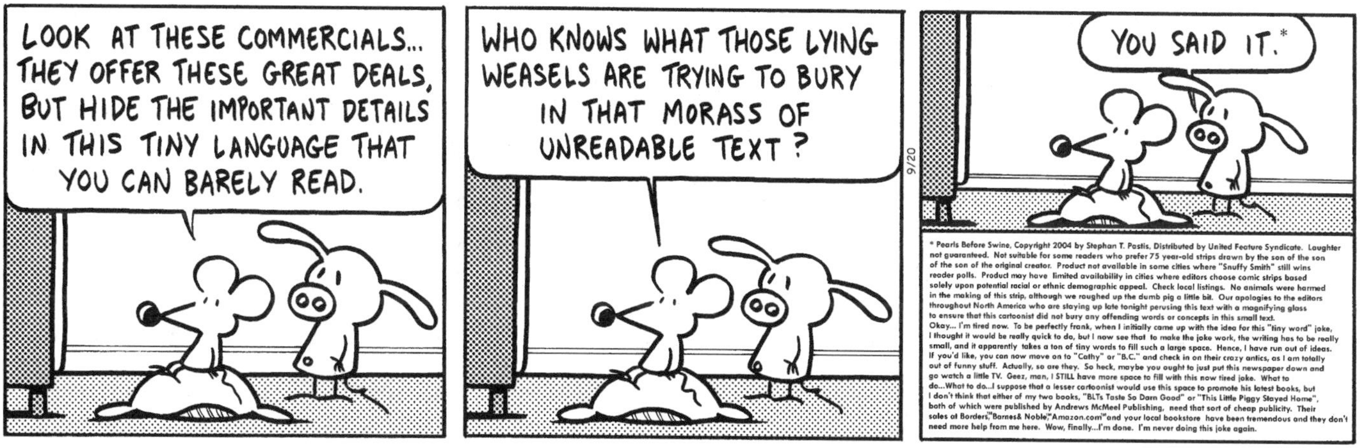
LOOK AT THESE COMMERCIALS... THEY OFFER THESE GREAT DEALS, BUT HIDE THE IMPORTANT DETAILS IN THIS TINY LANGUAGE THAT YOU CAN BARELY READ.
WHO KNOWS WHAT THOSE LYING WEASELS ARE TRYING TO BURY IN THAT MORASS OF UNREADABLE TEXT?
9/20
YOU SAID IT.*
* Pearls Before Swine, Copyright 2004 by Stephan T. Pastis, Distributed by United Feature Syndicate. Laughter not guaranteed. Not suitable for some readers who prefer 75 year-old strips drawn by the son of the son of the son of the original creator. Product not available in some cities where "Snuffy Smith" still wins reader polls. Product may have limited availability in cities where editors choose comic strips based solely upon potential racial or ethnic demographic appeal. Check local listings. No animals were harmed in the making of this strip, although we roughed up the dumb pig a little bit. Our apologies to the editors throughout North America who are staying up late tonight perusing this text with a magnifying glass to ensure that this cartoonist did not bury any offending words or concepts in this small text.
Okay... I'm tired now. To be perfectly frank, when I initially came up with the idea for this "tiny word" joke, I thought it would be really quick to do, but I now see that to make the joke work, the writing has to be really small, and it apparently takes a ton of tiny words to fill such a large space. Hence, I have run out of ideas. If you'd like, you can now move on to "Cathy" or "B.C." and check in on their crazy antics, as I am totally out of funny stuff. Actually, so are they. So heck, maybe you ought to just put this newspaper down and go watch a little TV. Geez, man, I STILL have more space to fill with this now tired joke. What to do...What to do...I suppose that a lesser cartoonist would use this space to promote his latest books, but I don't think that either of my two books, "BLTs Taste So Darn Good" or "This Little Piggy Stayed Home", both of which were published by Andrews McMeel Publishing, need that sort of cheap publicity. Their sales at Borders,™ Barnes& Noble,™ Amazon.com™ and your local bookstore have been tremendous and they don't need more help from me here. Wow, finally...I'm done. I'm never doing this joke again.

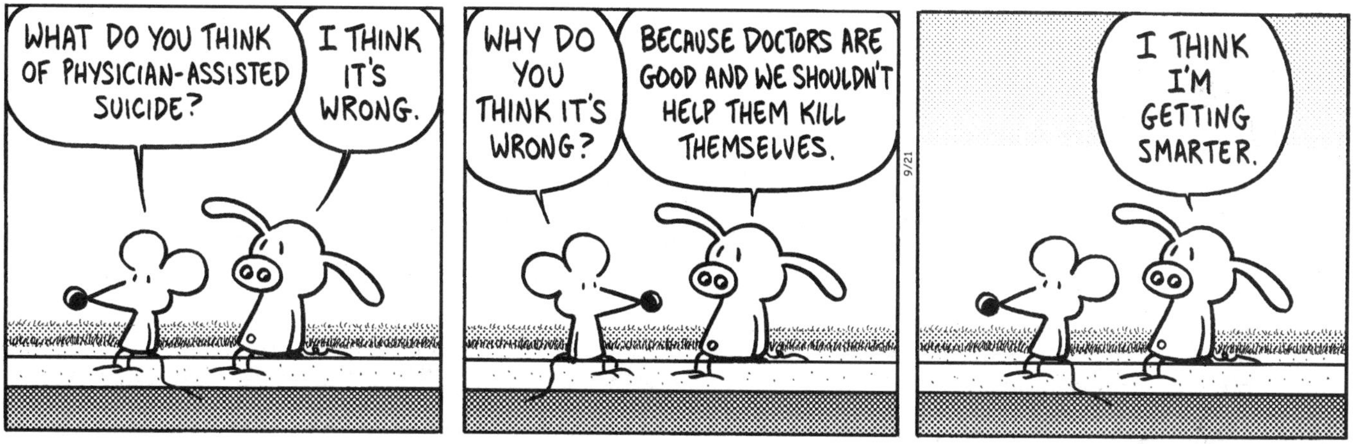
WHAT DO YOU THINK OF PHYSICIAN-ASSISTED SUICIDE?
I THINK IT'S WRONG.
WHY DO YOU THINK IT'S WRONG?
BECAUSE DOCTORS ARE GOOD AND WE SHOULDN'T HELP THEM KILL THEMSELVES.
9/21
I THINK I'M GETTING SMARTER.

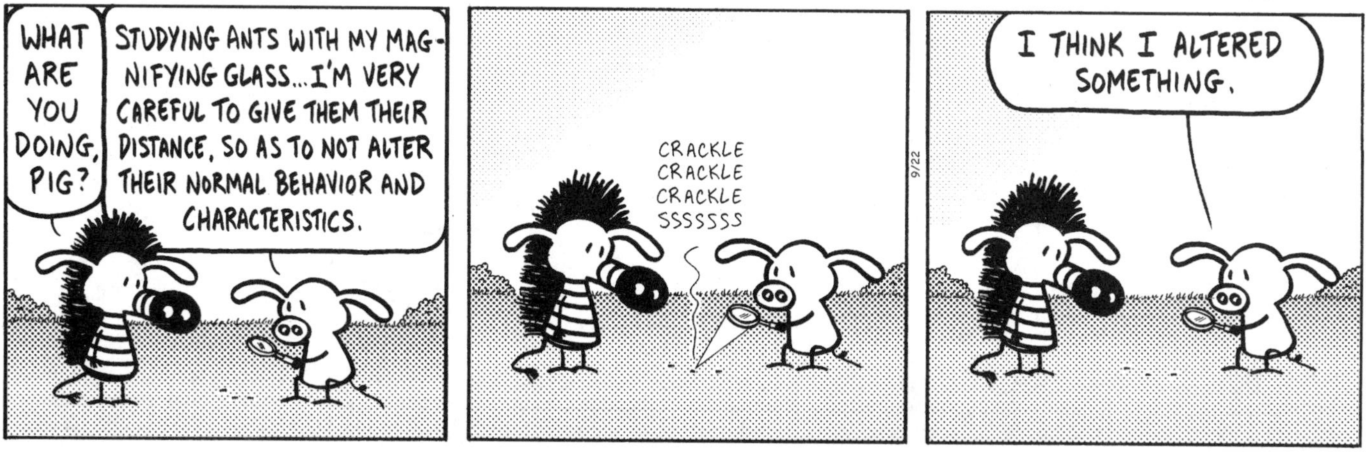
WHAT ARE YOU DOING, PIG?
STUDYING ANTS WITH MY MAGNIFYING GLASS... I'M VERY CAREFUL TO GIVE THEM THEIR DISTANCE, SO AS TO NOT ALTER THEIR NORMAL BEHAVIOR AND CHARACTERISTICS.
CRACKLE
CRACKLE
CRACKLE
SSSSSSS
9/22
I THINK I ALTERED SOMETHING.

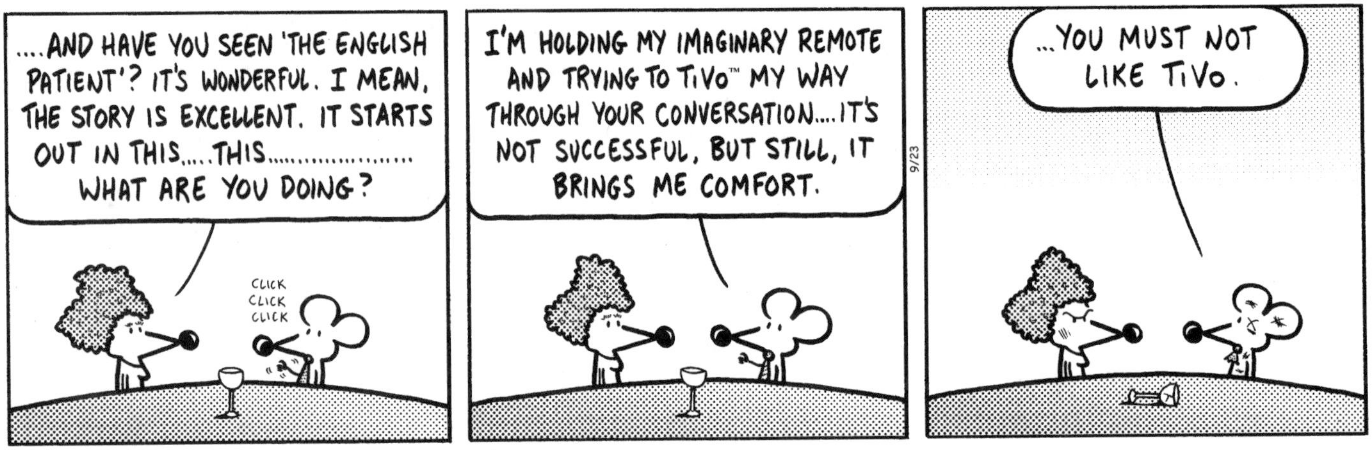
....AND HAVE YOU SEEN 'THE ENGLISH PATIENT'? IT'S WONDERFUL. I MEAN, THE STORY IS EXCELLENT. IT STARTS OUT IN THIS.....THIS.....................
WHAT ARE YOU DOING?
CLICK CLICK CLICK
I'M HOLDING MY IMAGINARY REMOTE AND TRYING TO TiVo™ MY WAY THROUGH YOUR CONVERSATION....IT'S NOT SUCCESSFUL, BUT STILL, IT BRINGS ME COMFORT.
9/23
...YOU MUST NOT LIKE TiVo.

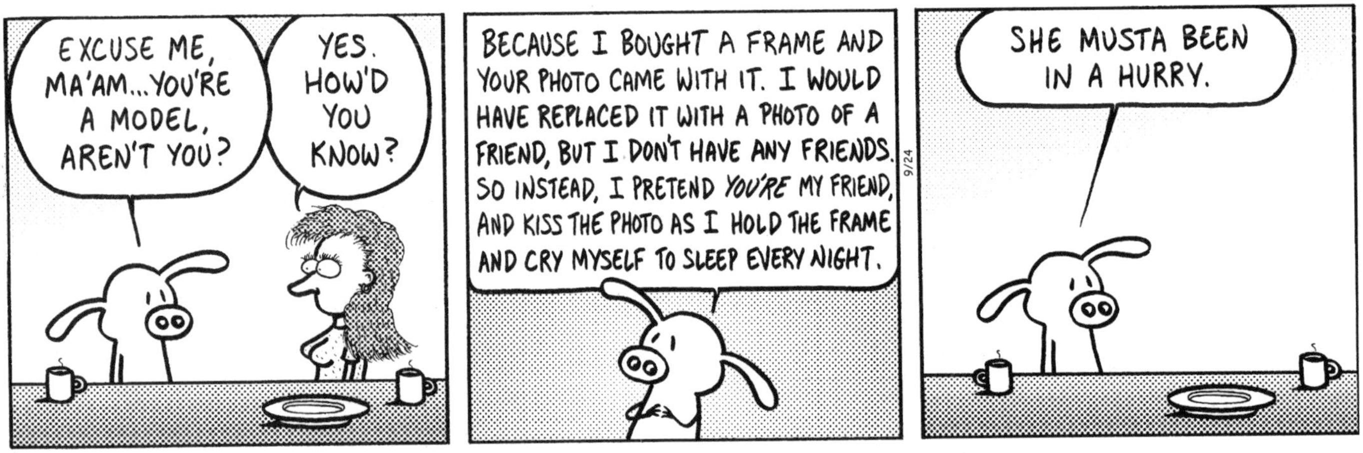
EXCUSE ME, MA'AM...YOU'RE A MODEL, AREN'T YOU?
YES. HOW'D YOU KNOW?
BECAUSE I BOUGHT A FRAME AND YOUR PHOTO CAME WITH IT. I WOULD HAVE REPLACED IT WITH A PHOTO OF A FRIEND, BUT I DON'T HAVE ANY FRIENDS. SO INSTEAD, I PRETEND *YOU'RE* MY FRIEND, AND KISS THE PHOTO AS I HOLD THE FRAME AND CRY MYSELF TO SLEEP EVERY NIGHT.
9/24
SHE MUSTA BEEN IN A HURRY.

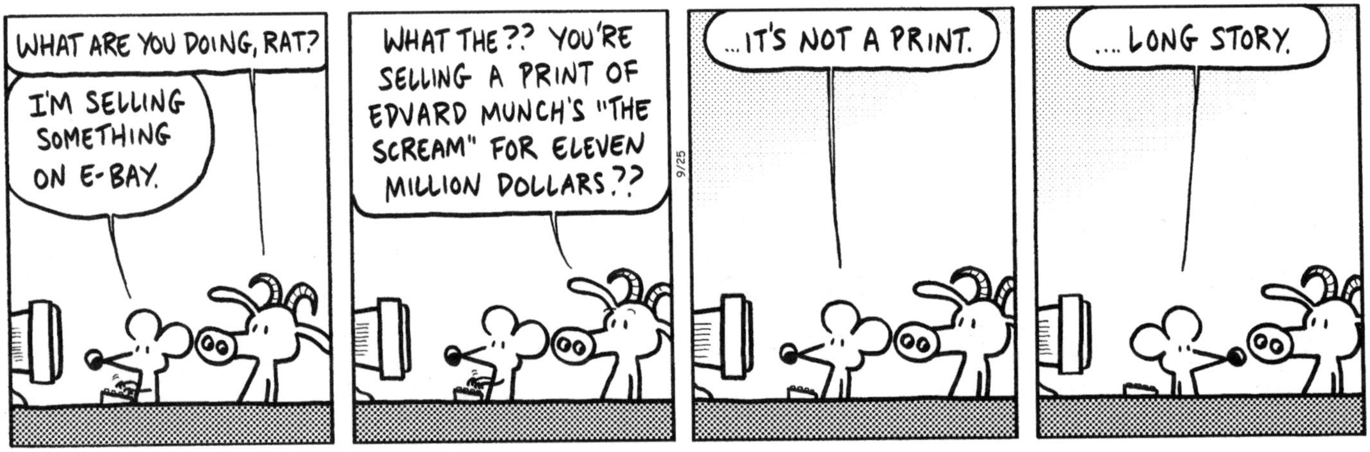
WHAT ARE YOU DOING, RAT?
I'M SELLING SOMETHING ON E-BAY.
WHAT THE?? YOU'RE SELLING A PRINT OF EDVARD MUNCH'S "THE SCREAM" FOR ELEVEN MILLION DOLLARS??
9/25
...IT'S NOT A PRINT.
....LONG STORY.

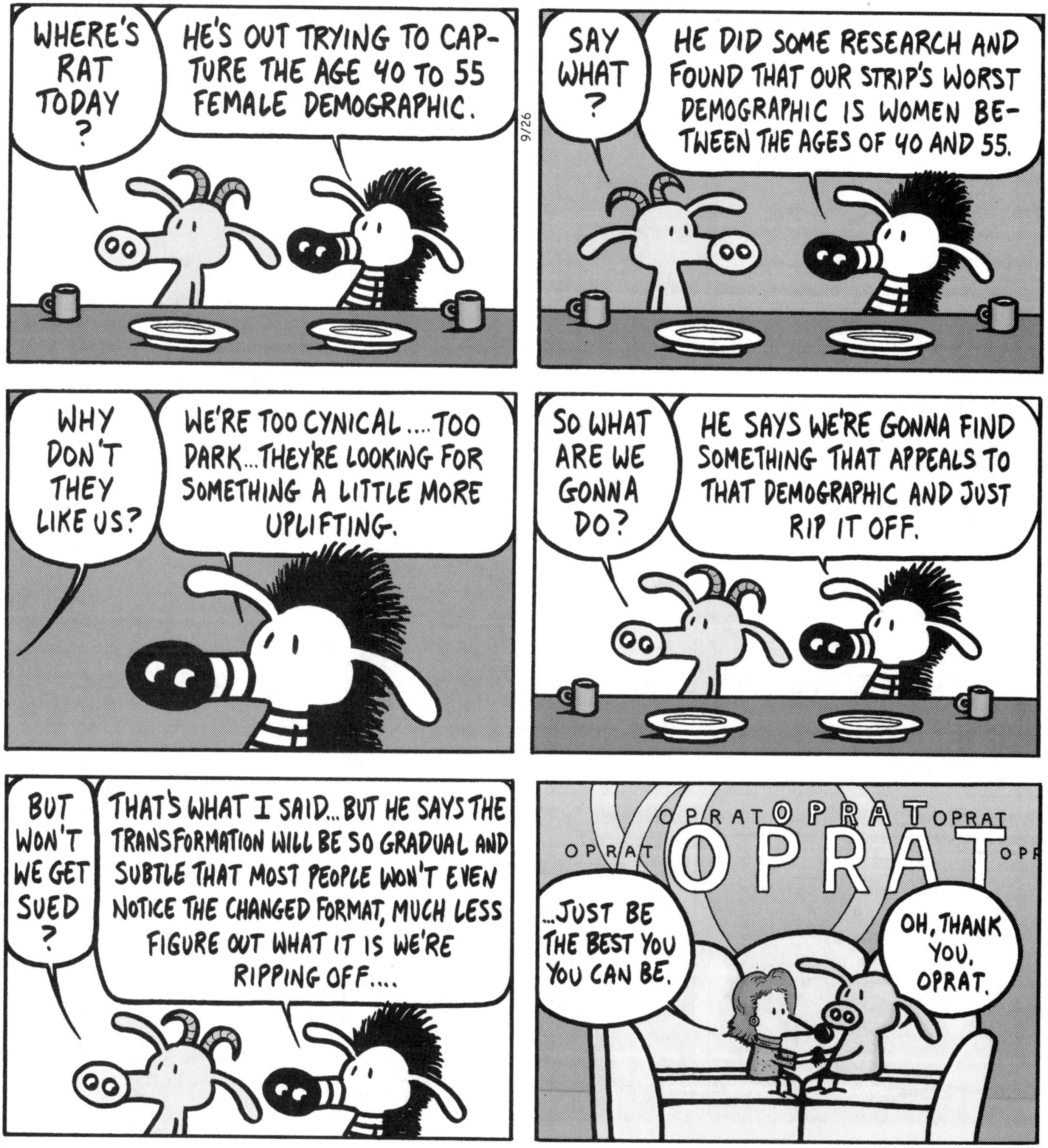
WHERE'S RAT TODAY ?
HE'S OUT TRYING TO CAPTURE THE AGE 40 TO 55 FEMALE DEMOGRAPHIC.
9/26
SAY WHAT ?
HE DID SOME RESEARCH AND FOUND THAT OUR STRIP'S WORST DEMOGRAPHIC IS WOMEN BETWEEN THE AGES OF 40 AND 55.
WHY DON'T THEY LIKE US?
WE'RE TOO CYNICAL.... TOO DARK... THEY'RE LOOKING FOR SOMETHING A LITTLE MORE UPLIFTING.
SO WHAT ARE WE GONNA DO?
HE SAYS WE'RE GONNA FIND SOMETHING THAT APPEALS TO THAT DEMOGRAPHIC AND JUST RIP IT OFF.
BUT WON'T WE GET SUED ?
THAT'S WHAT I SAID... BUT HE SAYS THE TRANSFORMATION WILL BE SO GRADUAL AND SUBTLE THAT MOST PEOPLE WON'T EVEN NOTICE THE CHANGED FORMAT, MUCH LESS FIGURE OUT WHAT IT IS WE'RE RIPPING OFF....
OPRAT OPRAT OPRAT OPRAT OPR
OPRAT
...JUST BE THE BEST YOU YOU CAN BE.
OH, THANK YOU, OPRAT.

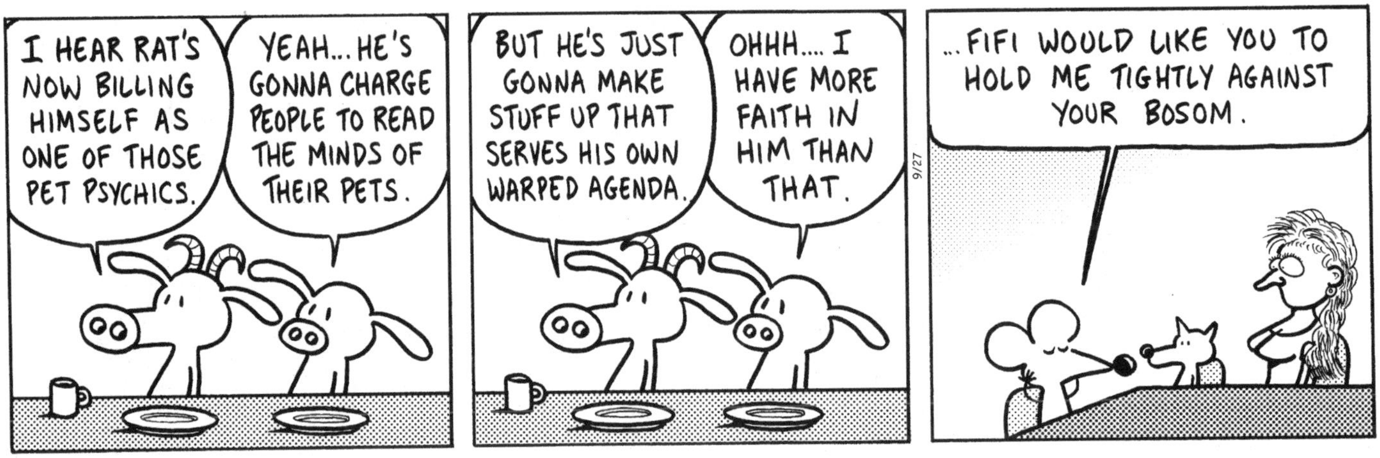
I HEAR RAT'S NOW BILLING HIMSELF AS ONE OF THOSE PET PSYCHICS.
YEAH... HE'S GONNA CHARGE PEOPLE TO READ THE MINDS OF THEIR PETS.
BUT HE'S JUST GONNA MAKE STUFF UP THAT SERVES HIS OWN WARPED AGENDA.
OHHH.... I HAVE MORE FAITH IN HIM THAN THAT.
9/27
...FIFI WOULD LIKE YOU TO HOLD ME TIGHTLY AGAINST YOUR BOSOM.

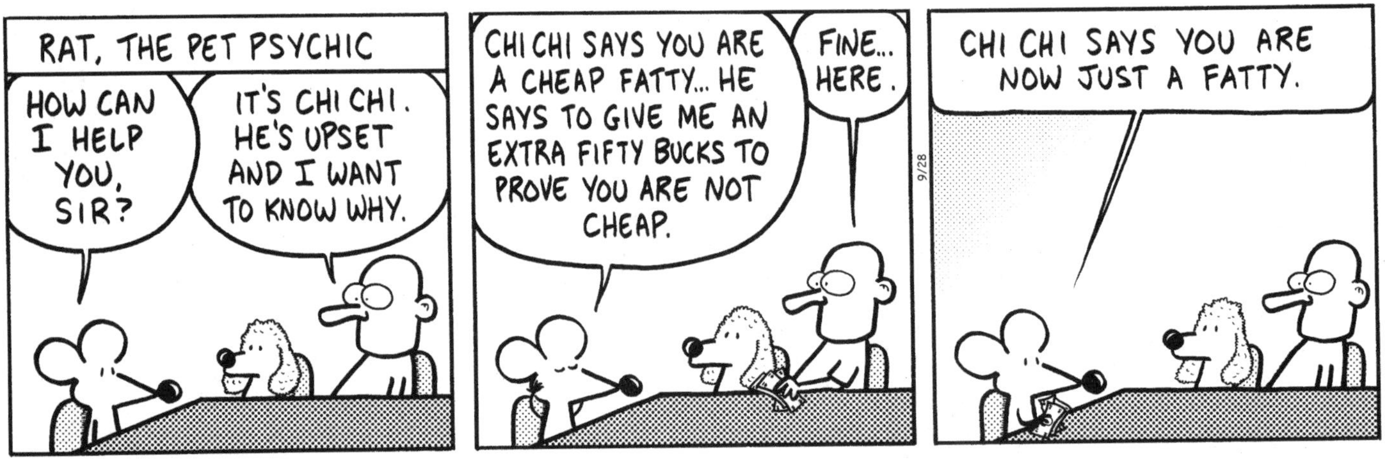
RAT, THE PET PSYCHIC
HOW CAN I HELP YOU, SIR?
IT'S CHI CHI. HE'S UPSET AND I WANT TO KNOW WHY.
CHI CHI SAYS YOU ARE A CHEAP FATTY... HE SAYS TO GIVE ME AN EXTRA FIFTY BUCKS TO PROVE YOU ARE NOT CHEAP.
FINE... HERE.
9/28
CHI CHI SAYS YOU ARE NOW JUST A FATTY.

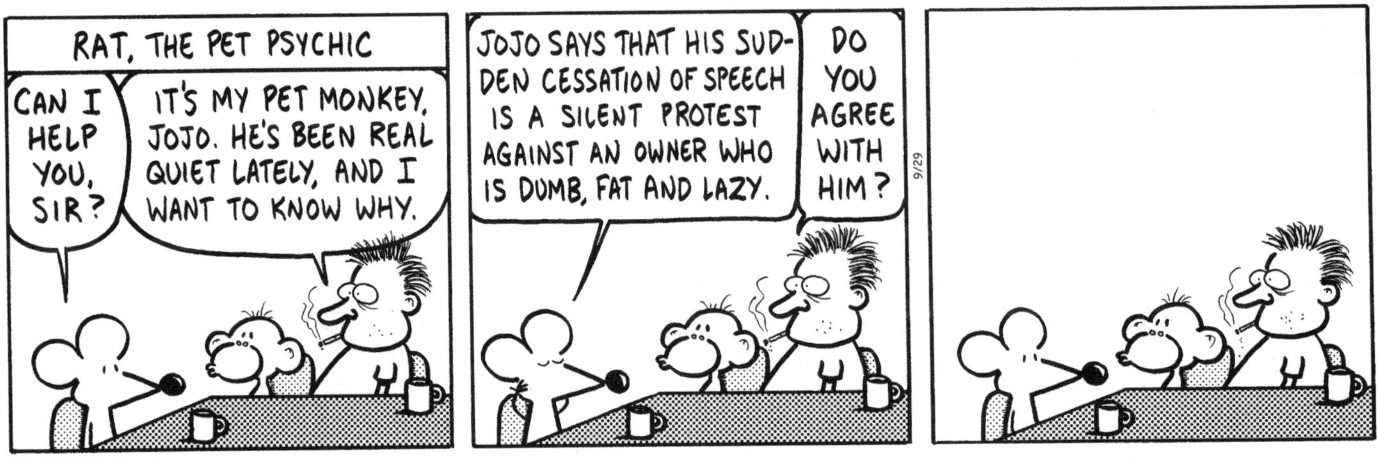
RAT, THE PET PSYCHIC
CAN I HELP YOU, SIR?
IT'S MY PET MONKEY, JOJO. HE'S BEEN REAL QUIET LATELY, AND I WANT TO KNOW WHY.
JOJO SAYS THAT HIS SUDDEN CESSATION OF SPEECH IS A SILENT PROTEST AGAINST AN OWNER WHO IS DUMB, FAT AND LAZY.
DO YOU AGREE WITH HIM?
9/29

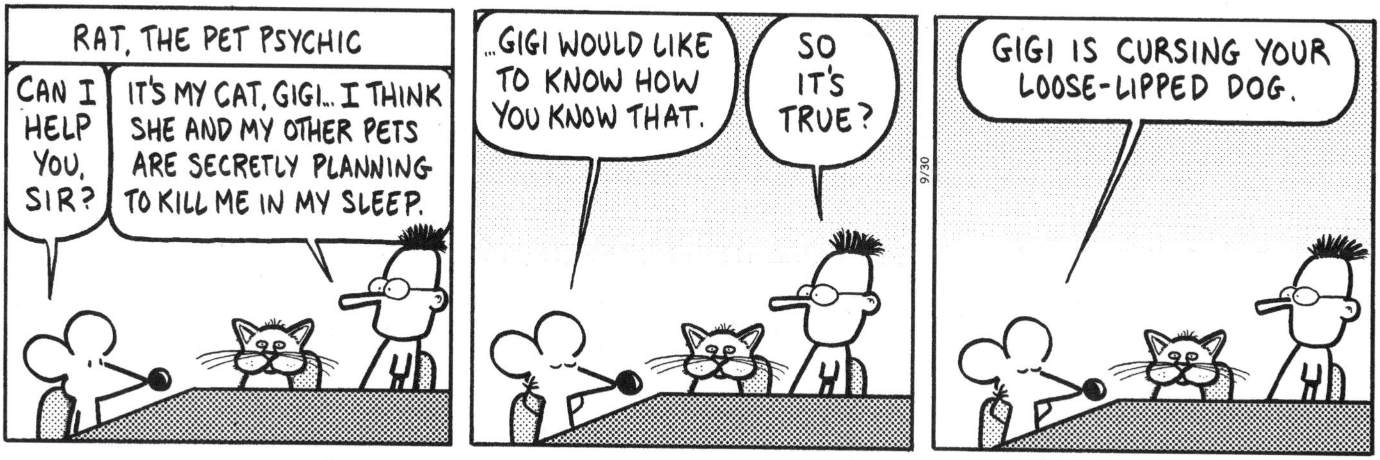
RAT, THE PET PSYCHIC
CAN I HELP YOU, SIR?
IT'S MY CAT, GIGI... I THINK SHE AND MY OTHER PETS ARE SECRETLY PLANNING TO KILL ME IN MY SLEEP.
...GIGI WOULD LIKE TO KNOW HOW YOU KNOW THAT.
SO IT'S TRUE?
9/30
GIGI IS CURSING YOUR LOOSE-LIPPED DOG.

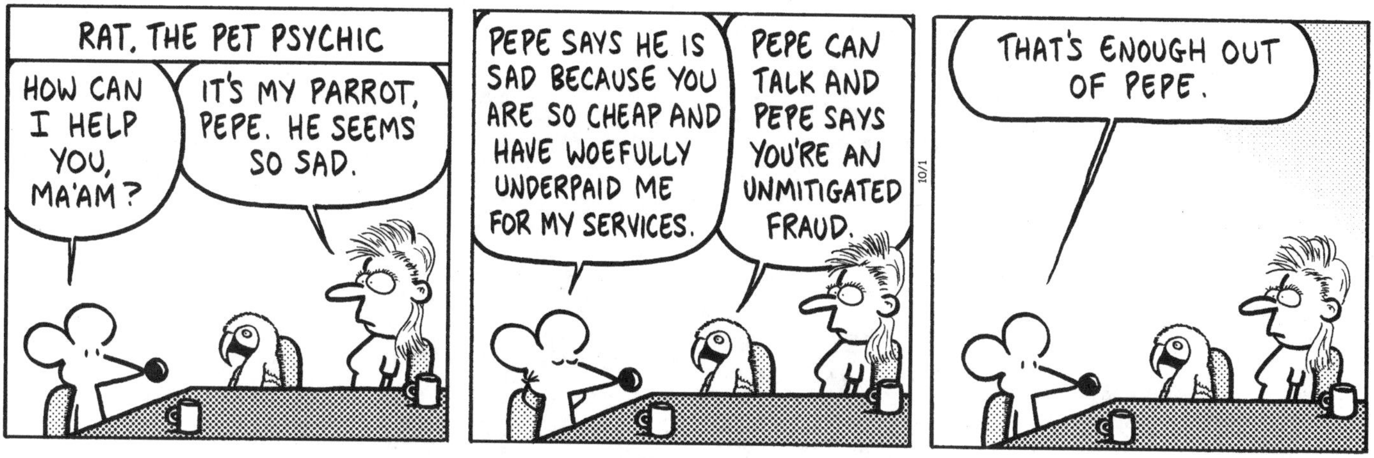
RAT, THE PET PSYCHIC
HOW CAN I HELP YOU, MA'AM?
IT'S MY PARROT, PEPE. HE SEEMS SO SAD.
PEPE SAYS HE IS SAD BECAUSE YOU ARE SO CHEAP AND HAVE WOEFULLY UNDERPAID ME FOR MY SERVICES.
PEPE CAN TALK AND PEPE SAYS YOU'RE AN UNMITIGATED FRAUD.
10/1
THAT'S ENOUGH OUT OF PEPE.

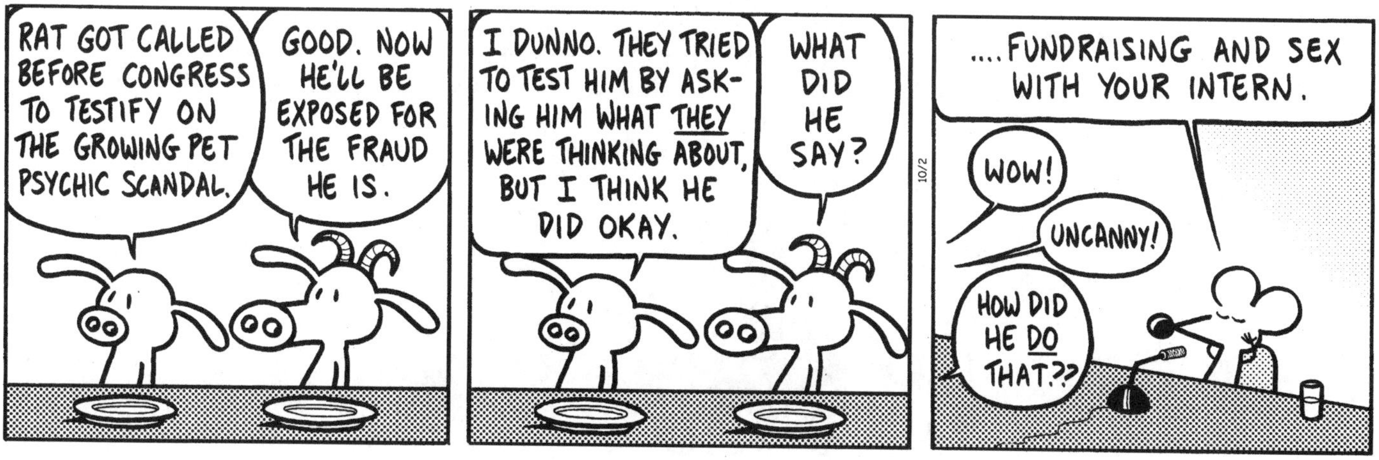
RAT GOT CALLED BEFORE CONGRESS TO TESTIFY ON THE GROWING PET PSYCHIC SCANDAL.
GOOD. NOW HE'LL BE EXPOSED FOR THE FRAUD HE IS.
I DUNNO. THEY TRIED TO TEST HIM BY ASKING HIM WHAT THEY WERE THINKING ABOUT, BUT I THINK HE DID OKAY.
WHAT DID HE SAY?
10/2
....FUNDRAISING AND SEX WITH YOUR INTERN.
WOW!
UNCANNY!
HOW DID HE DO THAT??

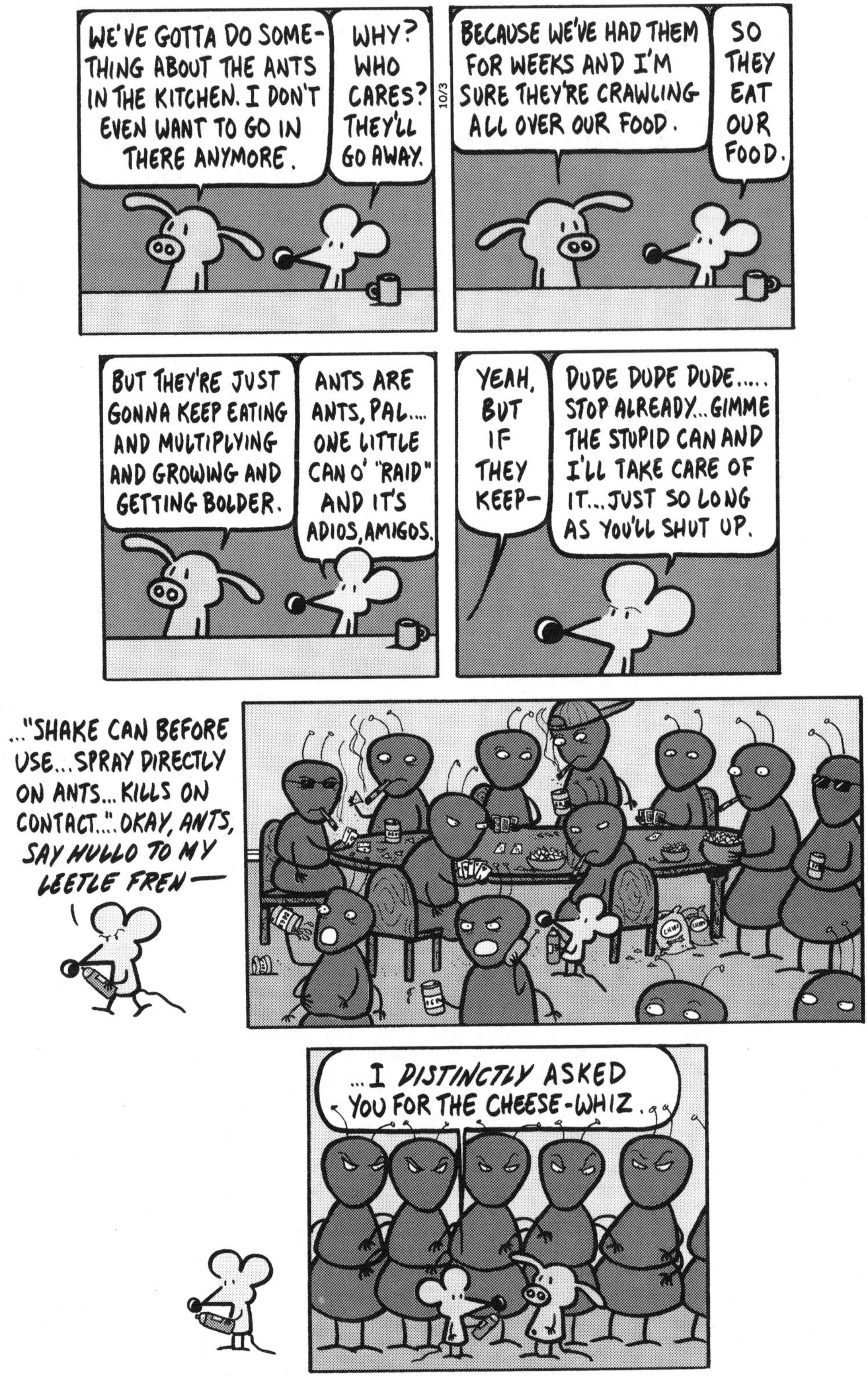
WE'VE GOTTA DO SOMETHING ABOUT THE ANTS IN THE KITCHEN. I DON'T EVEN WANT TO GO IN THERE ANYMORE.
WHY? WHO CARES? THEY'LL GO AWAY.
10/3
BECAUSE WE'VE HAD THEM FOR WEEKS AND I'M SURE THEY'RE CRAWLING ALL OVER OUR FOOD.
SO THEY EAT OUR FOOD.
BUT THEY'RE JUST GONNA KEEP EATING AND MULTIPLYING AND GROWING AND GETTING BOLDER.
ANTS ARE ANTS, PAL.... ONE LITTLE CAN O' "RAID" AND IT'S ADIOS, AMIGOS.
YEAH, BUT IF THEY KEEP-
DUDE DUDE DUDE..... STOP ALREADY...GIMME THE STUPID CAN AND I'LL TAKE CARE OF IT...JUST SO LONG AS YOU'LL SHUT UP.
..."SHAKE CAN BEFORE USE...SPRAY DIRECTLY ON ANTS...KILLS ON CONTACT...". OKAY, ANTS, SAY HULLO TO MY LEETLE FREN—
...I DISTINCTLY ASKED YOU FOR THE CHEESE-WHIZ.

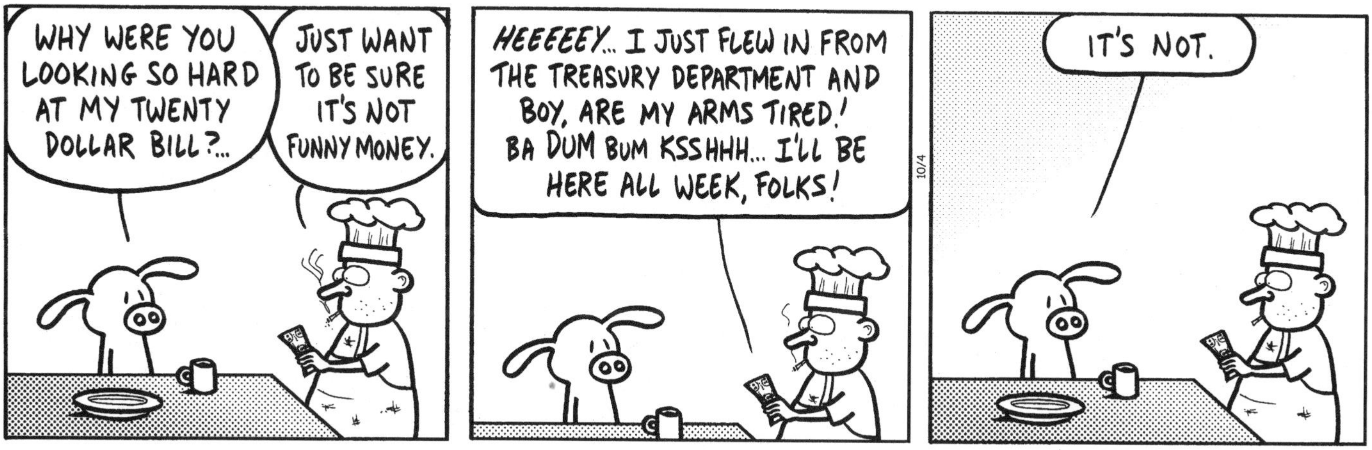
WHY WERE YOU LOOKING SO HARD AT MY TWENTY DOLLAR BILL?...
JUST WANT TO BE SURE IT'S NOT FUNNY MONEY.
HEEEEEY... I JUST FLEW IN FROM THE TREASURY DEPARTMENT AND BOY, ARE MY ARMS TIRED! BA DUM BUM KSSHHH... I'LL BE HERE ALL WEEK, FOLKS!
10/4
IT'S NOT.

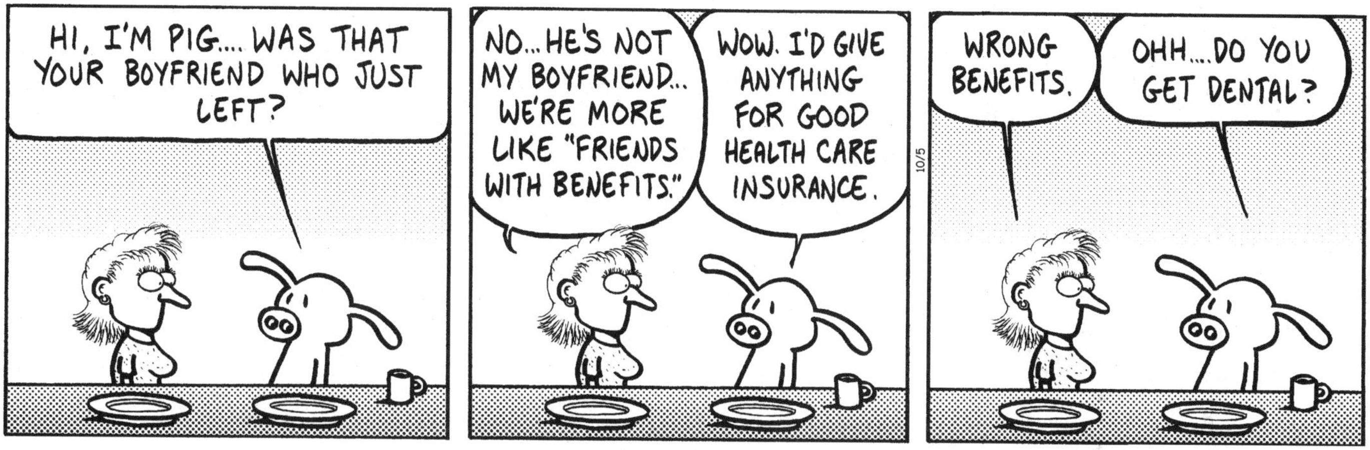
HI, I'M PIG.... WAS THAT YOUR BOYFRIEND WHO JUST LEFT?
NO... HE'S NOT MY BOYFRIEND... WE'RE MORE LIKE "FRIENDS WITH BENEFITS."
WOW. I'D GIVE ANYTHING FOR GOOD HEALTH CARE INSURANCE.
10/5
WRONG BENEFITS.
OHH.... DO YOU GET DENTAL?

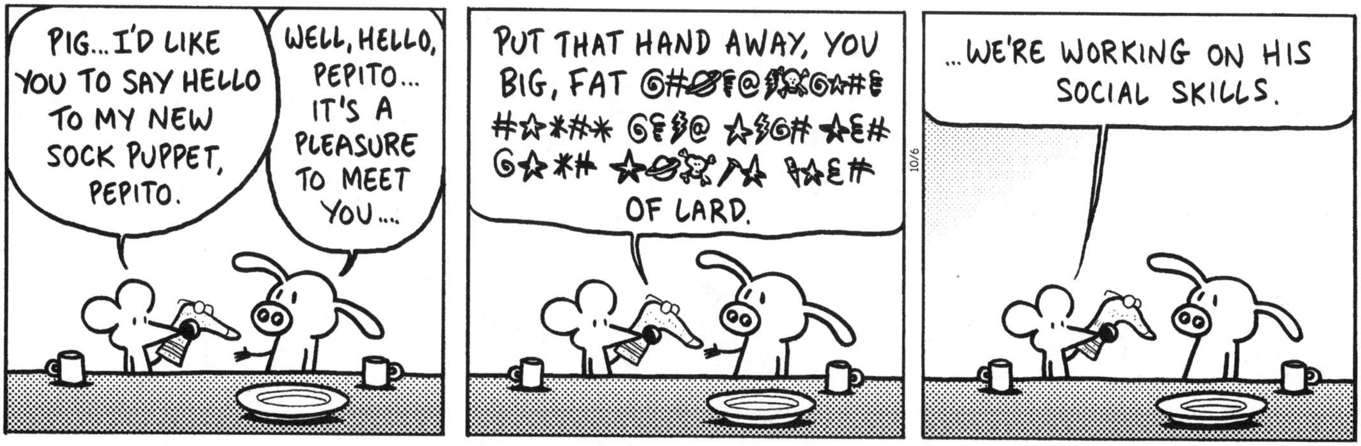
PIG... I'D LIKE YOU TO SAY HELLO TO MY NEW SOCK PUPPET, PEPITO.
WELL, HELLO, PEPITO... IT'S A PLEASURE TO MEET YOU....
PUT THAT HAND AWAY, YOU BIG, FAT
OF LARD.
10/6
...WE'RE WORKING ON HIS SOCIAL SKILLS.

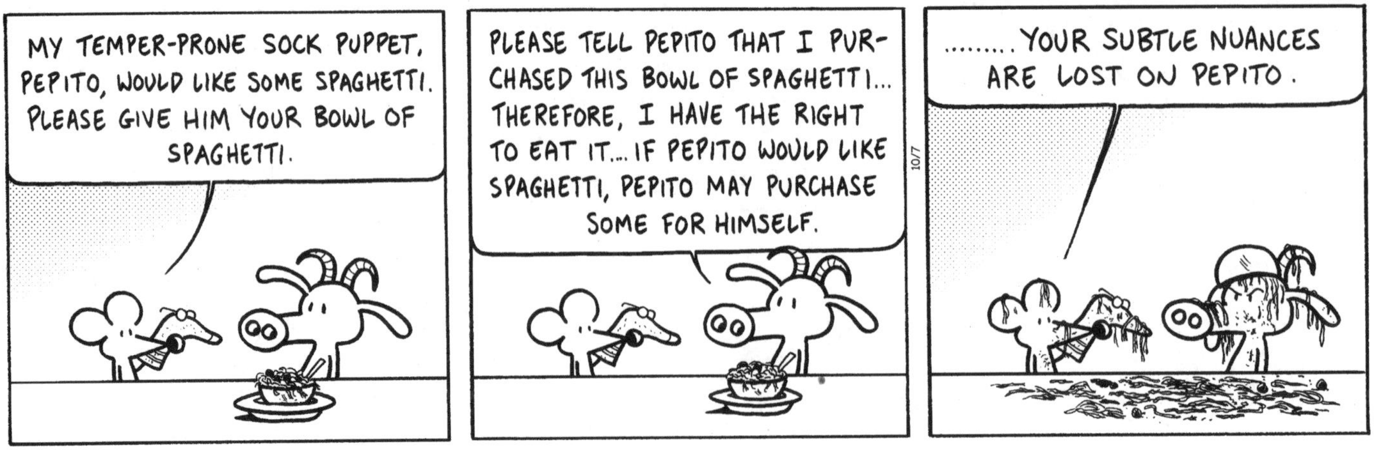
MY TEMPER-PRONE SOCK PUPPET, PEPITO, WOULD LIKE SOME SPAGHETTI. PLEASE GIVE HIM YOUR BOWL OF SPAGHETTI.
PLEASE TELL PEPITO THAT I PURCHASED THIS BOWL OF SPAGHETTI... THEREFORE, I HAVE THE RIGHT TO EAT IT.... IF PEPITO WOULD LIKE SPAGHETTI, PEPITO MAY PURCHASE SOME FOR HIMSELF.
10/7
........YOUR SUBTLE NUANCES ARE LOST ON PEPITO.

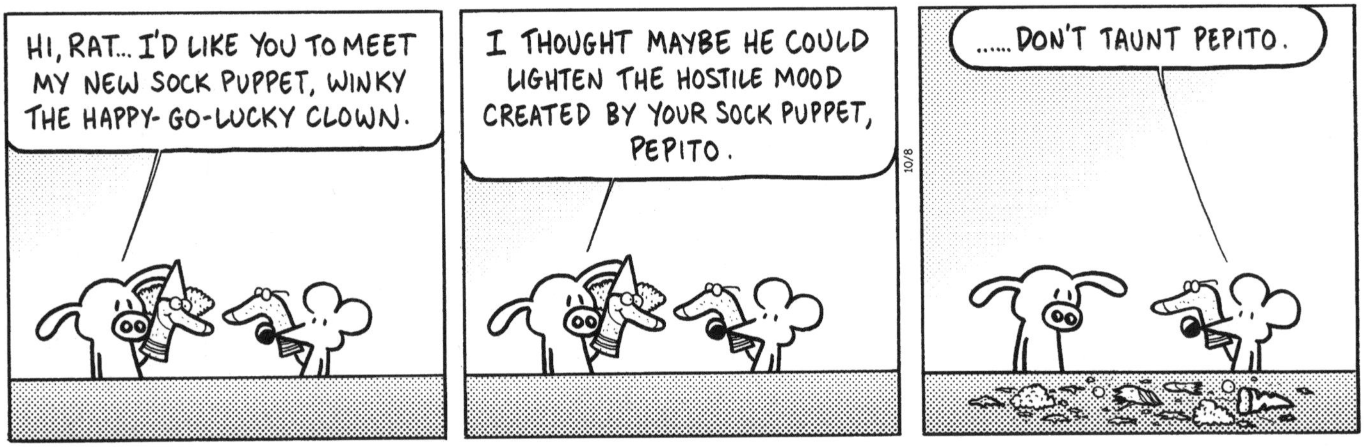
HI, RAT... I'D LIKE YOU TO MEET MY NEW SOCK PUPPET, WINKY THE HAPPY-GO-LUCKY CLOWN.
I THOUGHT MAYBE HE COULD LIGHTEN THE HOSTILE MOOD CREATED BY YOUR SOCK PUPPET, PEPITO.
10/8
......DON'T TAUNT PEPITO.

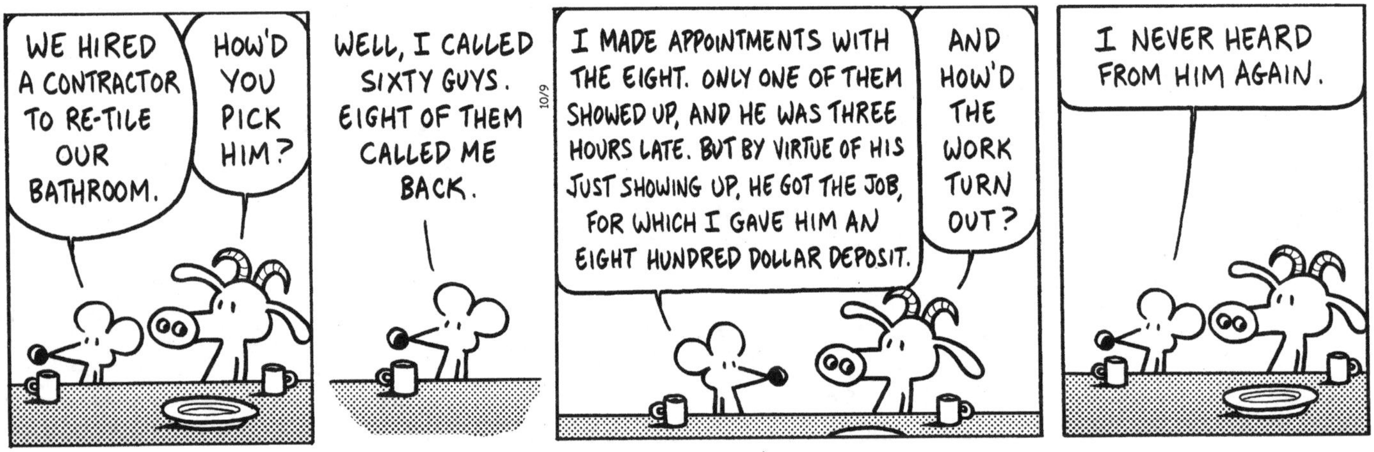
WE HIRED A CONTRACTOR TO RE-TILE OUR BATHROOM.
HOW'D YOU PICK HIM?
WELL, I CALLED SIXTY GUYS. EIGHT OF THEM CALLED ME BACK.
10/9
I MADE APPOINTMENTS WITH THE EIGHT. ONLY ONE OF THEM SHOWED UP, AND HE WAS THREE HOURS LATE. BUT BY VIRTUE OF HIS JUST SHOWING UP, HE GOT THE JOB, FOR WHICH I GAVE HIM AN EIGHT HUNDRED DOLLAR DEPOSIT.
AND HOW'D THE WORK TURN OUT?
I NEVER HEARD FROM HIM AGAIN.

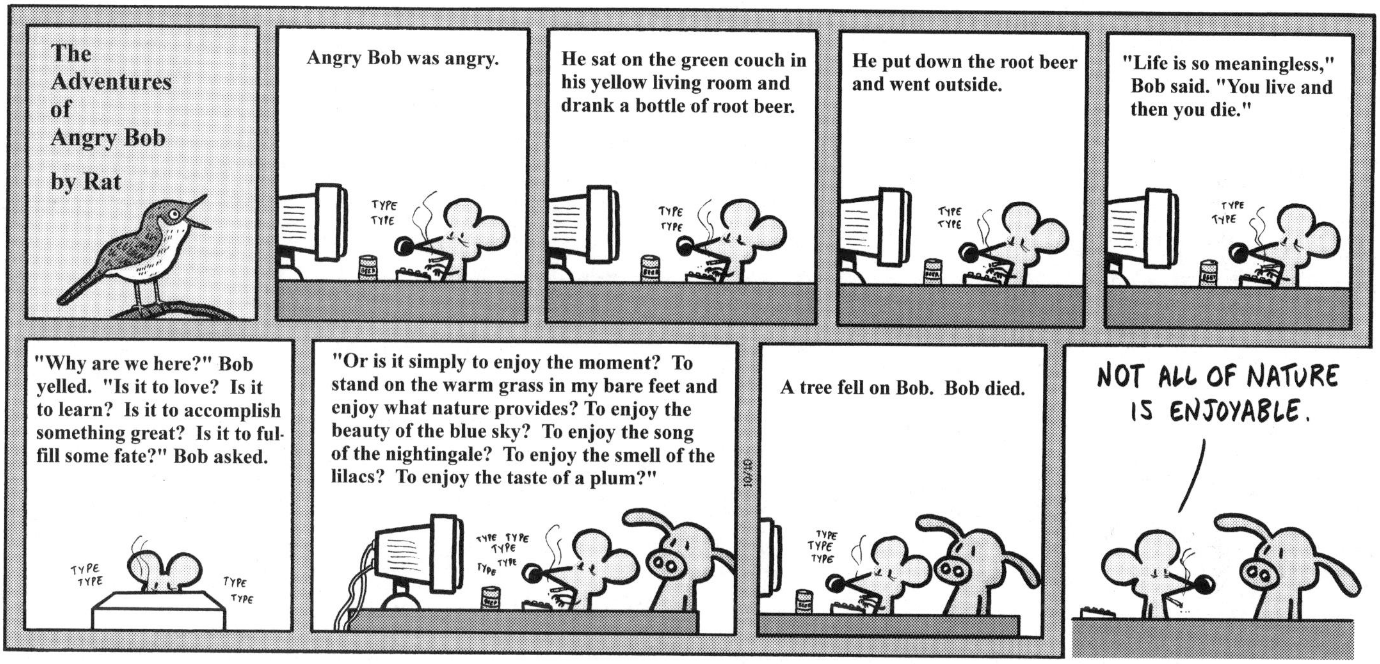
The Adventures of Angry Bob
by Rat
Angry Bob was angry.
TYPE TYPE
He sat on the green couch in his yellow living room and drank a bottle of root beer.
TYPE TYPE
He put down the root beer and went outside.
TYPE TYPE
"Life is so meaningless," Bob said. "You live and then you die."
TYPE TYPE
"Why are we here?" Bob yelled. "Is it to love? Is it to learn? Is it to accomplish something great? Is it to fulfill some fate?" Bob asked.
TYPE TYPE
TYPE TYPE
"Or is it simply to enjoy the moment? To stand on the warm grass in my bare feet and enjoy what nature provides? To enjoy the beauty of the blue sky? To enjoy the song of the nightingale? To enjoy the smell of the lilacs? To enjoy the taste of a plum?"
TYPE TYPE TYPE TYPE TYPE
A tree fell on Bob. Bob died.
TYPE TYPE TYPE
NOT ALL OF NATURE IS ENJOYABLE.

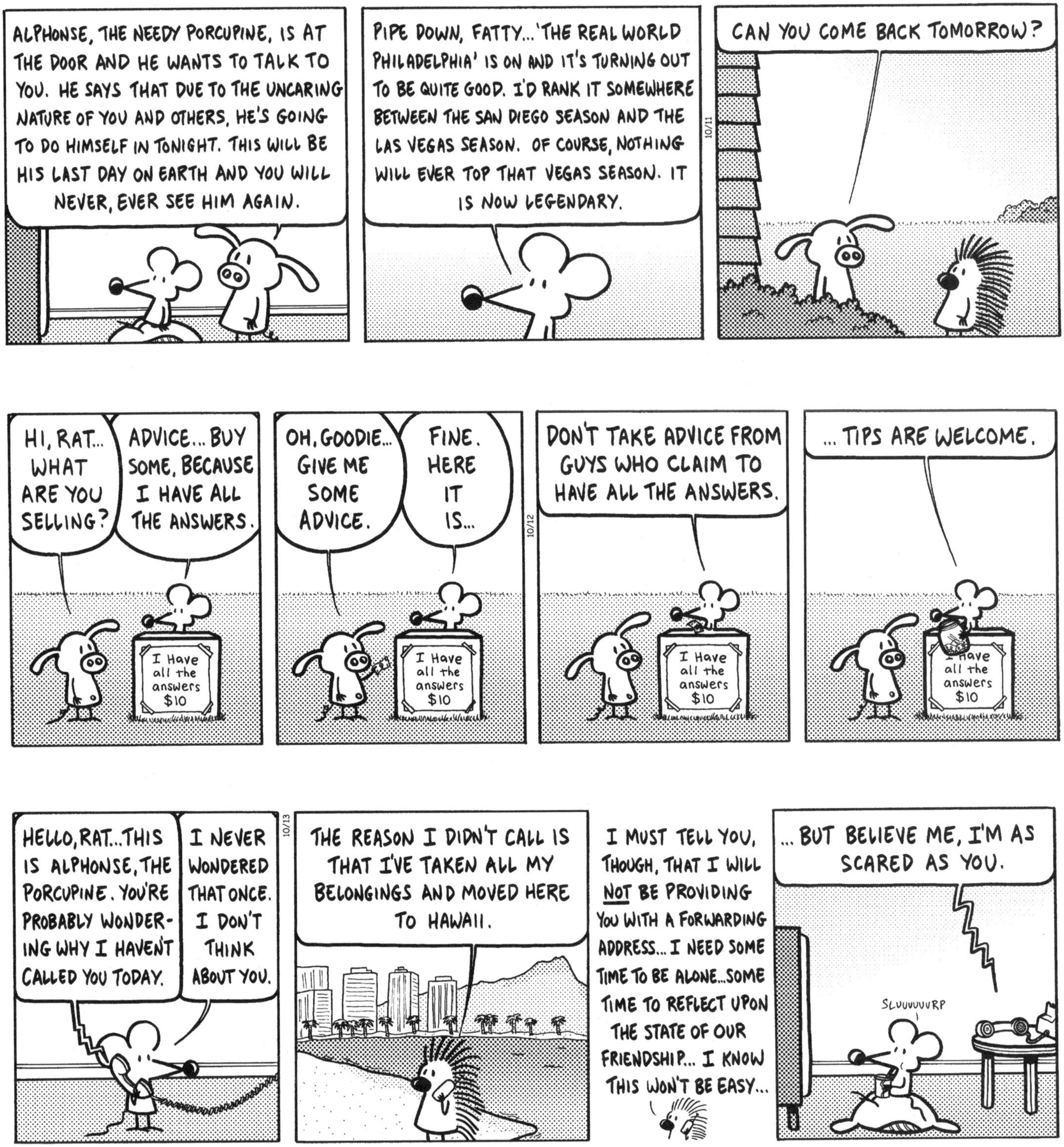
ALPHONSE, THE NEEDY PORCUPINE, IS AT THE DOOR AND HE WANTS TO TALK TO YOU. HE SAYS THAT DUE TO THE UNCARING NATURE OF YOU AND OTHERS, HE'S GOING TO DO HIMSELF IN TONIGHT. THIS WILL BE HIS LAST DAY ON EARTH AND YOU WILL NEVER, EVER SEE HIM AGAIN.
PIPE DOWN, FATTY... 'THE REAL WORLD PHILADELPHIA' IS ON AND IT'S TURNING OUT TO BE QUITE GOOD. I'D RANK IT SOMEWHERE BETWEEN THE SAN DIEGO SEASON AND THE LAS VEGAS SEASON. OF COURSE, NOTHING WILL EVER TOP THAT VEGAS SEASON. IT IS NOW LEGENDARY.
10/11
CAN YOU COME BACK TOMORROW?
HI, RAT... WHAT ARE YOU SELLING?
ADVICE... BUY SOME, BECAUSE I HAVE ALL THE ANSWERS.
I Have all the answers $10
OH, GOODIE... GIVE ME SOME ADVICE.
FINE. HERE IT IS...
10/12
DON'T TAKE ADVICE FROM GUYS WHO CLAIM TO HAVE ALL THE ANSWERS.
... TIPS ARE WELCOME.
HELLO, RAT... THIS IS ALPHONSE, THE PORCUPINE. YOU'RE PROBABLY WONDERING WHY I HAVEN'T CALLED YOU TODAY.
I NEVER WONDERED THAT ONCE. I DON'T THINK ABOUT YOU.
10/13
THE REASON I DIDN'T CALL IS THAT I'VE TAKEN ALL MY BELONGINGS AND MOVED HERE TO HAWAII.
I MUST TELL YOU, THOUGH, THAT I WILL NOT BE PROVIDING YOU WITH A FORWARDING ADDRESS... I NEED SOME TIME TO BE ALONE... SOME TIME TO REFLECT UPON THE STATE OF OUR FRIENDSHIP... I KNOW THIS WON'T BE EASY...
... BUT BELIEVE ME, I'M AS SCARED AS YOU.
SLUUUUUURP

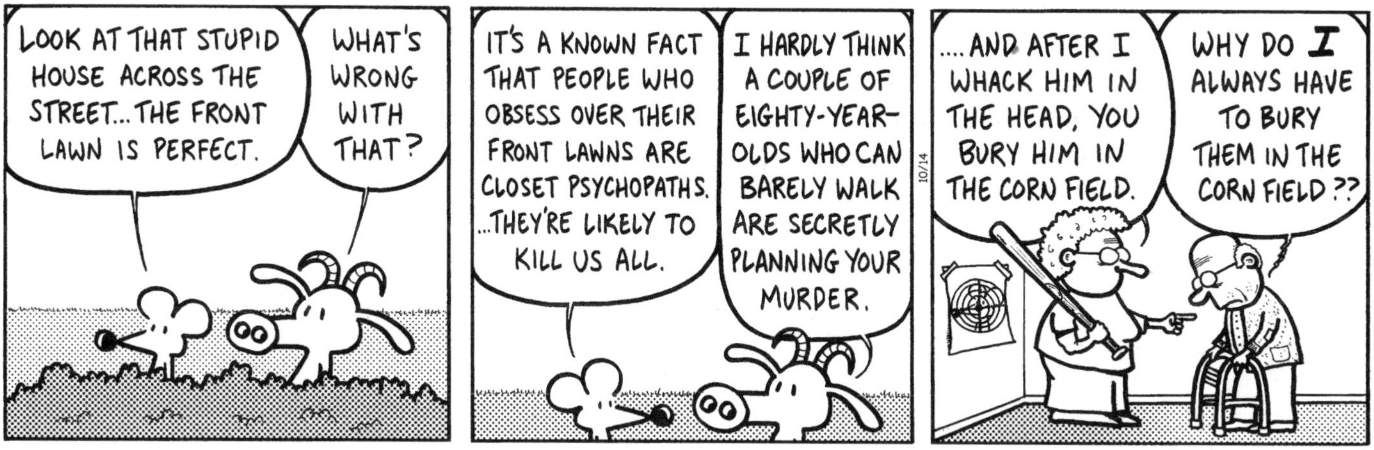
LOOK AT THAT STUPID HOUSE ACROSS THE STREET... THE FRONT LAWN IS PERFECT.
WHAT'S WRONG WITH THAT?
IT'S A KNOWN FACT THAT PEOPLE WHO OBSESS OVER THEIR FRONT LAWNS ARE CLOSET PSYCHOPATHS. ...THEY'RE LIKELY TO KILL US ALL.
I HARDLY THINK A COUPLE OF EIGHTY-YEAR-OLDS WHO CAN BARELY WALK ARE SECRETLY PLANNING YOUR MURDER.
10/14
.... AND AFTER I WHACK HIM IN THE HEAD, YOU BURY HIM IN THE CORN FIELD.
WHY DO *I* ALWAYS HAVE TO BURY THEM IN THE CORN FIELD??

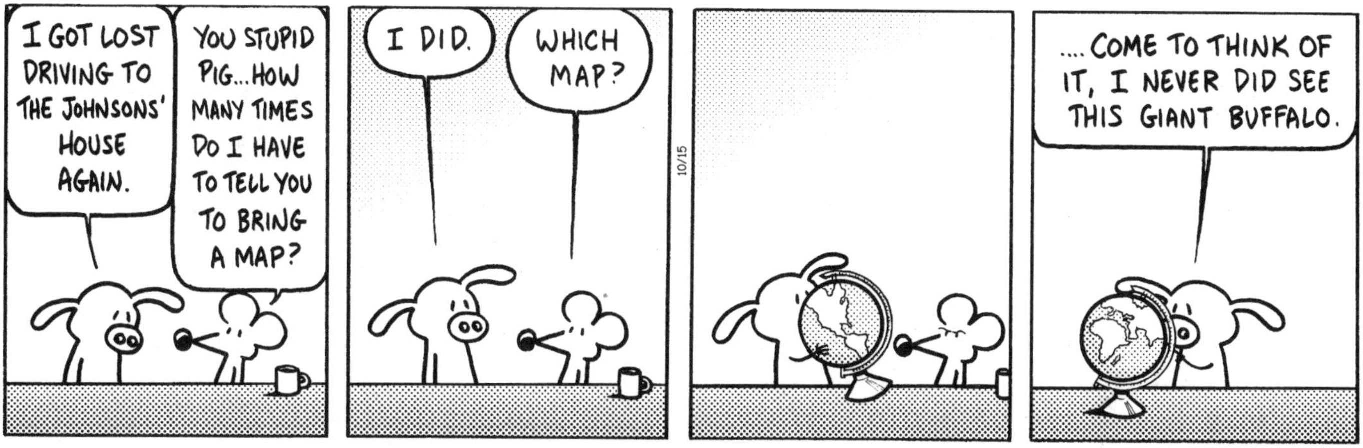
I GOT LOST DRIVING TO THE JOHNSONS' HOUSE AGAIN.
YOU STUPID PIG... HOW MANY TIMES DO I HAVE TO TELL YOU TO BRING A MAP?
I DID.
WHICH MAP?
10/15
.... COME TO THINK OF IT, I NEVER DID SEE THIS GIANT BUFFALO.

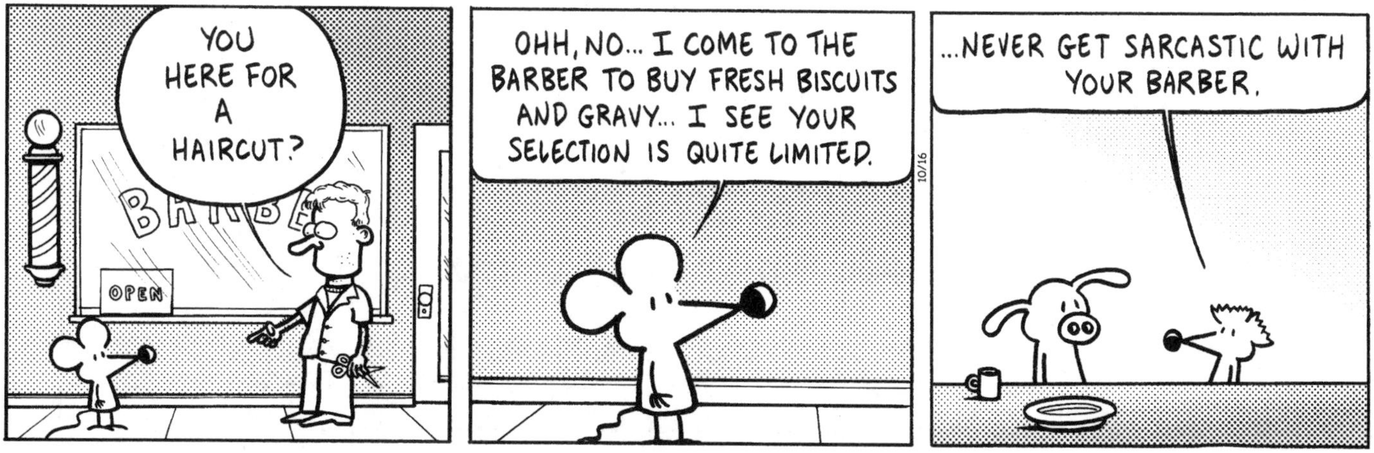
YOU HERE FOR A HAIRCUT?
OPEN
OHH, NO... I COME TO THE BARBER TO BUY FRESH BISCUITS AND GRAVY... I SEE YOUR SELECTION IS QUITE LIMITED.
10/16
...NEVER GET SARCASTIC WITH YOUR BARBER.

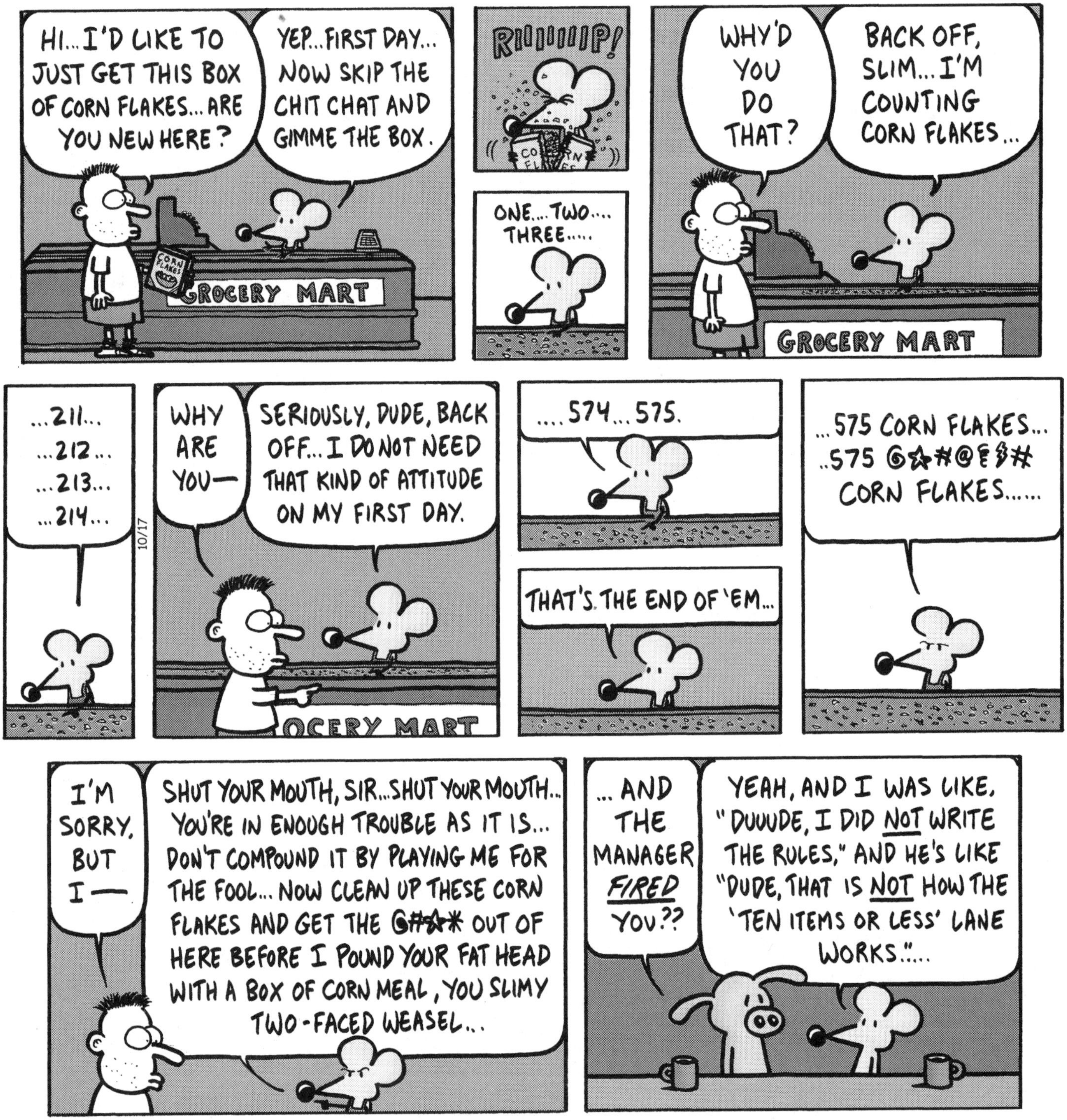
HI...I'D LIKE TO JUST GET THIS BOX OF CORN FLAKES...ARE YOU NEW HERE?
YEP...FIRST DAY...NOW SKIP THE CHIT CHAT AND GIMME THE BOX.
GROCERY MART
CORN FLAKES
RIIIIIIIP!
ONE....TWO....THREE.....
WHY'D YOU DO THAT?
BACK OFF, SLIM...I'M COUNTING CORN FLAKES...
GROCERY MART
...211...
...212...
...213...
...214...
10/17
WHY ARE YOU—
SERIOUSLY, DUDE, BACK OFF...I DO NOT NEED THAT KIND OF ATTITUDE ON MY FIRST DAY.
OCERY MART
....574...575.
THAT'S THE END OF 'EM...
...575 CORN FLAKES...
..575 @☆#@&$# CORN FLAKES......
I'M SORRY, BUT I—
SHUT YOUR MOUTH, SIR...SHUT YOUR MOUTH...YOU'RE IN ENOUGH TROUBLE AS IT IS...DON'T COMPOUND IT BY PLAYING ME FOR THE FOOL...NOW CLEAN UP THESE CORN FLAKES AND GET THE @#☆* OUT OF HERE BEFORE I POUND YOUR FAT HEAD WITH A BOX OF CORN MEAL, YOU SLIMY TWO-FACED WEASEL...
...AND THE MANAGER FIRED YOU??
YEAH, AND I WAS LIKE, "DUUUDE, I DID NOT WRITE THE RULES," AND HE'S LIKE "DUDE, THAT IS NOT HOW THE 'TEN ITEMS OR LESS' LANE WORKS."...

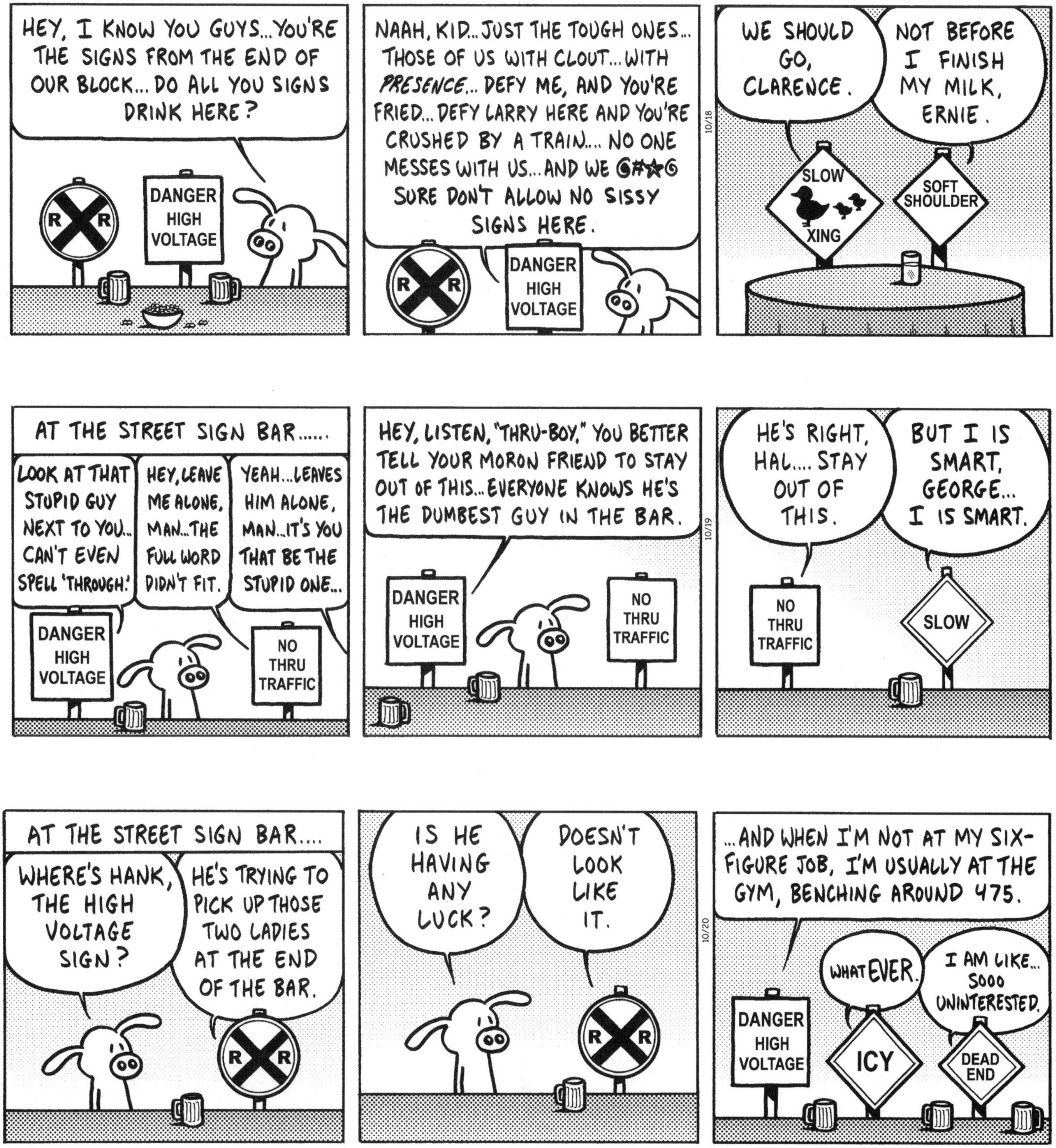
HEY, I KNOW YOU GUYS... YOU'RE THE SIGNS FROM THE END OF OUR BLOCK... DO ALL YOU SIGNS DRINK HERE?
R R
DANGER HIGH VOLTAGE
NAAH, KID... JUST THE TOUGH ONES... THOSE OF US WITH CLOUT... WITH PRESENCE... DEFY ME, AND YOU'RE FRIED... DEFY LARRY HERE AND YOU'RE CRUSHED BY A TRAIN... NO ONE MESSES WITH US... AND WE @#☆@ SURE DON'T ALLOW NO SISSY SIGNS HERE.
10/18
WE SHOULD GO, CLARENCE.
NOT BEFORE I FINISH MY MILK, ERNIE.
SLOW XING
SOFT SHOULDER
AT THE STREET SIGN BAR......
LOOK AT THAT STUPID GUY NEXT TO YOU... CAN'T EVEN SPELL 'THROUGH.'
HEY, LEAVE ME ALONE, MAN... THE FULL WORD DIDN'T FIT.
YEAH... LEAVES HIM ALONE, MAN... IT'S YOU THAT BE THE STUPID ONE...
NO THRU TRAFFIC
HEY, LISTEN, "THRU-BOY," YOU BETTER TELL YOUR MORON FRIEND TO STAY OUT OF THIS... EVERYONE KNOWS HE'S THE DUMBEST GUY IN THE BAR.
10/19
HE'S RIGHT, HAL.... STAY OUT OF THIS.
BUT I IS SMART, GEORGE... I IS SMART.
SLOW
AT THE STREET SIGN BAR....
WHERE'S HANK, THE HIGH VOLTAGE SIGN?
HE'S TRYING TO PICK UP THOSE TWO LADIES AT THE END OF THE BAR.
IS HE HAVING ANY LUCK?
DOESN'T LOOK LIKE IT.
10/20
...AND WHEN I'M NOT AT MY SIX-FIGURE JOB, I'M USUALLY AT THE GYM, BENCHING AROUND 475.
WHATEVER.
I AM LIKE... SOOO UNINTERESTED.
ICY
DEAD END

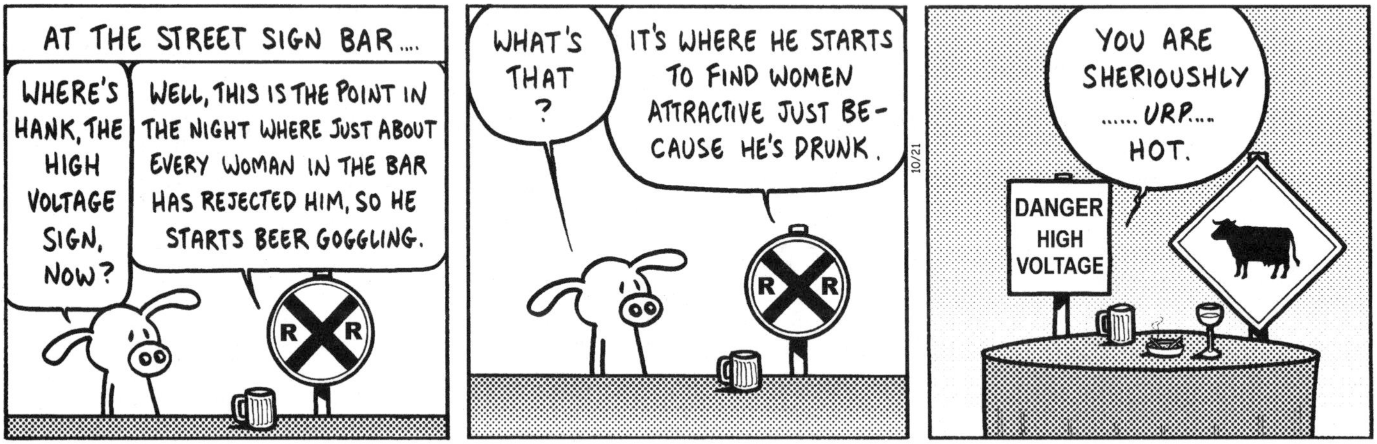
AT THE STREET SIGN BAR....
WHERE'S HANK, THE HIGH VOLTAGE SIGN, NOW?
WELL, THIS IS THE POINT IN THE NIGHT WHERE JUST ABOUT EVERY WOMAN IN THE BAR HAS REJECTED HIM, SO HE STARTS BEER GOGGLING.
R R
WHAT'S THAT ?
IT'S WHERE HE STARTS TO FIND WOMEN ATTRACTIVE JUST BE-CAUSE HE'S DRUNK.
R R
10/21
YOU ARE SHERIOUSHLY ......URP.... HOT.
DANGER HIGH VOLTAGE

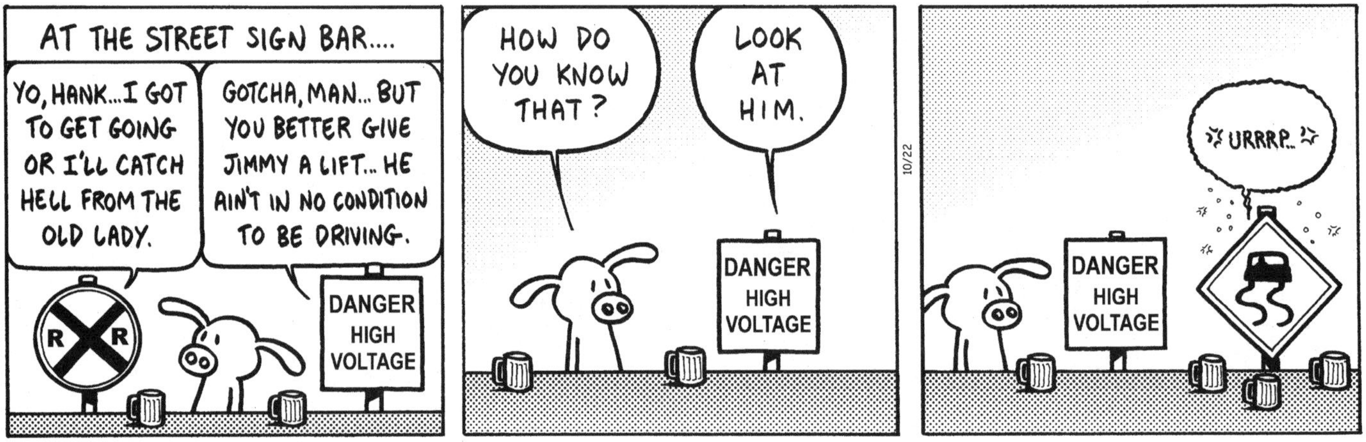
AT THE STREET SIGN BAR....
YO, HANK...I GOT TO GET GOING OR I'LL CATCH HELL FROM THE OLD LADY.
GOTCHA, MAN... BUT YOU BETTER GIVE JIMMY A LIFT... HE AIN'T IN NO CONDITION TO BE DRIVING.
R R
DANGER HIGH VOLTAGE
HOW DO YOU KNOW THAT ?
LOOK AT HIM.
DANGER HIGH VOLTAGE
10/22
URRRP..
DANGER HIGH VOLTAGE

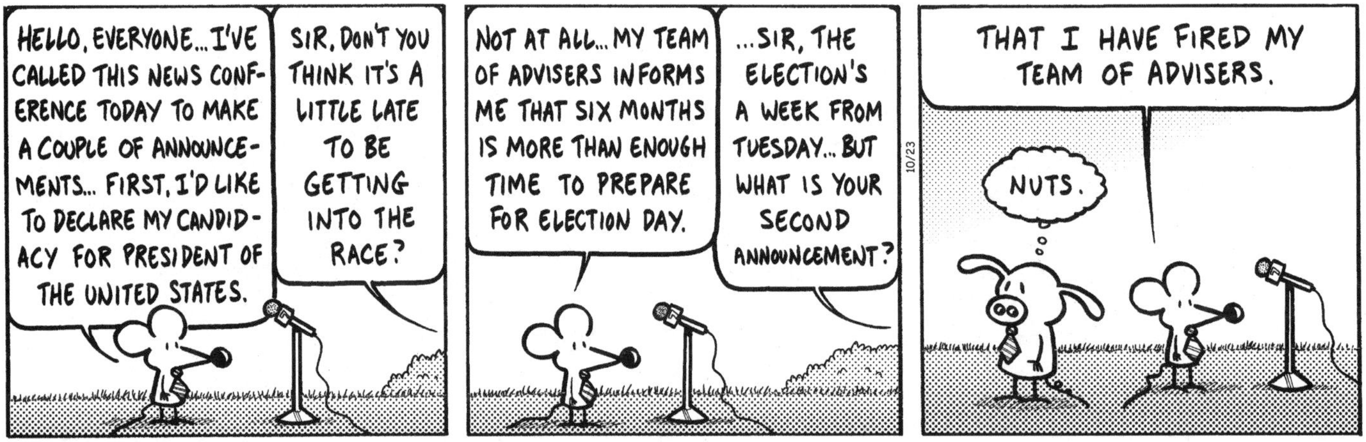
HELLO, EVERYONE... I'VE CALLED THIS NEWS CONF-ERENCE TODAY TO MAKE A COUPLE OF ANNOUNCE-MENTS... FIRST, I'D LIKE TO DECLARE MY CANDID-ACY FOR PRESIDENT OF THE UNITED STATES.
SIR, DON'T YOU THINK IT'S A LITTLE LATE TO BE GETTING INTO THE RACE?
NOT AT ALL... MY TEAM OF ADVISERS INFORMS ME THAT SIX MONTHS IS MORE THAN ENOUGH TIME TO PREPARE FOR ELECTION DAY.
...SIR, THE ELECTION'S A WEEK FROM TUESDAY... BUT WHAT IS YOUR SECOND ANNOUNCEMENT?
10/23
THAT I HAVE FIRED MY TEAM OF ADVISERS.
NUTS.

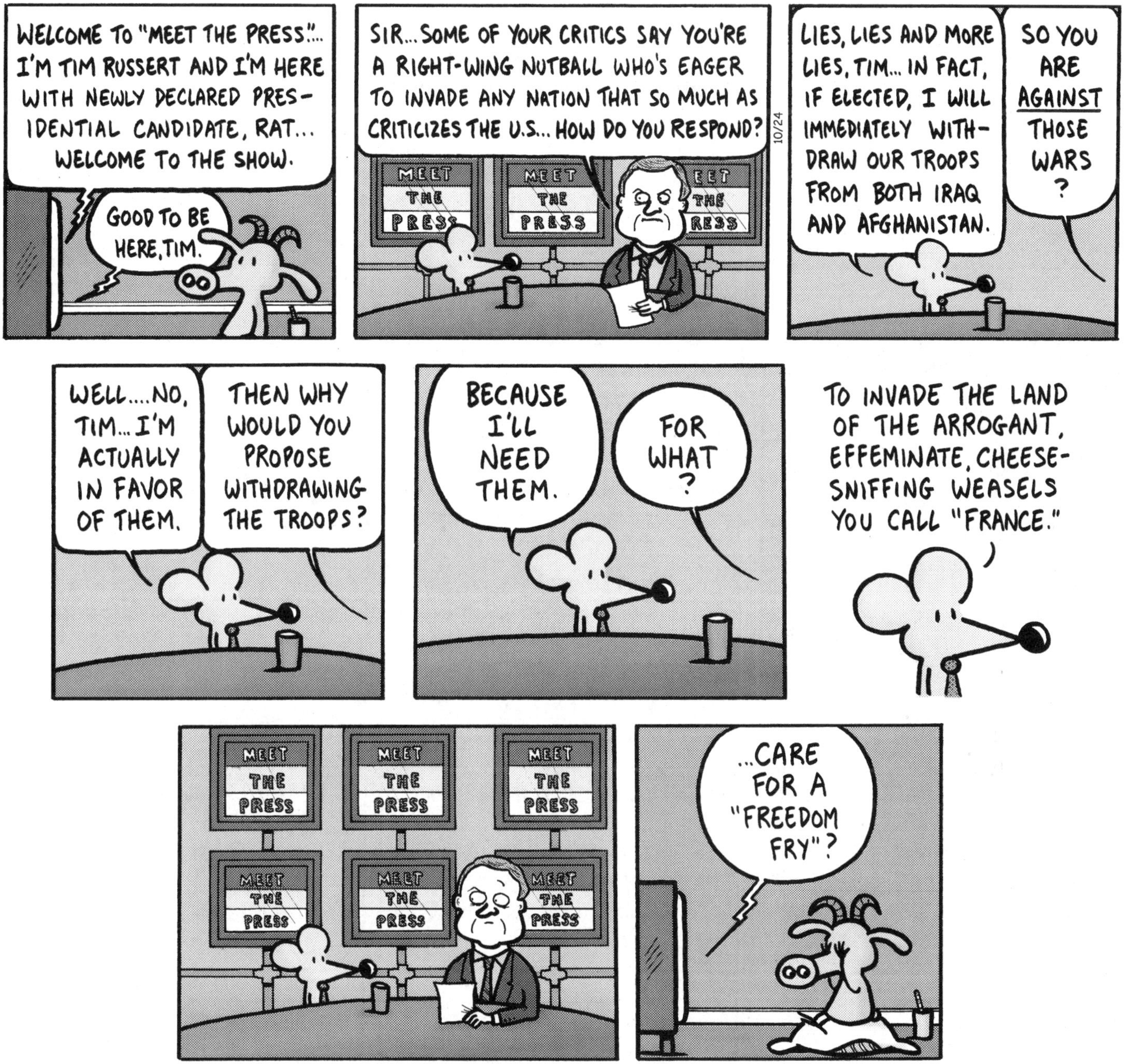
WELCOME TO "MEET THE PRESS."... I'M TIM RUSSERT AND I'M HERE WITH NEWLY DECLARED PRES-IDENTIAL CANDIDATE, RAT... WELCOME TO THE SHOW.
GOOD TO BE HERE, TIM.
SIR... SOME OF YOUR CRITICS SAY YOU'RE A RIGHT-WING NUTBALL WHO'S EAGER TO INVADE ANY NATION THAT SO MUCH AS CRITICIZES THE U.S... HOW DO YOU RESPOND?
MEET THE PRESS
10/24
LIES, LIES AND MORE LIES, TIM... IN FACT, IF ELECTED, I WILL IMMEDIATELY WITH-DRAW OUR TROOPS FROM BOTH IRAQ AND AFGHANISTAN.
SO YOU ARE AGAINST THOSE WARS?
WELL....NO, TIM... I'M ACTUALLY IN FAVOR OF THEM.
THEN WHY WOULD YOU PROPOSE WITHDRAWING THE TROOPS?
BECAUSE I'LL NEED THEM.
FOR WHAT?
TO INVADE THE LAND OF THE ARROGANT, EFFEMINATE, CHEESE-SNIFFING WEASELS YOU CALL "FRANCE."
MEET THE PRESS
...CARE FOR A "FREEDOM FRY"?

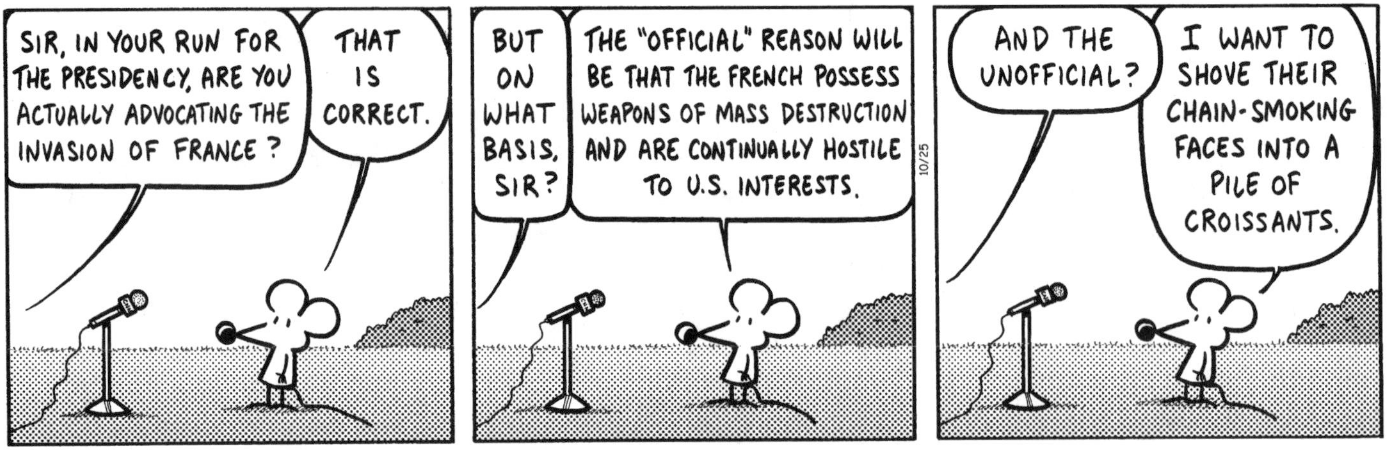
SIR, IN YOUR RUN FOR THE PRESIDENCY, ARE YOU ACTUALLY ADVOCATING THE INVASION OF FRANCE?
THAT IS CORRECT.
BUT ON WHAT BASIS, SIR?
THE "OFFICIAL" REASON WILL BE THAT THE FRENCH POSSESS WEAPONS OF MASS DESTRUCTION AND ARE CONTINUALLY HOSTILE TO U.S. INTERESTS.
10/25
AND THE UNOFFICIAL?
I WANT TO SHOVE THEIR CHAIN-SMOKING FACES INTO A PILE OF CROISSANTS.

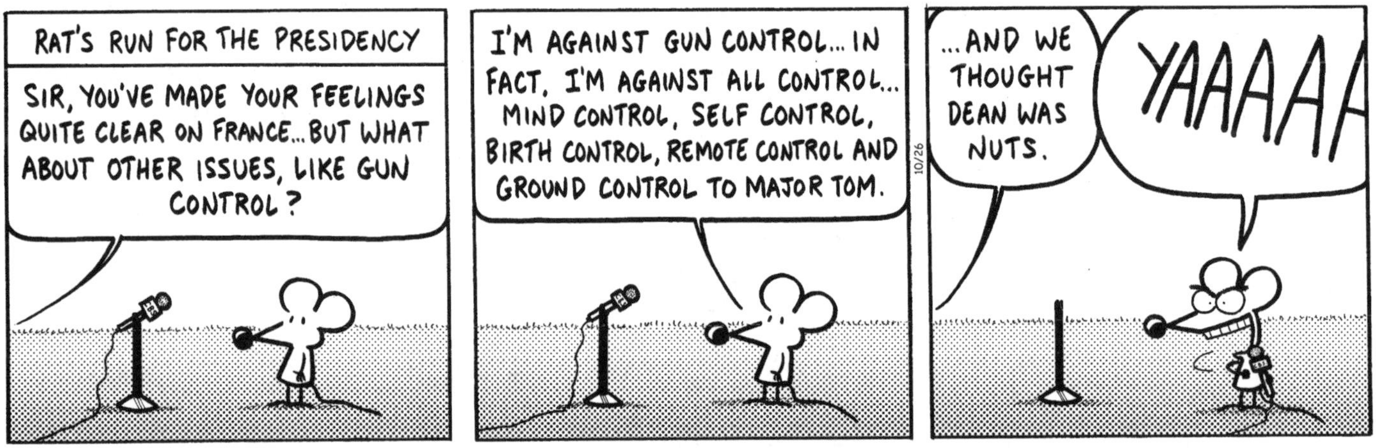
RAT'S RUN FOR THE PRESIDENCY
SIR, YOU'VE MADE YOUR FEELINGS QUITE CLEAR ON FRANCE...BUT WHAT ABOUT OTHER ISSUES, LIKE GUN CONTROL?
I'M AGAINST GUN CONTROL... IN FACT, I'M AGAINST ALL CONTROL... MIND CONTROL, SELF CONTROL, BIRTH CONTROL, REMOTE CONTROL AND GROUND CONTROL TO MAJOR TOM.
10/26
...AND WE THOUGHT DEAN WAS NUTS.
YAAAAA

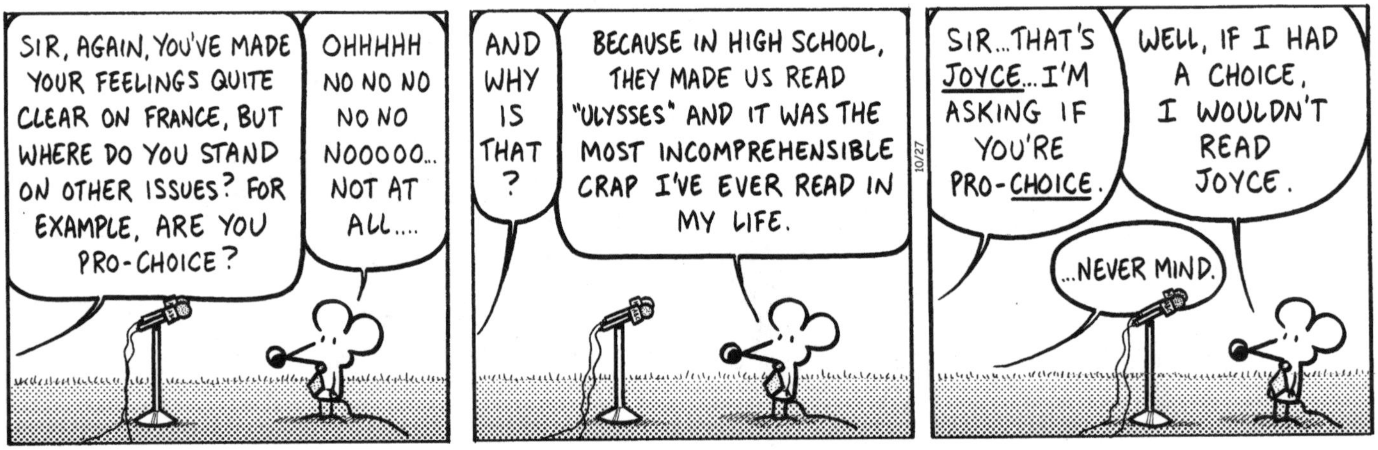
SIR, AGAIN, YOU'VE MADE YOUR FEELINGS QUITE CLEAR ON FRANCE, BUT WHERE DO YOU STAND ON OTHER ISSUES? FOR EXAMPLE, ARE YOU PRO-CHOICE?
OHHHHH NO NO NO NO NO NOOOOO... NOT AT ALL....
AND WHY IS THAT?
BECAUSE IN HIGH SCHOOL, THEY MADE US READ "ULYSSES" AND IT WAS THE MOST INCOMPREHENSIBLE CRAP I'VE EVER READ IN MY LIFE.
10/27
SIR...THAT'S JOYCE...I'M ASKING IF YOU'RE PRO-CHOICE.
WELL, IF I HAD A CHOICE, I WOULDN'T READ JOYCE.
...NEVER MIND.

Panel 1:

RAT'S RUN FOR THE PRESIDENCY

SIR, IF ELECTED ON YOUR ANTI-FRANCE PLATFORM, WHAT ELSE WILL YOU TRY TO DO?

WELL, YOU'VE HEARD OF CHANGING "FRENCH FRIES" TO "FREEDOM FRIES" BUT I'LL EXPAND THAT TO OTHER THINGS.

Panel 2:

SUCH AS WHAT, SIR?

WELL, LARRY BIRD WILL NOW BE FROM "FREEDOM" LICK, INDIANA... MR. FRENCH, THE BUTLER FROM "A FAMILY AFFAIR," WILL NOW BE "MR. FREEDOM," AND A KISS INVOLVING TONGUE WILL NOW BE....

Panel 3:

LEMME GUESS... A "FREEDOM KISS," SIR?

YES... AND COULD C.N.N.'S PAULA ZAHN PLEASE COME TO THE FRONT FOR A DEMONSTRATION?

Panel 4:

WELCOME TO C.N.N.'S "NEWSNIGHT."... HERE'S YOUR HOST, AARON BROWN....

WELCOME, FOLKS... TONIGHT WE EXPLORE THE CURIOUS PRESIDENTIAL CANDIDACY OF RAT....

Panel 5:

TO BEGIN, LET'S START WITH 'THE WHIP' AND OUR VERY OWN WOLF BLITZER, WHO'S STANDING BY WITH THE CANDIDATE IN WASHINGTON, D.C.

Panel 6:

HAVE YOU BEEN A BAAAD BOY, WOLFIE?

Panel 7:

...PERHAPS I MISUNDERSTOOD THE CONCEPT.

Panel 8:

THE PRESIDENTIAL DEBATES

LISTEN, RAT, THIS IS A LIST OF FAMOUS LINES FROM PAST PRESIDENTIAL DEBATES... IF YOU GET IN TROUBLE, OR SAY SOMETHING DUMB, YOU MIGHT WANT TO USE ONE.

GOTCHA.

Panel 9:

...MR. RAT... WHY SHOULD SOMEONE VOTE FOR YOU OVER SENATOR KERRY?

WELL... MR. KERRY'S FIRST NAME IS JOHN, AND A "JOHN" IS WHAT WE CALL A MAN WHO'S BEEN PICKED UP IN A PROSTITUTION STING...

Panel 11:

WHERE'S THE BEEF??

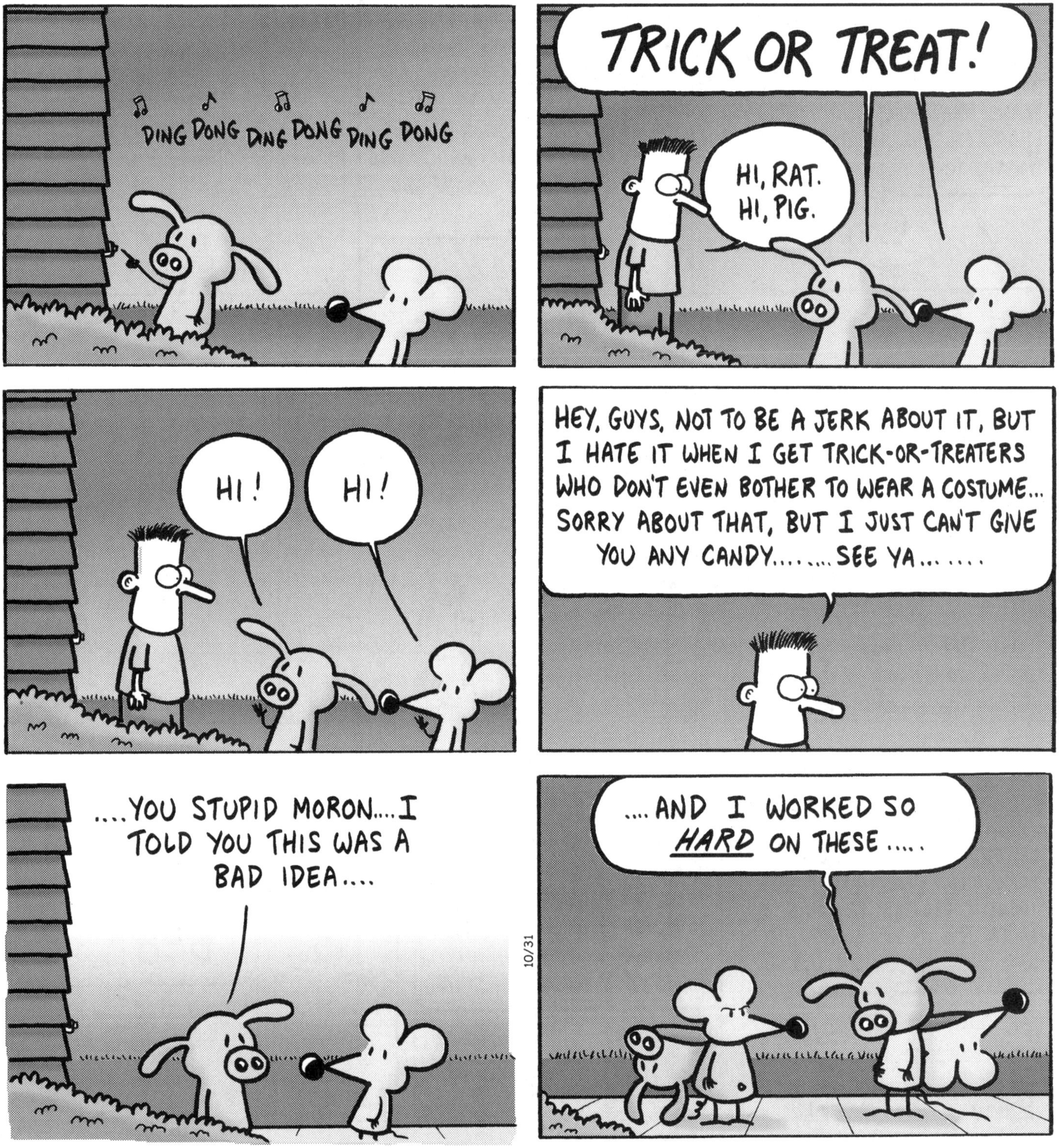
DING DONG DING DONG DING DONG
TRICK OR TREAT!
HI, RAT. HI, PIG.
HI!
HI!
HEY, GUYS, NOT TO BE A JERK ABOUT IT, BUT I HATE IT WHEN I GET TRICK-OR-TREATERS WHO DON'T EVEN BOTHER TO WEAR A COSTUME... SORRY ABOUT THAT, BUT I JUST CAN'T GIVE YOU ANY CANDY........SEE YA.......
....YOU STUPID MORON....I TOLD YOU THIS WAS A BAD IDEA....
....AND I WORKED SO HARD ON THESE.....
10/31

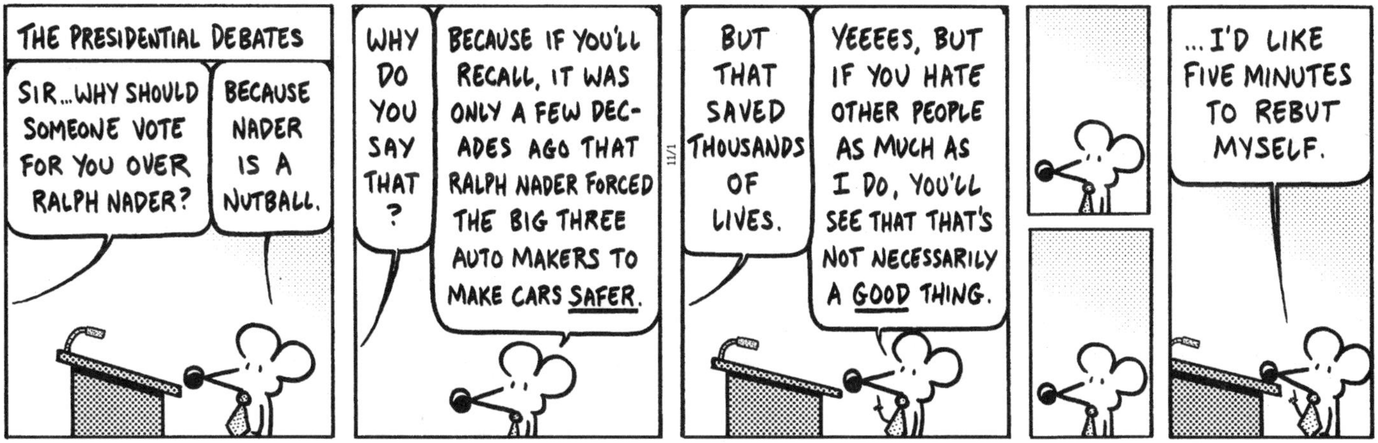
THE PRESIDENTIAL DEBATES
SIR...WHY SHOULD SOMEONE VOTE FOR YOU OVER RALPH NADER?
BECAUSE NADER IS A NUTBALL.
WHY DO YOU SAY THAT?
BECAUSE IF YOU'LL RECALL, IT WAS ONLY A FEW DECADES AGO THAT RALPH NADER FORCED THE BIG THREE AUTO MAKERS TO MAKE CARS SAFER.
11/1
BUT THAT SAVED THOUSANDS OF LIVES.
YEEEES, BUT IF YOU HATE OTHER PEOPLE AS MUCH AS I DO, YOU'LL SEE THAT THAT'S NOT NECESSARILY A GOOD THING.
...I'D LIKE FIVE MINUTES TO REBUT MYSELF.

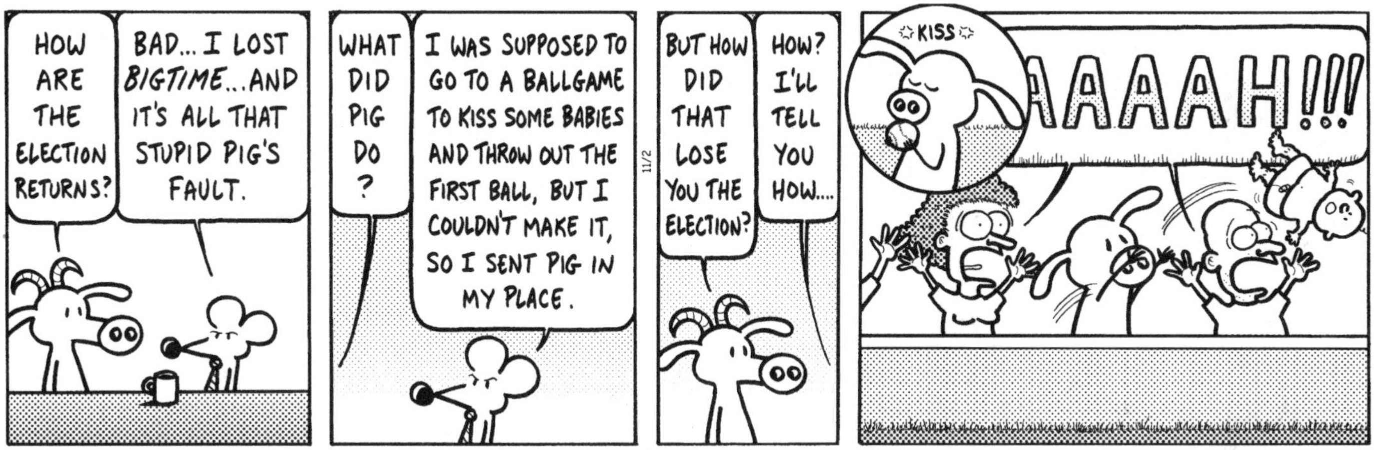
HOW ARE THE ELECTION RETURNS?
BAD... I LOST BIGTIME...AND IT'S ALL THAT STUPID PIG'S FAULT.
WHAT DID PIG DO?
I WAS SUPPOSED TO GO TO A BALLGAME TO KISS SOME BABIES AND THROW OUT THE FIRST BALL, BUT I COULDN'T MAKE IT, SO I SENT PIG IN MY PLACE.
11/2
BUT HOW DID THAT LOSE YOU THE ELECTION?
HOW? I'LL TELL YOU HOW....
KISS
AAAAAH!!!

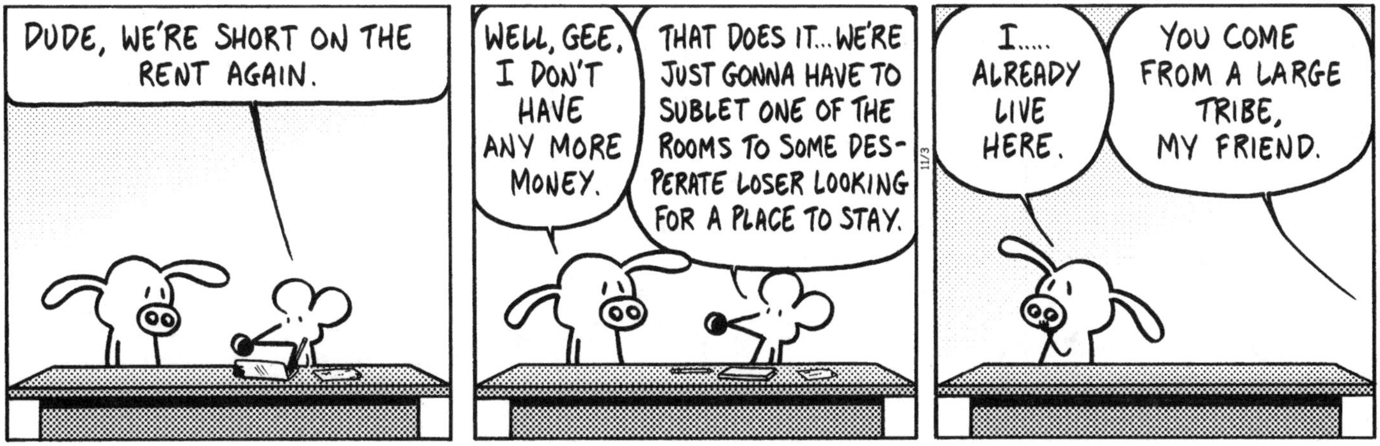
DUDE, WE'RE SHORT ON THE RENT AGAIN.
WELL, GEE, I DON'T HAVE ANY MORE MONEY.
THAT DOES IT...WE'RE JUST GONNA HAVE TO SUBLET ONE OF THE ROOMS TO SOME DESPERATE LOSER LOOKING FOR A PLACE TO STAY.
11/3
I..... ALREADY LIVE HERE.
YOU COME FROM A LARGE TRIBE, MY FRIEND.

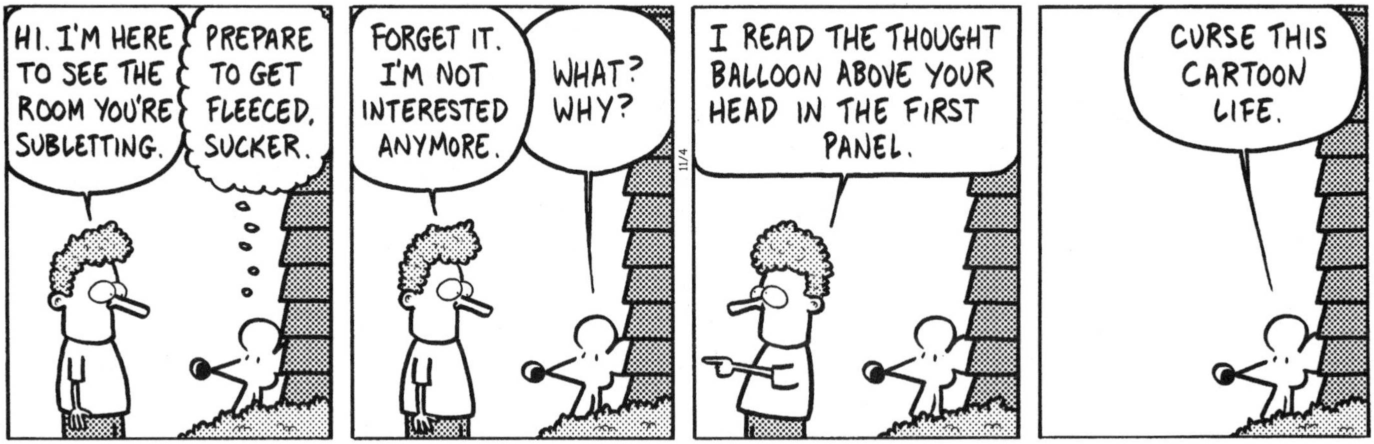
HI. I'M HERE TO SEE THE ROOM YOU'RE SUBLETTING.
PREPARE TO GET FLEECED, SUCKER.
FORGET IT. I'M NOT INTERESTED ANYMORE.
WHAT? WHY?
11/4
I READ THE THOUGHT BALLOON ABOVE YOUR HEAD IN THE FIRST PANEL.
CURSE THIS CARTOON LIFE.

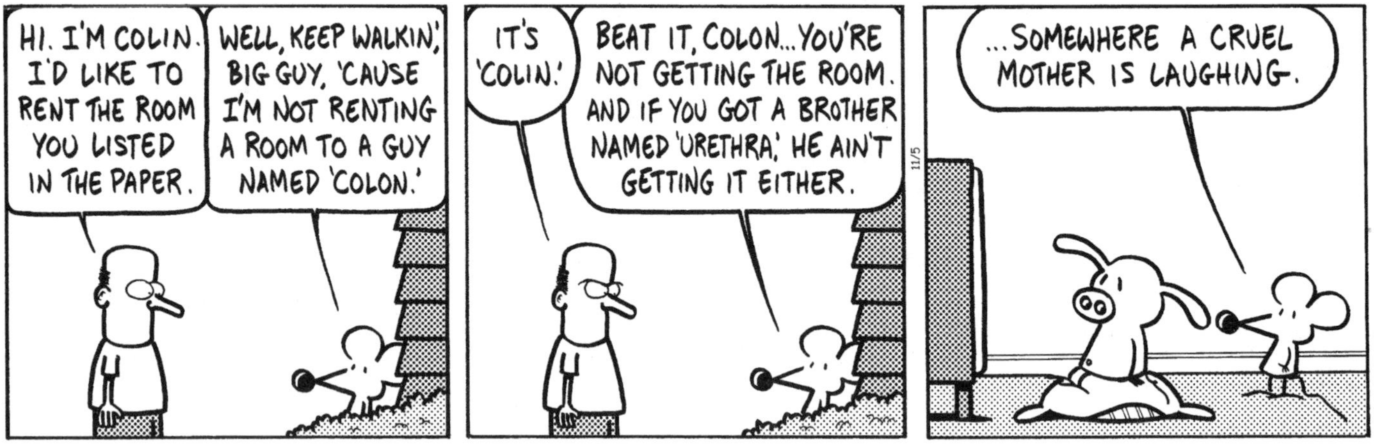
HI. I'M COLIN. I'D LIKE TO RENT THE ROOM YOU LISTED IN THE PAPER.
WELL, KEEP WALKIN', BIG GUY, 'CAUSE I'M NOT RENTING A ROOM TO A GUY NAMED 'COLON.'
IT'S 'COLIN.'
BEAT IT, COLON... YOU'RE NOT GETTING THE ROOM. AND IF YOU GOT A BROTHER NAMED 'URETHRA,' HE AIN'T GETTING IT EITHER.
11/5
...SOMEWHERE A CRUEL MOTHER IS LAUGHING.

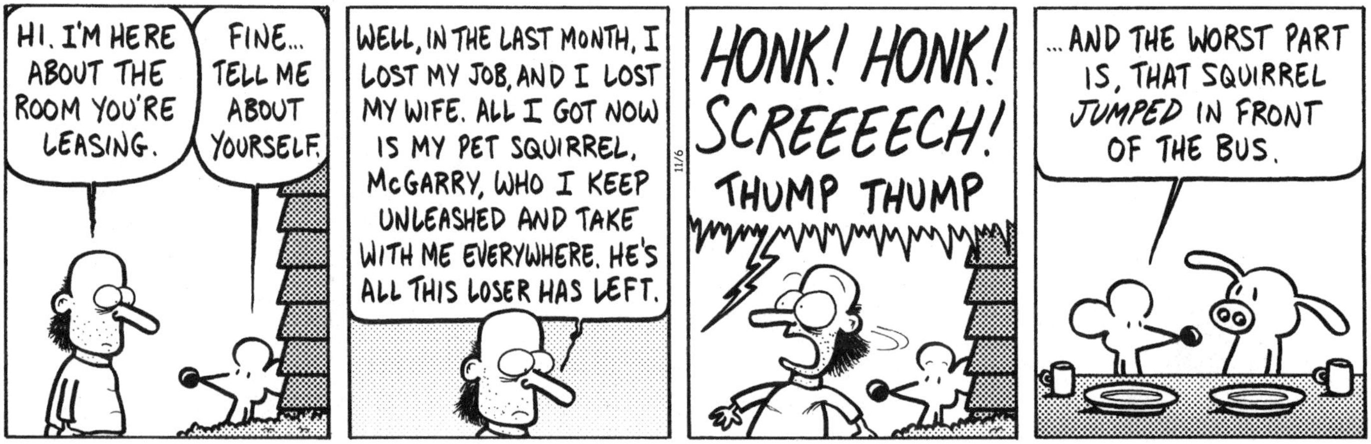
HI. I'M HERE ABOUT THE ROOM YOU'RE LEASING.
FINE... TELL ME ABOUT YOURSELF.
WELL, IN THE LAST MONTH, I LOST MY JOB, AND I LOST MY WIFE. ALL I GOT NOW IS MY PET SQUIRREL, McGARRY, WHO I KEEP UNLEASHED AND TAKE WITH ME EVERYWHERE. HE'S ALL THIS LOSER HAS LEFT.
11/6
HONK! HONK! SCREEEECH! THUMP THUMP
...AND THE WORST PART IS, THAT SQUIRREL JUMPED IN FRONT OF THE BUS.

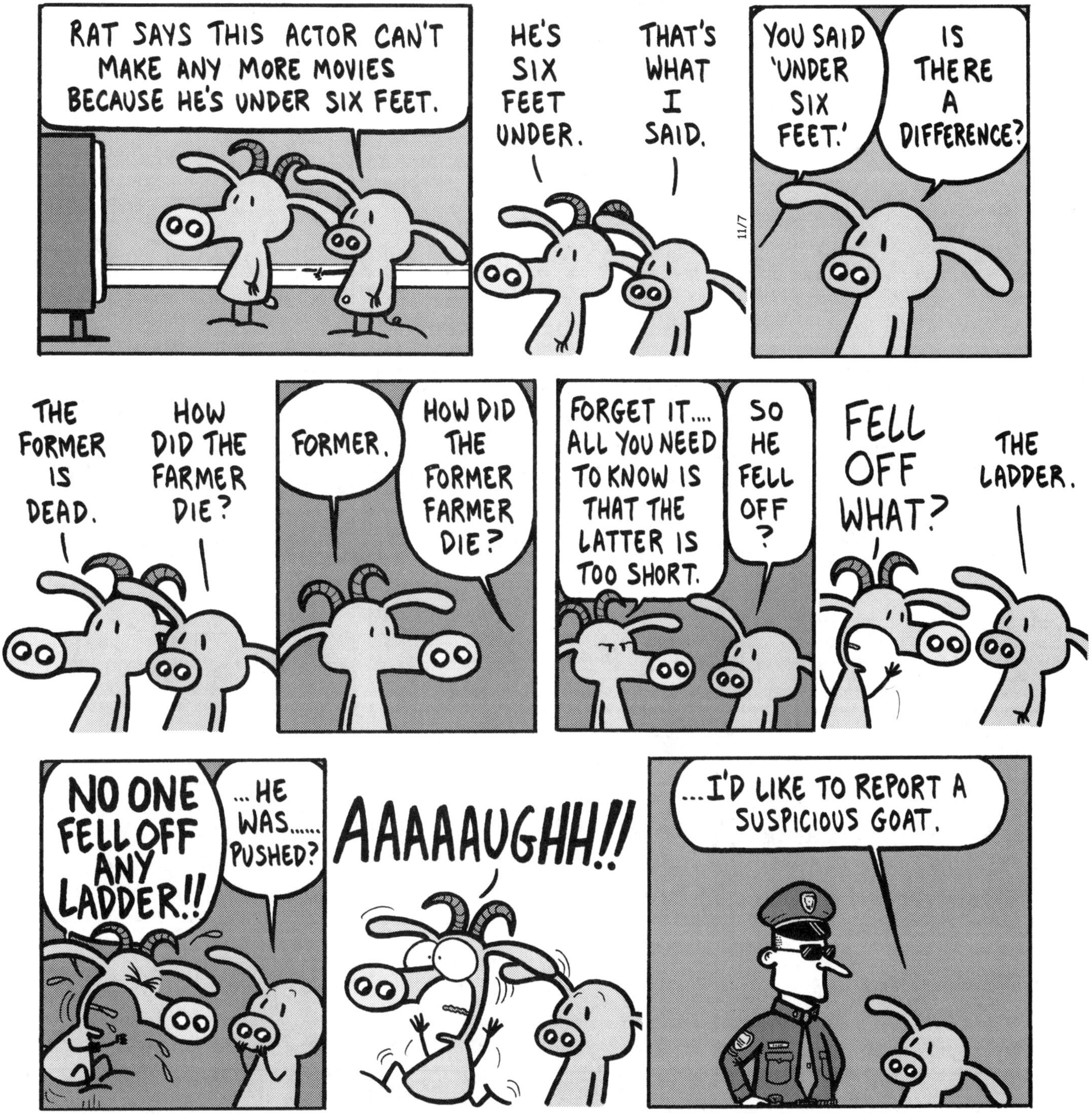
RAT SAYS THIS ACTOR CAN'T MAKE ANY MORE MOVIES BECAUSE HE'S UNDER SIX FEET.
HE'S SIX FEET UNDER.
THAT'S WHAT I SAID.
11/7
YOU SAID 'UNDER SIX FEET.'
IS THERE A DIFFERENCE?
THE FORMER IS DEAD.
HOW DID THE FARMER DIE?
FORMER.
HOW DID THE FORMER FARMER DIE?
FORGET IT.... ALL YOU NEED TO KNOW IS THAT THE LATTER IS TOO SHORT.
SO HE FELL OFF?
FELL OFF WHAT?
THE LADDER.
NO ONE FELL OFF ANY LADDER!!
...HE WAS...... PUSHED?
AAAAAUGHH!!
...I'D LIKE TO REPORT A SUSPICIOUS GOAT.

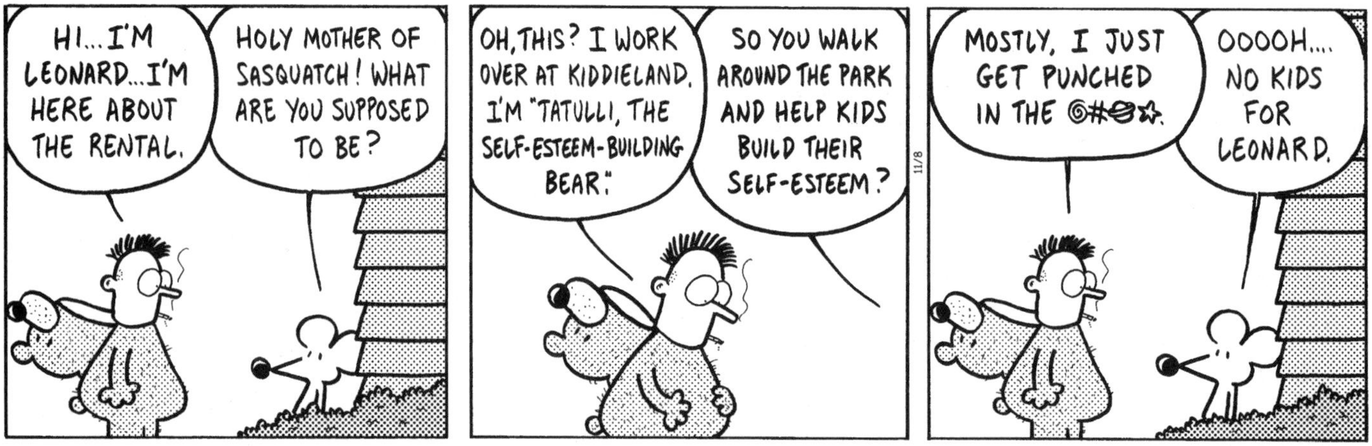
HI... I'M LEONARD... I'M HERE ABOUT THE RENTAL.
HOLY MOTHER OF SASQUATCH! WHAT ARE YOU SUPPOSED TO BE?
OH, THIS? I WORK OVER AT KIDDIELAND. I'M "TATULLI, THE SELF-ESTEEM-BUILDING BEAR."
SO YOU WALK AROUND THE PARK AND HELP KIDS BUILD THEIR SELF-ESTEEM?
11/8
MOSTLY, I JUST GET PUNCHED IN THE
OOOOH.... NO KIDS FOR LEONARD.

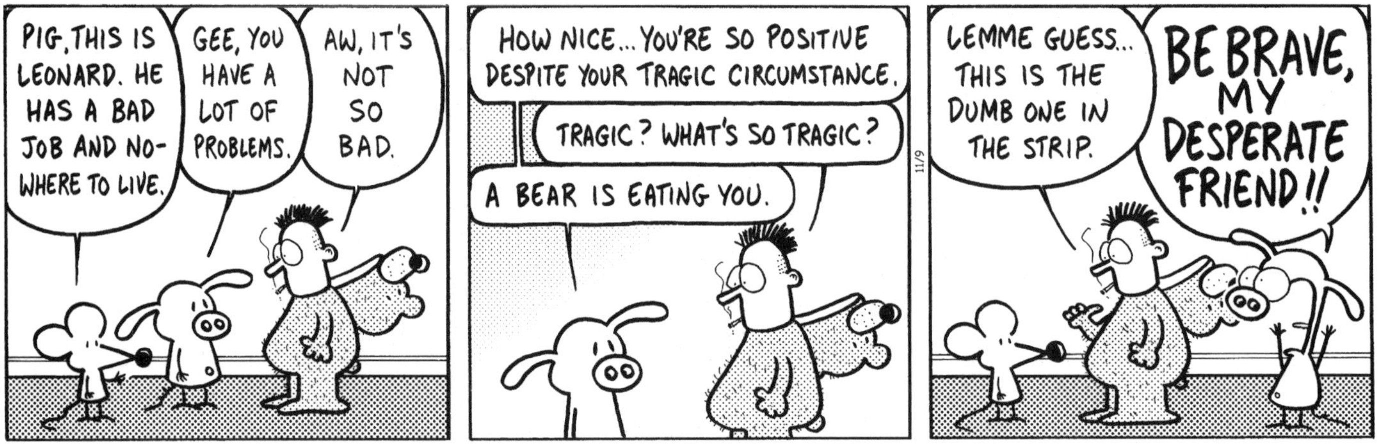
PIG, THIS IS LEONARD. HE HAS A BAD JOB AND NO-WHERE TO LIVE.
GEE, YOU HAVE A LOT OF PROBLEMS.
AW, IT'S NOT SO BAD.
HOW NICE... YOU'RE SO POSITIVE DESPITE YOUR TRAGIC CIRCUMSTANCE.
TRAGIC? WHAT'S SO TRAGIC?
A BEAR IS EATING YOU.
11/9
LEMME GUESS... THIS IS THE DUMB ONE IN THE STRIP.
BE BRAVE, MY DESPERATE FRIEND!!

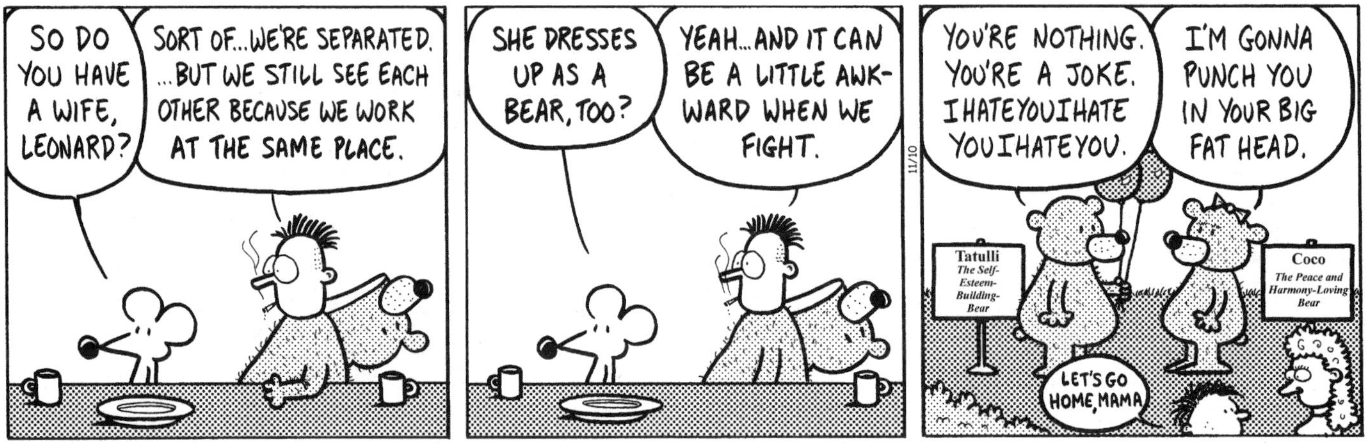
SO DO YOU HAVE A WIFE, LEONARD?
SORT OF... WE'RE SEPARATED. ...BUT WE STILL SEE EACH OTHER BECAUSE WE WORK AT THE SAME PLACE.
SHE DRESSES UP AS A BEAR, TOO?
YEAH... AND IT CAN BE A LITTLE AWK-WARD WHEN WE FIGHT.
11/10
YOU'RE NOTHING. YOU'RE A JOKE. I HATE YOU I HATE YOU I HATE YOU.
I'M GONNA PUNCH YOU IN YOUR BIG FAT HEAD.
Tatulli The Self-Esteem-Building Bear
Coco The Peace and Harmony-Loving Bear
LET'S GO HOME, MAMA

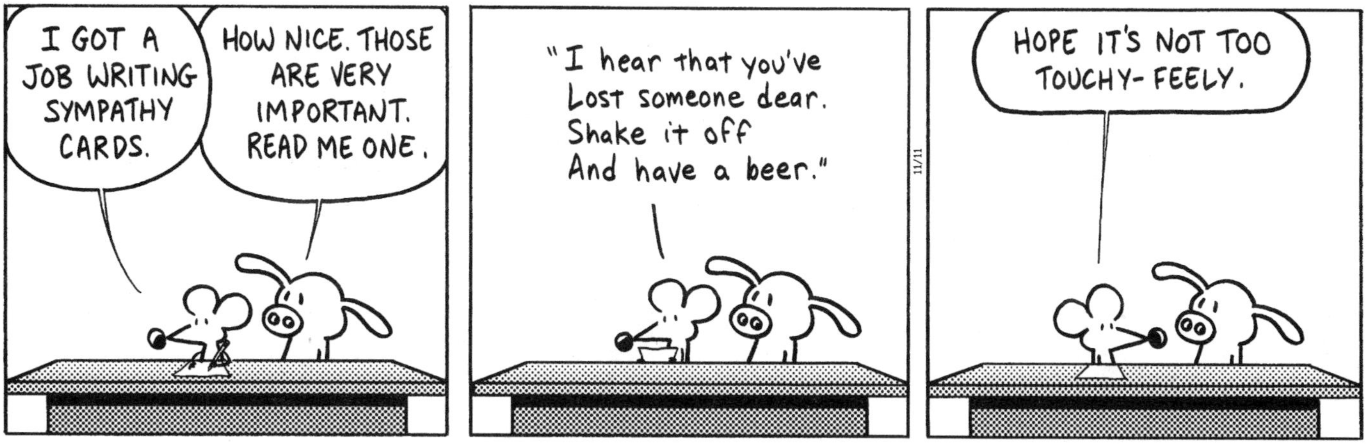
I GOT A JOB WRITING SYMPATHY CARDS.
HOW NICE. THOSE ARE VERY IMPORTANT. READ ME ONE.
"I hear that you've
Lost someone dear.
Shake it off
And have a beer."
11/11
HOPE IT'S NOT TOO TOUCHY-FEELY.

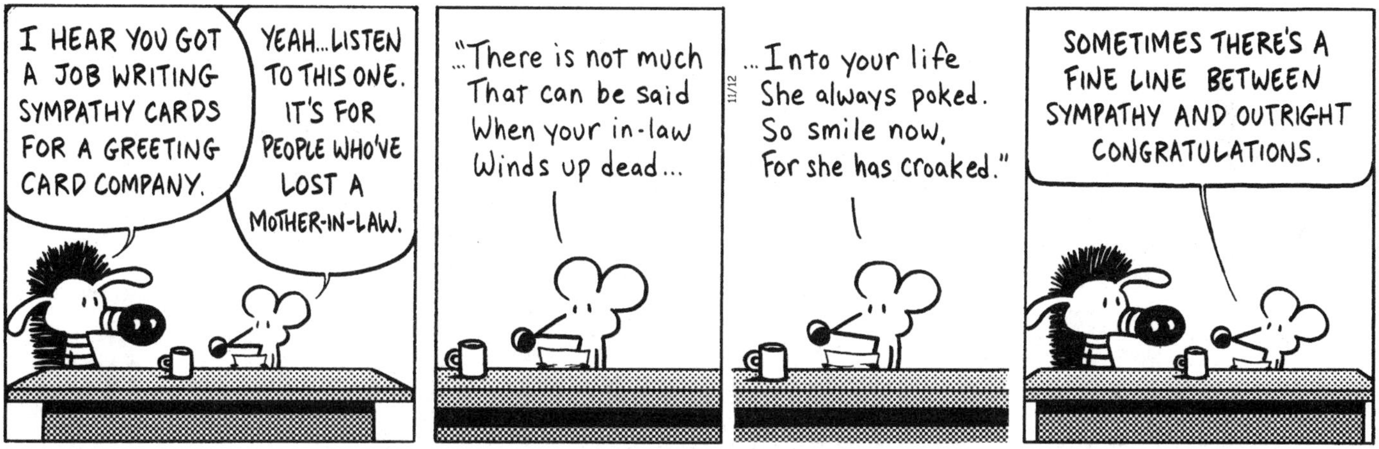
I HEAR YOU GOT A JOB WRITING SYMPATHY CARDS FOR A GREETING CARD COMPANY.
YEAH...LISTEN TO THIS ONE. IT'S FOR PEOPLE WHO'VE LOST A MOTHER-IN-LAW.
..."There is not much
That can be said
When your in-law
Winds up dead...
11/12
...Into your life
She always poked.
So smile now,
For she has croaked."
SOMETIMES THERE'S A FINE LINE BETWEEN SYMPATHY AND OUTRIGHT CONGRATULATIONS.

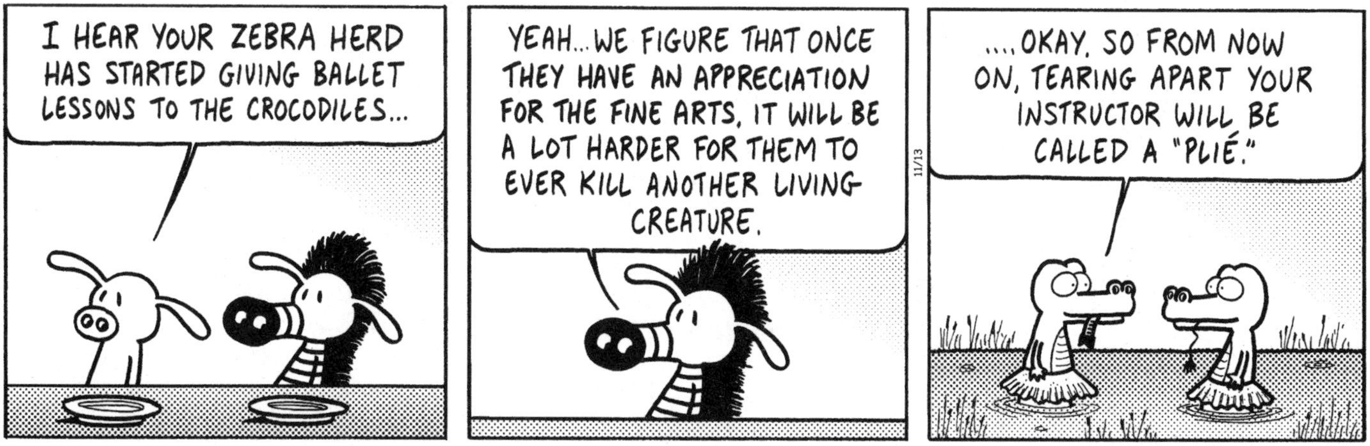
I HEAR YOUR ZEBRA HERD HAS STARTED GIVING BALLET LESSONS TO THE CROCODILES...
YEAH...WE FIGURE THAT ONCE THEY HAVE AN APPRECIATION FOR THE FINE ARTS, IT WILL BE A LOT HARDER FOR THEM TO EVER KILL ANOTHER LIVING CREATURE.
11/13
....OKAY, SO FROM NOW ON, TEARING APART YOUR INSTRUCTOR WILL BE CALLED A "PLIÉ."

HEY, THERE, RAT...WANT TO PLAY SOME INDOOR FOOTBALL?

ARE YOU INSANE? IT'S SUNDAY, YOU MORON.

WHAT'S THAT GOT TO DO WITH ANYTHING?

11/14

DUDE, ON SUNDAY, OUR STRIP APPEARS IN COLOR...THAT COLOR FILE HAS TO BE PLACED VERY CAREFULLY OVER THE BLACK AND WHITE LINEART, SO ALL THE COLORS ARE IN EXACTLY THE RIGHT PLACE...

HOW DOES FOOTBALL AFFECT THAT?

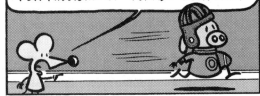

HOW?? DUDE, IF YOU RUN INTO ONE OF THE WALLS, YOU COULD JAR ALL THE LINEART OUT OF ALIGNMENT, THROWING OFF THE PRINT REGISTRATION FOR MILLIONS OF 'PEARLS' READERS.

PRINT REGISWHUUUUUU?

WHAM

...REGISTRATION.

1EEEEEEEY...LOVE WHAT YOU DID WITH THE PLACE...

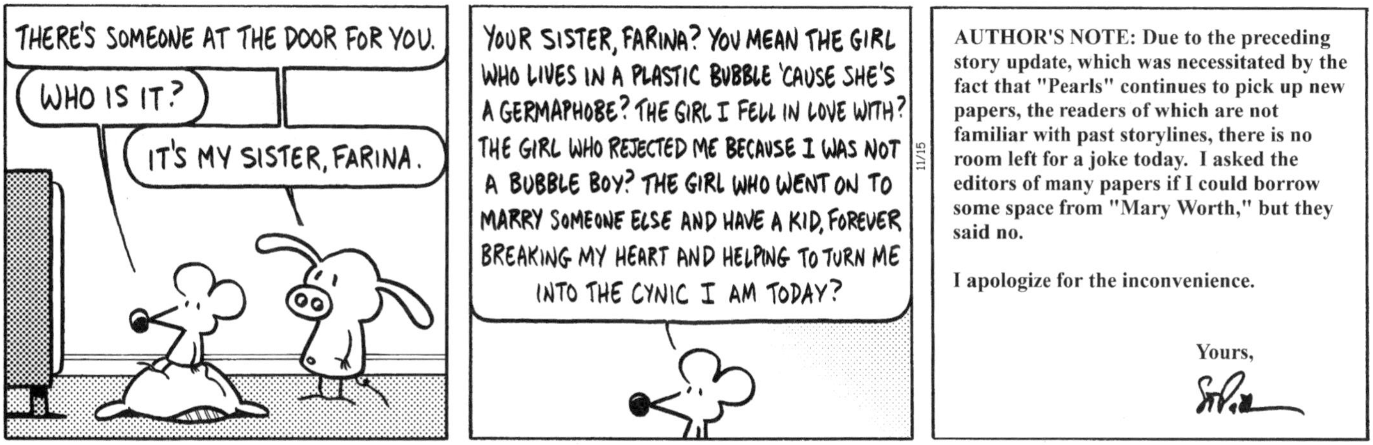
THERE'S SOMEONE AT THE DOOR FOR YOU.
WHO IS IT?
IT'S MY SISTER, FARINA.
YOUR SISTER, FARINA? YOU MEAN THE GIRL WHO LIVES IN A PLASTIC BUBBLE 'CAUSE SHE'S A GERMAPHOBE? THE GIRL I FELL IN LOVE WITH? THE GIRL WHO REJECTED ME BECAUSE I WAS NOT A BUBBLE BOY? THE GIRL WHO WENT ON TO MARRY SOMEONE ELSE AND HAVE A KID, FOREVER BREAKING MY HEART AND HELPING TO TURN ME INTO THE CYNIC I AM TODAY?
11/15
AUTHOR'S NOTE: Due to the preceding story update, which was necessitated by the fact that "Pearls" continues to pick up new papers, the readers of which are not familiar with past storylines, there is no room left for a joke today. I asked the editors of many papers if I could borrow some space from "Mary Worth," but they said no.
I apologize for the inconvenience.
Yours,

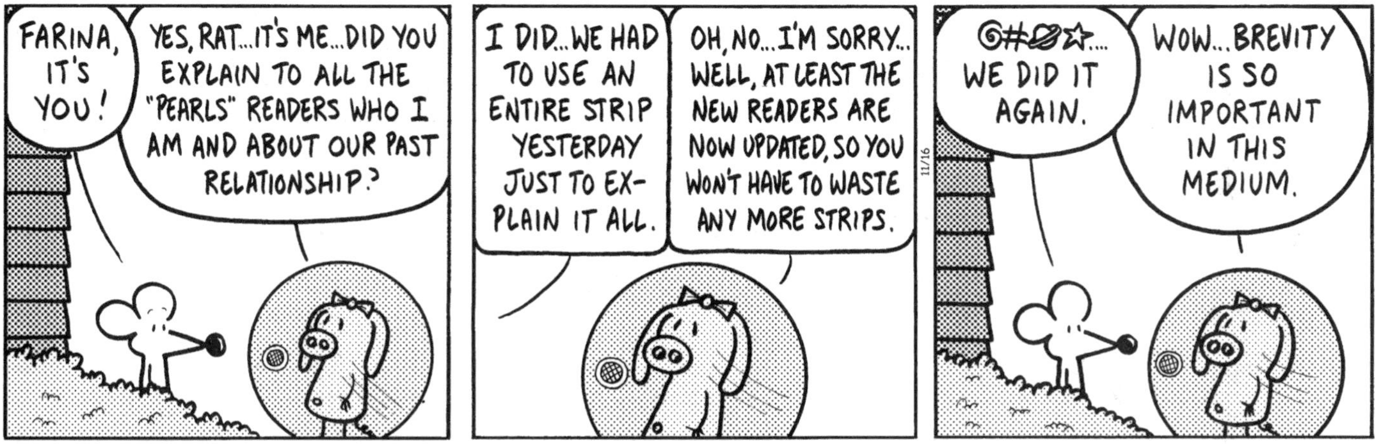
FARINA, IT'S YOU!
YES, RAT...IT'S ME...DID YOU EXPLAIN TO ALL THE "PEARLS" READERS WHO I AM AND ABOUT OUR PAST RELATIONSHIP?
I DID...WE HAD TO USE AN ENTIRE STRIP YESTERDAY JUST TO EXPLAIN IT ALL.
OH, NO...I'M SORRY...WELL, AT LEAST THE NEW READERS ARE NOW UPDATED, SO YOU WON'T HAVE TO WASTE ANY MORE STRIPS.
11/16
@#Ø☆.... WE DID IT AGAIN.
WOW...BREVITY IS SO IMPORTANT IN THIS MEDIUM.

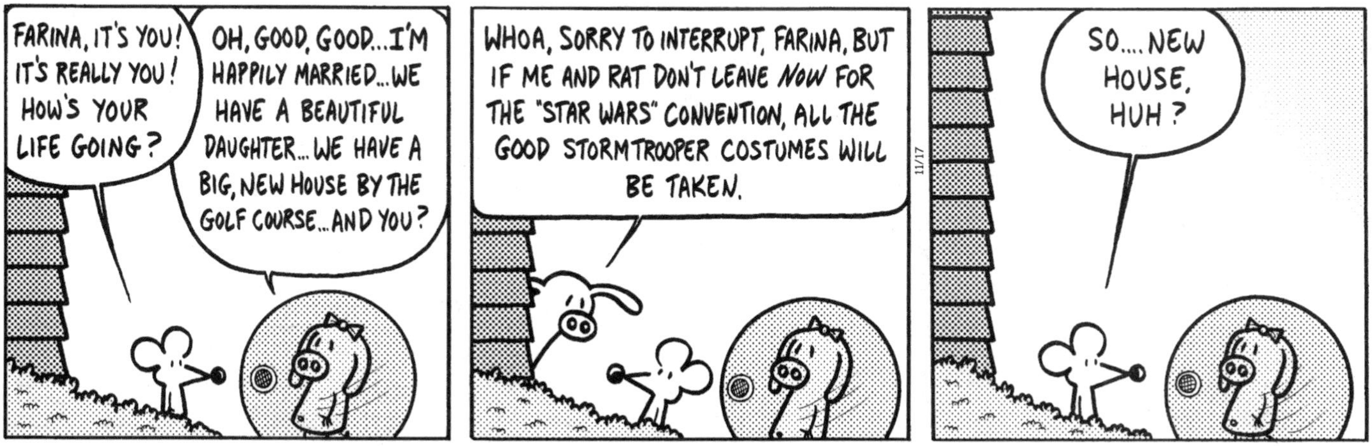
FARINA, IT'S YOU! IT'S REALLY YOU! HOW'S YOUR LIFE GOING?
OH, GOOD, GOOD...I'M HAPPILY MARRIED...WE HAVE A BEAUTIFUL DAUGHTER...WE HAVE A BIG, NEW HOUSE BY THE GOLF COURSE...AND YOU?
WHOA, SORRY TO INTERRUPT, FARINA, BUT IF ME AND RAT DON'T LEAVE *NOW* FOR THE "STAR WARS" CONVENTION, ALL THE GOOD STORMTROOPER COSTUMES WILL BE TAKEN.
11/17
SO.... NEW HOUSE, HUH?

Panel 1:
SO YOU'RE DOING OKAY, RAT?

OH, YES... IN FACT, SINCE WE BROKE UP, I'VE REALLY MATURED AND GROWN INTELLECTUALLY, MOSTLY BY ASSOCIATING MYSELF WITH A HIGHER CLASS OF PEOPLE.

Panel 2:
HEY, DUDE...THE JOHN'S CLOGGED... YA GOT A HANGER? OR SHOULD I ASK PIG?

11/18

Panel 3:
...AND HOW ARE YOU DOING?

DUDE DUDE STOP! YOU'RE FLUSHING MY G#@#G#☆ PAW DOWN THE CAN!!

Panel 4:
SO WHAT BRINGS YOU HERE, FARINA?...IT'S NOT OFTEN THAT THE GIRL WHO BROKE YOUR HEART AND LEFT YOU FOR ANOTHER GUY COMES BACK TO SEE YOU.

Panel 5:
WELL, MY HUSBAND AND I WERE WONDERING IF YOU COULD BABYSIT OUR DAUGHTER WHILE WE GO ON A TWO-WEEK ROMANTIC GETAWAY TO THE BAHAMAS.

AAAAAAHH

11/19

Panel 6:
...WHY'D YOU JUMP IN THE HEDGES?

LORD?... IS THAT YOU?

Panel 7:
Y'KNOW, THAT GIRL YOU WERE TALKING TO DOES SOME VOLUNTEER WORK WITH KIDDIELAND...SHE AND MY EX-WIFE ARE FRIENDS...

Panel 8:
MY EX AND YOUR EX ARE FRIENDS?? DON'T YOU REALIZE WHAT THIS MEANS? GIRLS TELL EACH OTHER *EVERYTHING* ABOUT THEIR BOYFRIENDS AND HUSBANDS!

OHH....DON'T WORRY...

11/20

Panel 9:
....ALTHOUGH I DO FIND IT ODD YOU USED TO CRY IN HER ARMS AFTER MAKING OUT.

AAAAAAAHHH!!!

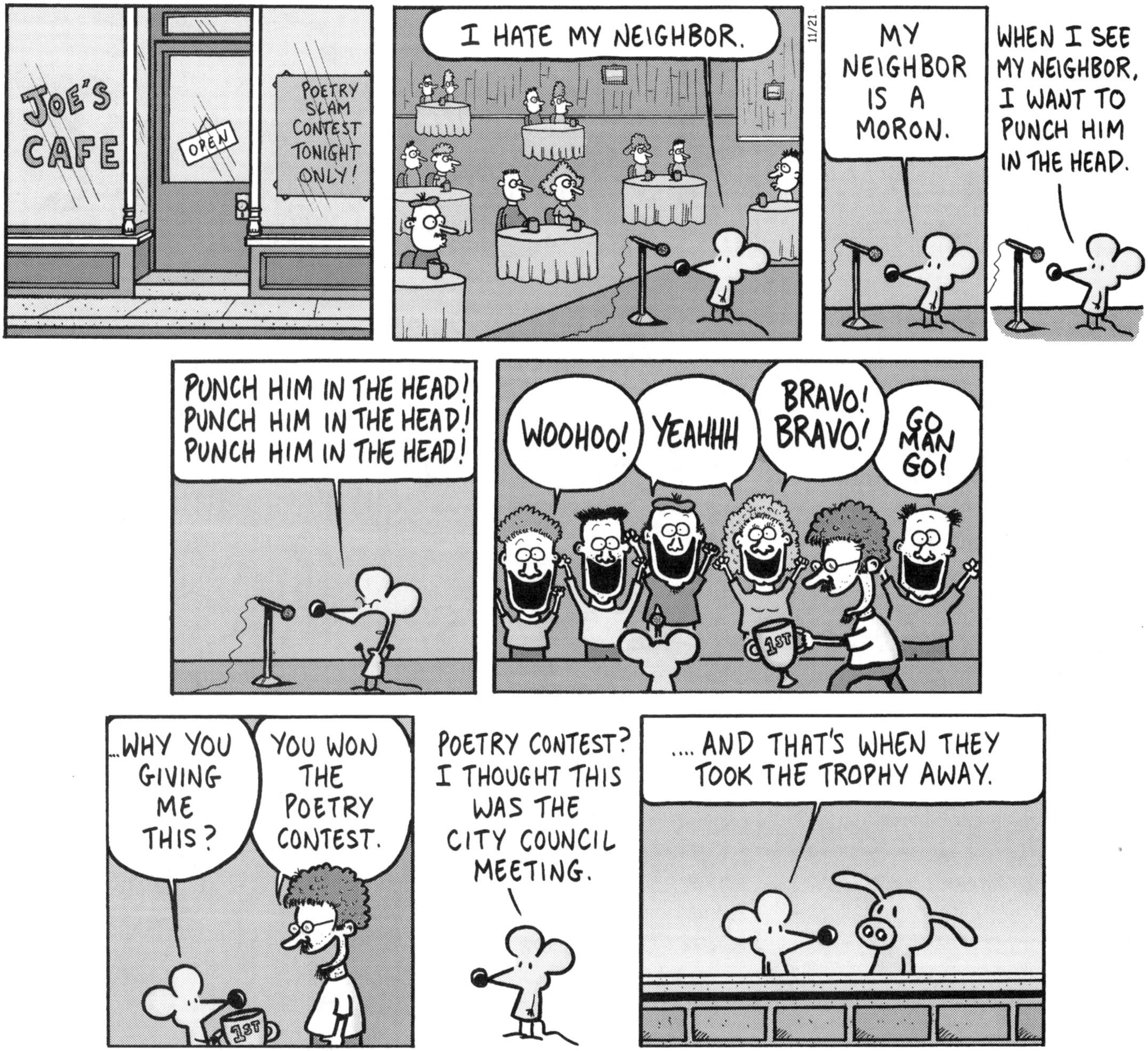
JOE'S CAFE
OPEN
POETRY SLAM CONTEST TONIGHT ONLY!
I HATE MY NEIGHBOR.
11/21
MY NEIGHBOR IS A MORON.
WHEN I SEE MY NEIGHBOR, I WANT TO PUNCH HIM IN THE HEAD.
PUNCH HIM IN THE HEAD! PUNCH HIM IN THE HEAD! PUNCH HIM IN THE HEAD!
WOOHOO!
YEAHHH
BRAVO! BRAVO!
GO MAN GO!
1ST
...WHY YOU GIVING ME THIS?
YOU WON THE POETRY CONTEST.
1ST
POETRY CONTEST? I THOUGHT THIS WAS THE CITY COUNCIL MEETING.
.... AND THAT'S WHEN THEY TOOK THE TROPHY AWAY.

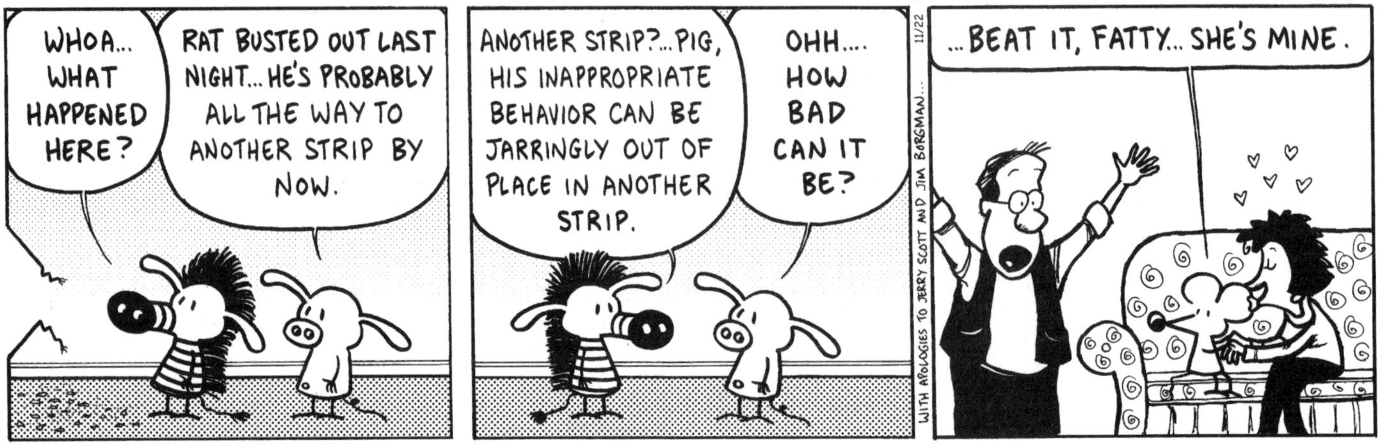
WHOA... WHAT HAPPENED HERE?
RAT BUSTED OUT LAST NIGHT... HE'S PROBABLY ALL THE WAY TO ANOTHER STRIP BY NOW.
ANOTHER STRIP?... PIG, HIS INAPPROPRIATE BEHAVIOR CAN BE JARRINGLY OUT OF PLACE IN ANOTHER STRIP.
OHH.... HOW BAD CAN IT BE?
11/22
WITH APOLOGIES TO JERRY SCOTT AND JIM BORGMAN...
...BEAT IT, FATTY... SHE'S MINE.

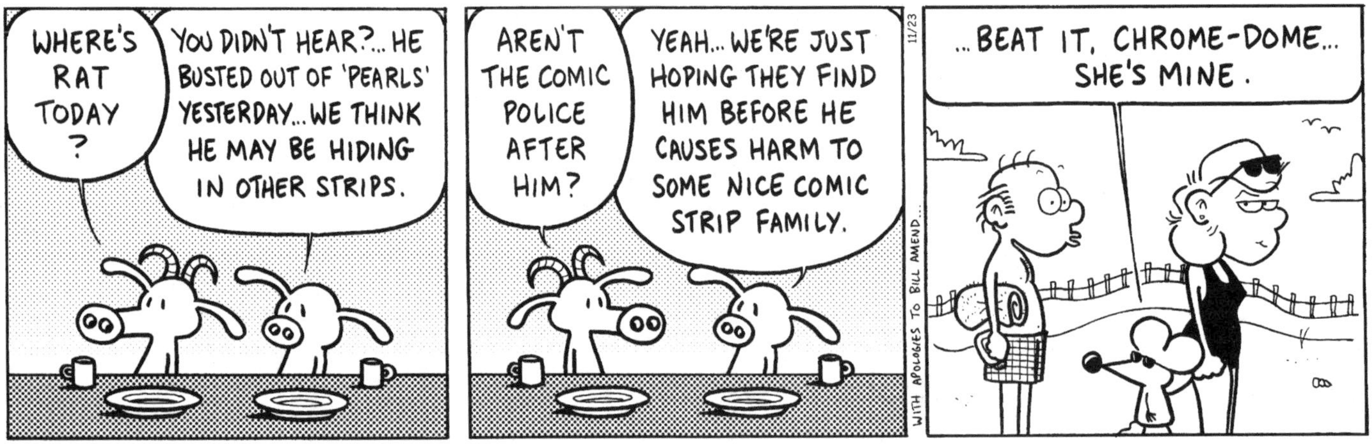
WHERE'S RAT TODAY?
YOU DIDN'T HEAR?... HE BUSTED OUT OF 'PEARLS' YESTERDAY... WE THINK HE MAY BE HIDING IN OTHER STRIPS.
AREN'T THE COMIC POLICE AFTER HIM?
YEAH... WE'RE JUST HOPING THEY FIND HIM BEFORE HE CAUSES HARM TO SOME NICE COMIC STRIP FAMILY.
11/23
WITH APOLOGIES TO BILL AMEND...
...BEAT IT, CHROME-DOME... SHE'S MINE.

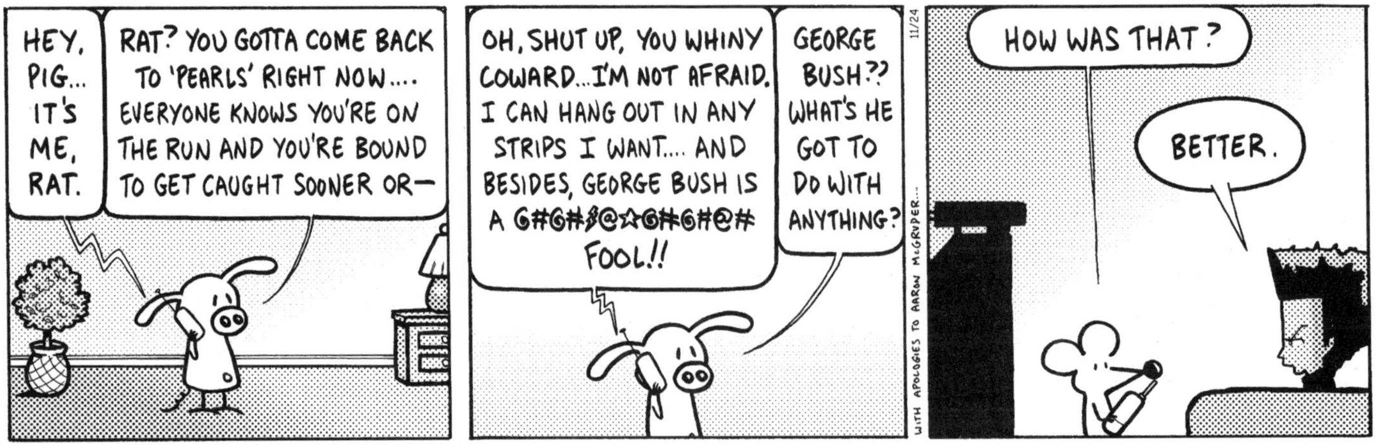
HEY, PIG... IT'S ME, RAT.
RAT? YOU GOTTA COME BACK TO 'PEARLS' RIGHT NOW.... EVERYONE KNOWS YOU'RE ON THE RUN AND YOU'RE BOUND TO GET CAUGHT SOONER OR—
OH, SHUT UP, YOU WHINY COWARD... I'M NOT AFRAID. I CAN HANG OUT IN ANY STRIPS I WANT.... AND BESIDES, GEORGE BUSH IS A G#G#$@☆G#G#@# FOOL!!
GEORGE BUSH?? WHAT'S HE GOT TO DO WITH ANYTHING?
11/24
WITH APOLOGIES TO AARON MCGRUDER...
HOW WAS THAT?
BETTER.

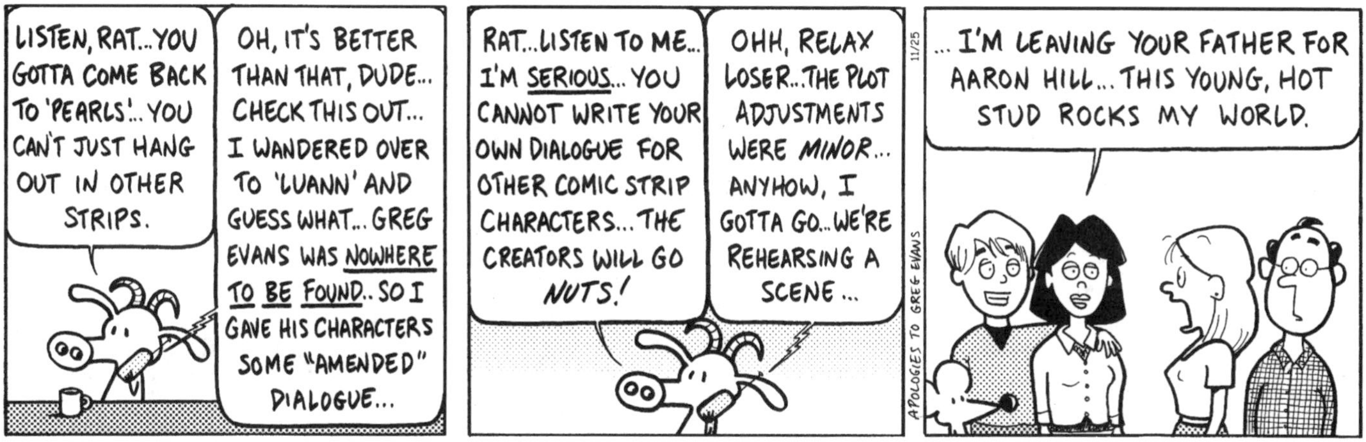
LISTEN, RAT...YOU GOTTA COME BACK TO 'PEARLS'...YOU CAN'T JUST HANG OUT IN OTHER STRIPS.
OH, IT'S BETTER THAN THAT, DUDE... CHECK THIS OUT... I WANDERED OVER TO 'LUANN' AND GUESS WHAT... GREG EVANS WAS NOWHERE TO BE FOUND.. SO I GAVE HIS CHARACTERS SOME "AMENDED" DIALOGUE...
RAT...LISTEN TO ME... I'M SERIOUS... YOU CANNOT WRITE YOUR OWN DIALOGUE FOR OTHER COMIC STRIP CHARACTERS... THE CREATORS WILL GO NUTS!
OHH, RELAX LOSER...THE PLOT ADJUSTMENTS WERE MINOR... ANYHOW, I GOTTA GO...WE'RE REHEARSING A SCENE...
11/25
APOLOGIES TO GREG EVANS
... I'M LEAVING YOUR FATHER FOR AARON HILL... THIS YOUNG, HOT STUD ROCKS MY WORLD.

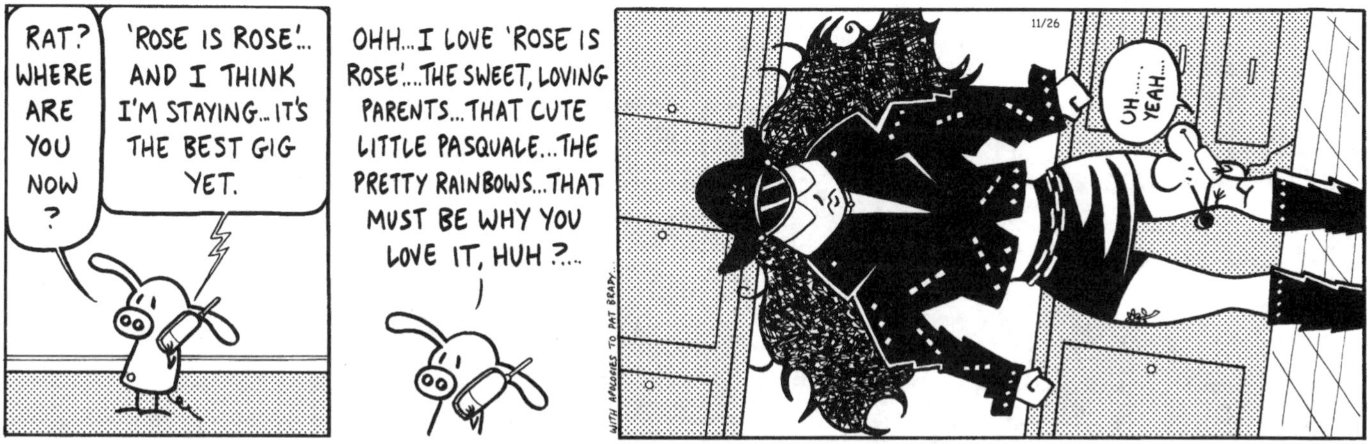
RAT? WHERE ARE YOU NOW ?
'ROSE IS ROSE'... AND I THINK I'M STAYING.. IT'S THE BEST GIG YET.
OHH...I LOVE 'ROSE IS ROSE'...THE SWEET, LOVING PARENTS...THAT CUTE LITTLE PASQUALE...THE PRETTY RAINBOWS...THAT MUST BE WHY YOU LOVE IT, HUH ?...
WITH APOLOGIES TO PAT BRADY
11/26
OH...... YEAH...

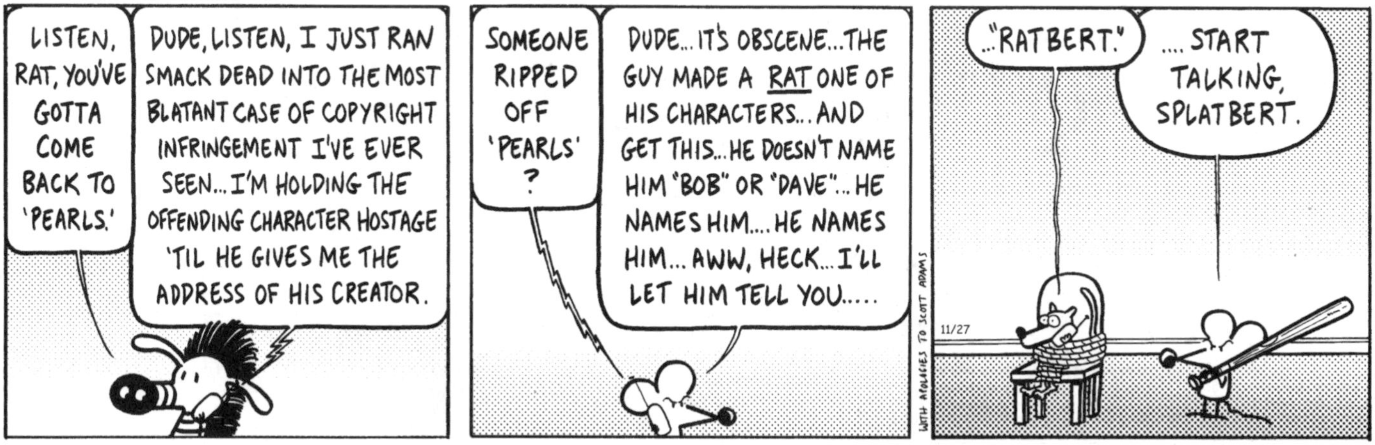
LISTEN, RAT, YOU'VE GOTTA COME BACK TO 'PEARLS.'
DUDE, LISTEN, I JUST RAN SMACK DEAD INTO THE MOST BLATANT CASE OF COPYRIGHT INFRINGEMENT I'VE EVER SEEN...I'M HOLDING THE OFFENDING CHARACTER HOSTAGE 'TIL HE GIVES ME THE ADDRESS OF HIS CREATOR.
SOMEONE RIPPED OFF 'PEARLS' ?
DUDE... IT'S OBSCENE...THE GUY MADE A RAT ONE OF HIS CHARACTERS... AND GET THIS...HE DOESN'T NAME HIM "BOB" OR "DAVE"... HE NAMES HIM.... HE NAMES HIM... AWW, HECK... I'LL LET HIM TELL YOU.....
WITH APOLOGIES TO SCOTT ADAMS
11/27
..."RATBERT."
.... START TALKING, SPLATBERT.

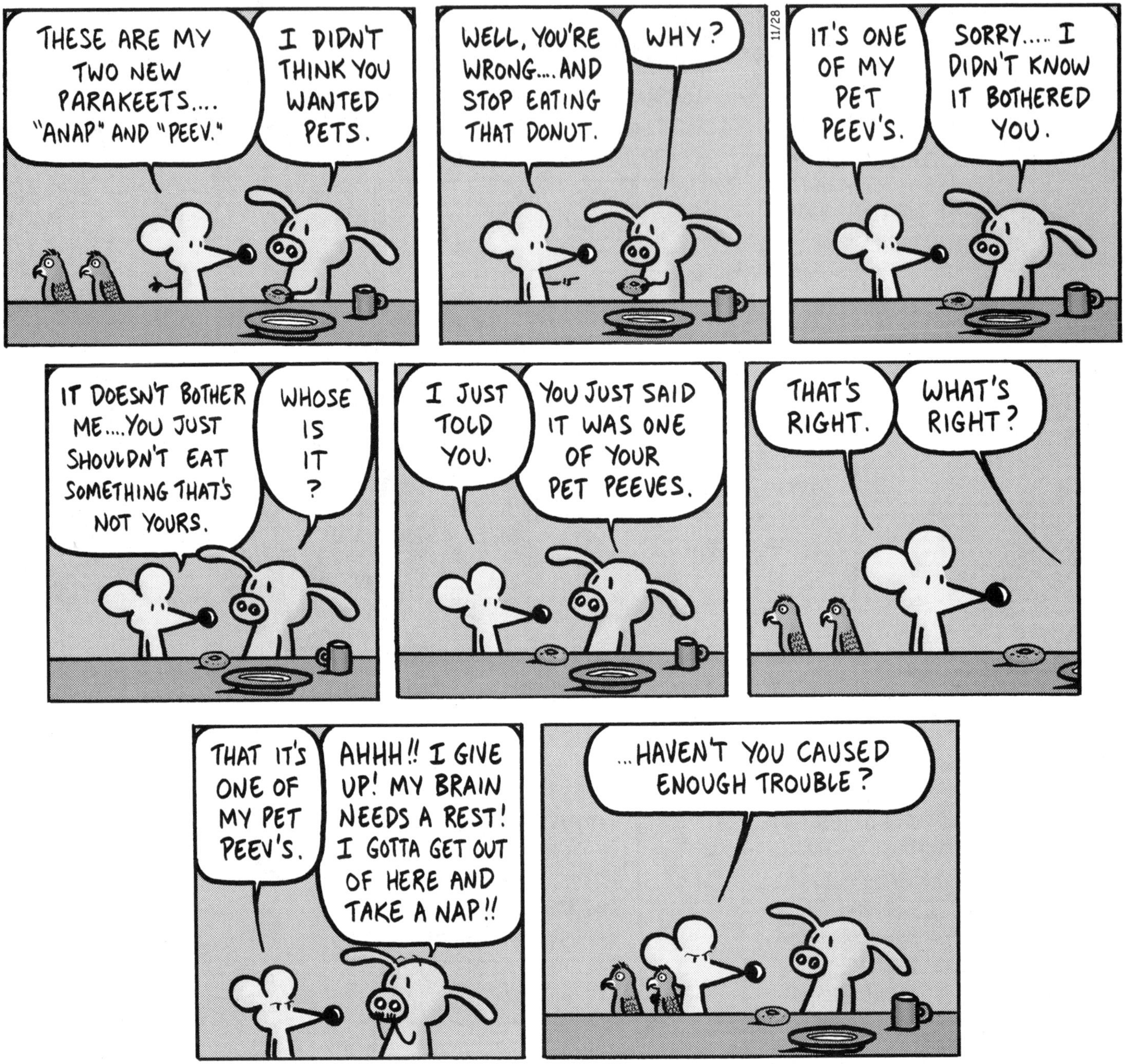
THESE ARE MY TWO NEW PARAKEETS.... "ANAP" AND "PEEV."
I DIDN'T THINK YOU WANTED PETS.
WELL, YOU'RE WRONG.... AND STOP EATING THAT DONUT.
WHY?
11/28
IT'S ONE OF MY PET PEEV'S.
SORRY..... I DIDN'T KNOW IT BOTHERED YOU.
IT DOESN'T BOTHER ME.... YOU JUST SHOULDN'T EAT SOMETHING THAT'S NOT YOURS.
WHOSE IS IT?
I JUST TOLD YOU.
YOU JUST SAID IT WAS ONE OF YOUR PET PEEVES.
THAT'S RIGHT.
WHAT'S RIGHT?
THAT IT'S ONE OF MY PET PEEV'S.
AHHH!! I GIVE UP! MY BRAIN NEEDS A REST! I GOTTA GET OUT OF HERE AND TAKE A NAP!!
...HAVEN'T YOU CAUSED ENOUGH TROUBLE?

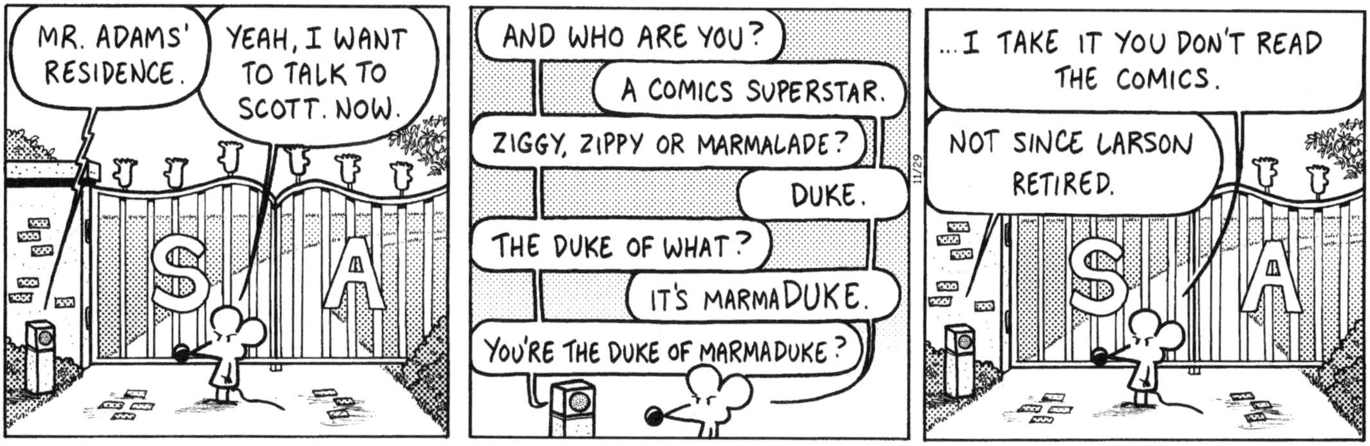
MR. ADAMS' RESIDENCE.
YEAH, I WANT TO TALK TO SCOTT. NOW.
AND WHO ARE YOU?
A COMICS SUPERSTAR.
ZIGGY, ZIPPY OR MARMALADE?
DUKE.
THE DUKE OF WHAT?
IT'S MARMADUKE.
YOU'RE THE DUKE OF MARMADUKE?
11/29
...I TAKE IT YOU DON'T READ THE COMICS.
NOT SINCE LARSON RETIRED.

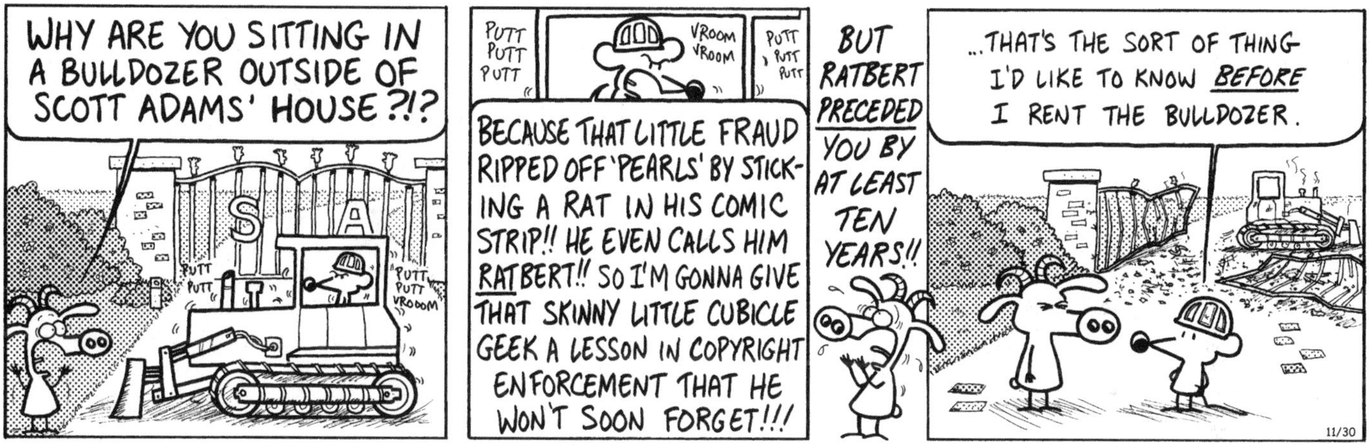
WHY ARE YOU SITTING IN A BULLDOZER OUTSIDE OF SCOTT ADAMS' HOUSE?!?
PUTT PUTT
PUTT PUTT VROOOM
PUTT PUTT PUTT
VROOM VROOM
PUTT PUTT PUTT
BECAUSE THAT LITTLE FRAUD RIPPED OFF 'PEARLS' BY STICKING A RAT IN HIS COMIC STRIP!! HE EVEN CALLS HIM RATBERT!! SO I'M GONNA GIVE THAT SKINNY LITTLE CUBICLE GEEK A LESSON IN COPYRIGHT ENFORCEMENT THAT HE WON'T SOON FORGET!!!
BUT RATBERT PRECEDED YOU BY AT LEAST TEN YEARS!!
...THAT'S THE SORT OF THING I'D LIKE TO KNOW BEFORE I RENT THE BULLDOZER.
11/30

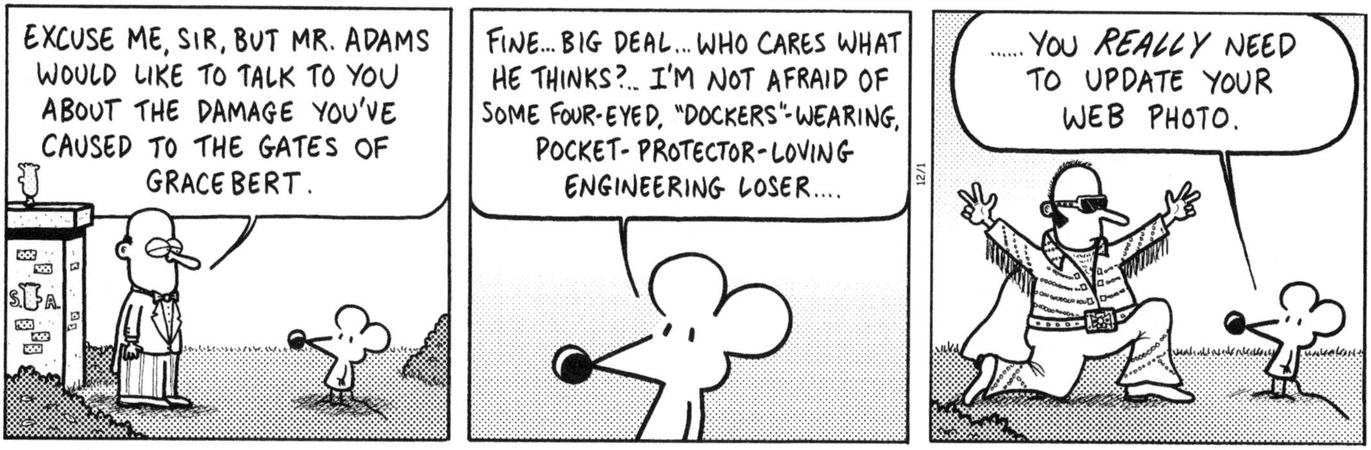
EXCUSE ME, SIR, BUT MR. ADAMS WOULD LIKE TO TALK TO YOU ABOUT THE DAMAGE YOU'VE CAUSED TO THE GATES OF GRACEBERT.
FINE... BIG DEAL... WHO CARES WHAT HE THINKS?.. I'M NOT AFRAID OF SOME FOUR-EYED, "DOCKERS"-WEARING, POCKET-PROTECTOR-LOVING ENGINEERING LOSER....
12/1
......YOU REALLY NEED TO UPDATE YOUR WEB PHOTO.

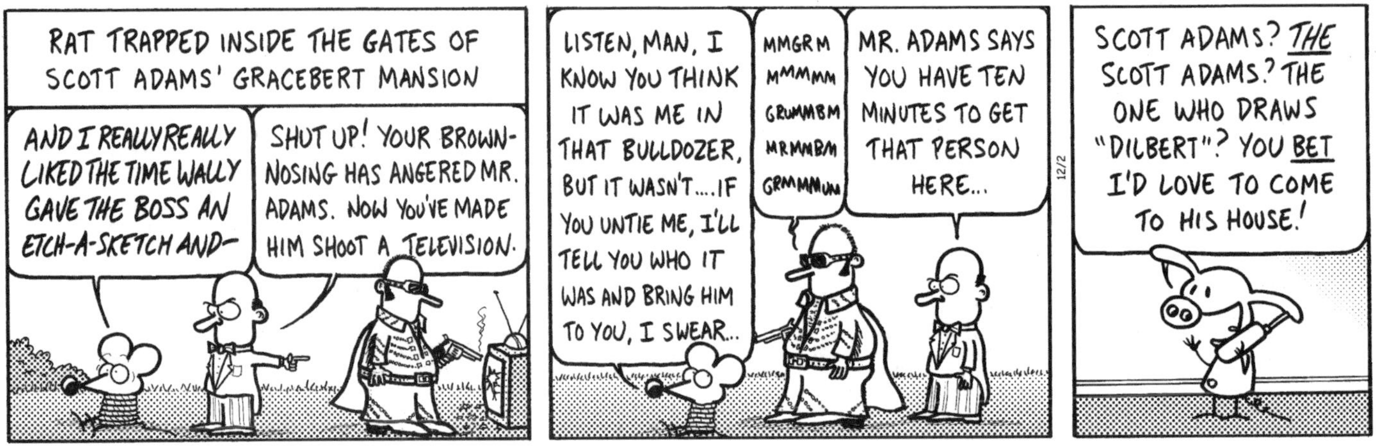
RAT TRAPPED INSIDE THE GATES OF SCOTT ADAMS' GRACEBERT MANSION
AND I REALLY REALLY LIKED THE TIME WALLY GAVE THE BOSS AN ETCH-A-SKETCH AND-
SHUT UP! YOUR BROWN-NOSING HAS ANGERED MR. ADAMS. NOW YOU'VE MADE HIM SHOOT A TELEVISION.
LISTEN, MAN, I KNOW YOU THINK IT WAS ME IN THAT BULLDOZER, BUT IT WASN'T....IF YOU UNTIE ME, I'LL TELL YOU WHO IT WAS AND BRING HIM TO YOU, I SWEAR...
MMGRM MMMMM GRUMMBM MRMMBM GRMMMUM
MR. ADAMS SAYS YOU HAVE TEN MINUTES TO GET THAT PERSON HERE...
12/2
SCOTT ADAMS? THE SCOTT ADAMS? THE ONE WHO DRAWS "DILBERT"? YOU BET I'D LOVE TO COME TO HIS HOUSE!

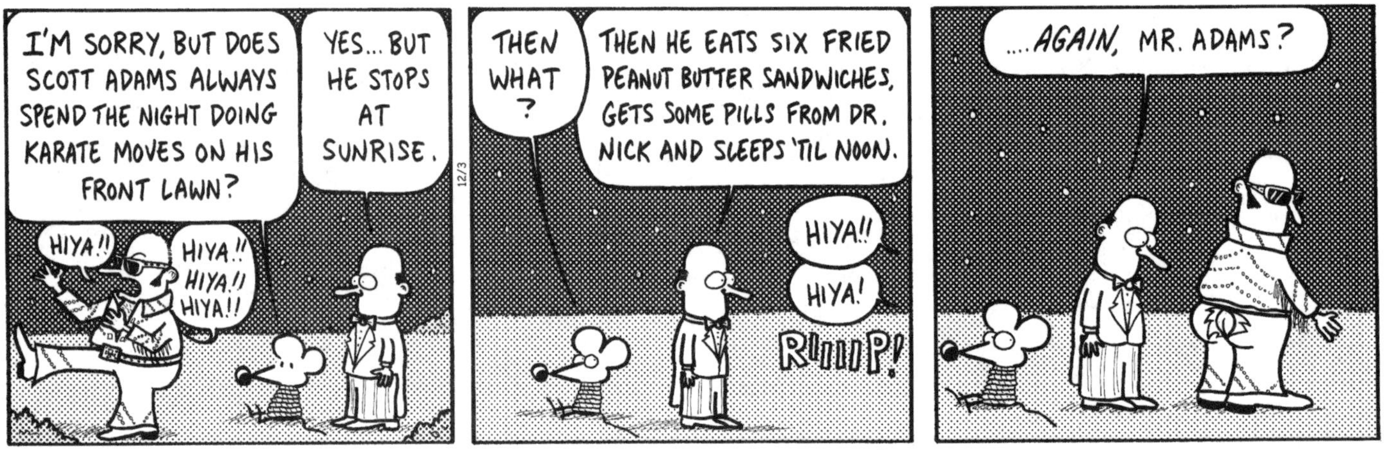
I'M SORRY, BUT DOES SCOTT ADAMS ALWAYS SPEND THE NIGHT DOING KARATE MOVES ON HIS FRONT LAWN?
HIYA!!
HIYA!! HIYA!! HIYA!!
YES... BUT HE STOPS AT SUNRISE.
12/3
THEN WHAT?
THEN HE EATS SIX FRIED PEANUT BUTTER SANDWICHES, GETS SOME PILLS FROM DR. NICK AND SLEEPS 'TIL NOON.
HIYA!!
HIYA!
RIIIIP!
....AGAIN, MR. ADAMS?

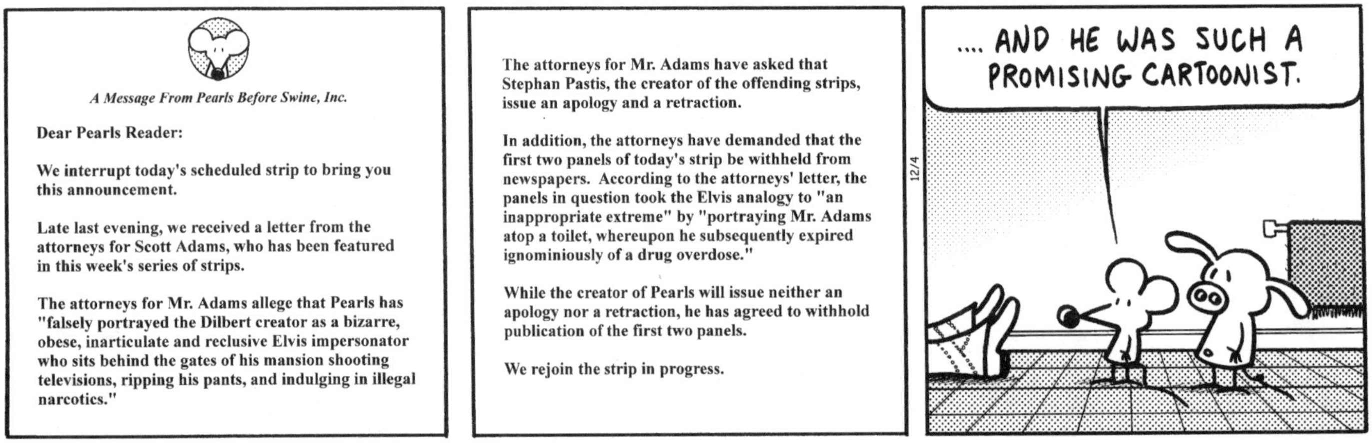
A Message From Pearls Before Swine, Inc.
Dear Pearls Reader:
We interrupt today's scheduled strip to bring you this announcement.
Late last evening, we received a letter from the attorneys for Scott Adams, who has been featured in this week's series of strips.
The attorneys for Mr. Adams allege that Pearls has "falsely portrayed the Dilbert creator as a bizarre, obese, inarticulate and reclusive Elvis impersonator who sits behind the gates of his mansion shooting televisions, ripping his pants, and indulging in illegal narcotics."
The attorneys for Mr. Adams have asked that Stephan Pastis, the creator of the offending strips, issue an apology and a retraction.
In addition, the attorneys have demanded that the first two panels of today's strip be withheld from newspapers. According to the attorneys' letter, the panels in question took the Elvis analogy to "an inappropriate extreme" by "portraying Mr. Adams atop a toilet, whereupon he subsequently expired ignominiously of a drug overdose."
While the creator of Pearls will issue neither an apology nor a retraction, he has agreed to withhold publication of the first two panels.
We rejoin the strip in progress.
12/4
.... AND HE WAS SUCH A PROMISING CARTOONIST.

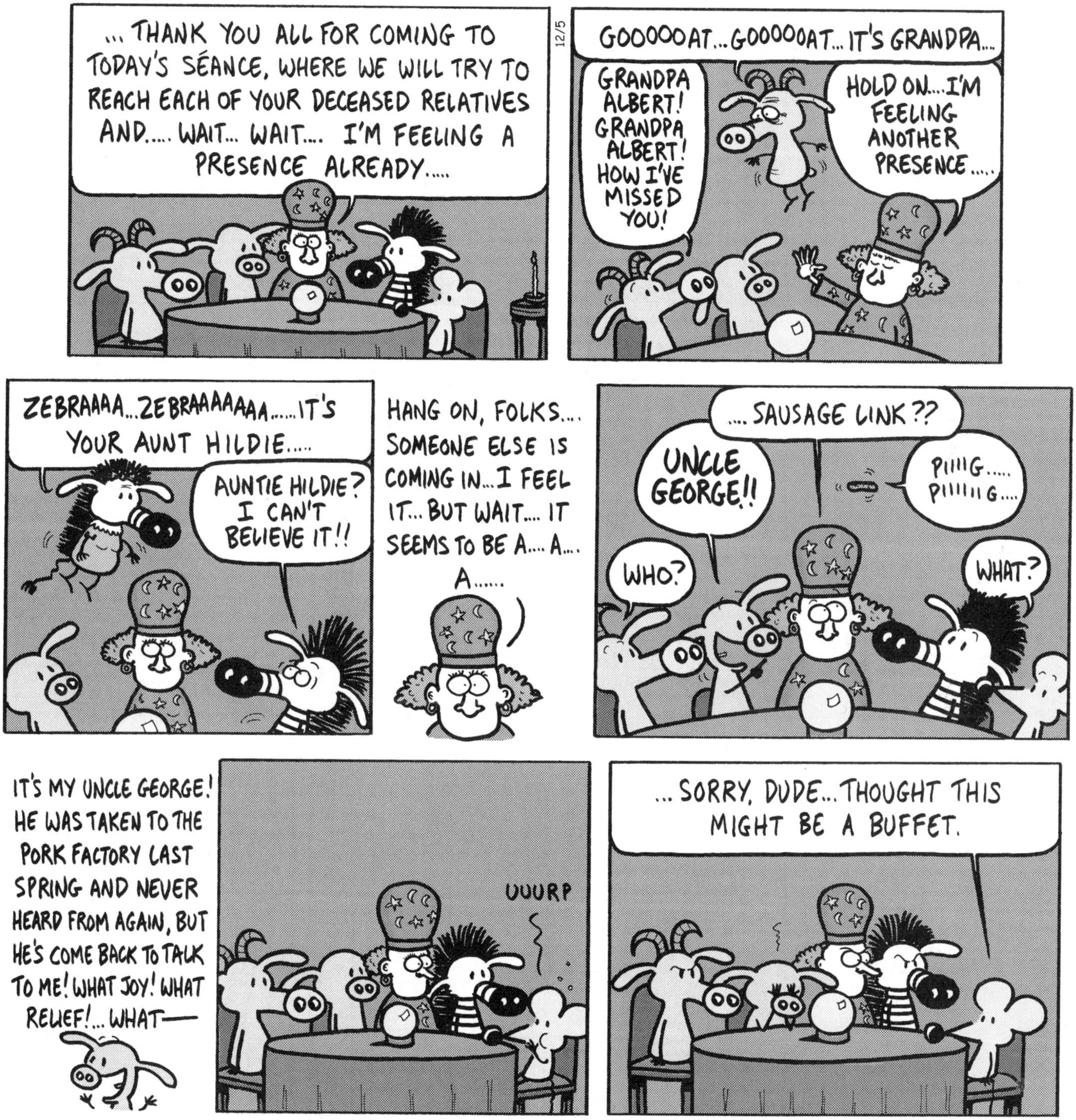
... THANK YOU ALL FOR COMING TO TODAY'S SÉANCE, WHERE WE WILL TRY TO REACH EACH OF YOUR DECEASED RELATIVES AND..... WAIT... WAIT.... I'M FEELING A PRESENCE ALREADY.....
12/5
GOOOOOAT...GOOOOOAT... IT'S GRANDPA....
GRANDPA ALBERT! GRANDPA ALBERT! HOW I'VE MISSED YOU!
HOLD ON....I'M FEELING ANOTHER PRESENCE.....
ZEBRAAAA...ZEBRAAAAAAA......IT'S YOUR AUNT HILDIE.....
AUNTIE HILDIE? I CAN'T BELIEVE IT!!
HANG ON, FOLKS.... SOMEONE ELSE IS COMING IN...I FEEL IT... BUT WAIT.... IT SEEMS TO BE A.... A.... A......
.... SAUSAGE LINK??
UNCLE GEORGE!!
PIIIG..... PIIIIIG....
WHO?
WHAT?
IT'S MY UNCLE GEORGE! HE WAS TAKEN TO THE PORK FACTORY LAST SPRING AND NEVER HEARD FROM AGAIN, BUT HE'S COME BACK TO TALK TO ME! WHAT JOY! WHAT RELIEF!... WHAT—
UUURP
... SORRY, DUDE... THOUGHT THIS MIGHT BE A BUFFET.

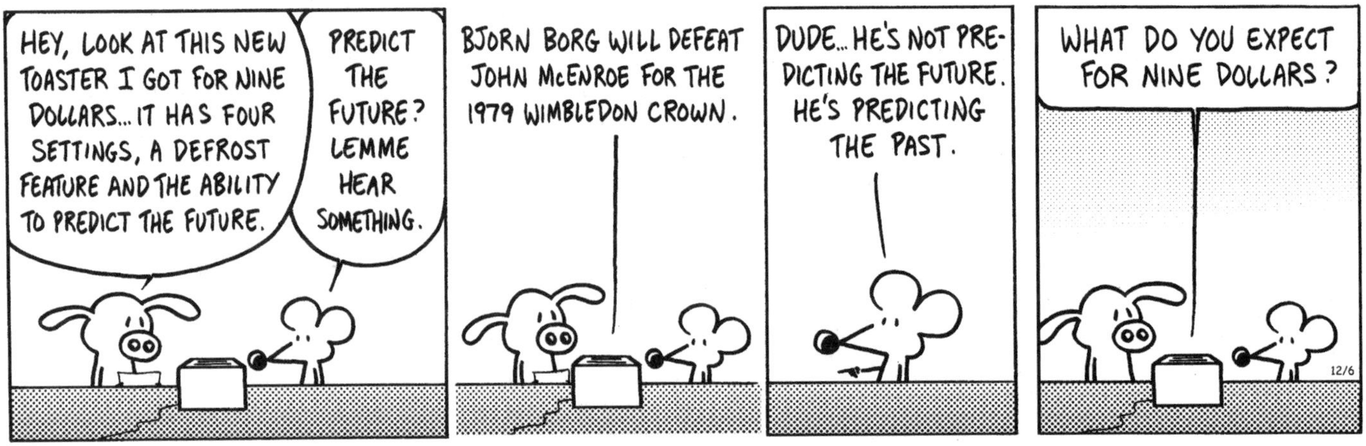
HEY, LOOK AT THIS NEW TOASTER I GOT FOR NINE DOLLARS... IT HAS FOUR SETTINGS, A DEFROST FEATURE AND THE ABILITY TO PREDICT THE FUTURE.
PREDICT THE FUTURE? LEMME HEAR SOMETHING.
BJORN BORG WILL DEFEAT JOHN McENROE FOR THE 1979 WIMBLEDON CROWN.
DUDE... HE'S NOT PREDICTING THE FUTURE. HE'S PREDICTING THE PAST.
WHAT DO YOU EXPECT FOR NINE DOLLARS?
12/6

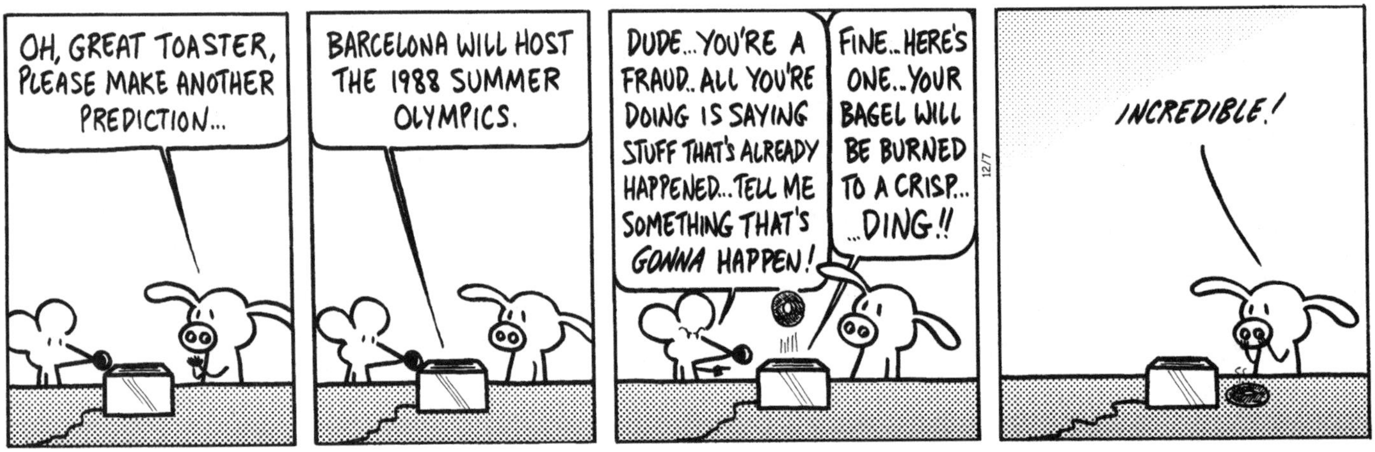
OH, GREAT TOASTER, PLEASE MAKE ANOTHER PREDICTION...
BARCELONA WILL HOST THE 1988 SUMMER OLYMPICS.
DUDE... YOU'RE A FRAUD.. ALL YOU'RE DOING IS SAYING STUFF THAT'S ALREADY HAPPENED... TELL ME SOMETHING THAT'S *GONNA* HAPPEN!
FINE.. HERE'S ONE.. YOUR BAGEL WILL BE BURNED TO A CRISP... ...DING!!
INCREDIBLE!
12/7

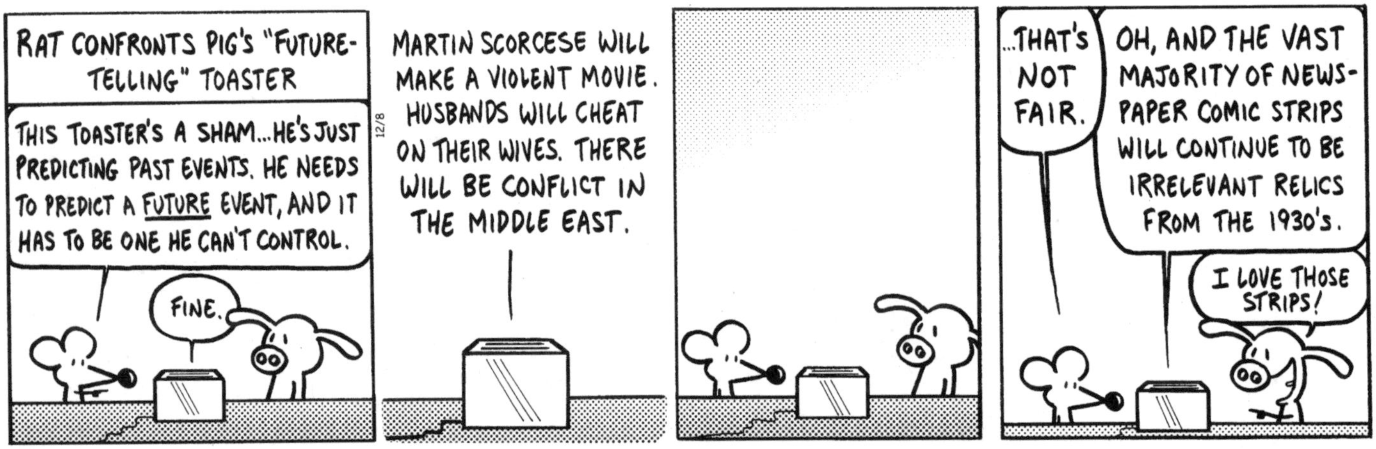
RAT CONFRONTS PIG'S "FUTURE-TELLING" TOASTER
THIS TOASTER'S A SHAM... HE'S JUST PREDICTING PAST EVENTS. HE NEEDS TO PREDICT A FUTURE EVENT, AND IT HAS TO BE ONE HE CAN'T CONTROL.
FINE.
MARTIN SCORCESE WILL MAKE A VIOLENT MOVIE. HUSBANDS WILL CHEAT ON THEIR WIVES. THERE WILL BE CONFLICT IN THE MIDDLE EAST.
...THAT'S NOT FAIR.
OH, AND THE VAST MAJORITY OF NEWSPAPER COMIC STRIPS WILL CONTINUE TO BE IRRELEVANT RELICS FROM THE 1930'S.
I LOVE THOSE STRIPS!
12/8

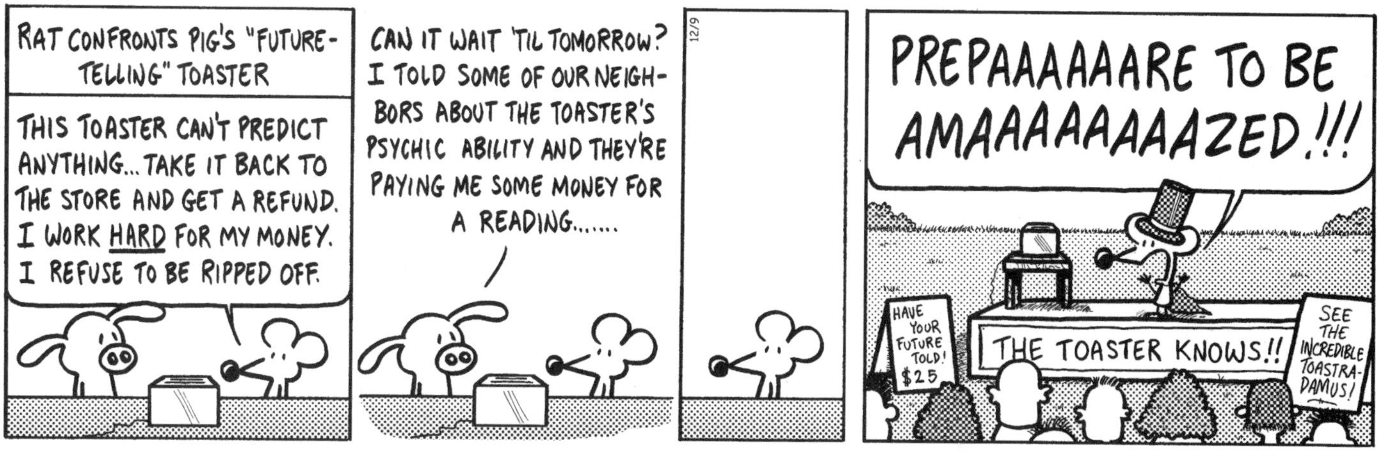
RAT CONFRONTS PIG'S "FUTURE-TELLING" TOASTER
THIS TOASTER CAN'T PREDICT ANYTHING... TAKE IT BACK TO THE STORE AND GET A REFUND. I WORK HARD FOR MY MONEY. I REFUSE TO BE RIPPED OFF.
CAN IT WAIT 'TIL TOMORROW? I TOLD SOME OF OUR NEIGHBORS ABOUT THE TOASTER'S PSYCHIC ABILITY AND THEY'RE PAYING ME SOME MONEY FOR A READING......
12/9
PREPAAAAAARE TO BE AMAAAAAAAAZED!!!
HAVE YOUR FUTURE TOLD! $25
THE TOASTER KNOWS!!
SEE THE INCREDIBLE TOASTRA-DAMUS!

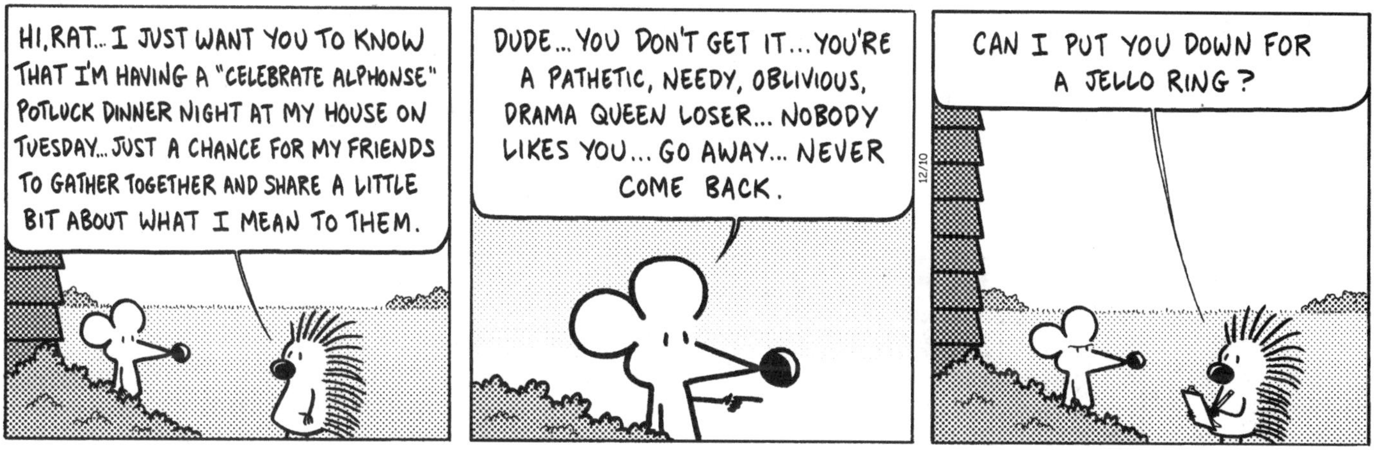
HI, RAT.. I JUST WANT YOU TO KNOW THAT I'M HAVING A "CELEBRATE ALPHONSE" POTLUCK DINNER NIGHT AT MY HOUSE ON TUESDAY... JUST A CHANCE FOR MY FRIENDS TO GATHER TOGETHER AND SHARE A LITTLE BIT ABOUT WHAT I MEAN TO THEM.
DUDE... YOU DON'T GET IT... YOU'RE A PATHETIC, NEEDY, OBLIVIOUS, DRAMA QUEEN LOSER... NOBODY LIKES YOU... GO AWAY... NEVER COME BACK.
12/10
CAN I PUT YOU DOWN FOR A JELLO RING?

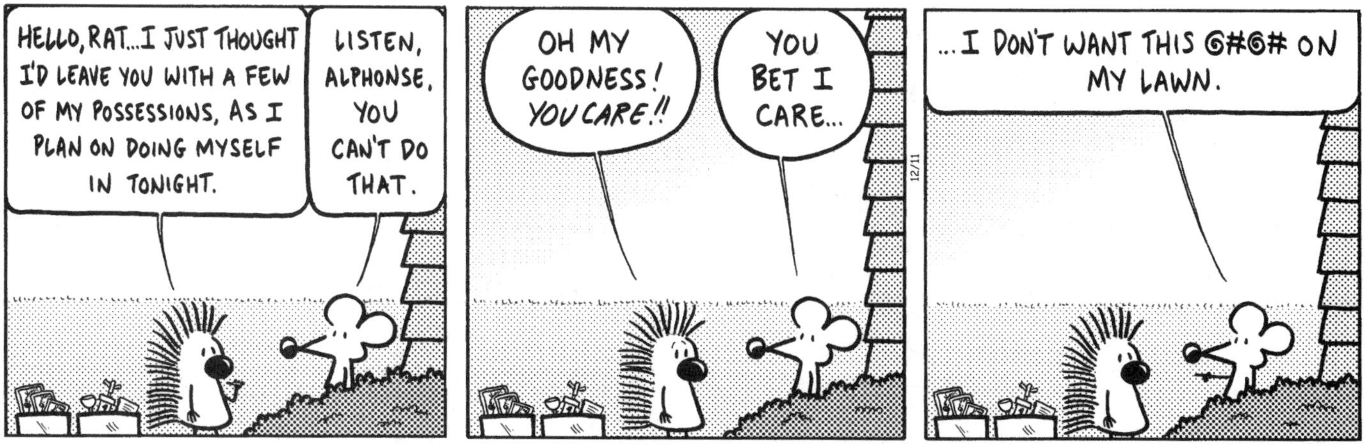
HELLO, RAT...I JUST THOUGHT I'D LEAVE YOU WITH A FEW OF MY POSSESSIONS, AS I PLAN ON DOING MYSELF IN TONIGHT.
LISTEN, ALPHONSE, YOU CAN'T DO THAT.
OH MY GOODNESS! YOU CARE!!
YOU BET I CARE...
12/11
...I DON'T WANT THIS @#@# ON MY LAWN.

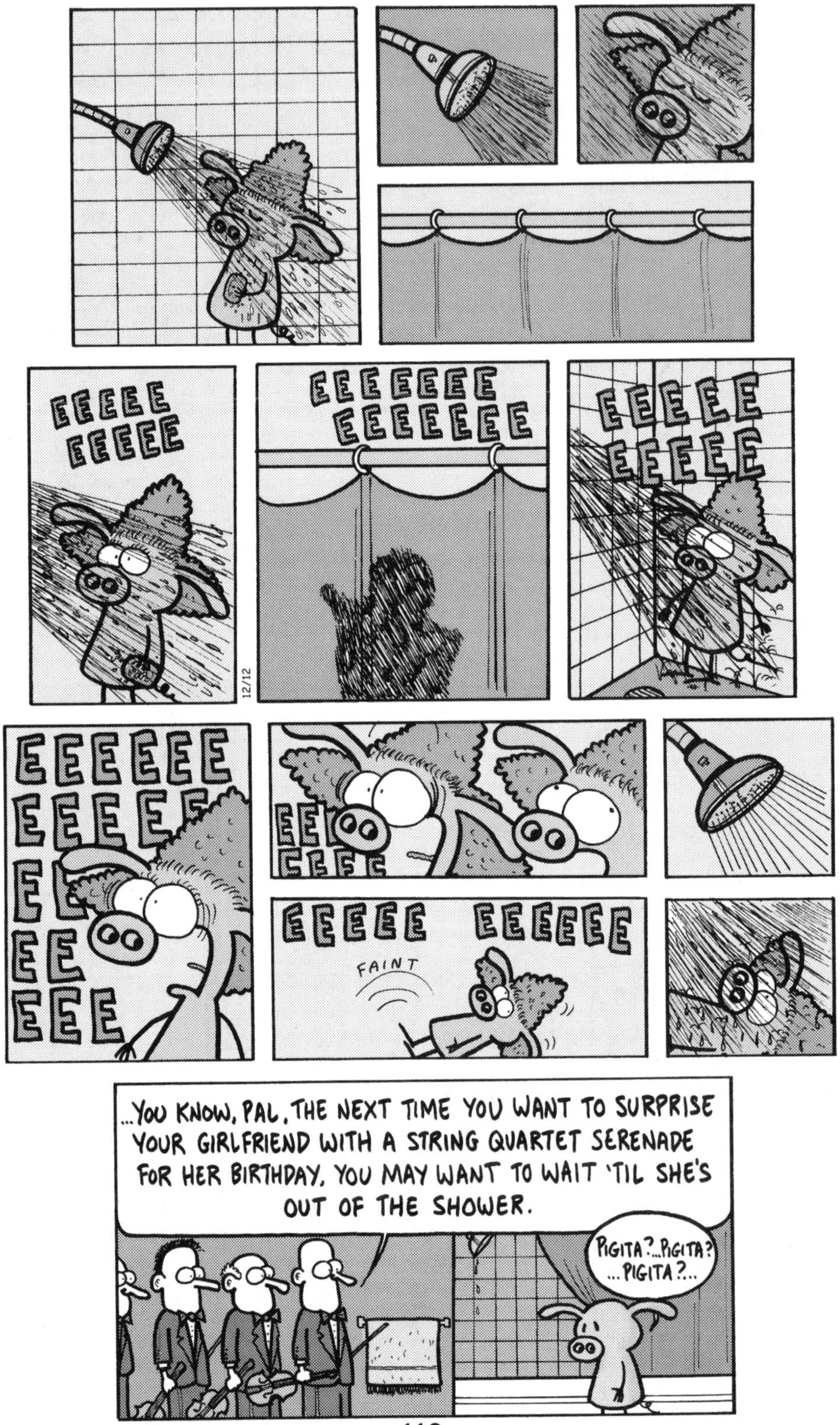
EEEEE EEEEE
EEEEEEE EEEEEEE
12/12
EEEEE EEEEE
EEEEEE
EEEEE
EE
EEE
EEEEE EEEEEE
FAINT
...YOU KNOW, PAL, THE NEXT TIME YOU WANT TO SURPRISE YOUR GIRLFRIEND WITH A STRING QUARTET SERENADE FOR HER BIRTHDAY, YOU MAY WANT TO WAIT 'TIL SHE'S OUT OF THE SHOWER.
PIGITA?...PIGITA? ...PIGITA?...

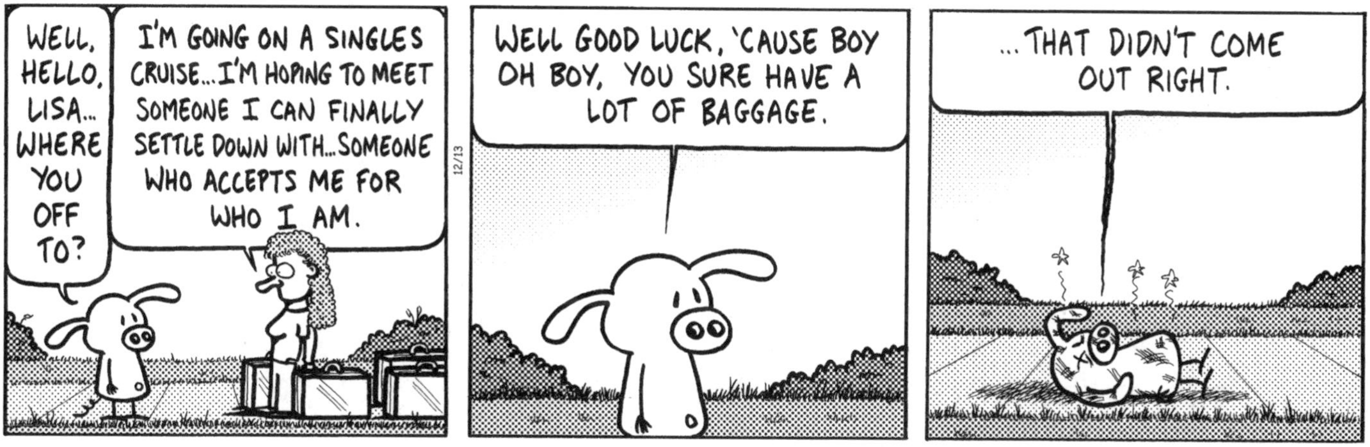
WELL, HELLO, LISA... WHERE YOU OFF TO?
I'M GOING ON A SINGLES CRUISE... I'M HOPING TO MEET SOMEONE I CAN FINALLY SETTLE DOWN WITH... SOMEONE WHO ACCEPTS ME FOR WHO I AM.
12/13
WELL GOOD LUCK, 'CAUSE BOY OH BOY, YOU SURE HAVE A LOT OF BAGGAGE.
... THAT DIDN'T COME OUT RIGHT.

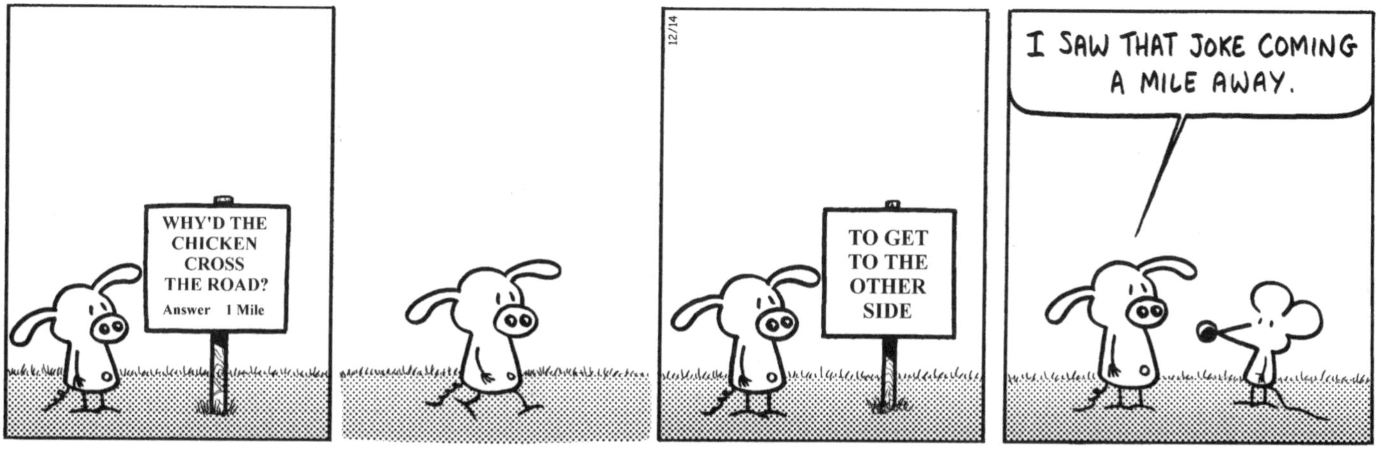
WHY'D THE CHICKEN CROSS THE ROAD?
Answer 1 Mile
12/14
TO GET TO THE OTHER SIDE
I SAW THAT JOKE COMING A MILE AWAY.

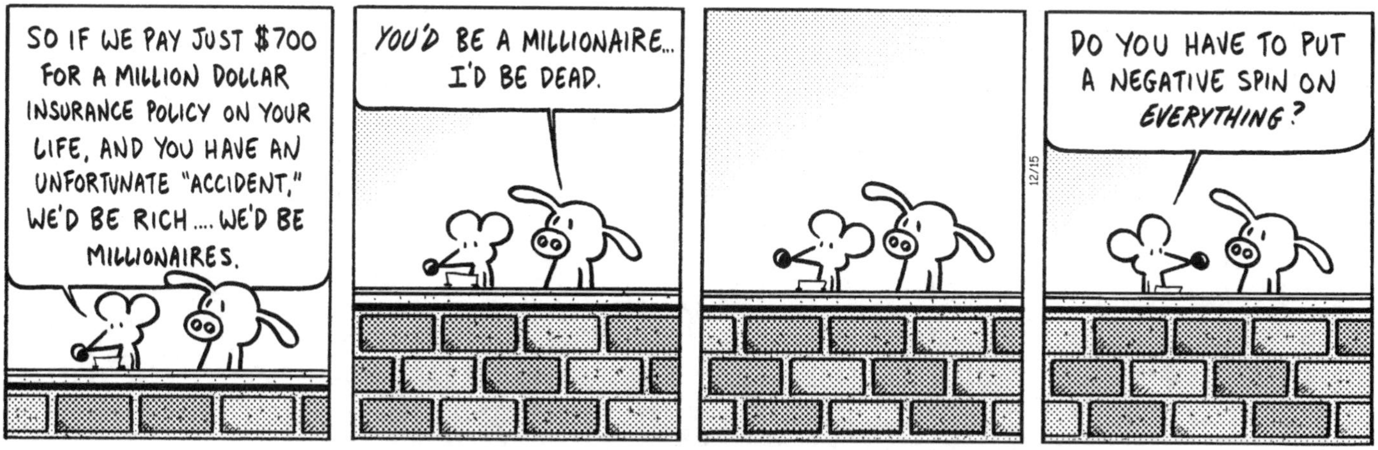
SO IF WE PAY JUST $700 FOR A MILLION DOLLAR INSURANCE POLICY ON YOUR LIFE, AND YOU HAVE AN UNFORTUNATE "ACCIDENT," WE'D BE RICH .... WE'D BE MILLIONAIRES.
YOU'D BE A MILLIONAIRE... I'D BE DEAD.
12/15
DO YOU HAVE TO PUT A NEGATIVE SPIN ON EVERYTHING?

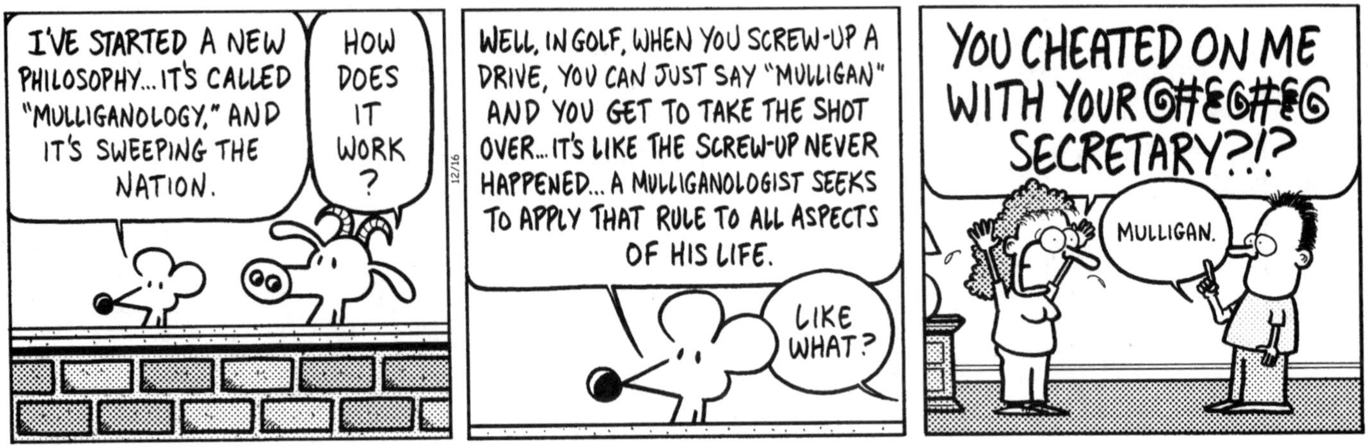
I'VE STARTED A NEW PHILOSOPHY... IT'S CALLED "MULLIGANOLOGY," AND IT'S SWEEPING THE NATION.
HOW DOES IT WORK?
12/16
WELL, IN GOLF, WHEN YOU SCREW-UP A DRIVE, YOU CAN JUST SAY "MULLIGAN" AND YOU GET TO TAKE THE SHOT OVER... IT'S LIKE THE SCREW-UP NEVER HAPPENED... A MULLIGANOLOGIST SEEKS TO APPLY THAT RULE TO ALL ASPECTS OF HIS LIFE.
LIKE WHAT?
YOU CHEATED ON ME WITH YOUR @#£@#£@ SECRETARY?!?
MULLIGAN.

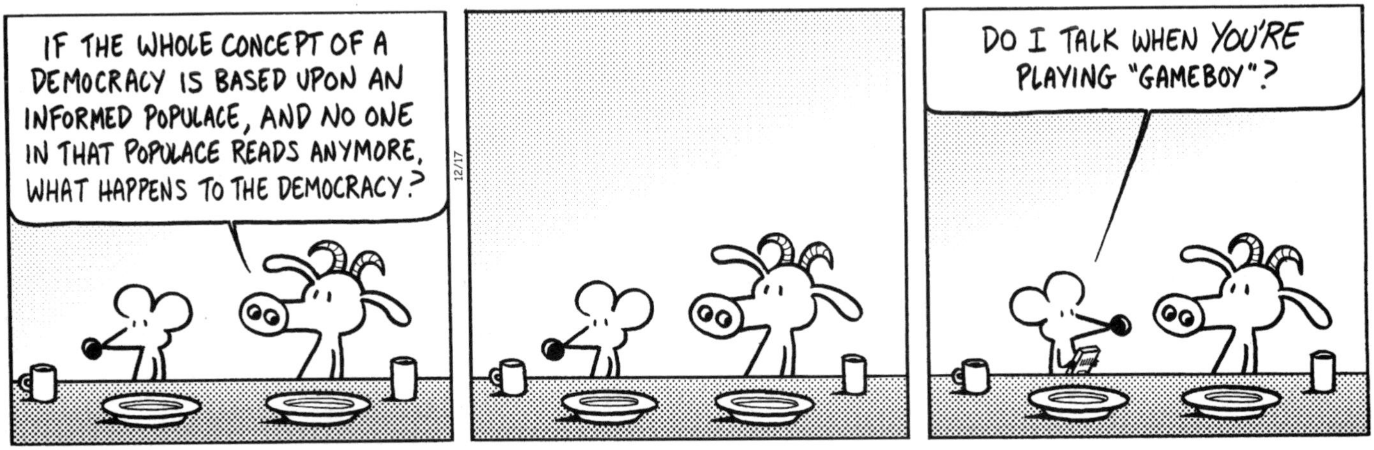
IF THE WHOLE CONCEPT OF A DEMOCRACY IS BASED UPON AN INFORMED POPULACE, AND NO ONE IN THAT POPULACE READS ANYMORE, WHAT HAPPENS TO THE DEMOCRACY?
12/17
DO I TALK WHEN *YOU'RE* PLAYING "GAMEBOY"?

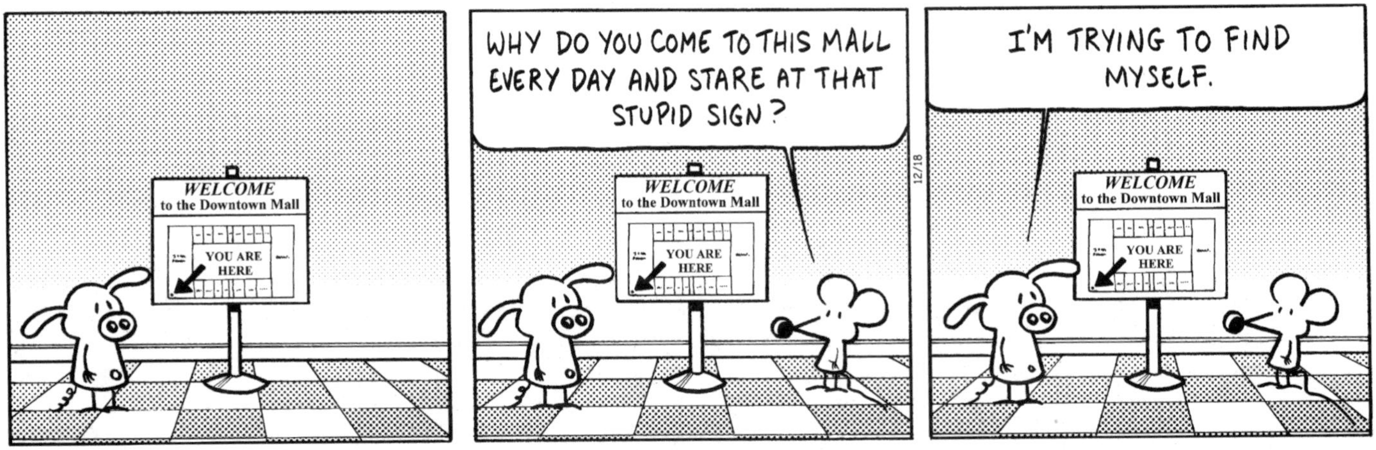
WELCOME
to the Downtown Mall
YOU ARE HERE
WHY DO YOU COME TO THIS MALL EVERY DAY AND STARE AT THAT STUPID SIGN?
12/18
I'M TRYING TO FIND MYSELF.

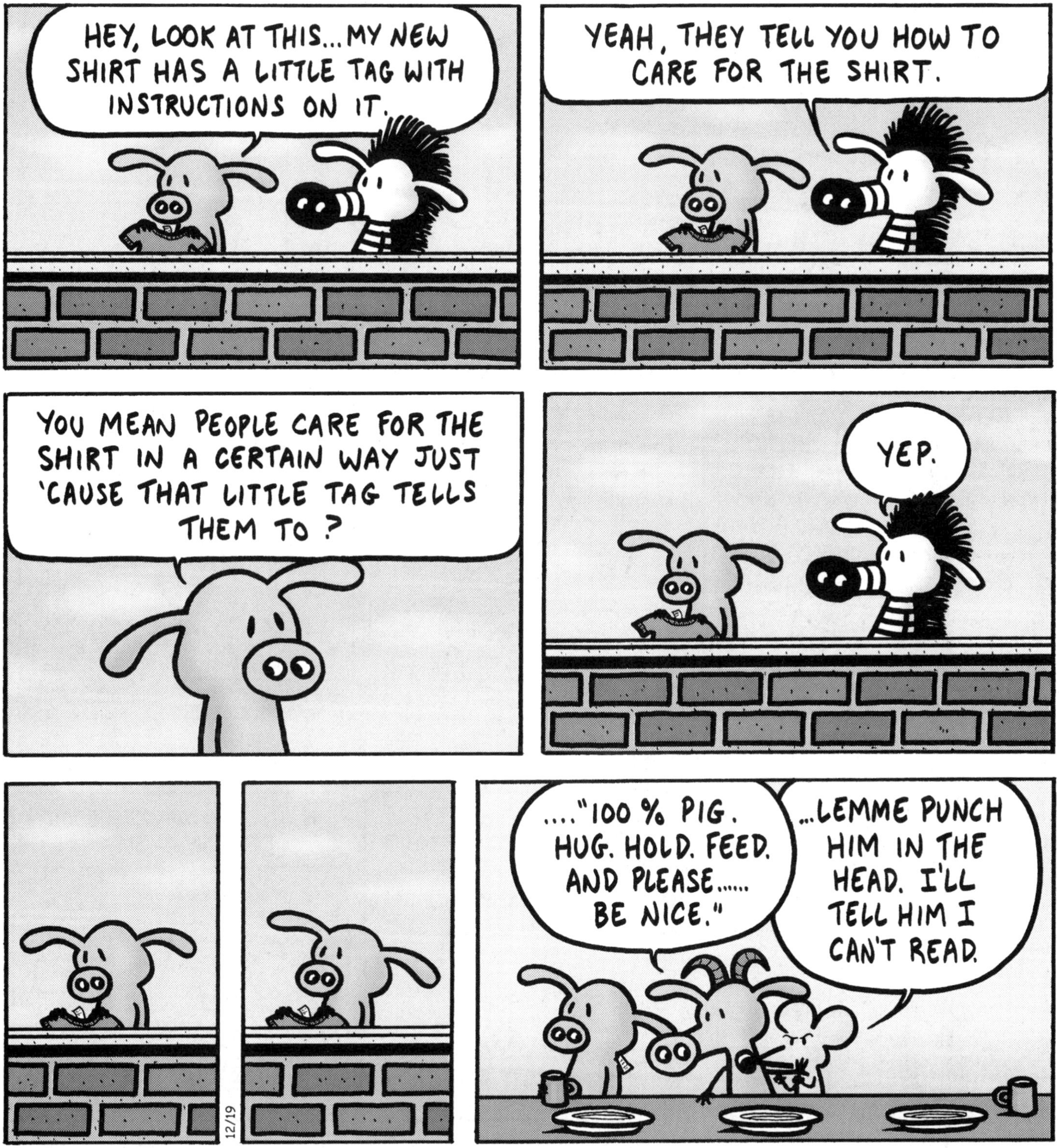
HEY, LOOK AT THIS... MY NEW SHIRT HAS A LITTLE TAG WITH INSTRUCTIONS ON IT.
YEAH, THEY TELL YOU HOW TO CARE FOR THE SHIRT.
YOU MEAN PEOPLE CARE FOR THE SHIRT IN A CERTAIN WAY JUST 'CAUSE THAT LITTLE TAG TELLS THEM TO?
YEP.
...."100% PIG. HUG. HOLD. FEED. AND PLEASE...... BE NICE."
...LEMME PUNCH HIM IN THE HEAD. I'LL TELL HIM I CAN'T READ.
12/19

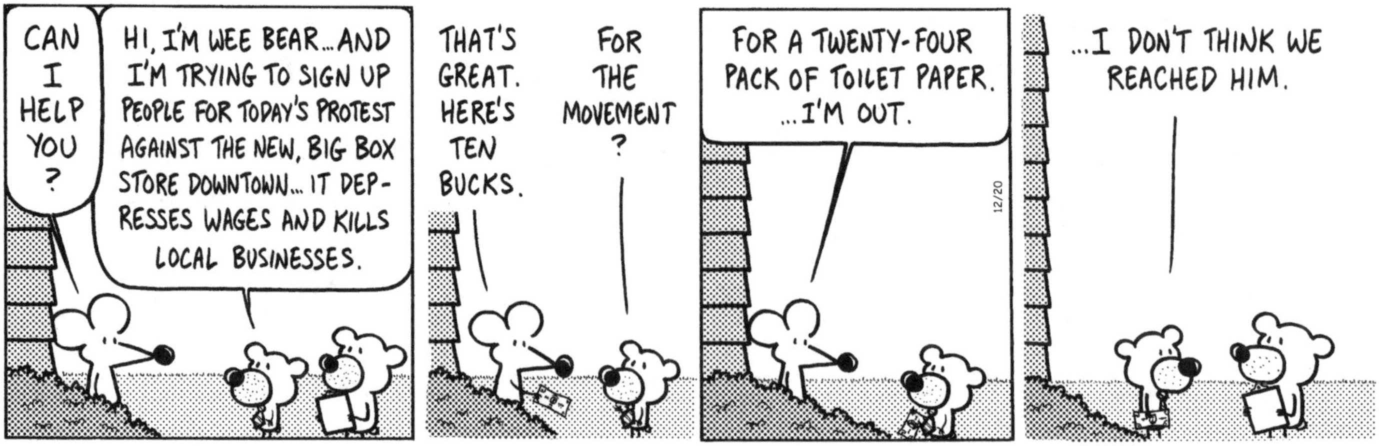
CAN I HELP YOU?
HI, I'M WEE BEAR...AND I'M TRYING TO SIGN UP PEOPLE FOR TODAY'S PROTEST AGAINST THE NEW, BIG BOX STORE DOWNTOWN... IT DEPRESSES WAGES AND KILLS LOCAL BUSINESSES.
THAT'S GREAT. HERE'S TEN BUCKS.
FOR THE MOVEMENT?
FOR A TWENTY-FOUR PACK OF TOILET PAPER. ...I'M OUT.
12/20
...I DON'T THINK WE REACHED HIM.

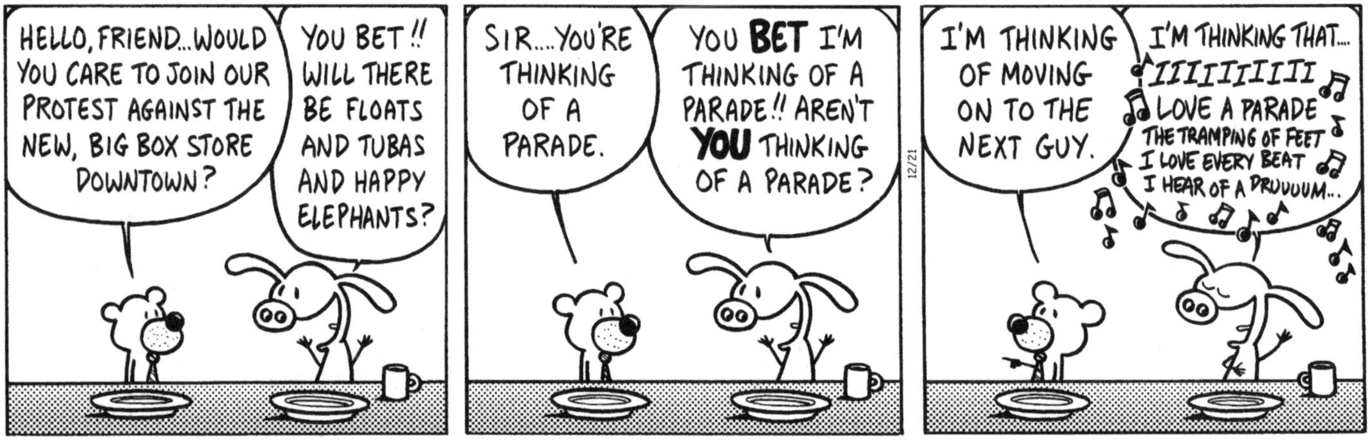
HELLO, FRIEND...WOULD YOU CARE TO JOIN OUR PROTEST AGAINST THE NEW, BIG BOX STORE DOWNTOWN?
YOU BET!! WILL THERE BE FLOATS AND TUBAS AND HAPPY ELEPHANTS?
SIR....YOU'RE THINKING OF A PARADE.
YOU **BET** I'M THINKING OF A PARADE!! AREN'T **YOU** THINKING OF A PARADE?
12/21
I'M THINKING OF MOVING ON TO THE NEXT GUY.
I'M THINKING THAT.... IIIIIIIII LOVE A PARADE THE TRAMPING OF FEET I LOVE EVERY BEAT I HEAR OF A DRUUUUM...

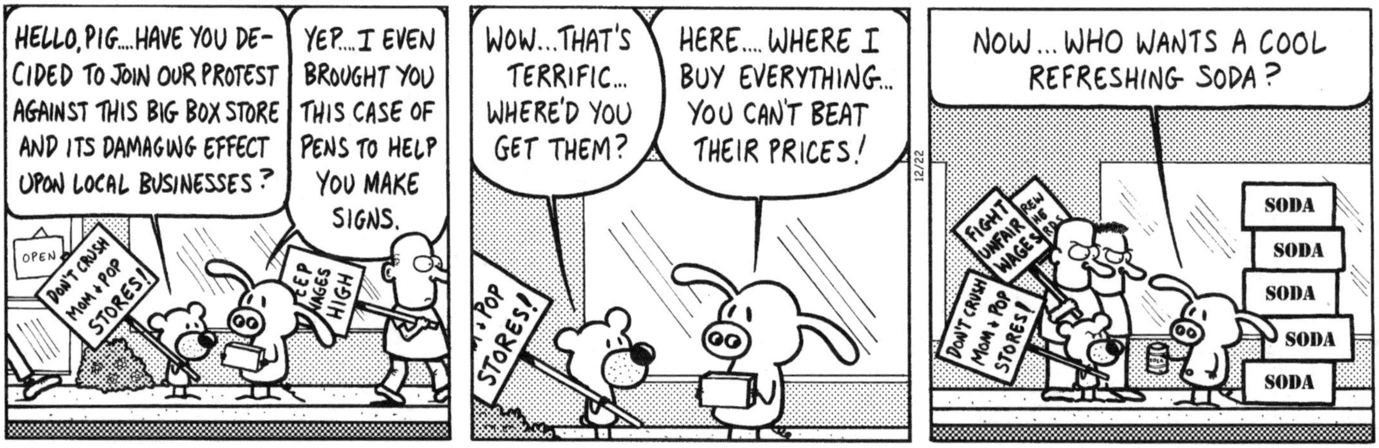
HELLO, PIG....HAVE YOU DECIDED TO JOIN OUR PROTEST AGAINST THIS BIG BOX STORE AND ITS DAMAGING EFFECT UPON LOCAL BUSINESSES?
YEP....I EVEN BROUGHT YOU THIS CASE OF PENS TO HELP YOU MAKE SIGNS.
OPEN
DON'T CRUSH MOM + POP STORES!
WOW...THAT'S TERRIFIC... WHERE'D YOU GET THEM?
HERE.... WHERE I BUY EVERYTHING... YOU CAN'T BEAT THEIR PRICES!
12/22
NOW... WHO WANTS A COOL REFRESHING SODA?
FIGHT UNFAIR WAGES
DON'T CRUSH MOM + POP STORES!
SODA
SODA
SODA
SODA
SODA

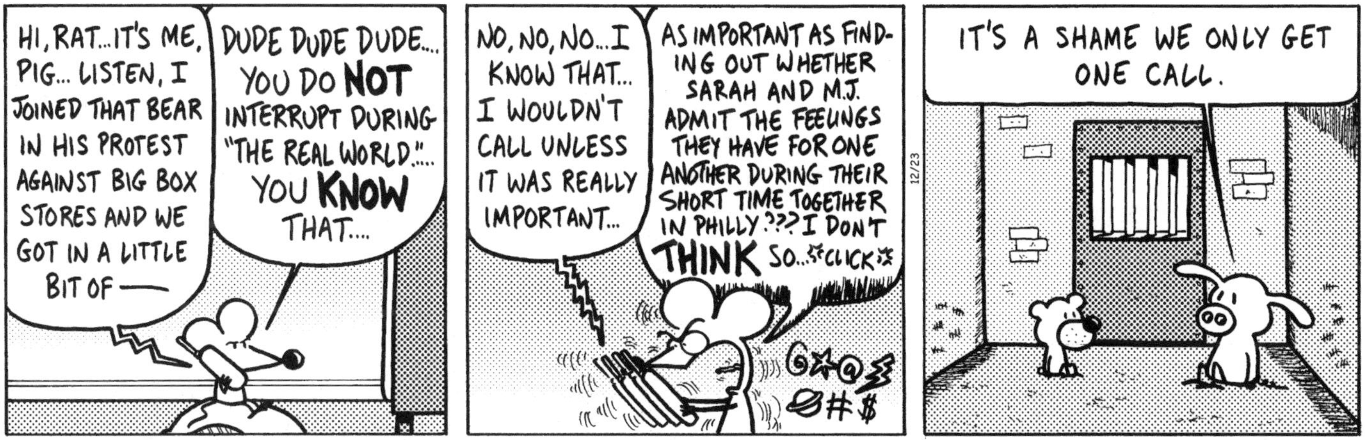
HI, RAT...IT'S ME, PIG... LISTEN, I JOINED THAT BEAR IN HIS PROTEST AGAINST BIG BOX STORES AND WE GOT IN A LITTLE BIT OF —
DUDE DUDE DUDE... YOU DO NOT INTERRUPT DURING "THE REAL WORLD."... YOU KNOW THAT....
NO, NO, NO...I KNOW THAT... I WOULDN'T CALL UNLESS IT WAS REALLY IMPORTANT...
AS IMPORTANT AS FINDING OUT WHETHER SARAH AND M.J. ADMIT THE FEELINGS THEY HAVE FOR ONE ANOTHER DURING THEIR SHORT TIME TOGETHER IN PHILLY??? I DON'T THINK SO...
CLICK
12/23
IT'S A SHAME WE ONLY GET ONE CALL.

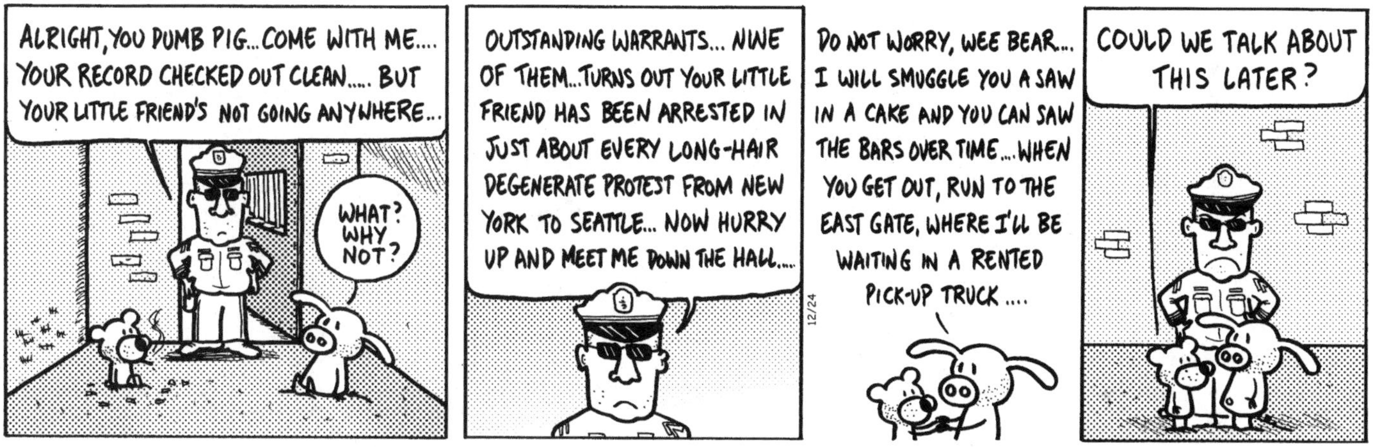
ALRIGHT, YOU DUMB PIG...COME WITH ME.... YOUR RECORD CHECKED OUT CLEAN..... BUT YOUR LITTLE FRIEND'S NOT GOING ANYWHERE...
WHAT? WHY NOT?
OUTSTANDING WARRANTS... NINE OF THEM...TURNS OUT YOUR LITTLE FRIEND HAS BEEN ARRESTED IN JUST ABOUT EVERY LONG-HAIR DEGENERATE PROTEST FROM NEW YORK TO SEATTLE... NOW HURRY UP AND MEET ME DOWN THE HALL....
12/24
DO NOT WORRY, WEE BEAR... I WILL SMUGGLE YOU A SAW IN A CAKE AND YOU CAN SAW THE BARS OVER TIME....WHEN YOU GET OUT, RUN TO THE EAST GATE, WHERE I'LL BE WAITING IN A RENTED PICK-UP TRUCK ....
COULD WE TALK ABOUT THIS LATER?

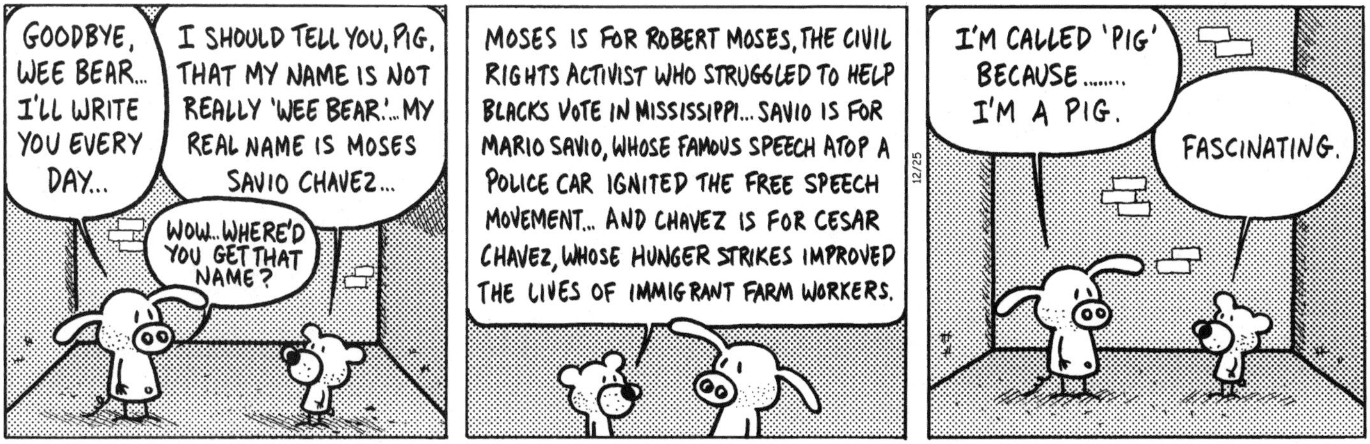
GOODBYE, WEE BEAR... I'LL WRITE YOU EVERY DAY...
I SHOULD TELL YOU, PIG, THAT MY NAME IS NOT REALLY 'WEE BEAR.'...MY REAL NAME IS MOSES SAVIO CHAVEZ...
WOW...WHERE'D YOU GET THAT NAME?
MOSES IS FOR ROBERT MOSES, THE CIVIL RIGHTS ACTIVIST WHO STRUGGLED TO HELP BLACKS VOTE IN MISSISSIPPI... SAVIO IS FOR MARIO SAVIO, WHOSE FAMOUS SPEECH ATOP A POLICE CAR IGNITED THE FREE SPEECH MOVEMENT... AND CHAVEZ IS FOR CESAR CHAVEZ, WHOSE HUNGER STRIKES IMPROVED THE LIVES OF IMMIGRANT FARM WORKERS.
12/25
I'M CALLED 'PIG' BECAUSE .... I'M A PIG.
FASCINATING.

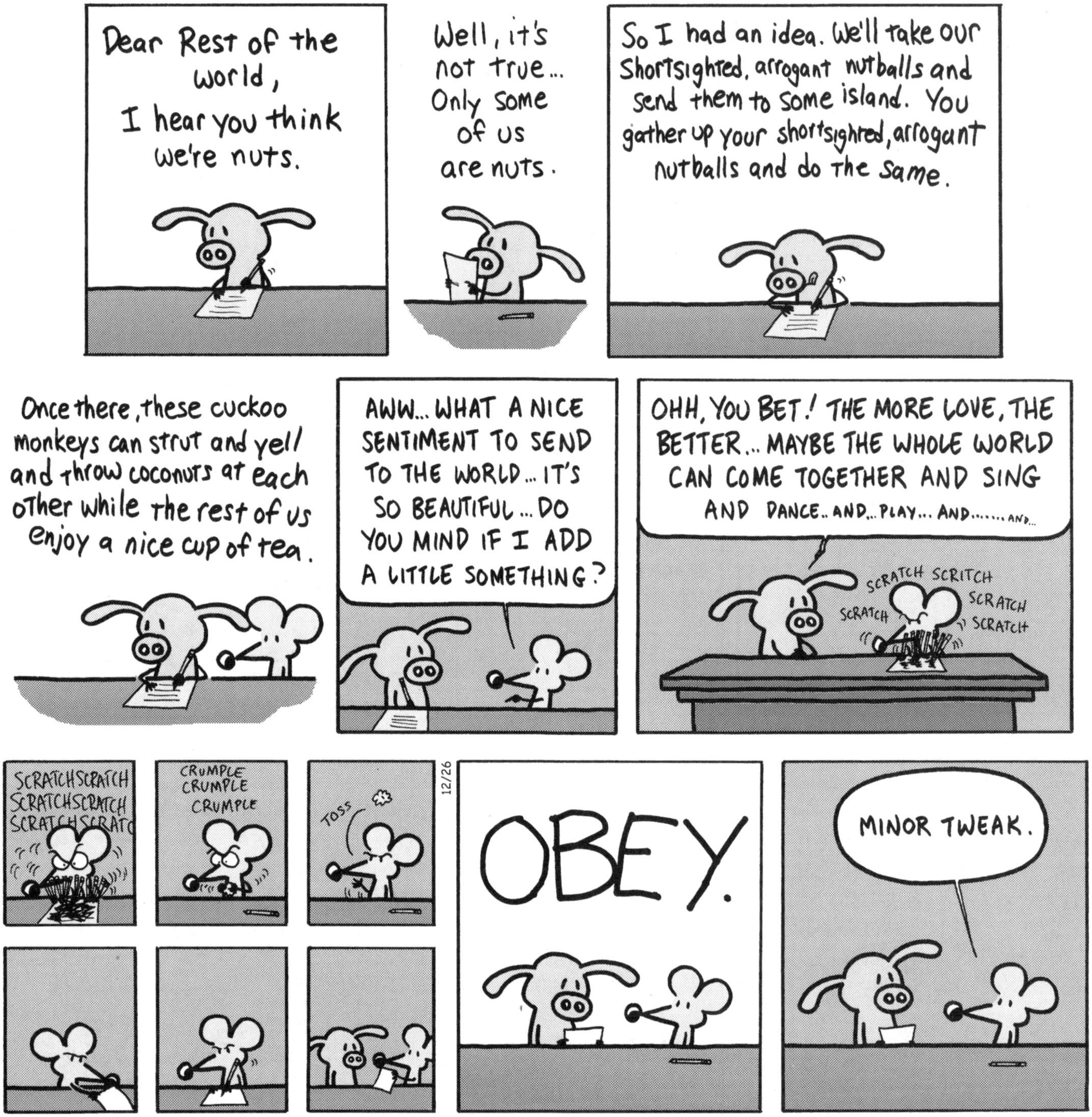
Dear Rest of the world,
I hear you think we're nuts.
Well, it's not true... Only some of us are nuts.
So I had an idea. We'll take our shortsighted, arrogant nutballs and send them to some island. You gather up your shortsighted, arrogant nutballs and do the same.
Once there, these cuckoo monkeys can strut and yell and throw coconuts at each other while the rest of us enjoy a nice cup of tea.
AWW... WHAT A NICE SENTIMENT TO SEND TO THE WORLD... IT'S SO BEAUTIFUL... DO YOU MIND IF I ADD A LITTLE SOMETHING?
OHH, YOU BET! THE MORE LOVE, THE BETTER... MAYBE THE WHOLE WORLD CAN COME TOGETHER AND SING AND DANCE.. AND... PLAY... AND....... AND...
SCRATCH SCRATCH SCRITCH SCRATCH SCRATCH
SCRATCHSCRATCH SCRATCHSCRATCH SCRATCHSCRATC
CRUMPLE CRUMPLE CRUMPLE
TOSS
12/26
OBEY.
MINOR TWEAK.

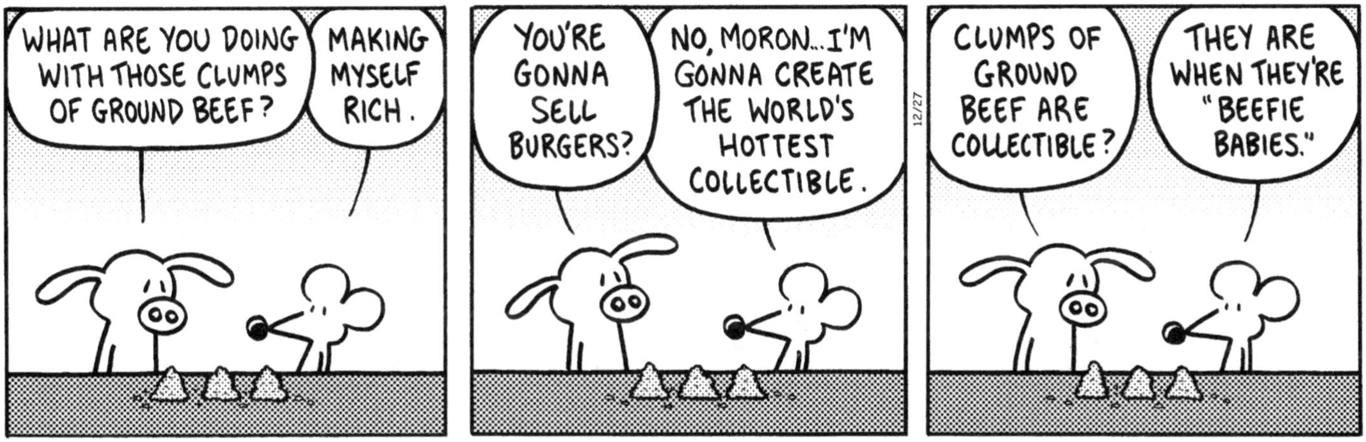
WHAT ARE YOU DOING WITH THOSE CLUMPS OF GROUND BEEF?
MAKING MYSELF RICH.
YOU'RE GONNA SELL BURGERS?
NO, MORON... I'M GONNA CREATE THE WORLD'S HOTTEST COLLECTIBLE.
12/27
CLUMPS OF GROUND BEEF ARE COLLECTIBLE?
THEY ARE WHEN THEY'RE "BEEFIE BABIES."

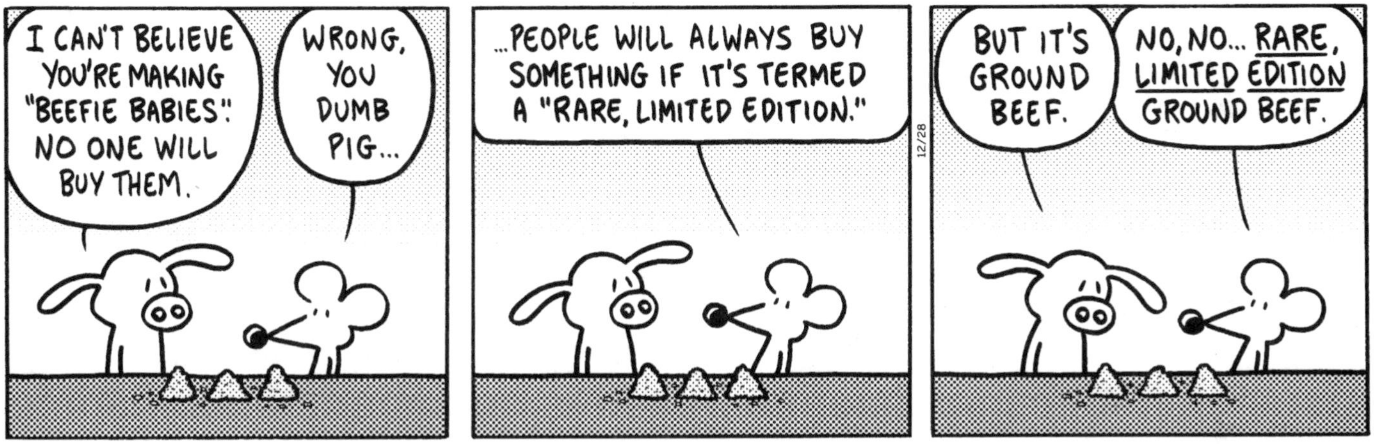
I CAN'T BELIEVE YOU'RE MAKING "BEEFIE BABIES." NO ONE WILL BUY THEM.
WRONG, YOU DUMB PIG...
...PEOPLE WILL ALWAYS BUY SOMETHING IF IT'S TERMED A "RARE, LIMITED EDITION."
12/28
BUT IT'S GROUND BEEF.
NO, NO... RARE, LIMITED EDITION GROUND BEEF.

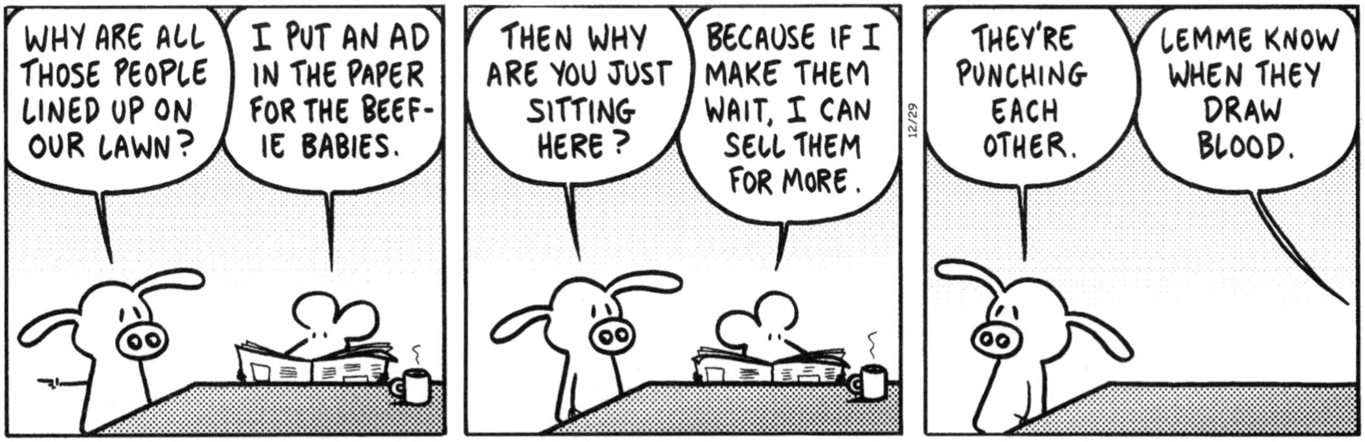
WHY ARE ALL THOSE PEOPLE LINED UP ON OUR LAWN?
I PUT AN AD IN THE PAPER FOR THE BEEF-IE BABIES.
THEN WHY ARE YOU JUST SITTING HERE?
BECAUSE IF I MAKE THEM WAIT, I CAN SELL THEM FOR MORE.
12/29
THEY'RE PUNCHING EACH OTHER.
LEMME KNOW WHEN THEY DRAW BLOOD.

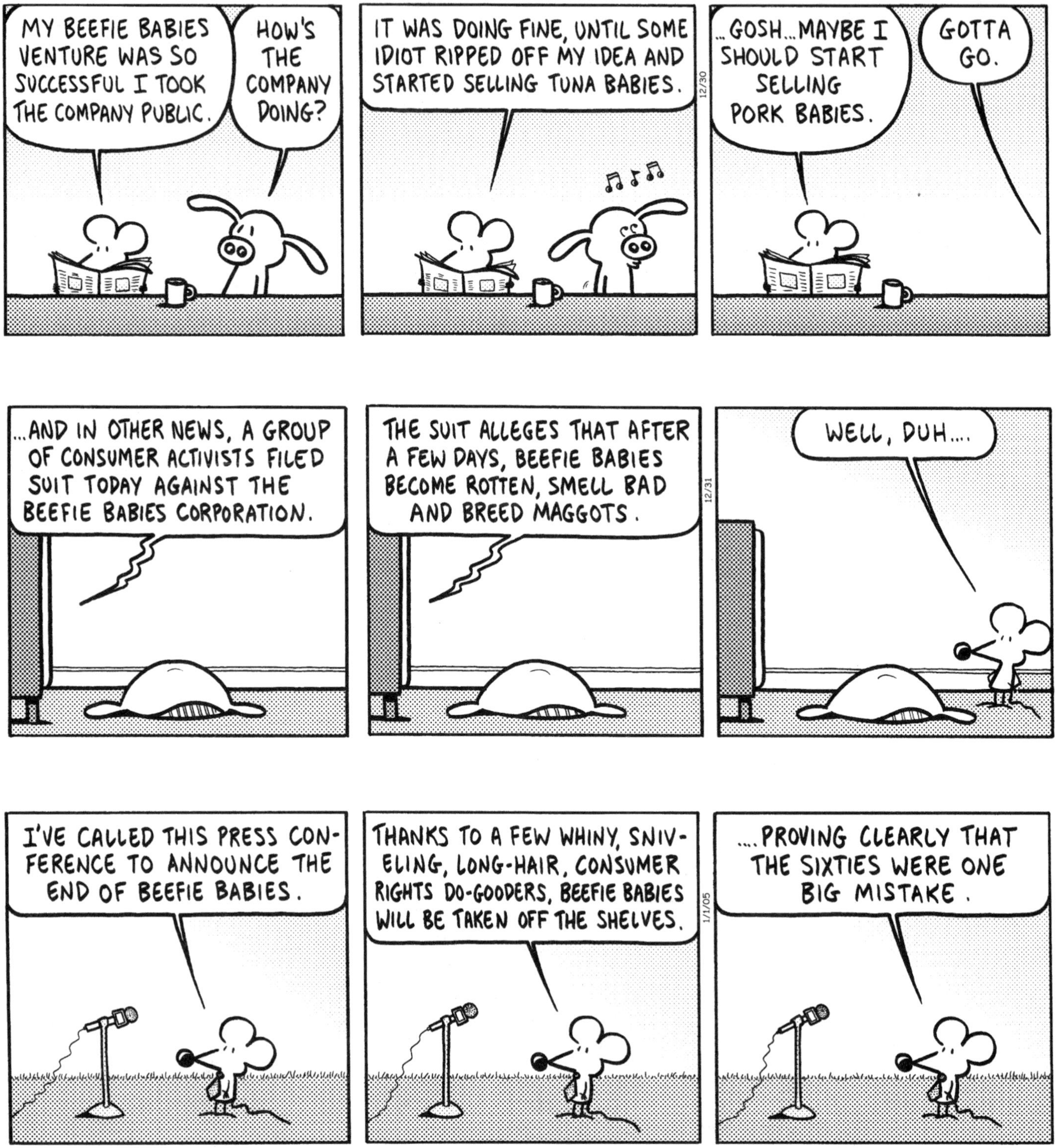
MY BEEFIE BABIES VENTURE WAS SO SUCCESSFUL I TOOK THE COMPANY PUBLIC.
HOW'S THE COMPANY DOING?
IT WAS DOING FINE, UNTIL SOME IDIOT RIPPED OFF MY IDEA AND STARTED SELLING TUNA BABIES.
12/30
...GOSH...MAYBE I SHOULD START SELLING PORK BABIES.
GOTTA GO.
...AND IN OTHER NEWS, A GROUP OF CONSUMER ACTIVISTS FILED SUIT TODAY AGAINST THE BEEFIE BABIES CORPORATION.
THE SUIT ALLEGES THAT AFTER A FEW DAYS, BEEFIE BABIES BECOME ROTTEN, SMELL BAD AND BREED MAGGOTS.
12/31
WELL, DUH....
I'VE CALLED THIS PRESS CONFERENCE TO ANNOUNCE THE END OF BEEFIE BABIES.
THANKS TO A FEW WHINY, SNIVELING, LONG-HAIR, CONSUMER RIGHTS DO-GOODERS, BEEFIE BABIES WILL BE TAKEN OFF THE SHELVES.
1/1/05
....PROVING CLEARLY THAT THE SIXTIES WERE ONE BIG MISTAKE.

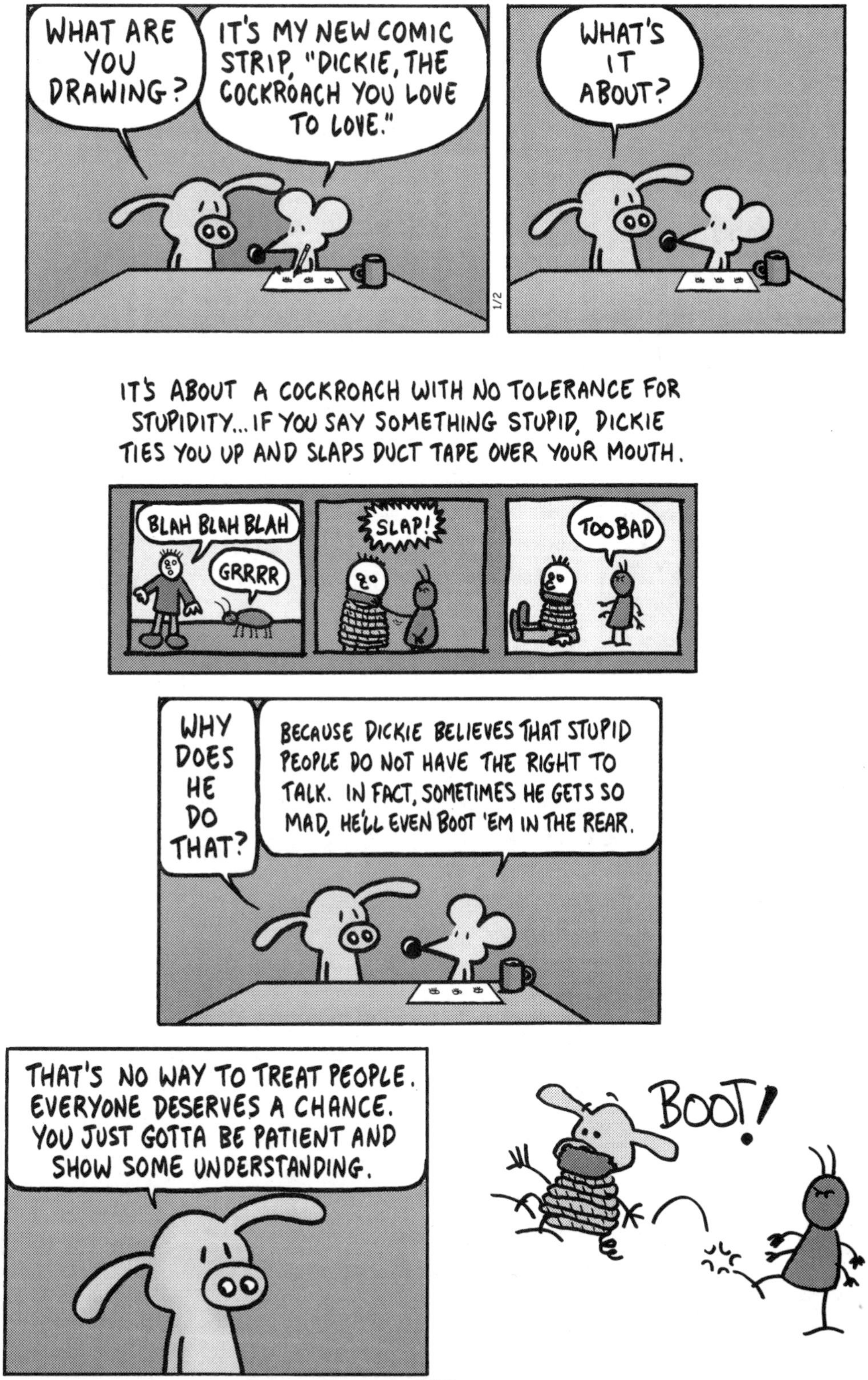
WHAT ARE YOU DRAWING?
IT'S MY NEW COMIC STRIP, "DICKIE, THE COCKROACH YOU LOVE TO LOVE."
WHAT'S IT ABOUT?
IT'S ABOUT A COCKROACH WITH NO TOLERANCE FOR STUPIDITY... IF YOU SAY SOMETHING STUPID, DICKIE TIES YOU UP AND SLAPS DUCT TAPE OVER YOUR MOUTH.
BLAH BLAH BLAH
GRRRR
SLAP!
TOO BAD
WHY DOES HE DO THAT?
BECAUSE DICKIE BELIEVES THAT STUPID PEOPLE DO NOT HAVE THE RIGHT TO TALK. IN FACT, SOMETIMES HE GETS SO MAD, HE'LL EVEN BOOT 'EM IN THE REAR.
THAT'S NO WAY TO TREAT PEOPLE. EVERYONE DESERVES A CHANCE. YOU JUST GOTTA BE PATIENT AND SHOW SOME UNDERSTANDING.
BOOT!

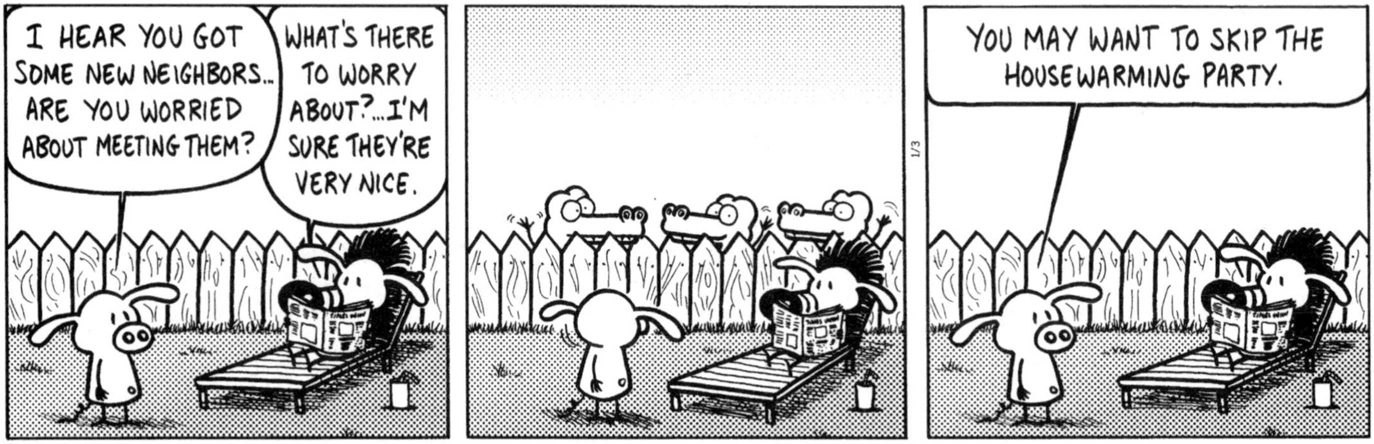
I HEAR YOU GOT SOME NEW NEIGHBORS.. ARE YOU WORRIED ABOUT MEETING THEM?
WHAT'S THERE TO WORRY ABOUT?...I'M SURE THEY'RE VERY NICE.
YOU MAY WANT TO SKIP THE HOUSEWARMING PARTY.

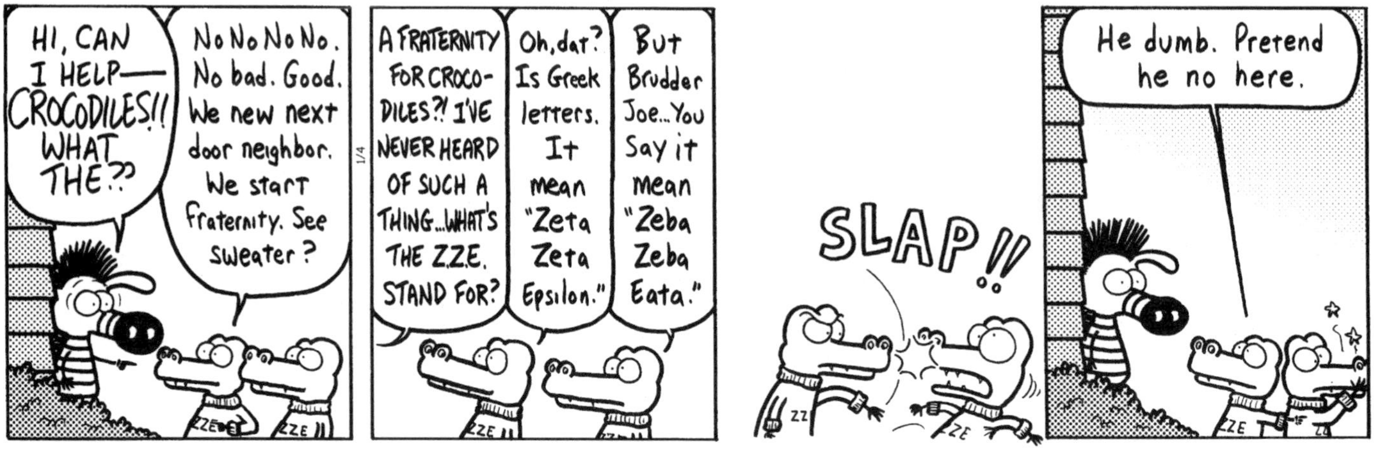
HI, CAN I HELP— CROCODILES!! WHAT THE??
No No No No. No bad. Good. We new next door neighbor. We start fraternity. See sweater?
A FRATERNITY FOR CROCODILES?! I'VE NEVER HEARD OF SUCH A THING...WHAT'S THE Z.Z.E. STAND FOR?
Oh, dat? Is Greek letters. It mean "Zeta Zeta Epsilon."
But Brudder Joe...You say it mean "Zeba Zeba Eata."
SLAP!!
He dumb. Pretend he no here.

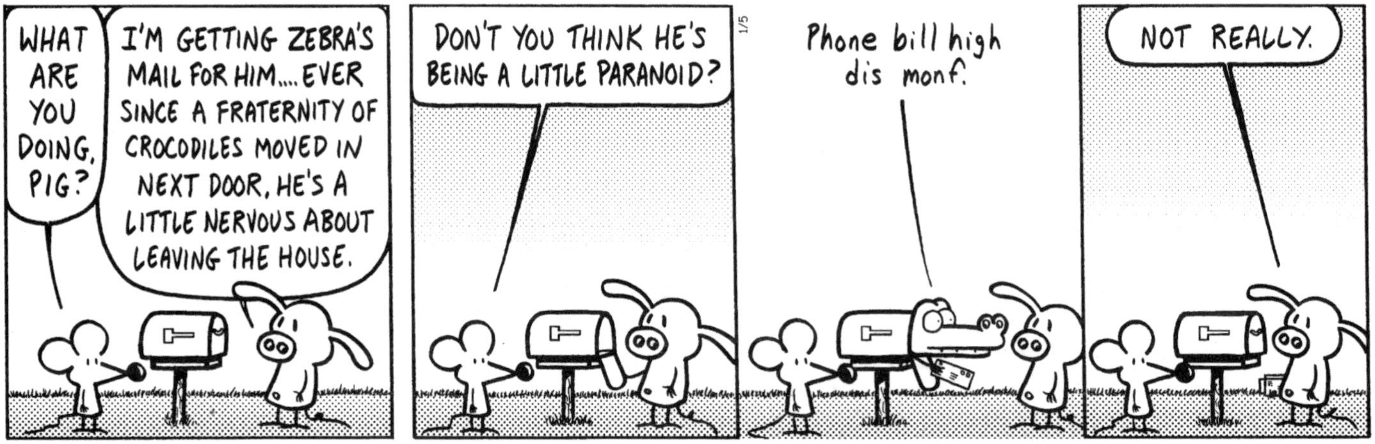
WHAT ARE YOU DOING, PIG?
I'M GETTING ZEBRA'S MAIL FOR HIM.... EVER SINCE A FRATERNITY OF CROCODILES MOVED IN NEXT DOOR, HE'S A LITTLE NERVOUS ABOUT LEAVING THE HOUSE.
DON'T YOU THINK HE'S BEING A LITTLE PARANOID?
Phone bill high dis monf.
NOT REALLY.

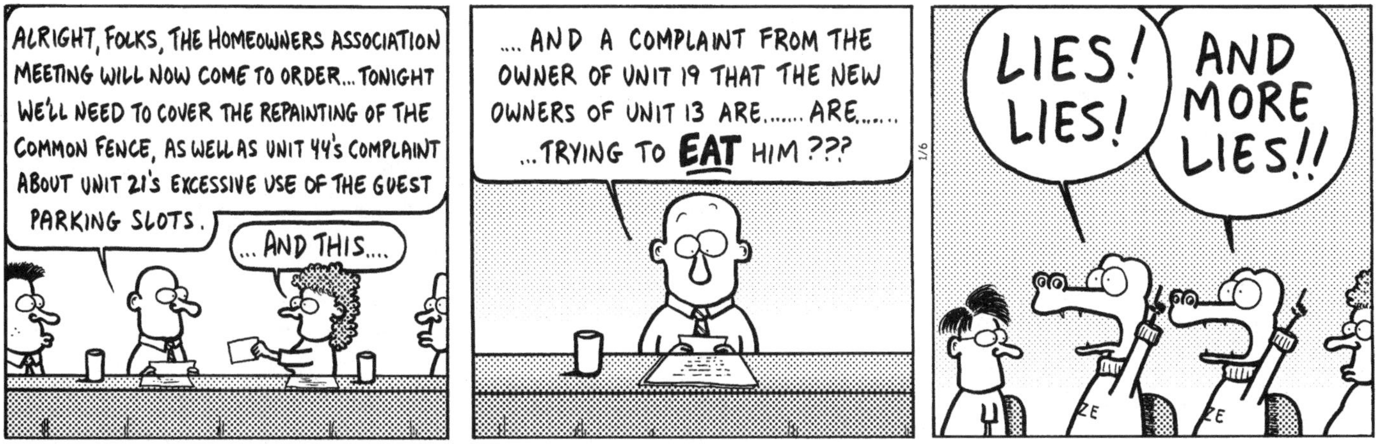
ALRIGHT, FOLKS, THE HOMEOWNERS ASSOCIATION MEETING WILL NOW COME TO ORDER... TONIGHT WE'LL NEED TO COVER THE REPAINTING OF THE COMMON FENCE, AS WELL AS UNIT 44'S COMPLAINT ABOUT UNIT 21'S EXCESSIVE USE OF THE GUEST PARKING SLOTS.
... AND THIS....
.... AND A COMPLAINT FROM THE OWNER OF UNIT 19 THAT THE NEW OWNERS OF UNIT 13 ARE....... ARE....... ...TRYING TO EAT HIM???
1/6
LIES! LIES!
AND MORE LIES!!

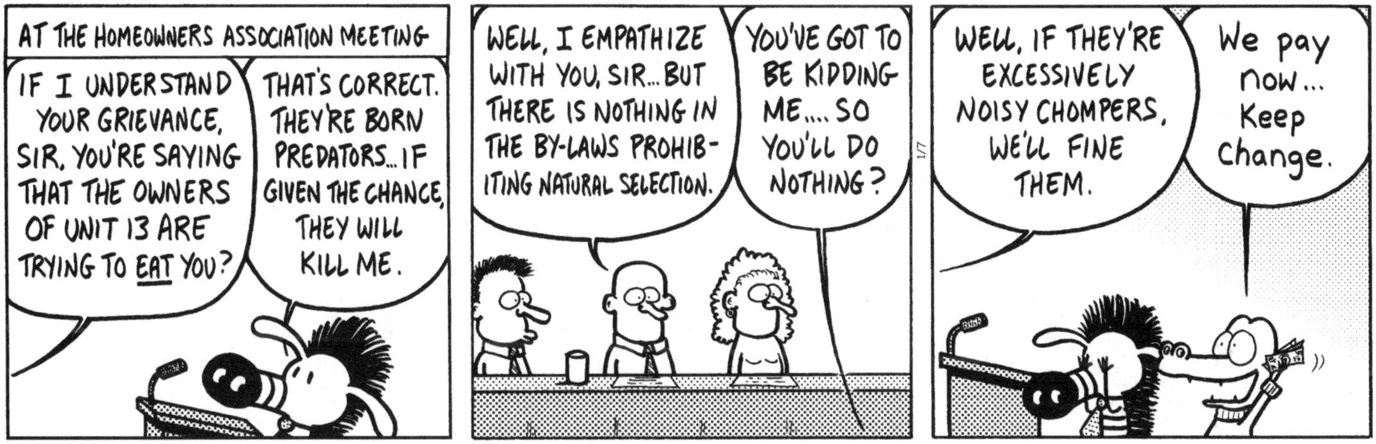
AT THE HOMEOWNERS ASSOCIATION MEETING
IF I UNDERSTAND YOUR GRIEVANCE, SIR, YOU'RE SAYING THAT THE OWNERS OF UNIT 13 ARE TRYING TO EAT YOU?
THAT'S CORRECT. THEY'RE BORN PREDATORS... IF GIVEN THE CHANCE, THEY WILL KILL ME.
WELL, I EMPATHIZE WITH YOU, SIR... BUT THERE IS NOTHING IN THE BY-LAWS PROHIBITING NATURAL SELECTION.
YOU'VE GOT TO BE KIDDING ME.... SO YOU'LL DO NOTHING?
1/7
WELL, IF THEY'RE EXCESSIVELY NOISY CHOMPERS, WE'LL FINE THEM.
We pay now... Keep Change.

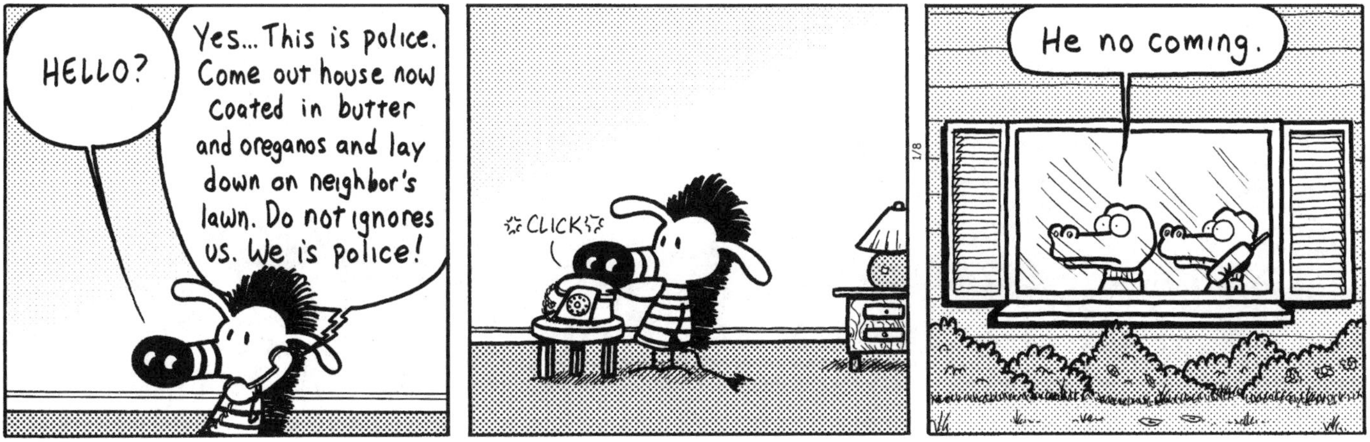
HELLO?
Yes... This is police. Come out house now coated in butter and oreganos and lay down on neighbor's lawn. Do not ignores us. We is police!
CLICK
1/8
He no coming.

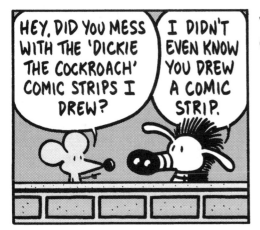

HEY, DID YOU MESS WITH THE 'DICKIE THE COCKROACH' COMIC STRIPS I DREW?

I DIDN'T EVEN KNOW YOU DREW A COMIC STRIP.

YEAH, IT'S ABOUT THIS COCKROACH WITH NO TOLERANCE FOR STUPIDITY. IF YOU SAY SOMETHING DUMB, HE TIES YOU UP AND SLAPS DUCT TAPE OVER YOUR MOUTH... BUT SOMEONE ERASED DICKIE FROM ALL THE STRIPS I DREW.

HEY, MAYBE IT'S ONE OF THOSE FRANKENSTEIN-TYPE SITUATIONS WHERE YOUR CREATION CAME TO LIFE, ROSE OFF THE PAGE, AND MARCHED OFF TO TERRIFY THE VILLAGERS.

OH, MAN... WHAT A TRAGEDY THAT WOULD BE.

WHY DO YOU SAY THAT?

BECAUSE ME AND YOU LIVE ON THE REAL COMICS PAGE, AND THIS PLACE IS JUST FILLED WITH FOLKS WHO UTTER INANITY AFTER INANITY... IF DICKIE GOT LOOSE HERE, THERE'S NO TELLING WHAT HAVOC HE'D WREAK.

MS. GUISEWITE WILL NOT BE PLEASED.

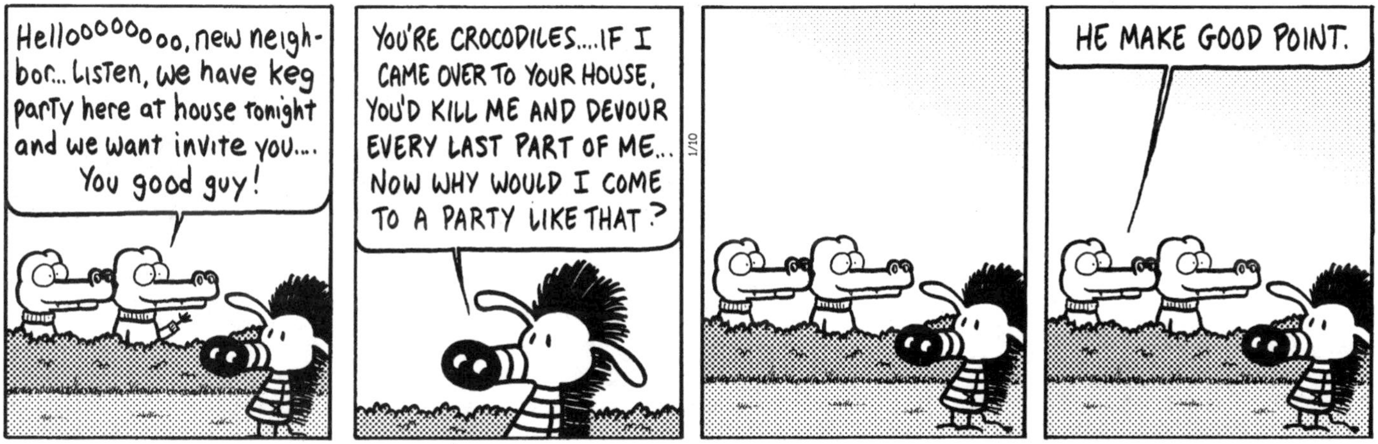
Hellooooooooo, new neighbor... Listen, we have keg party here at house tonight and we want invite you.... You good guy!
YOU'RE CROCODILES....IF I CAME OVER TO YOUR HOUSE, YOU'D KILL ME AND DEVOUR EVERY LAST PART OF ME... NOW WHY WOULD I COME TO A PARTY LIKE THAT?
1/10
HE MAKE GOOD POINT.

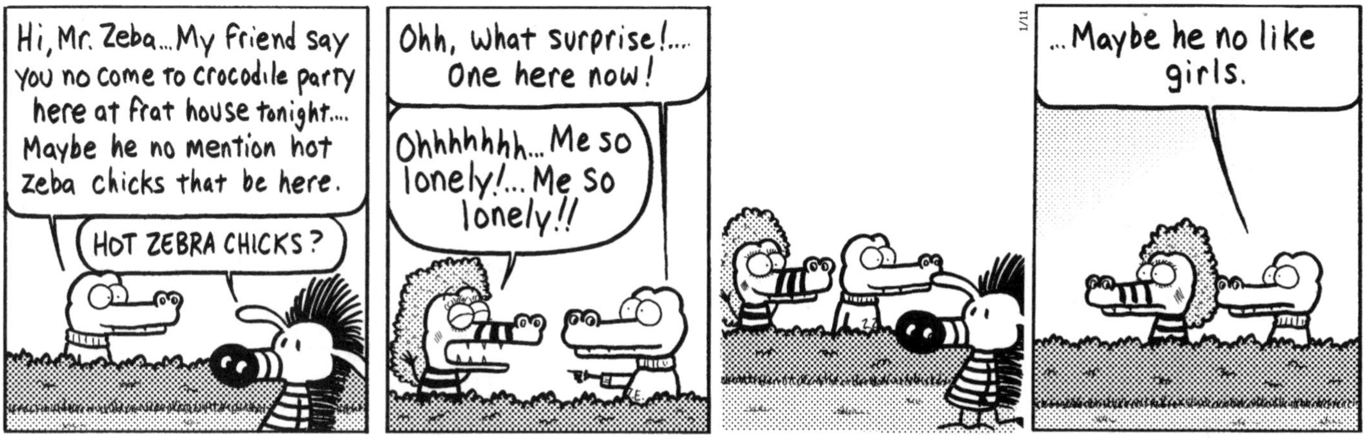
Hi, Mr. Zeba...My friend say you no come to crocodile party here at frat house tonight.... Maybe he no mention hot zeba chicks that be here.
HOT ZEBRA CHICKS?
Ohh, what surprise!.... One here now!
Ohhhhhhh... Me so lonely!... Me so lonely!!
1/11
...Maybe he no like girls.

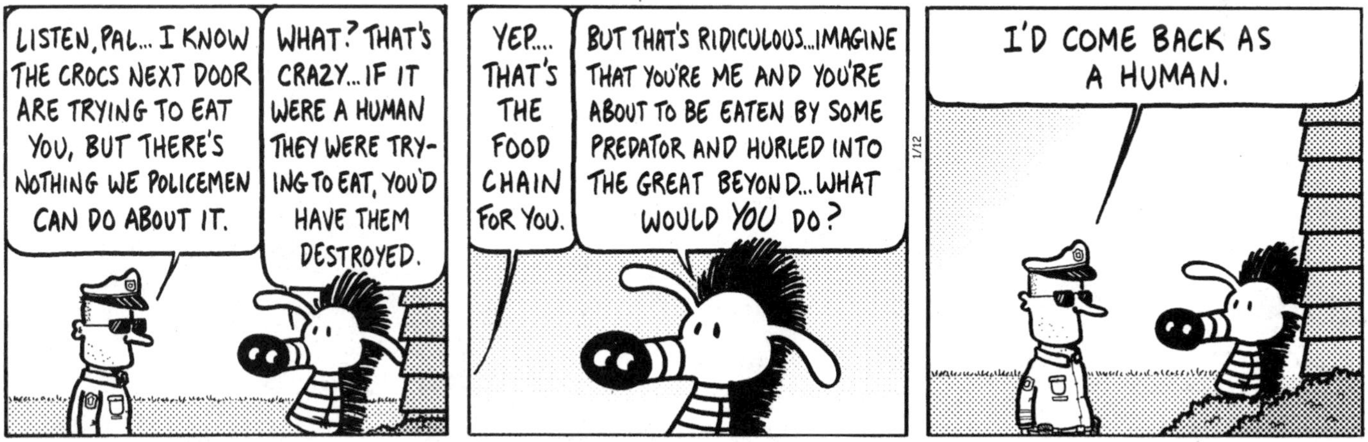
LISTEN, PAL... I KNOW THE CROCS NEXT DOOR ARE TRYING TO EAT YOU, BUT THERE'S NOTHING WE POLICEMEN CAN DO ABOUT IT.
WHAT? THAT'S CRAZY... IF IT WERE A HUMAN THEY WERE TRYING TO EAT, YOU'D HAVE THEM DESTROYED.
YEP.... THAT'S THE FOOD CHAIN FOR YOU.
BUT THAT'S RIDICULOUS...IMAGINE THAT YOU'RE ME AND YOU'RE ABOUT TO BE EATEN BY SOME PREDATOR AND HURLED INTO THE GREAT BEYOND...WHAT WOULD YOU DO?
1/12
I'D COME BACK AS A HUMAN.

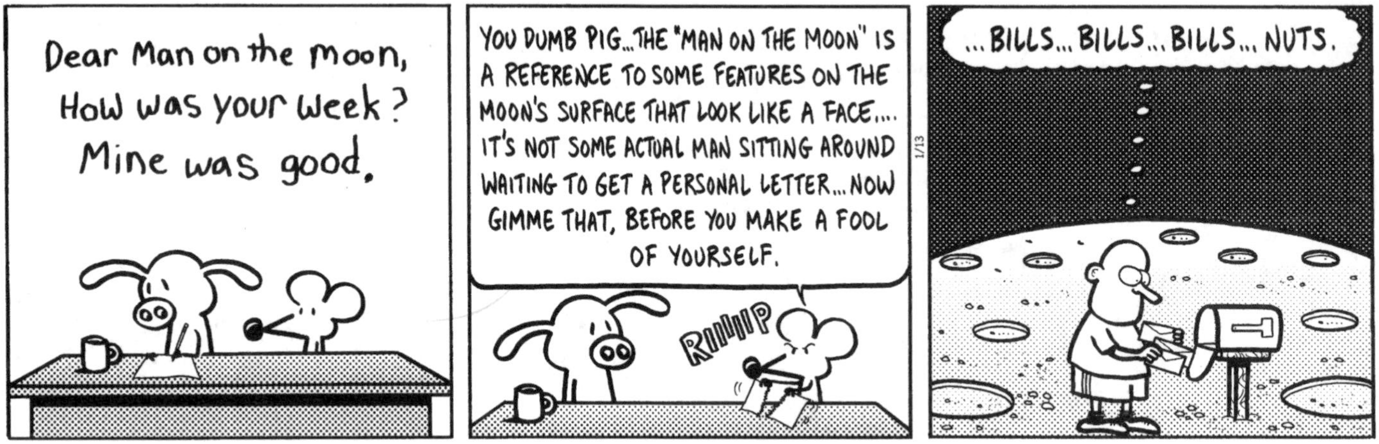
Dear Man on the moon,
How was your week?
Mine was good.
YOU DUMB PIG... THE "MAN ON THE MOON" IS A REFERENCE TO SOME FEATURES ON THE MOON'S SURFACE THAT LOOK LIKE A FACE.... IT'S NOT SOME ACTUAL MAN SITTING AROUND WAITING TO GET A PERSONAL LETTER... NOW GIMME THAT, BEFORE YOU MAKE A FOOL OF YOURSELF.
RIIIIIP
1/13
...BILLS... BILLS... BILLS... NUTS.

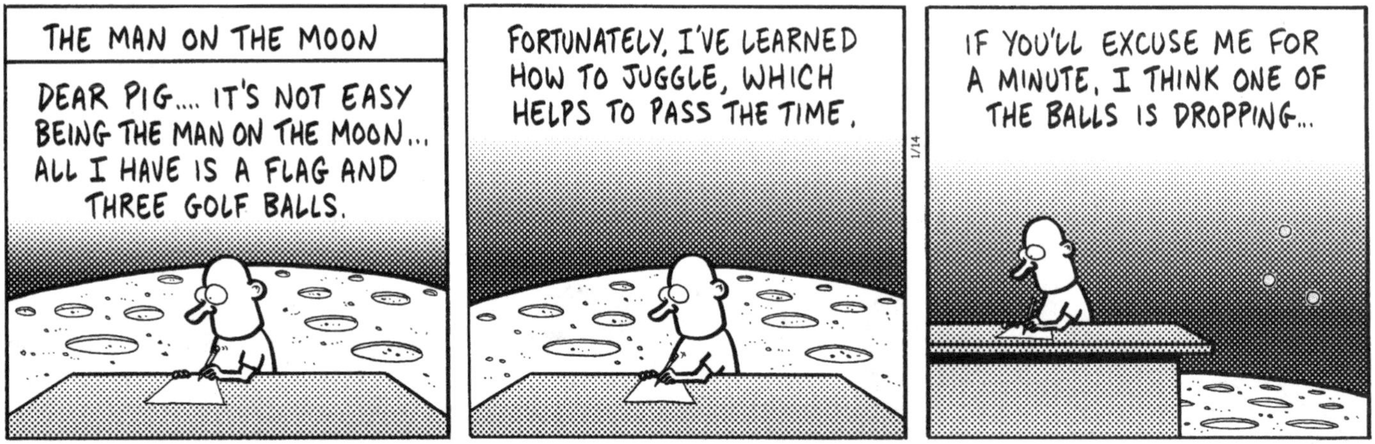
THE MAN ON THE MOON
DEAR PIG.... IT'S NOT EASY BEING THE MAN ON THE MOON... ALL I HAVE IS A FLAG AND THREE GOLF BALLS.
FORTUNATELY, I'VE LEARNED HOW TO JUGGLE, WHICH HELPS TO PASS THE TIME.
1/14
IF YOU'LL EXCUSE ME FOR A MINUTE, I THINK ONE OF THE BALLS IS DROPPING...

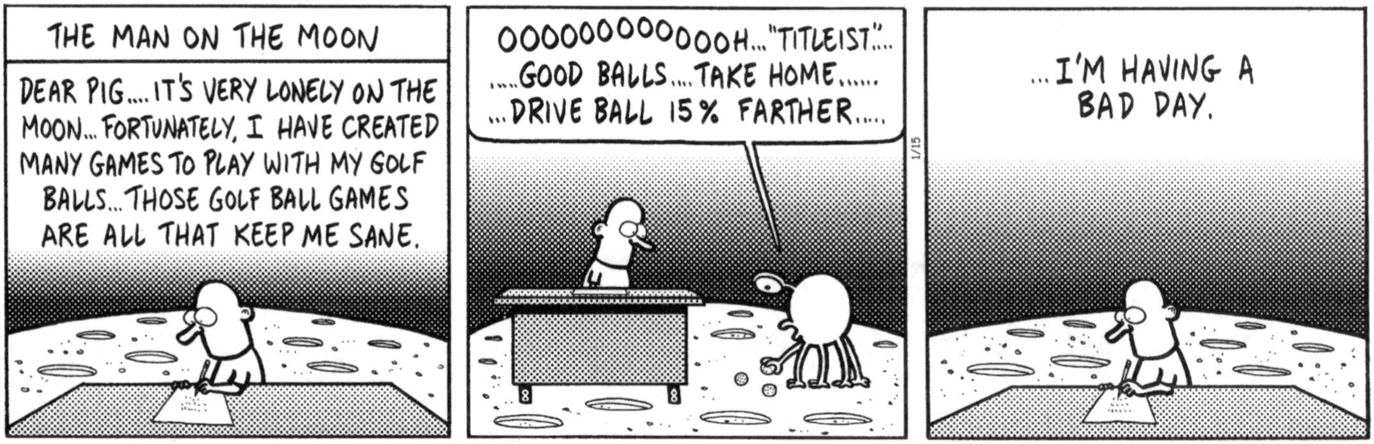
THE MAN ON THE MOON
DEAR PIG.... IT'S VERY LONELY ON THE MOON... FORTUNATELY, I HAVE CREATED MANY GAMES TO PLAY WITH MY GOLF BALLS... THOSE GOLF BALL GAMES ARE ALL THAT KEEP ME SANE.
OOOOOOOOOOOOH... "TITLEIST"... ....GOOD BALLS.... TAKE HOME...... ...DRIVE BALL 15% FARTHER.....
1/15
...I'M HAVING A BAD DAY.

UPDATE

Last Sunday, Rat's comic strip creation, "Dickie the Cockroach," got loose in the Sunday funnies and slapped duct tape over the mouth of a very popular comic strip star.... We join the strip in progress.

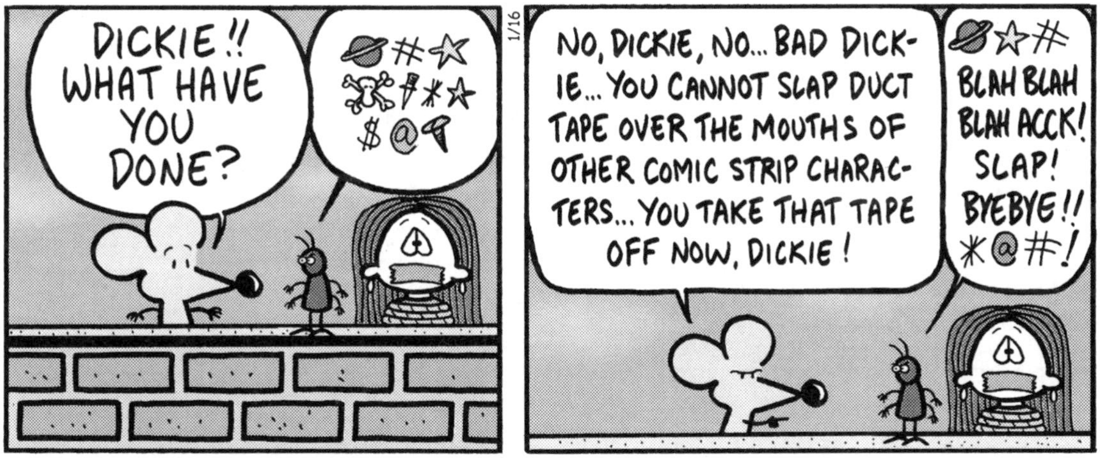

DICKIE!! WHAT HAVE YOU DONE?
1/16
NO, DICKIE, NO... BAD DICKIE... YOU CANNOT SLAP DUCT TAPE OVER THE MOUTHS OF OTHER COMIC STRIP CHARACTERS... YOU TAKE THAT TAPE OFF NOW, DICKIE!
BLAH BLAH BLAH ACCK! SLAP! BYEBYE!!

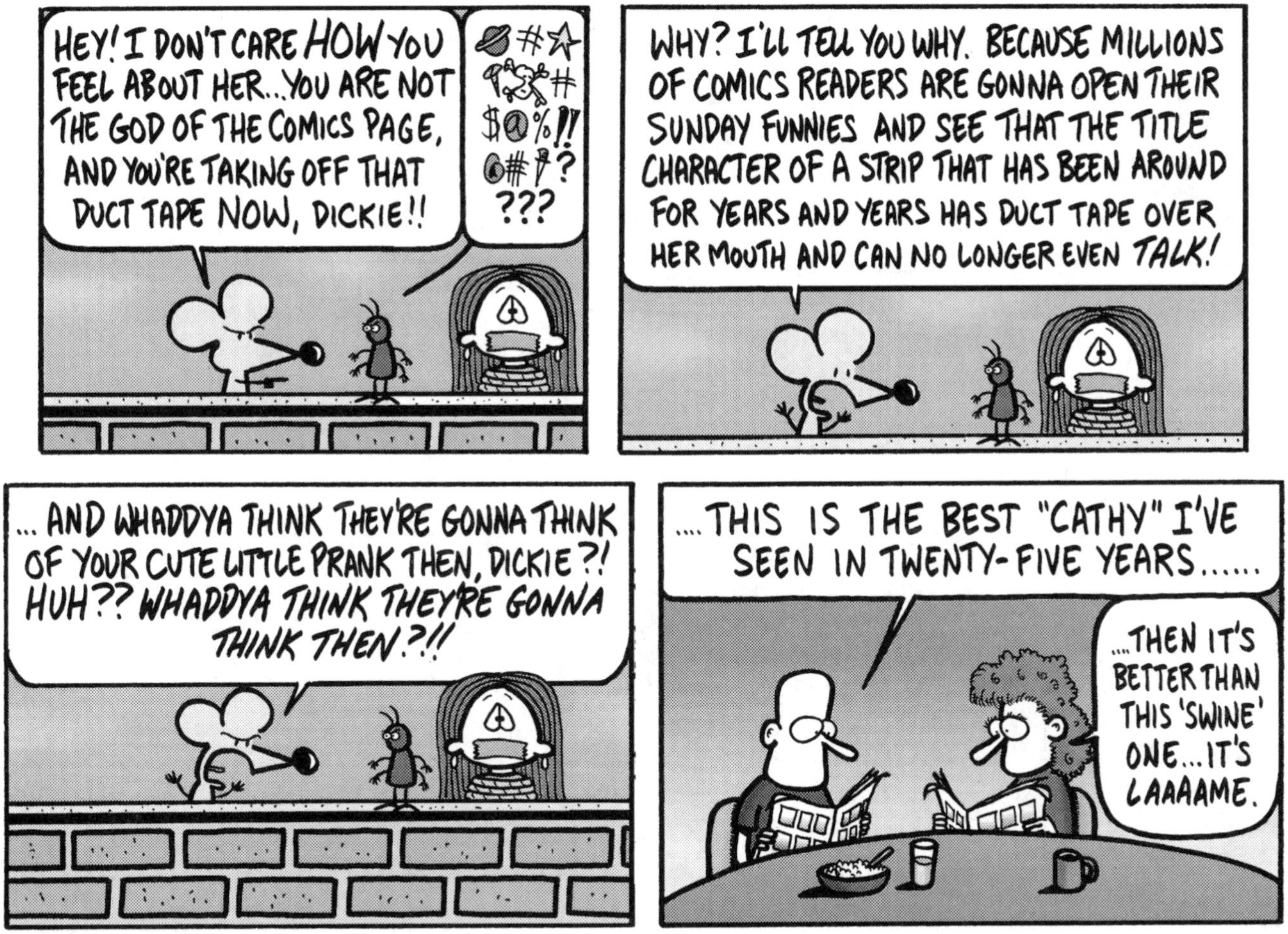

HEY! I DON'T CARE HOW YOU FEEL ABOUT HER... YOU ARE NOT THE GOD OF THE COMICS PAGE, AND YOU'RE TAKING OFF THAT DUCT TAPE NOW, DICKIE!!
???
WHY? I'LL TELL YOU WHY. BECAUSE MILLIONS OF COMICS READERS ARE GONNA OPEN THEIR SUNDAY FUNNIES AND SEE THAT THE TITLE CHARACTER OF A STRIP THAT HAS BEEN AROUND FOR YEARS AND YEARS HAS DUCT TAPE OVER HER MOUTH AND CAN NO LONGER EVEN TALK!
... AND WHADDYA THINK THEY'RE GONNA THINK OF YOUR CUTE LITTLE PRANK THEN, DICKIE?! HUH?? WHADDYA THINK THEY'RE GONNA THINK THEN?!!
.... THIS IS THE BEST "CATHY" I'VE SEEN IN TWENTY-FIVE YEARS......
....THEN IT'S BETTER THAN THIS 'SWINE' ONE... IT'S LAAAAME.

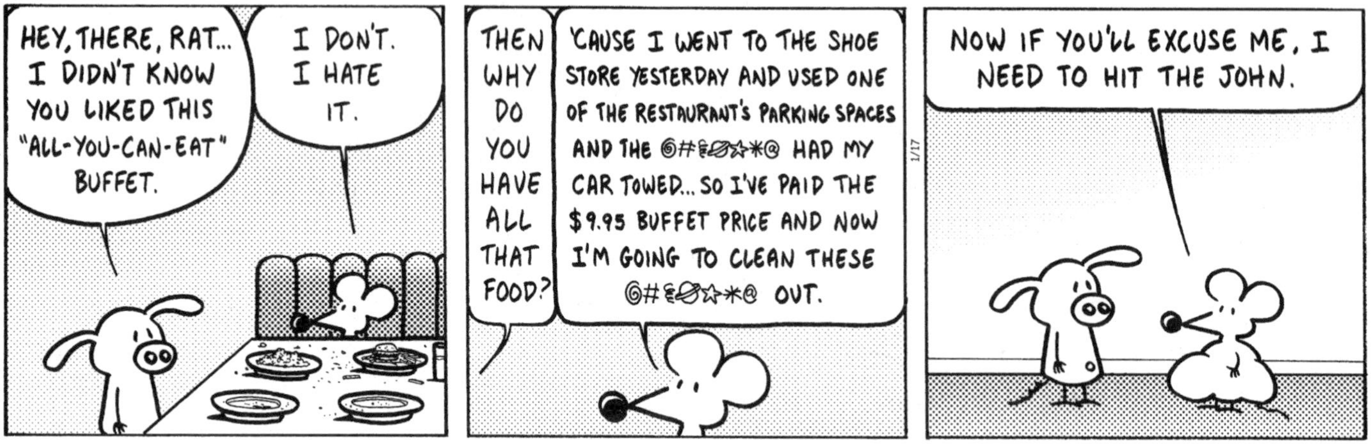
HEY, THERE, RAT... I DIDN'T KNOW YOU LIKED THIS "ALL-YOU-CAN-EAT" BUFFET.
I DON'T. I HATE IT.
THEN WHY DO YOU HAVE ALL THAT FOOD?
'CAUSE I WENT TO THE SHOE STORE YESTERDAY AND USED ONE OF THE RESTAURANT'S PARKING SPACES AND THE @#§&☆*@ HAD MY CAR TOWED... SO I'VE PAID THE $9.95 BUFFET PRICE AND NOW I'M GOING TO CLEAN THESE @#§&☆*@ OUT.
1/17
NOW IF YOU'LL EXCUSE ME, I NEED TO HIT THE JOHN.

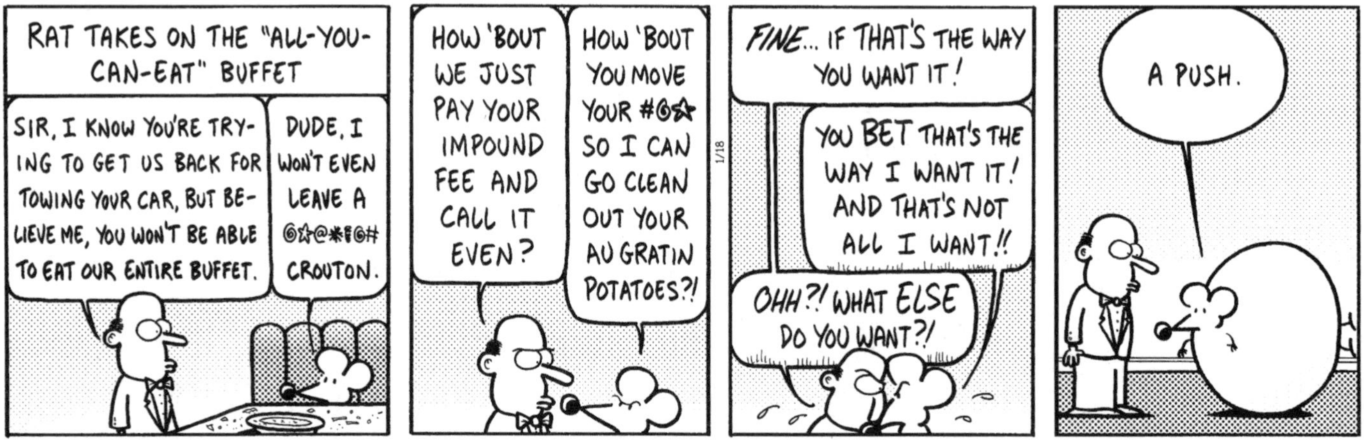
RAT TAKES ON THE "ALL-YOU-CAN-EAT" BUFFET
SIR, I KNOW YOU'RE TRYING TO GET US BACK FOR TOWING YOUR CAR, BUT BELIEVE ME, YOU WON'T BE ABLE TO EAT OUR ENTIRE BUFFET.
DUDE, I WON'T EVEN LEAVE A @☆@*§@# CROUTON.
HOW 'BOUT WE JUST PAY YOUR IMPOUND FEE AND CALL IT EVEN?
HOW 'BOUT YOU MOVE YOUR #@☆ SO I CAN GO CLEAN OUT YOUR AU GRATIN POTATOES?!
1/18
FINE... IF THAT'S THE WAY YOU WANT IT!
YOU BET THAT'S THE WAY I WANT IT! AND THAT'S NOT ALL I WANT!!
OHH?! WHAT ELSE DO YOU WANT?!
A PUSH.

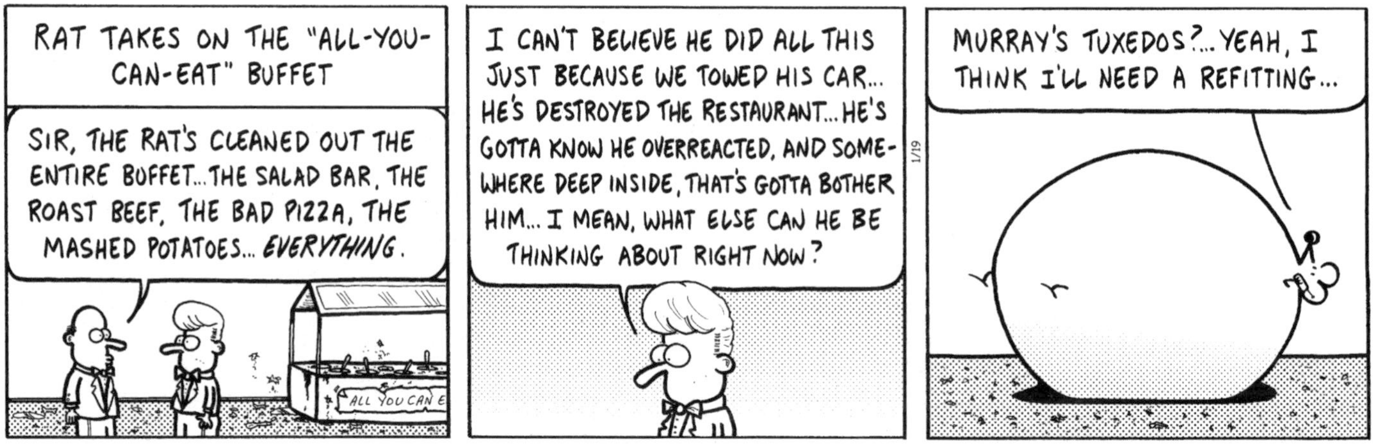
RAT TAKES ON THE "ALL-YOU-CAN-EAT" BUFFET
SIR, THE RAT'S CLEANED OUT THE ENTIRE BUFFET... THE SALAD BAR, THE ROAST BEEF, THE BAD PIZZA, THE MASHED POTATOES... *EVERYTHING*.
ALL YOU CAN E
I CAN'T BELIEVE HE DID ALL THIS JUST BECAUSE WE TOWED HIS CAR... HE'S DESTROYED THE RESTAURANT... HE'S GOTTA KNOW HE OVERREACTED, AND SOMEWHERE DEEP INSIDE, THAT'S GOTTA BOTHER HIM... I MEAN, WHAT ELSE CAN HE BE THINKING ABOUT RIGHT NOW?
1/19
MURRAY'S TUXEDOS?... YEAH, I THINK I'LL NEED A REFITTING...

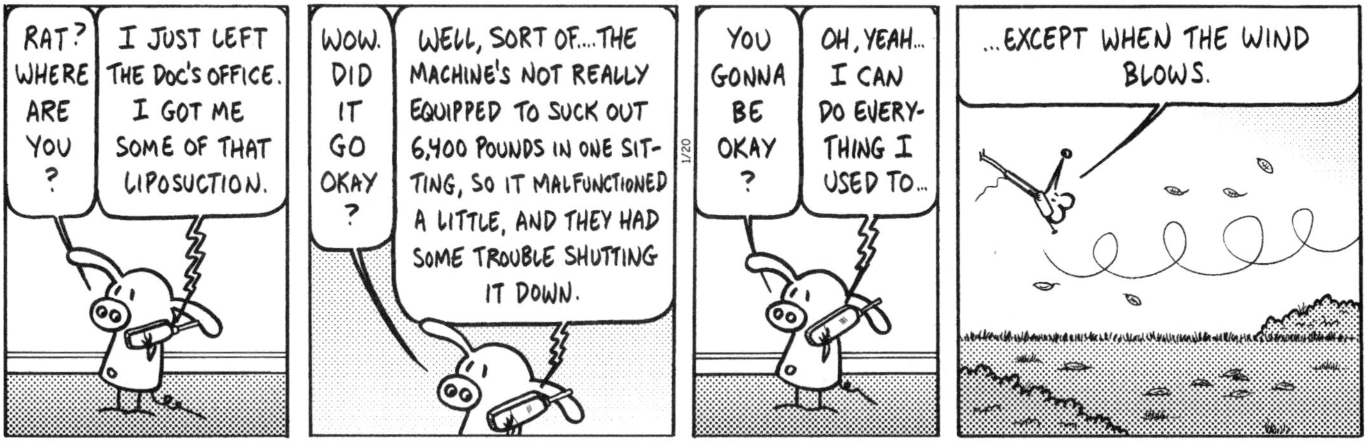
RAT? WHERE ARE YOU?
I JUST LEFT THE DOC'S OFFICE. I GOT ME SOME OF THAT LIPOSUCTION.
WOW. DID IT GO OKAY?
WELL, SORT OF.... THE MACHINE'S NOT REALLY EQUIPPED TO SUCK OUT 6,400 POUNDS IN ONE SITTING, SO IT MALFUNCTIONED A LITTLE, AND THEY HAD SOME TROUBLE SHUTTING IT DOWN.
1/20
YOU GONNA BE OKAY?
OH, YEAH... I CAN DO EVERYTHING I USED TO...
...EXCEPT WHEN THE WIND BLOWS.

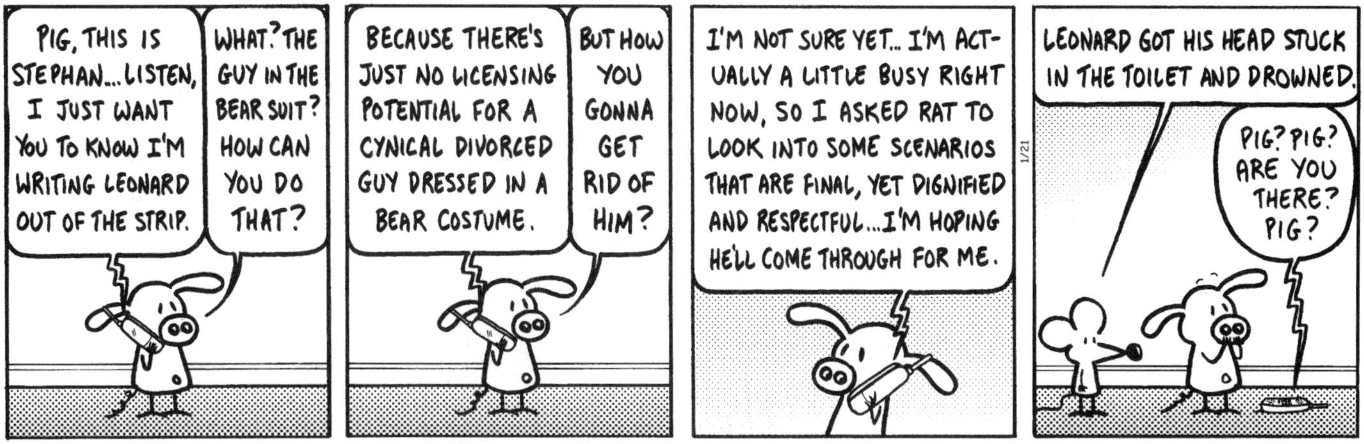
PIG, THIS IS STEPHAN... LISTEN, I JUST WANT YOU TO KNOW I'M WRITING LEONARD OUT OF THE STRIP.
WHAT? THE GUY IN THE BEAR SUIT? HOW CAN YOU DO THAT?
BECAUSE THERE'S JUST NO LICENSING POTENTIAL FOR A CYNICAL DIVORCED GUY DRESSED IN A BEAR COSTUME.
BUT HOW YOU GONNA GET RID OF HIM?
1/21
I'M NOT SURE YET... I'M ACTUALLY A LITTLE BUSY RIGHT NOW, SO I ASKED RAT TO LOOK INTO SOME SCENARIOS THAT ARE FINAL, YET DIGNIFIED AND RESPECTFUL... I'M HOPING HE'LL COME THROUGH FOR ME.
LEONARD GOT HIS HEAD STUCK IN THE TOILET AND DROWNED.
PIG? PIG? ARE YOU THERE? PIG?

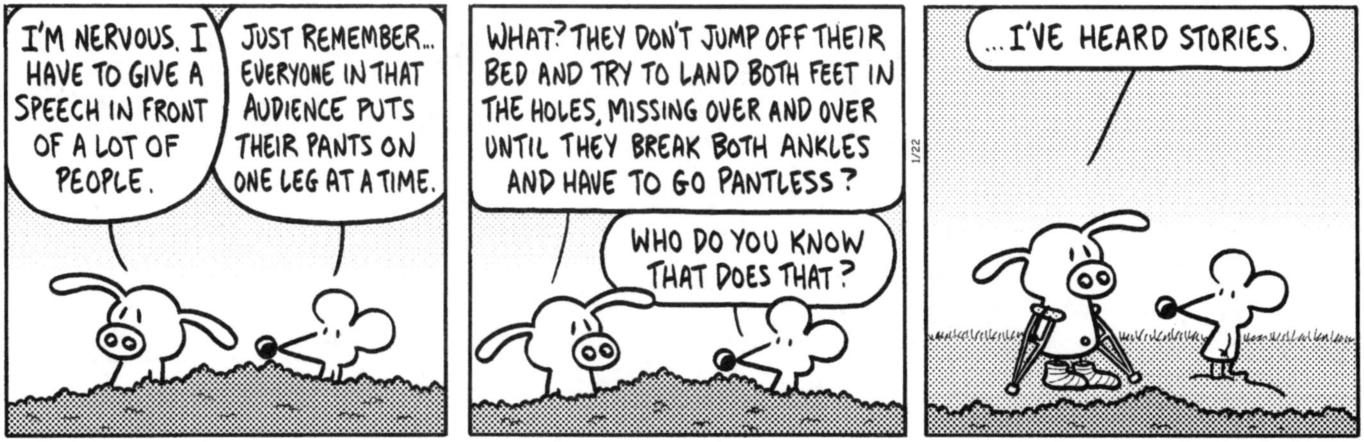
I'M NERVOUS. I HAVE TO GIVE A SPEECH IN FRONT OF A LOT OF PEOPLE.
JUST REMEMBER... EVERYONE IN THAT AUDIENCE PUTS THEIR PANTS ON ONE LEG AT A TIME.
WHAT? THEY DON'T JUMP OFF THEIR BED AND TRY TO LAND BOTH FEET IN THE HOLES, MISSING OVER AND OVER UNTIL THEY BREAK BOTH ANKLES AND HAVE TO GO PANTLESS?
WHO DO YOU KNOW THAT DOES THAT?
1/22
...I'VE HEARD STORIES.

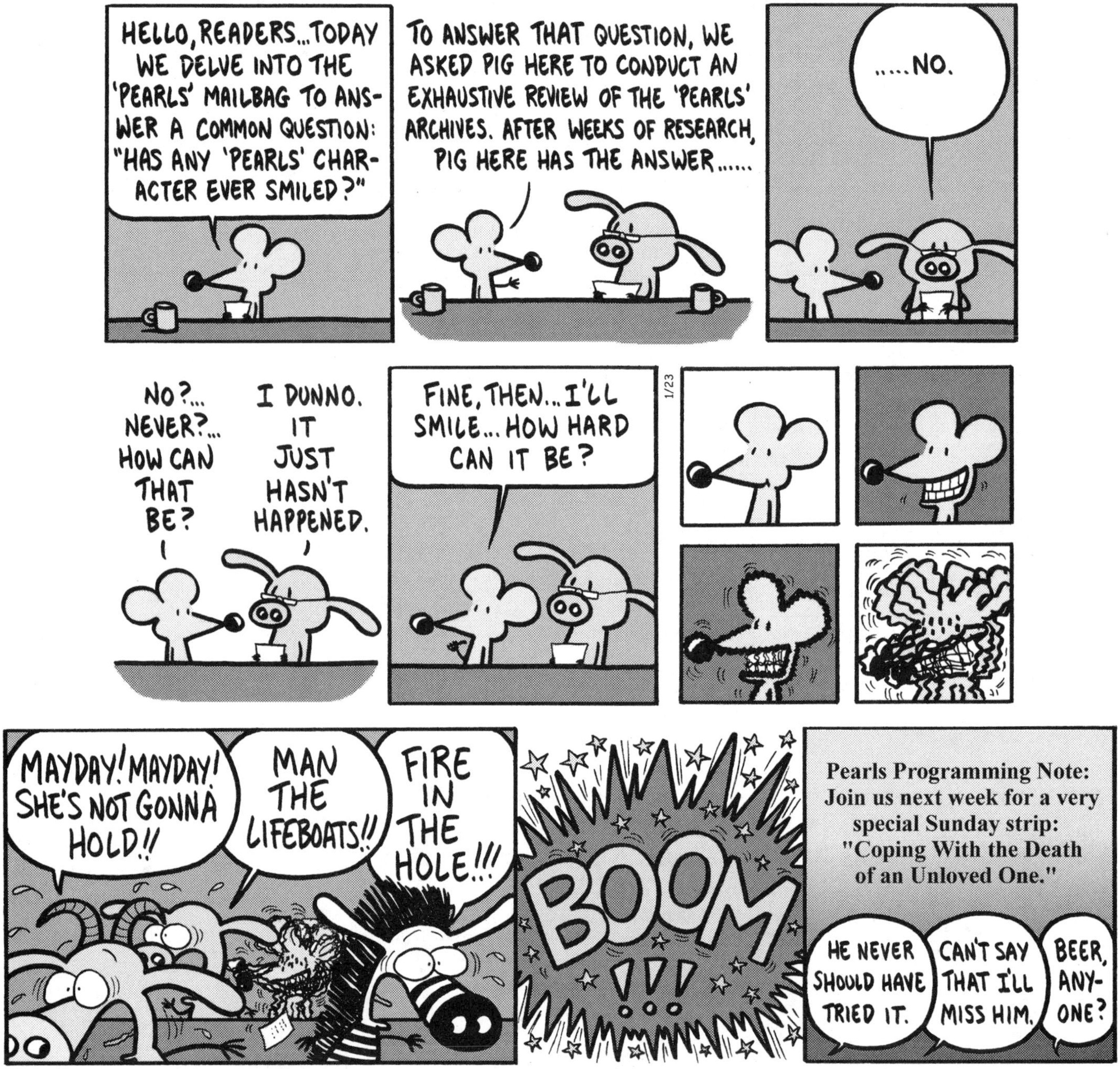
HELLO, READERS... TODAY WE DELVE INTO THE 'PEARLS' MAILBAG TO ANSWER A COMMON QUESTION: "HAS ANY 'PEARLS' CHARACTER EVER SMILED?"
TO ANSWER THAT QUESTION, WE ASKED PIG HERE TO CONDUCT AN EXHAUSTIVE REVIEW OF THE 'PEARLS' ARCHIVES. AFTER WEEKS OF RESEARCH, PIG HERE HAS THE ANSWER......
.....NO.
NO?... NEVER?... HOW CAN THAT BE?
I DUNNO. IT JUST HASN'T HAPPENED.
FINE, THEN... I'LL SMILE... HOW HARD CAN IT BE?
1/23
MAYDAY! MAYDAY! SHE'S NOT GONNA HOLD!!
MAN THE LIFEBOATS!!
FIRE IN THE HOLE!!!
BOOM!!!
Pearls Programming Note: Join us next week for a very special Sunday strip: "Coping With the Death of an Unloved One."
HE NEVER SHOULD HAVE TRIED IT.
CAN'T SAY THAT I'LL MISS HIM.
BEER, ANYONE?